# PASSIONATE ENLIGHTENMENT

## WOMEN IN TANTRIC BUDDHISM

*Miranda Shaw*

PRINCETON UNIVERSITY PRESS PRINCETON, NEW JERSEY

Published by Princeton University Press, 41 William Street,
Princeton, New Jersey 08540
In the United Kingdom: Princeton University Press,
Chichester, West Sussex


*Library of Congress Cataloging-in-Publication Data*

Shaw, Miranda Eberle, 1954–
Passionate enlightenment: women in Tantric Buddhism /
Miranda Shaw.
p. cm.
Includes bibliographical references and index.
ISBN 0-691-03380-3
1. Women in Tantric Buddhism—India.
BQ8915.S53 1994
294.3′925′082—dc20 93-31407

This book has been composed in Adobe Palatino

Princeton University Press books are printed
on acid-free paper and meet the guidelines for
permanence and durability of the Committee
on Production Guidelines for Book Longevity
of the Council on Library Resources

Printed in the United States of America

Third printing, with corrections, 1994

5 7 9 10 8 6 4

བླ་མ་བསོད་ནམས་འབྱོར་འཕེལ་རིན་པོ་ཆེ་

ཡང་དག་པའི་དེད་དཔོན་ཆེན་པོ་མཆོག་གི་

ཐུགས་བརྩེ་དང་བཀའ་དྲིན་རྗེས་དྲན་དུ་

འབུལ་བ་ལགས་སོ།།

*(To Lama Sonam Jorphel Rinpoche,*
*consummate Tantric guide,*
*for unforgettable kindness*
*and rare compassion)*

# Contents

# *List of Illustrations*

# *Acknowledgments*

MY MENTOR, Masatoshi Nagatomi, supported this project long before it showed concrete promise. He sets an unattainable standard of passionate, rigorous scholarship that is ever an inspiration. Diana Eck's astute questions have challenged and deepened my thought, while Tu Weiming lent invaluable theoretical insights. Elisabeth Schüssler Fiorenza provided inspiration through her feminist historical work on early Christianity. It was her courageous example that spurred my decisive commitment to this project.

I would like to acknowledge several valued companions in exploration. John Huntington's enthusiastic introduction to Tantric Buddhist art awakened my lifelong fascination with the subject. He and Susan Huntington introduced me to the joys of scholarship and adventures of research. Robert Thurman was my unforgettable and peerless guide first to Madhyamaka texts and later to the Tantric genre. Frédérique Apffel Marglin has been a constant advisor since our first meeting in Orissa. I cannot overestimate my debt of gratitude to her for helping to forge insights that shape every page of this work.

Gaining entree to any religious tradition requires the cooperation of adherents of that tradition, and that necessity is heightened in the case of an esoteric tradition like Tantric Buddhism. Therefore, I want to thank all the yoginis, yogis, lamas, monks, scholars, and lay people who graciously opened their monasteries, temples, rituals, homes, hermitages, pilgrimages, and hearts to me. I went to them for information and came away deeply enriched with both knowledge and affection.

Among the lamas to be thanked for assisting me, the foremost is His Holiness the Dalai Lama, for giving his approval, offers of assistance, and an indispensable interview. The following lamas assisted my research in various ways: in the dGe-lugs order, Lati Rinpoche, Tara Tulku Rinpoche, and Gungru Tulku; in the 'Bri-gung bKa'-brgyud order, H. H. Chetsang Rinpoche, Ayang Rinpoche, and Khenpo Konchog Gyaltsen; in the Karma bKa'-brgyud order, H. H. Shamarpa Rinpoche, Pawo Rinpoche, and Trangu Rinpoche; in the Sa-skya school, H. H. Sakya Trizin, Jetsun Chime Luding, Luding Khen Rinpoche, and Khenpo Abbe; and in the rNying-ma tradition, H. H. Dilgo Khyentse Rinpoche, Minglin Trichen, Tulku Thondup, and Lama Tsultrim. Several of these venerable teachers have subsequently passed away, and I am honored that their memory is woven into these pages. Sonam Sangpo helped me locate some manuscripts in exceptionally hot weather in Kathmandu and then helped me translate them after we had found them. Ngawang Jorden of Sakya College, Dehra Dun, fortuitously came to Harvard at the same time that I returned from the field and has remained a willing and knowledgeable advisor ever since.

When I was in India, it was a privilege to have the brilliant historian Bitendra Nath Mukherjee as my project advisor. The inimitable Narendra Nath Bhattacharyya offered his piquant insights over many cups of Indian tea. Abhijit Ghosh shared his philological expertise during many enjoyable hours of reading Hindu *tantras* and Sanskrit fiction. I am grateful to the staff of the United States Educational Foundation in India, at both the New Delhi and Calcutta offices, for assistance with the arcane world of Indian bureaucracy and for a myriad of indispensable arrangements when I was in the field.

The institutions whose directors, staffs, and libraries greatly aided my research include the Indian Institute for Advanced Studies, Simla; Tibet House, New Delhi; Lokesh Chandra, International Academy of Indian Culture, New Delhi; Sahitya Akademii, Delhi; Central Institute of Higher Tibetan Studies, Sarnath; Library of Tibetan Works and Archives, Dharamsala; Orissa State Museum Library; The National Library, Calcutta; The Asiatic Society, Calcutta; Ramakrishna Mission Institute of Culture, Calcutta; and Yenching Institute, Harvard University. I am also grateful to Joseph Loizzo for the loan of his bsTan-'gyur for the duration of this project, to Melbourne Taliaferro for procuring copies of some essential texts, and to Musashi Tachikawa for a timely gift of the *rGyud sde kun btus*.

This project required fieldwork, archival research, and time for translation and writing free from other obligations. All this would not have been possible without the funding provided by the dean of Radcliffe College, the Harvard Center for the Study of World Religions under the directorship of John Carman, the Fulbright-Hays Foundation, the Charlotte W. Newcombe Foundation, the Mrs. Giles Whiting Foundation, and the Faculty Research Committee of the University of Richmond. Steven Zimmerman and Pamela Russell also deserve special thanks for two crucial trips to Nepal.

For advice, encouragement, helpful references, and editorial advice I am indebted to Tsultrim Allione, Paula Kane Arai, Theodore Bergren, Agehananda Bharati, Annie Dillard, Sherab Drolma, John Dunne, Elinor Gadon, Herbert Guenther, Adelheid Hermann-Pfandt, Toni Kenyon, Cliff Leftwich, Miriam Levering, Sara McClintock, Mildred Munday, Robin Rao, Shinichi Tsuda, and Alex Wayman. Special appreciation is due to Prajwal Ratna Vajracharya for luminous dance interpretations of the comportment of Tantric deities. Emily Martindale gave the project a final infusion of energy with her exquisite line-drawn renderings of Tibetan paintings and woodblock prints.

My deepest gratitude goes to Lama Sonam Jorphel Rinpoche, a 'Bri-gung bKa'-brgyud lineage holder, for sharing the precious resource of his time and the abundant stores of his kindness and erudition during three months at his mountain hermitage in Ladakh, hundreds of hours of discussions in the following months, and two months going over the fine points of the manuscript in Kathmandu. Nothing can ever repay this debt.

Finally, to the family that nurtured and supported me: my grandmother, Frances Wilson Eberle, who taught me the importance of books; my mother, Merry Gant Norris, whose appreciation sweetens every accomplishment; and Kenneth Rose, companion in life and intellectual journeying, whose numerous personal and scholarly ministrations helped to bring this book into being.

## Guide to Transliteration

SANSKRIT WORDS that can be found in English dictionaries generally occur without diacritical marks or italicization (e.g., karma, mantra, yogi, yogini). In the interests of devising a readable format, I have tried to use English words whenever possible. When the context is Indian, the Sanskrit term will generally be given in the body of the text or in a note. When the context is Tibet or the Himalayas, the Sanskrit and/or Tibetan terms will be given.

Tibetan words are transliterated according to the Wylie system.* Few Tibetan personal names are used, and they are spelled without hyphens and according to a widespread and recognizable usage (e.g., Tsongkhapa, Milarepa, Rechungpa). In the cases of other Tibetan proper nouns, such as the titles of texts, sects, and lesser-known names, the Tibetan names are transliterated and hyphenated.

Tantric adepts have multiple names, and the problems in identification raised by this, particularly in the tendency to name people after great masters of the past, are compounded by the variety of spellings that occur in Sanskrit and Tibetan sources. Therefore, it has been necessary to standardize names in the absence of certainty regarding the original names.

Tibetans generally add the suffix *-pa* to Sanskrit names, which helps to identify them as names. At times I include this suffix, when it has become part of the common form of the name and readers will find the name in that form in other works and indices (e.g., Nāropa, Luipa, and Tilopa), but in the case of lesser-known persons and whenever possible I have omitted this suffix.

The editions of Sanskrit and Tibetan texts upon which translations are based are cited in the endnotes. In most cases multiple versions have been consulted, but only one version is cited in the note, since this is adequate documentation for another researcher seeking to retrace my steps. In the case of Tibetan canonical texts, my first preference was for the sDe-dge edition; however, in some cases because of availability, greater legibility, or a significant variation I have translated from another edition and have specified the edition in the endnotes and bibliography. The sDe-dge numbers used in the notes and bibliography correspond to the Tōhoku catalogue of the sDe-dge edition, while the Peking numbers and folio references refer to the Ōtani edition. Unless otherwise indicated, all translations are my own.

* See Turrell Wylie, "A Standard System of Tibetan Transcription."

# PASSIONATE ENLIGHTENMENT

CHAPTER ONE

# Seeking the Traces of Sky-Dancers

ANYONE WHO READS a Tantric text or enters a Tantric temple immediately encounters a dazzling array of striking female imagery. One discovers a pantheon of female Buddhas and a host of female enlighteners known as *ḍākinīs*. The *ḍākinīs* leap and fly, unfettered by clothing, encircled by billowing hair, their bodies curved in sinuous dance poses. Their eyes blaze with passion, ecstasy, and ferocious intensity. One can almost hear the soft clacking of their intricate bone jewelry and feel the wind stirred by their rainbow-colored scarves as they soar through the Tantric Buddhist landscape. These unrestrained damsels appear to revel in freedom of every kind. Expressions of this motif in Tantric literature describe yoginis with magical powers, powerful enchantresses with the ability to change shape at will, and enlightened women who can spark a direct experience of reality with a precisely aimed word or gesture.

These female figures, with their exuberant air of passion and freedom, communicate a sense of mastery and spiritual power. They inspired my initial interest in the Tantric tradition and served as the lodestar of my explorations throughout. It seemed to me that the yoginis who grace Tantric literature and gaze so compellingly from Tantric paintings and statuary may provide evidence of the women of Tantric Buddhism—their historical existence, spiritual liberation, and religious insights. The present study is the fruit of my search for the women who inspired and helped to create these evocative female images.

Interpreters of Tantric art and literature have maintained that the positive female imagery does not reflect women's lives or accomplishments. Rather, historians have held that Tantric Buddhism was an oppressive movement in which women were at best marginal and subordinate and at worst degraded and exploited. The prevalent view is that the human counterparts of the exuberant yoginis of Tantric iconography were downtrodden prostitutes and low-caste women exploited for ritual purposes. This assessment is not surprising, for statements that discount women's religious lives are seen in all fields of historical study before significant research on women has been undertaken. For instance, similar assertions were made about the lowly estate of women in medieval European Christianity, before the first trickle of historical interest several decades ago became a rushing stream of increasingly specialized and methodologically sophisticated studies. Such statements also resemble those made about Australian Aboriginal women before female ethnographers discovered the rich world of women's myth and ritual from which men—including male researchers—are excluded. Therefore, casual assumptions made in passing about the marginality of women in Tantric circles need not discourage deeper inquiry; they simply underscore the need for further research.

This volume challenges the prevailing view of the women of Tantric Buddhism by bringing forth new historical and textual evidence and reinterpreting central motifs and doctrines in light of that evidence. There is extensive evidence that women participated fully in the emerging Tantric movement. Tantric biographies portray bold, outspoken, independent women. Tantric texts prescribe how women should be respected, served, and ritually worshipped. Tantric literature introduces practices performed solely by women and others performed by women and men together. Tantric theory advances an ideal of cooperative, mutually liberative relationships between women and men. Where interpretive categories previously applied to practices, doctrines, gender relations, and social groups discussed herein have been found to be inadequate, they have been critiqued and either modified or abandoned in order to develop the following analyses.

## SCHOLARLY CONTEXTS

Buddhist studies has lagged behind other fields in the use of gender as an analytic category. Male dominance has long been accepted as an ahistorical, immutable principle of Buddhist history. Since women have been present throughout all epochs of Buddhist history for over two and a half millennia and their presence inevitably had an impact on the ongoing creation of the tradition, there is little justification for continuing to neglect this dimension of Buddhist history. In the case of Indo-Tibetan Buddhism, some progress has been made in the areas of women in early Buddhism,[1] monasticism,[2] and Mahāyāna Buddhism.[3] Two articles have seriously broached the topic of women in Indian Tantric Buddhism,[4] while somewhat more attention has been devoted to Tibetan nuns[5] and lay yoginis.[6]

By concentrating on women in Tantric Buddhism in India, this study provides a basis for differentiating gender relations during the Indian phase of the movement from historical developments in Tibet.[7] The emergence of powerful Buddhist dynasties, the consolidation of a priestly hierarchy that dominated the economic and political life of the country, the inauguration of an incarnation system that allowed male hierarchs to reproduce themselves without marrying, and a thriving eremitic subculture all affected the participation of women in ways that have yet to be studied in depth.[8] The more radical Tantric teachings, such as those involving sexual practices, encountered official resistance in Tibet, resulting in restrictions upon the translation of offending texts.[9] Nonetheless, the full spectrum of Tantric teachings survived and flourished in the Land of Snows. The Tantric ideal of inclusivism and the utopian vision of men and women as companions in the spiritual quest were like embers that could be fanned into flame whenever a teacher or cultural setting supported their expression.[10] Conflicts between celibate and noncelibate partisans, clerical authority and charismatic leadership, and hierarchical and egalitarian tendencies added greatly to the vitality of the Tibetan tradition. The present book also considers the degree to which the female pioneers of the Tantric movement are remembered and credited for their innovations by their spiritual heirs in Tibet.

This book is located within an expanding body of literature on women and religion and presents material relevant to cross-cultural inquiry in areas such as cultural constructions of gender, the self, the body, sexuality, and ritual. In the area of feminist theology, some scholars have articulated Buddhist principles that may complement, inform, and be informed by Western feminism, particularly by offering alternative models of selfhood and power. These scholars—most notably Anne Klein and Rita Gross—have concentrated on central Buddhist philosophical concepts and psychological insights, such as Buddhist understandings of nonself, interdependence, and meditative awareness.[11] Tantric understandings of embodiment, ecstasy, and the transformative dimensions of passion and intimacy may enrich this dialogue.

One of the foremost aims of this volume is to contribute a chapter on Tantric Buddhism to the religious history of Indian women. In the study of women and religion in India, as in other parts of the world, previous opinions are being revised and overturned by careful attention to women's lives and religious expressions. Indologists in the past have tended to accept male religiosity as normative and universally representative. Many factors have predisposed scholars to fail to recognize the existence of women's religious activities, such as an uncritical acceptance of the reports of male informants in the field, unwitting participation in sectarian polemics, an inability to gain access to women's gatherings and religious practices (particularly in a highly gender-stratified society like that of India), and a concentration upon written sources at the expense of ritual and oral traditions. Scholars have begun to document the existence of religious traditions in India in which women are the custodians of treasuries of cultural knowledge, ritual and meditative arts, and oral and local traditions.[12] The impressive results of such pioneering studies reveal that the religious history of Indian women has just begun to be told.

Tantra in both its Hindu and Buddhist sectarian varieties appears to represent an arena in which Indian women can engage in religious disciplines freely, seriously, and at their own initiative. This is the conviction primarily of Indian scholars and of Westerners like Sir John Woodroffe and Lilian Silburn who have spent long periods in India as Tantric novitiates. These native and engaged scholars report that women can be gurus and perform rituals of initiation in Tantric traditions,[13] and in some Tantric lineages women are regarded as preferable to men as gurus.[14] Proponents also point out that male Tantrics are required to respect, venerate, and ritually worship women.[15] In view of the generally high status of women in Tantric circles, several Indian scholars suggest that Tantra (both Hindu and Buddhist) originated among the priestesses and shamanesses of matrilineal tribal and rural societies.[16]

Rare firsthand accounts have provided an intriguing glimpse of women in Tantra as a living tradition. For instance, the feisty female Śākta and Vaiṣṇava Tantrics interviewed by anthropologist Bholanath Bhattacharya displayed a complete lack of subservience to their male companions and belie any suggestion that they practice Tantra for the sake of someone other than themselves.[17] In her anthropological fieldwork on women ascetics in Benares, Lynn Denton found the female Tantrics to be unconstrained by social conventions and freely and forthrightly to choose their own male partners and life patterns.[18] In his spiritual autobiography, Brajamadhava Bhattacharya describes the instruction and initiations he received from his Tantric guru, the "Lady in Saffron," a coconut-vendor in his native village who initiated and taught disciples independently of any male authority.[19] Indologist Lilian Silburn's technical descriptions of sexual yoga in Kashmir Śaivism, enriched by teachings she received as an initiate, demonstrate the complete reciprocity of male and female adepts in the performance of advanced *kuṇḍalinī* practices, for which both partners must be comparably qualified and from which they derive equal benefit.[20] These studies, while not directly relevant to the question of women in medieval Buddhist Tantra, confirm that women can be active, independently motivated participants in Tantric movements.

These positive assessments by native and engaged scholars find no echo in most Western scholarship on Tantric Buddhism. When writing about its reformist tendencies, scholars stress the egalitarianism and radical inclusiveness of the emerging movement, but when discussing women, they assert the sexist oppressiveness and exploitativeness of Tantric circles, without explaining this dramatic inconsistency. Most Western scholars insist that the genuine, serious practitioners of Tantra were men and that women were only admitted to rituals when their "services" were required by male Tantrics. These authors depict the Tantric yoginis in derogatory, even contemptuous, terms:

> The feminine partner . . . is in effect used as a means to an end, which is experienced by the yogin himself.[21]
>
> We get the impression that they [men] are the main actors, and . . . their female companions are passive counterparts, participating solely to help bring about spiritual insights on part [*sic*] of the yogins.[22]
>
> In . . . Tantrism . . . woman is means, an alien object, without possibility of mutuality or real communication.[23]
>
> The goal of Sahajayāna *sādhanā* is . . . to destroy the female.[24]
>
> Women . . . are assumed to be recruited on each occasion and are made to participate in the assembly.[25]
>
> The "slut" or "*Ḍombī*" refers to a woman of the despised, low Ḍom caste—they earned their living as laundresses, vendors and prostitutes. . . . Tantric *yogins* employed them for the performance of sexual rituals.[26]
>
> The role played by girls of low caste and courtesans in the tantric "orgies" (*cakra,* the tantric wheel) is well known. The more depraved and debauched the woman, the more fit she is for the rite.[27]
>
> Their presence was essential to the performance of the psycho-sexual rites and their activities generally are so gruesome and obscene as to earn them quite properly the name witch.[28]

Similar pronouncements have been made about women and Tantra in general:

> Their attitude toward the woman is . . . she is to be used as a ritual object and then cast aside.[29]
>
> The chief role of women in the Śākta Tantric cult . . . is to act as female partners (*śakti, dūtī*) of the male adepts.[30]

These speculations are all offered in passing and treated as self-evident, without benefit of documentation or analysis. The scenario that these scholars have agreed upon is unambiguous. The men are religious seekers, and the women are "passive counterparts" who are "employed," "available," and "used" as a "ritual object" or "alien object." Apparently the men had a religious motivation, but the women did not. The explanation offered for the women's behavior is that they are "sluts," "lewd," "depraved and debauched," "gruesome and obscene." Although this scenario seems to have been crafted to elevate men as the true practitioners of the tradition, it has the presumably unintended consequence of creating an image of ruthless, self-serving Tantric yogis who will use anything—even the bodies of other human beings—in their pursuit of spiritual perfection.

## THEORETICAL CONSIDERATIONS

The consistent disparity between indigenous and Western assessments of female Tantrics is telling. Several theoretical presuppositions have created a lens or prism that refracts the images in a predictable way. This refraction is now familiar as the pattern of colonial reactions to aspects of India that seemed incomprehensible, repugnant, or irreducibly alien. For instance, the disdainful appraisal of female Tantric practitioners is reminiscent of colonialist judgments of the Indian *devadāsīs* as "temple prostitutes." These women, who are artists, scholars, and performers of ritual dance and worship, presented an unfamiliar and apparently disquieting sight to the colonial gaze. Since British civil servants and missionaries could not comprehend the religious offices of these temple votaries, they labeled them as "strumpets" and "harlots" and proceeded to outlaw the *devadāsī* tradition. Such judgments reflected not only a lack of knowledge of the colonialized peoples but also deep antipathy for some of their cultural values.[31] This judgment prevailed until quite recently, when an anthropologist exploring the lives of the surviving remnant of the *devadāsīs* of Puri, in the coastal state of Orissa, discovered a tradition of economically independent, learned, and venerated temple dancers whose ritual services were essential to the maintenance of a well-run Indian kingdom. As embodiments of female divinity and power, the dancers received lavish gifts for their services, and worshippers coveted the very dust from their feet.[32]

Analyses of the colonial encounter in India have exposed ways in which the colonial and indigenous worldviews clashed in the traits they attribute to maleness and femaleness. The Indian worldview does not mirror Western values but includes a profound respect and veneration for the magical potencies and divine powers inherent in womanhood.[33] This veneration is accentuated in the overlapping realms of Śāktism and Tantra that the *devadāsīs* and women of Tantric Buddhism inhabit. Perhaps the scholarly characterizations of the Tantric Buddhist yoginis as "lewd," "sluts," and "depraved and debauched" betray a vestige of Victorian indignation not only at nonmarital sexual activity of women but also at the religious exaltation and worship of women. Theologian Hans Küng acknowledges that religious awe of women is so antithetical to Jewish and Christian values that it poses a major barrier to understanding:

> It is especially hard for the Christian theologian to discuss . . . Shaktist Tantrism with its orientation toward female power or divinity. . . . No one could fail to see that all the Tantric systems, and the Shaktist practices especially, are extraordinarily alien to Christians, more alien than anything we have met thus far in Buddhism or Hinduism.[34]

These attitudes are so alien in part because they epitomize a cultural realm that is animated by dualities that are entirely different from those shaping the Western interpretations of Tantra. Indian society and religion revolve on the axial values of purity and pollution and auspiciousness and inauspiciousness; they do not share the prevalent Western dualisms of nature and culture, matter and spirit, and humanity and divinity. The association of women with "nature," "matter," and "humanity"—particularly as devalued halves of these dualities—is misplaced here.

The interpretation of women's religious practices in Buddhist Tantra requires correctly locating their realm of cultural meaning rather than recasting them into something more in keeping with the interpreters' understandings of gender, sexuality, and power. Herbert Guenther attributes the pattern of interpretation cited above to "Western dominance psychology," which has resulted in what he calls the "paranoid Western conception about Tantrism," namely, the projection of the preoccupations of "the paranoid who is obsessed with his sexual potency and attempts to compel the object to come towards him."[35] The interpretations cited here do reproduce specific Western androcentric constructions of gender in an almost embarrassingly simplistic way: men are active agents, women are passive victims; men are powerful and exploit, women are powerless and exploited; male sexual prowess is admirable, female promiscuity is reprehensible; men are defined by intellectual and spiritual criteria, women are inescapably biological. These dualisms have a particularity and distinctively European pedigree that disallows attributing them uncritically to all cultures. Further, these interpretations assume conflictual, antagonistic relations between the sexes and the inevitable dominance of one over the other in any social arrangement, again disallowing for cultural variations.[36]

The indiscriminate application of selectively Western categories ignores the thoroughly culturally constituted nature of gender traits and relations. Other cultures have very different understandings of gender, power, status, and religious advancement. There is no cross-cultural uniformity of gender relations that allows one to speak in global, ahistorical, universalizing terms without reference to specific cultural constructions of status and power. Anthropologist Shelly Errington asserts the inadequacy of simplistic models of gender to describe the complexity of gender relations encountered throughout the world: "At best, no simple content or criterion of high status or low can measure the status and power of women cross-culturally. At worst, our most unconscious common-sense ideas about 'power,' and with it 'status,' may have to be turned inside out if we are to understand the relations between men and women in some parts of the world."[37] Dominance, exploitation, and power are highly nuanced cultural constructs that rarely correspond directly to gender categories (e.g., men have power and exploit, women are powerless and exploited, etc.) and rarely are vested in individual persons or classes of persons, but rather are configured in complex matrices of ever-shifting positions.

In addition to the imposition of Western understandings of gender, sexuality, and power, even more fundamental ideas of selfhood are imposed in the interpretations of women and Tantric ritual cited above. A situation is postulated in which women are depersonalized and exploited. The postulated depersonalization of the women is predicated upon their possession of an individual self as it is constructed in the mainstream of Western thought. This notion of selfhood understands the self to be a substance, bounded by flesh, that may undergo certain changes but nonetheless retains an identity and remains a bounded entity throughout the life span. This concept of selfhood allows a process of objectification or commodification that turns the "self" into a "thing," "object," or "commodity" that can be "used" by another person as a means to an end.[38] This commodified self is at variance with traditional Indian and Buddhist understandings of personhood. Further, this exercise in "commodity fetishism," or commodity logic, which assumes that women's bodies were used as a physical instrument of male purposes, implies a Cartesian dualism of mind and body, a separability of spirit and matter, that is alien to the Indian context, which has a much more fluidic, dynamic, and organismic understanding of living entities and their orchestrally rich interactions, including all ritual, social, and biological exchanges.[39] The superimposition of prevailing Western categories—such as an atomistic, substantialist self—upon a medieval Indian movement necessarily must result in a distorted analysis, although the distortion will tend to go unnoticed because of the intuitive familiarity of the categories for Western interpreters and their audience. It is difficult to become aware of the structuring principles of one's own thought; however, the interpretation of Buddhist Tantra and women's roles in it requires that the tradition's own understandings of femaleness and gender relations be consulted.

I argue that Tantric Buddhism offers not a model of exploitation but one of complementarity and mutuality. Rather than offering a justification to oppress women or to use them sexually, Tantric texts encourage a sense of reliance upon women as a source of spiritual power. They express a sense of esteem and respect for women, which will be discussed in detail in later chapters, and evince a genuine concern for finding and showing the proper deference toward religiously advanced, spiritually powerful women. Western scholars have taken this concern as demonstrating that the Tantric methods serve only for male liberation and privilege men while exploiting women. This book advances a different interpretation.

In the interpretations cited above, Western cultural categories and preoccupations have been universalized and applied to the Tantric context without investigating whether the Tantric tradition echoes these preoccupations or whether it may offer a radically different understanding of the possibilities for liberating relationships between men and women. There is no demonstrable need to take recourse to an ethnocentric, Euro-American interpretive framework, because the Tantric Buddhist tradition is quite articulate regarding male-female relationships. This study will demonstrate that Tantric Buddhism presents a distinctive understanding of femaleness and maleness and of the ideal, or spiritually transformative, relations that can be attained between them. Authors of the classical *yoginī-tantra* texts discuss these critical topics at length.[40]

Exponents of the tradition also write in depth and with precision about embodiment, which is understood to be not a "soul" in a "body" but rather a multilayered mind-body continuum of corporeality, affectivity, cognitivity, and spirituality whose layers are subtly interwoven and mutually interactive. This nonessentialist self is seen not as a boundaried or static entity but as the site of a host of energies, inner winds and flames, dissolutions, meltings, and flowings that can bring about dramatic transformations in embodied experience and provide a bridge between humanity and divinity. It is in light of this model of a dynamic, permeable self without fixed boundaries that the Tantric Buddhist paradigm must be interpreted. Herbert Guenther, alone among Western scholars, has placed spiritual companionship in Tantra in the context of Buddhist metaphysics, and this book continues that pattern of analysis.[41]

## METHODOLOGY

The interpretive principles I have found most useful are those put forward in the context of feminist historiography, particularly in the work of Gerda Lerner, Elizabeth Schüssler Fiorenza, and Joan Scott.[42] One of the principles upon which feminist historians have come to agree is the need to reclaim the historical agency of women, that is, to concentrate upon how women acted rather than how they were acted upon and to consider how women viewed events rather than how women were viewed.[43] Therefore, one of my operative principles is to view women as active shapers of history and interpreters of their own experience rather than as passive objects or victims of history. Women had powers of assent and dissent and were users and interpreters of symbols, performers and innovators of ritual and meditation practices, writers and teachers, religious specialists, and enlightened preceptors. My intent has been insofar as possible to discover and present the agency, creativity, and self-understanding of the women of Tantric Buddhism. I am secondarily interested in how men may have viewed or treated women, to the extent that this may shed light on gender dynamics in the movement.

It is crucial to restore to historical accounts the eminent women whose importance can be measured in terms of conventional historiographic models, but it is also necessary to redefine historical importance so that women's lives and concerns are included. This requires refashioning regnant historical models to accommodate the activities, contributions, and points of view of women. It also requires that a historian evaluate events and movements from the perspectives of the women present.[44] In seeking to recover women's history, it is important to recognize that cultural creations are often the products of both men and women.[45] In the case of Tantric Buddhism, this involves recognizing that women's views about the Tantric movement and their participation in it are found not only in texts by women but also in the literature produced by the communities of which they were a part. Therefore, I approach Tantric texts and iconography as the products of communities of men and women, not of solitary men. Reading them as evidence of the experiences and insights of both women and men yields a different interpretation from reading them as cultural creations of men who are indistinguishable in philosophy, morality, and behavior from a selective group of modern Western men.

Historical research that focuses on women may proceed with different assumptions from conventional history. One of the differences is that records of women's lives are preserved in disproportionately small amounts. Therefore, available information about women cannot be accepted as numerically representative but rather, in Elisabeth Schüssler Fiorenza's words, "should be read as the tip of an iceberg indicating how much historical information we have lost."[46] Even when documents from the past are irredeemably androcentric, this cannot be taken as evidence that women were not present or that women did not have their own views of their lives.[47] Misogynistic sources do not necessarily reflect the reality of women's lives, but they do tell something about the environments in which women lived.

Thus, this study participates in an effort to recover women's own religious writings, views, practices, and self-understanding.[48] In trying to recover women's history, one needs first of all to compile records left by women: visual arts, crafts, inscriptions, autobiographies, treatises, *belles-lettres*, popular literatures, folklore, correspondence, and oral traditions.[49] These documents provide a basis for a pattern of interpretation that uses women's insights and experiences as its organizing principles and overall design. Subsequently, evidence not directly attributed to women can be interpreted in light of this design. According to historian Elisabeth Schüssler Fiorenza, "A historically adequate translation and interpretation of androcentric texts . . . must not view the texts referring explicitly to women as patchwork pieces within an androcentric design, but must articulate a feminist model of historical reconstruction that can understand them as the highlights and colors within a feminist design."[50]

Eliciting a gynocentric design often requires the application of creative hermeneutical strategies, such as strategies for reading texts to extract information about women. Women's presence and points of view can sometimes be reconstructed by going beyond the statements made in a text to imagine the world of discourse in which the text occurs, controversies to which it is responding, practices or social arrangements it seeks to legitimize, and assumptions it leaves unstated. For example, Tantric passages on the classification of women have been construed as androcentric because they reflect men's desire to find certain types of women and thus presumably express male interests rather than female ones. However, these passages can be interpreted from numerous perspectives. One perspective is that of a yogi looking for a particular kind of yogini, but one must also inquire about the historical settings that would render the meeting of such a woman necessary, and one possibility is a movement in which men apprentice themselves to women. Further, it is easy to imagine the scene from the perspective of a woman who is so sought, because the texts describe how a man is to approach her, what he is to offer her, and what forms of respect and obeisance he is to show. Thus, these passages can be read as records of what female Tantrics demanded of male apprentices and as a basis upon which women could claim certain acts of tribute as their due. Although these passages have been dismissed as androcentric and thus unsuited to the purposes of feminist reconstruction, they actually provide a wealth of information about women and gender relations in the Tantric movement. Therefore, the term "androcentric" refers more properly to the way they have been read than to the texts themselves. Although at times it is necessary to critique previous readings, this study is devoted more directly to the positive task of reconstructing the world of the texts and recovering women's place in it.

This study is based on a range of sources, including women's writings, Tantric scriptures, Indian and Tibetan commentarial traditions, oral traditions, and field research. The strongest evidence of the women of Tantric Buddhism derives from writings by the women themselves. This work draws on about forty texts by women that were discovered in the course of my archival research. The search for a text by a woman typically began with the name of a specific woman, a mention of a work by a woman in another source, or a search through catalog lists of authors for female names or feminine gender markers. In this way many candidates for texts of female authorship were found. The next step was to locate and examine the texts. At this stage many texts were eliminated, unless the colophon or internal evidence of the text—and preferably both—supported female authorship. Subsequently additional forms of confirmation, such as mention of the woman's life or teachings in other sources, were sought. About one-fifth of the leads yielded a text that could be confirmed by several forms of supporting evidence to be of female authorship or to be the teachings of a woman as recorded by her disciples.[51] After the completion of this spadework, which took several years and spanned two continents, an even more demanding process followed, namely, gaining familiarity with a range of literary forms, topics, and meditation practices in order to be able to read the women's diverse and specialized writings. Additional historical and field research was then required to investigate the historical role and surviving influence of those works. They provide invaluable insight into women's religious practices, teachings, and levels of expertise.

This study also draws upon the revealed scriptures produced by the communities of which these women were a part. The esoteric texts termed *yoginī-tantras* and *mahāyoga-tantras* (later classified collectively as *anuttara-yoga*, or "unexcelled yoga," *tantras*) are most relevant for this study because they are the ones that describe spiritual companionship between men and women and sexual union as a vehicle of religious transformation. The major texts are well established as those that are featured in the biographies of the great Indian adepts and have remained at the forefront of contemplation, ritual, and interpretation throughout the Himalayan Buddhist sphere. The major *yoginī-tantras,* whose contents are discussed herein, are the *Cakrasaṃvara, Hevajra,* and *Caṇḍamahāroṣaṇa.* The translations are with few exceptions from previously untranslated texts or portions of texts. At times I consult Indian and Tibetan written commentaries to see how passages on women and the female images have been interpreted. Exegetical and sectarian traditions do not evince unanimity on these issues or any other topic. Thus, this study documents one of the living streams among the diverse voices and communities of this international tradition.

My journey has been both intellectual and physical. The physical journey was the field research I conducted during sixteen months in India, several weeks in Japan, and six subsequent months in Nepal. Before I went into the field I corresponded with the Dalai Lama about the advisability of my project and gained his official approval. I received additional advice from him during an interview at his residence in Dharamsala, India. His approval of my project and subsequent approval by other Tibetan Buddhist sectarian leaders were very helpful in securing cooperation, interviews, and access to manuscript collections. In India I also consulted with Indian historians and scholars of Tantra, most notably Narendra Nath Bhattacharyya and Lokesh Chandra. These scholars encouraged my research by affirming my vision of Tantra and sharing their own research and libraries with me.

I also traveled and interviewed numerous lamas and Tantric yogis and yoginis regarding the roles of women in Tantra, attitudes to women, and the interpretation of relevant textual passages. Part of this time was spent in a Tibetan monastery, and another period was spent at Lama Yuru, Ladakh, in a tiny hermitage on a cliff perch that is dwarfed by the surrounding Himalayan mountains. A meditation cave once used by the famed Nāropa is hollowed into the rocks below, and the dramatically carved cliffs all around are riddled with caves that have been used by Tantric yogis and yoginis over the centuries. This remote and lofty location was a perfect setting for exploring the highly esoteric Tantric teachings.

The challenges of field research on an esoteric tradition include those inherent in all field research, such as finding appropriate field collaborators, gaining admittance to communities and religious events, and winning the trust and cooperation of a wide range of people. There are ethical concerns like respecting the informants' privacy and protecting their interests. However, research on an esoteric tradition presents additional challenges as well. The elements of the Tantric tradition in which I was most interested are counted among its most esoteric and closely guarded features, namely, the worship of women and the practice of sexual intimacy as a form of spiritual discipline. Gaining access to this aspect of the tradition is not simply a matter of finding relevant texts. Tantric written sources are not self-explanatory, and oral commentarial traditions are regarded as more authoritative than the printed word of ancient manuscripts. Therefore, it is necessary to obtain access to an oral commentarial tradition that is secreted in the minds and hearts of living masters (both male and female) of the tradition. Even after doing so, one must respect the fact that those who speak of esoteric practices often do so with the understanding that they will never be quoted by name and that on some points they will not be quoted at all.

In the Tantric Buddhist context, initiation is another requirement for receiving esoteric instruction. Initiation has three levels: ritual empowerment (*abhiṣeka*), reading transmission (*āgama*), and secret oral instruction (*upadeśa*). The ritual empowerment is a somatic and aesthetic immersion in a process that concentrates in symbolic form the truths that the initiate will experience in her future journeying. The reading transmission, consisting of a ceremonial reading, grants permission to study and is given in order to prepare the mind for insight into the tradition. I received empowerments for several key teachings and reading transmissions for others, and this technically qualified me to receive secret oral instructions. On my part, initiation confirmed my respect for the tradition, commitment to gain a sympathetic understanding, and resolve to do justice to the profundity of the Tantric teachings as an ancient and sophisticated religious tradition that has been followed and prized by many sincere and remarkable people for many centuries.

I am most grateful that the experts and practitioners I met generously shared some of the most closely guarded aspects of their tradition. Although I met the technical requirement of receiving initiation, individual masters had to decide upon their own authority whether to assist me and how openly to talk to me, because of the deep responsibility inherent in guarding and giving the esoteric teachings.[52] It was clear that those whose assistance I sought were intent to discern my motives and seriousness of purpose. The fact that I was a doctoral student at Harvard carried little weight, since most of those I met had never heard of Harvard. Being a scholar garnered some respect but was not in itself regarded as a sufficient qualification for gaining Tantric teachings. However, the physical hardships of the journey I had undertaken proved my passion to understand, and in some cases I was asked to relate my recent dreams or to explain my motivations. Other signs might be sought concerning the advisability of assisting my work. A rainbow, strange cloud formation, or unusual precipitation would be regarded as confirmation.

To give an example, late one afternoon when a lama was deliberating about instructing me, we left a darkening shrine room and emerged into the luminosity of a bright pink and golden sunset over snow-topped Himalayan peaks. As we paused at the door to admire the flaming panorama, a light snow suddenly began to fall out of a cloudless sky. The snowflakes reflected the colors of the sky and filled the air with a delicate, shimmering shower of pink and gold. This unearthly and magical snowfall continued for five minutes and then stopped just as suddenly, leaving us breathless at the uncanny timing. It seemed to be a clear sign of the blessings of the female spirits called *ḍākinīs*, the special guardians of Tantric knowledge. This supernatural seal of approval opened the way for some invaluable teachings. On other occasions, rainbows, dreams, and other portents provided the needed authorization. It made sense to my informants that, being female themselves, *ḍākinīs* would naturally be more favorably disposed to women than to men and apparently had chosen to entrust a transmission of the secret *yoginī-tantra* teachings to a woman at this time.

Since the *yoginī-tantra*, or *anuttara-yoga*, teachings represent the pinnacle of the Tantric curriculum, I required more than the cooperation of educated persons and novice practitioners and more even than a series of interviews with highly accomplished masters. Ultimately I required the guidance of a master of an extremely advanced course of meditation, study, and personal realization. It is hard enough to find such a master and rarer still to find one who is willing and has the time to teach. It took six months of searching throughout India before I found one who was qualified, willing, and available to provide the extensive instruction I sought. My main mentor in the field was a master of the 'Bri-gung (often written Drikung) bKa'-brgyud sect, Lama Sonam Jorphel Rinpoche, a saintly and charismatic teacher with whom I spent hundreds of hours. Because of his greater involvement in my research, he felt a greater sense of responsibility for the outcome and thus had a deeper interest in my intentions. In the course of our long association he came to understand more fully the complexity of my motivations and commitments, such as my hunger to discover accomplished women of the past, to savor words they had written, and to be nourished by inspiring understandings of female embodiment. Ultimately it was his bodhisattva-like empathy with my aspirations that induced him to share with me some of the gems of his hard-won knowledge and to open the portals of the visionary world of Tantra to such a modestly qualified seeker.

FIGURE 1. Yogini reveling in skylike freedom

As is well known in anthropology, different field settings and the gathering of different types of data require varying levels of involvement, even in the course of a single project. The degrees of participation on different occasions may span complete nonparticipation, or detached observation, through levels of passive, moderate, active, and complete participation.[53] In addition, one alternates among different degrees of insider and outsider perspectives, an alternation that makes it possible both to gain empathetic insight and to maintain critical distance and perspective.[54] There were times when my observer status fell away, such as when I found myself in the company of an exquisitely sagacious person or an irresistibly ebullient yogi or yogini. Other such times were ritual settings, when I set my camera, note pad, and dictionary aside and sought to experience an event in a more holistic way. On these occasions I immersed myself in a chosen setting so that the memories would be imprinted in my blood, flesh, and bones and would enliven my language, increasing its evocative power and poetic depth. Although I base my discussion on written sources whenever possible, I have confirmed or observed the survival, in the living tradition, of the practices and beliefs I describe in this work.

The women of Tantric Buddhism and their divine counterparts are often called *ḍākinīs,* translatable as women who dance in space, or women who revel in the freedom of emptiness (figure 1). As their name suggests, these are not ladies who leave a heavily beaten path. At times their trail disappears into thin air where they took flight and embarked on their enlightenment adventures, but sometimes the trail resumes in the dense underbrush of ancient texts, amidst the tangled vines of Tibetan lineage histories, or among the embers of the bonfires of fame of their renowned students. The traces of the women of Tantric Buddhism are sometimes obscure, enigmatic, even hidden and disguised, but they are accessible to anyone who discovers where to look for them. Once found, their traces are incandescent, exhilarating, and provocative as they beckon to their seekers from a spacious realm of skylike freedom.

CHAPTER TWO

# Tantric Buddhism in India

## *RELIGIOUS AND HISTORICAL INTRODUCTION*

Tantric Buddhism was the crowning cultural achievement of Pāla period India (eighth through twelfth centuries) and an internationally influential movement that swept throughout Asia, where it has survived in many countries to the present day.[1] Tantric Buddhism arose when Mahāyāna Buddhism was enjoying a period of great philosophical productivity and intellectual influence. Flourishing monastic universities offered a life of study and contemplation but also provided a direct route to tremendous wealth, political influence, and social prestige. Chinese pilgrims to India attested to the potential rewards of renunciation, as in the following accounts:

> As the state holds men of learning and genius in esteem, and the people respect those who have high intelligence, the honours and praises of such men are conspicuously abundant, and the attentions private and official paid to them are very considerable. Hence men . . . force themselves to a thorough acquisition of knowledge.[2]

> [The monastics] proceed to the king's court. . . . There they present their schemes and show their (political) talent, seeking to be appointed in the practical government. . . . They receive grants of land, and are advanced to a high rank; their famous names are, as a reward, written in white on their lofty gates. After this they can follow whatever occupation they like.[3]

A monk who enjoyed a successful academic career might be given land, servants, animals, buildings, precious metals, jewels, furnishings, art, and the privilege of riding on an elephant in official processions.[4] Admiring patrons offered these gifts as tokens of their esteem and as a way to gain religious merit. One monk was even offered the income from eighty villages by an enthusiastic royal patron. The monk declined.[5]

Building upon the great achievements of Mahāyāna philosophy, yet impelled by a spirit of critique, Tantric Buddhism arose outside the powerful Buddhist monasteries as a protest movement initially championed by lay people rather than monks and nuns. Desiring to return to classical Mahāyāna universalism, the Tantric reformers protested against ecclesiastical privilege and arid scholasticism and sought to forge a religious system that was more widely accessible and socially inclusive. The Tantrics believed that self-mastery was to be tested amidst family life, the tumult of town and marketplace, the awesome spectacles of a cremation ground, and the dangers of isolated wilderness areas. The new breed of Buddhists also insisted that desire, passion, and ecstasy should be embraced on the religious path. Since they sought to master desires by immersion in them rather than flight from them, the Tantrics styled themselves as "heroes" (*vīra*) and "heroines" (*vīrā*) who bravely dive deep into the ocean of the passions in order to harvest the pearls of enlightenment. In consonance with Tantra's daring assertion that enlightenment can be found in all activities, sexual intimacy became a major paradigm of Tantric ritual and meditation.

The Tantric revolution gained popular and royal support and eventually made its way into the curriculum of monastic universities like Nālandā, Vikramaśīla, Odantapurī, and Somapurī. These institutes of higher learning were patronized and attended by both Hindus and Buddhists. They featured philology, literature, medicine, mathematics, astronomy, and art, as well as the "inner sciences" of meditation, psychology, and philosophy.[6] While the monasteries served as the institutional strongholds of the faith, wandering lay Tantrics carried Buddhism to the villages, countryside, tribal areas, and border regions, providing an interface at which new populations could bring their practices, symbols, and deities into the Buddhist fold. Practices that had great antiquity in India's forests, mountains, and rural areas, among tribal peoples, villagers, and the lower classes, were embraced and redirected to Buddhist ends.[7] The renewed social inclusiveness and incorporation of an eclectic array of religious practices reshaped Buddhism into a tradition once again worthy of the loyalty of people from all sectors of Indian society. Tantric Buddhism drew adherents from competing faiths, expanded geographically into every region of the Indian subcontinent, and continued outward on a triumphal sweep of the Himalayas, East Asia, and Southeast Asia.

## TANTRIC BUDDHIST THOUGHT AND PRACTICE

The Tantric movement represented a radical revision of the reigning values, practices, and symbols of Buddhism. As a new religious paradigm, Tantric Buddhism stimulated vigorous literary and artistic creativity. Tantric adherents introduced a new body of scriptures called *tantras*, for which they claimed the status of divine revelation. Tapping into the same wellspring as Hindu Tantric and Śākta (goddess-worshipping) movements, the Buddhist *tantras* arose from a dynamic interchange among diverse elements of society that revitalized Buddhism with fresh infusions of cultural energy. These works introduced a dramatic and colorful array of rituals, initiations, magic, mantras, yoga, sacramental feasting, and ecstatic practices.

The social backgrounds and life patterns of the Tantric adherents were richly diverse. Some were princes, royal ministers, and wealthy merchants who pursued Tantric meditation while fulfilling their social obligations. Other adepts of royal or aristocratic background, like Princess Lakṣmīṅkarā, left positions of privilege and comfort to pursue arduous Tantric disciplines in remote caves, forests, and cremation grounds. Some took up lowly forms of livelihood in order to lead a simple life more amenable to Tantric practice, like the scholar Tilopa, who became a pounder of sesame seeds. The monk Saraha abandoned his monastic vows, found a spiritual companion, and adopted her trade, becoming an arrow-maker. He celebrated his humble, noncelibate life-style as the perfect context for religious practice. The day he united with the arrow-maker he exulted, "Today I have become a true monk!"[8] One of his famous verses gives voice to a lesson he learned from her:

> Without meditating, without renouncing the world,
> Stay at home in the company of your mate.
> Perfect knowledge can only be attained
> While one is enjoying the pleasures of the senses.[9]

Some Tantrics were already from lowly backgrounds—cobblers, bird-catchers, weavers, innkeepers—and continued in their current occupations, living inconspicuously while cultivating ecstatic inner freedom. Among these we find Maṇibhadrā, a housewife who pursued Tantric meditation while fulfilling her domestic duties. Maṇibhadrā even attained enlightenment in the performance of a household task, for one day she dropped a pitcher of water she was carrying from the village well, and as the water gushed forth her consciousness flowed out and merged with all of reality (figure 2). The Tantric movement embraced people not ordinarily credited with spiritual knowledge or refinement, namely, outcasts and social rejects like rag-pickers, street-sweepers, thieves, gamblers, bartenders, entertainers, and menial laborers of all types. There were also tribal people in remote wilderness areas, like the huntresses Padmalocanā and Jñānalocanā. Some, like Saraha, defected from their monasteries to immerse themselves more fully in the emotions and sensations of worldly life. Others remained in the monastery and tried to carry on Tantric practices in secret—an attempt that often failed, judging from the fame of some of their Tantric exploits.

FIGURE 2. Maṇibhadrā attaining enlightenment

As a branch of Mahāyāna, Tantric Buddhism derives its philosophy from the Mahāyāna tradition. The insights of Madhyamaka, Yogācāra, and Tathāgatagarbha philosophy and the ideals of altruistic motivation and dedication to compassionate service form the theoretical core of Tantric practice. Nonetheless, the intellectual continuity between the two movements is sometimes belied by a dramatic divergence of methodologies. Mahāyāna teaches that the world, which seems so flawed to unenlightened awareness, is actually a sparkling Buddha-land and indeed is just one jewel in an infinite lattice of interlacing Buddha-lands. Tantra shares this ontological perspective but developed different methods for its realization. Whereas Mahāyāna offers a gradual process of purification over many lifetimes of perfecting wisdom, compassion, patience, and other virtues, Tantric Buddhism insisted that enlightenment is attainable in a single lifetime. Tantric practices challenge practitioners immediately to see all things and all experiences as intrinsically pure and innately perfect. Many Tantric methods seek to break down conventional, dualistic thought patterns swiftly and directly, in a very immediate way. These may include situations meant to shock, repulse, or terrify in order to evoke a powerful reaction and draw forth the primal contents of the psyche. Every corner of the mind and heart will be illuminated, and all the shadows and dark recesses will be exposed. This is why Tantra is considered a "quick path" to enlightenment. It is accelerated by methods that force self-confrontation, and as the self is confronted, the spiritual guide provides the necessary tools for self-transformation.

Mahāyāna sees the emotions as the nourishing mud in which the lotuses of compassion, generosity, and sensitivity can take root and blossom, as proclaimed in the *Vimalakīrtinirdeśa-sūtra*: "Flowers like the blue lotus, the red lotus, the white lotus . . . do not grow on the dry ground in the wilderness, but do grow in the swamps and mud banks. Just so, the Buddha-qualities . . . grow in those living beings who are like swamps and mudbanks of passions."[10] Building upon this valuation of the emotions, Tantra affirms the passions, desire, and sense experience as intrinsically pure. Indeed, Tantra prides itself on being a path for intense, passionate people. Therefore, the Tantric path is not without pitfalls, because passion becomes an obstacle for one who does not have purity of heart and mind. However, for yogis and yoginis who have cultivated detachment and are motivated by compassion, passion provides the fuel and energy for meditation upon emptiness. "Emptiness" (*śūnyatā*) is a Buddhist term for the rainbowlike insubstantiality and illusory nature of all phenomena. The Tantric goal is to maintain a clear realization of emptiness in the midst of passion, for this makes it possible to turn passion into supreme bliss. Therefore, many Tantric practices are aimed at putting the yogi or yogini back in contact with the ongoing stream of direct, immediate experience. Further, Tantra offers many methods for heightening, channeling, and offering bliss, including ritual feasts, spontaneous poetry, esoteric dance and song, inner fire offerings, sacraments like meat and alcohol, and yogic practices performed by women and men together. These practices are described in more detail in the chapters that follow.

Because the path to enlightenment requires a fearless confrontation of every aspect of the psyche, including primal levels of anger, desire, and fear, an experienced guide is required. That guide is the Tantric master, or guru. The guru bestows initiation, provides instruction, and applies precise psychological insight to the training of each disciple. At the outset of the path, the guru performs an initiation (*abhiṣeka*) that permits and prepares the disciple to receive esoteric teachings. The initiation can be a short, private ceremony or an elaborate ritual lasting many days. It places a seal of commitment and sacred trust upon whatever transpires in the master-disciple relationship. The relationship can become quite intimate as the guru oversees the disciple's psychological journey and leaves no psychic stone unturned, probing the personality, long-hidden memories, childhood disappointments and sorrows, and buried sources of pain from the present and previous lifetimes, stripping away all personal and cultural pretensions. The goal of this journey is not only freedom from suffering but an expanded capacity for creativity, clarity, and joy.

Tantra can be practiced in any setting. Although Tantric Buddhism offers many practices, no single method is formally required. What is sought is a way to cut through ordinary awareness as directly as possible, in order to attain enlightenment in a single lifetime. The best method for doing this will be different for each person, so teachers assign whatever practices they consider most appropriate for a particular student. Strenuous methods of purification like prostrations and mantra recitation are often prescribed at the outset, in order to prepare the mind for the disciplines to follow. The Tantric pioneers developed meditations that could be done in the midst of any activity. Homemakers, artisans, and laborers of all types were taught how to transform their awareness in the midst of their daily occupations. A jeweler could meditate by envisioning that everything is as pure and radiant as shimmering gold; a winemaker might picture herself as distilling bliss from the grapes of experience; a shoemaker could imagine that he was sewing the leather of passion with the thread of freedom to produce shoes of enlightenment.

For example, Sahajavajrā was a wandering wine-seller in Uḍḍiyāna who catered to the Tantric yogis there. She had misgivings about the compatibility of her livelihood with the pursuit of enlightenment. When she was actively seeking an answer to this dilemma, the guru Padmavajra saw that she was on the verge of full awakening and gave her a meditation based on the selling of wine:

> All the Buddhas drink wine that isn't made by human hands, and it is inexhaustible. . . . That is to be known as the inexhaustible treasure-box,

> the entrance into the sphere of all Buddhas. It is also called the sphere beyond thought. Buddha-daughter, remain in that meditative state, and you will taste the primordial wine of innately spontaneous realization (*sahaja*) that all the Buddhas drink. It will quench your thirst, and you will be able to serve it to all beings.[11]

As a Tantric practitioner, Sahajavajrā did not have to abandon her livelihood. Her guru provided her with a method whereby she could integrate her work and her meditation discipline.

Some Tantric methodologies create with language, image, or ritual an aesthetic realm that the practitioner initially enters by means of meditation and ritual, and of which she eventually gains a direct awareness. One of these aesthetic, or imaginative, techniques is deity yoga (*devayoga*), in which the meditator envisions herself as a deity, such as Tārā, Mañjuśrī, or Avalokiteśvara. The purpose of this practice is to awaken and discover enlightened qualities within, be it the maternal protectiveness of Tārā, the shining wisdom of Mañjuśrī, or the unfailing compassion of Avalokiteśvara. A meditator might expand this practice and visualize all beings as Buddhas, the environment as the residence of a Buddha, all sounds as the voice of a Buddha, and all events as the liberating activities of a Buddha.

One of the main Tantric images used to remodel the practitioner's subjective reality is the *maṇḍala*. The *maṇḍala* provides a blueprint for enlightened vision. Ordinarily each person experiences a world that reflects her cultural background, personal neuroses and attachments, and habitual patterns of thought and behavior (known as *karma*). Meditation on a *maṇḍala* replaces the habitually dulled way of seeing the world with a bright, crystalline world of radiant colors, beautiful forms, and divine images and sounds. The basic pattern of the *maṇḍala* is a palace resting on a lotus flower that rises out of the cosmic sea. The *maṇḍala* palace is envisioned not as solid but rather as made of crystallized light, or as translucent, like jewels with light shining through them: sapphire blue, topaz yellow, ruby red, emerald green, and diamond white. Each of the walls has a large ornamental gate and is decorated with vases, canopies, pearl garlands, and victory banners. The journey through the *maṇḍala* symbolically re-creates the journey to enlightenment. The meditator enters by the eastern gate and encounters a series of Buddhas that represent different aspects of the personality and their enlightened counterparts. In this process, visualization and imagination are used to turn the five poisons of self-centered existence into the five nectars, or Buddha-wisdoms. Anger is transformed into mirrorlike wisdom, arrogance becomes the wisdom of equality, desire becomes discriminating awareness, jealousy turns into all-accomplishing wisdom, and ignorance becomes the panoramic wisdom of all-encompassing space.[12]

The Buddhist pantheon expanded under Tantric inspiration, introducing new deities and new types of deities. Female Buddhas added a dramatic new dimension to Buddhist iconography and soteriology, explicitly affirming the possibility of attaining Buddhahood in a female body.[13] Early Buddhist texts maintain that women can attain enlightenment, but deny that there could ever be a female Buddha: "It is impossible, it cannot come to pass that a woman who is a perfected one could be a complete and perfect Buddha."[14] Since the attainment of Buddhahood was regarded as a rare event that occurred only at cosmic intervals, this proscription did not necessarily represent a serious limitation for women. Mahāyāna Buddhism also upheld the ability of a woman to attain enlightenment but denied the possibility of a female Buddha. However, since Mahāyāna made Buddhahood the universal goal of all practitioners, the denial of female Buddhas had more problematic implications. When a woman attained enlightenment, she would become a male Buddha, apparently the only kind of Buddha known to Mahāyāna.[15] The *Bodhisattvabhūmi*, a fourth-century text, argues:

> Completely perfected Buddhas are not women. And why? Precisely because a bodhisattva [i.e., one on his way to complete enlightenment] . . . has completely abandoned the state of womanhood. Ascending to the most excellent throne of enlightenment, he is never again reborn as a woman. All women are by nature full of defilement and of weak intelligence. And not by one who is by nature full of defilement and of weak intelligence, is completely perfected Buddhahood attained.[16]

Although Mahāyāna texts did express positive views toward women in other regards,[17] this belief had negative implications for women insofar as it communicated the insufficiency of the female body as a locus of enlightenment.

The appearance of female Buddhas in Tantric iconography functioned positively for women in various ways. The introduction of female Buddhas was particularly felicitous in view of the Tantric doctrine that Buddhahood can be attained in the present lifetime and present body. Since bodies are both male and female, the absence of a female Buddha would effectively exclude women from the Tantric goal of Buddhahood in the present body. Instead, an earlier doctrine of innate Buddhahood is elaborated into a Tantric identification of men as male Buddhas and women as female Buddhas. Thus, in the *Caṇḍamahāroṣaṇa-tantra*, wherein a male and female Buddha converse, the male Buddha announces:

I am the son of Māyā [i.e., Śākyamuni],
Now in the form of Caṇḍamahāroṣaṇa.
You are the exalted Gopā [wife of Śākyamuni],
Identical to Lady Perfection of Wisdom.
All women in the universe
Are your embodiments, and
All men are my embodiments.[18]

Perhaps the foremost female Buddha is Vajrayoginī. She is blood red and has loosely flowing black hair; she is dancing, wears bone ornaments, and brandishes a skull-cup brimming with ambrosia. She is beautiful, passionate, and untamed. Sometimes this supreme liberator tramples corpses underfoot (figure 3), and sometimes she soars in the sky. Vajrayoginī often appears alone, but sometimes she is portrayed with a retinue of yoginis, and occasionally she has a male partner. Another important female Buddha, Nairātmyā, is the color of the sky, symbolizing her transcendence of ego-centered existence. She dances with her crescent-shaped knife aloft to cut off self-centered mind-states wherever they occur.

Another innovation of Tantric iconography is the introduction of fierce, or wrathful, Buddhas and other deities. The wrathful deities (*krodhakāya*), sometimes known as Herukas, or "blood-drinkers,"[19] generally have bloodshot eyes, an angry glare, dark blue skin, a tiger-skin garment belted with a snake, and jewelry made of bones and skulls. The wrathful category includes male Buddhas, like Hevajra, and female Buddhas, like the lion-faced Siṃhamukhā (figure 4). Tantric yogis and yoginis, patterning themselves after deities, also wear tiger skins and bone ornaments and drink out of skull-cups. Wrathful deities dance upon the negative forces they have overcome and laugh as they feast on the raw, painful negativity that unenlightened people regard as frightening demons. Such Buddhas may appear menacing, but Buddhas by definition act only to benefit sentient beings. Wrathful deities demonstrate that there is pure energy even at the heart of aggression. The meditator must cease seeing fearsome and hostile appearances as threats to the ego and realize that they are patterns of pure energy, devoid of negativity. As a female Tantric of the eighth century taught:

Activities that are graceful, heroic, terrifying,
Compassionate, furious, and peaceful—
And passion, anger, greed, pride, and envy—
All these things without exception
Are the perfected forms
Of pure, self-illuminating wisdom.[20]

FIGURE 3. Female Buddha Vajrayoginī

FIGURE 4. Siṃhamukhā, wrathful female Buddha

Wrath and anger are not totally eliminated on the spiritual path because at times it may be necessary to wield the appearance of wrath in order to rescue, liberate, or protect someone. For example, Caṇḍamahāroṣaṇa proclaims to his beloved Dveśavajrī that he carries his weapons so that he can protect women from men who fail to honor and serve them.[21]

Buddha couples, consisting of a male and a female Buddha in sacred union (*maithuna*), and other divine couples were another innovation of Tantric iconography. These deity couples occur in both peaceful and more wrathful forms. The divine consorts experience bliss and passion in their enraptured embrace, yet their facial expressions are tender and tranquil, showing the complete fruition of their wisdom. Buddhas do not reify the experience of union, approach it selfishly, or allow it to create neurotic attachment, for their passion is transposed to a higher octave by the realization of emptiness. The Buddha couples embody passionate enlightenment.

## CULTURAL BACKGROUND OF THE TANTRIC MOVEMENT

One of the reasons for the vigor and viability of Tantric Buddhism was its skillful synthesis of diverse elements of Indian culture. There was no Indian religious movement from which Tantric Buddhism did not draw something of value. Vedic ritual and mantra, Upaniṣadic mystical theory, *hatha-yoga*, *kuṇḍalinī-yoga*, Śaivite iconography, and Śākta beliefs all found a place in the Tantric repertoire. *Hatha-yoga* contributed physical disciplines and breathing exercises to enhance the flexibility, control, and longevity of the body. *Kuṇḍalinī-yoga* offered a range of techniques to harness the powerful psycho-physical energy coursing through the body. In India it is believed that this energy can be channeled for procreation, sexuality, creativity, or spiritual experience and heightened awareness. Most people simply allow the energy to churn a cauldron of chaotic thoughts and emotions or dissipate the energy in a superficial pursuit of pleasure, but a yogi or yogini consciously accumulates and then directs it for specified purposes. This energy generates warmth as it accumulates and becomes an inner fire or inner heat (*caṇḍālī*) that burns away the dross of ignorance and ego-clinging.

Foremost among the pan-Indian influences were those of the Śākta (goddess-worshipping) and Śaivite traditions. Tantric Buddhists encountered their Hindu counterparts at the cremation grounds and pilgrimage places where they congregated, for these were also the gathering spots of yoginis and yogis of Śaivite and Śākta persuasion. To this day the Tantric Buddhists and Śaivite and Śākta movements share many sacred places in common and use the same term for them (*pīṭha* rather than *tīrtha*). Their meetings provided ample opportunity for mutual influence and borrowing.[22]

The influence of Śaivite traditions is readily visible in Tantric Buddhist iconography. The Hindu deity Śiva is known as the lord of yogis. He lives in a cremation ground where no one will disturb his meditations, and he gets everything he needs from the cremation ground. He rubs ashes on his body, wears rags from corpses, lets snakes curl around him as ornaments, sits on a tiger skin or antelope skin, drinks and eats from a bowl made from a human skull, and makes his jewelry and musical instruments out of human bone. He is not celibate, and his mate Pārvatī is also a great meditator and practitioner of yoga. Some of the traits of Śiva were incorporated into Buddhist symbolism, most notably in the iconography of Heruka Buddhas like Cakrasaṃvara and Hevajra.

The participation of Tantric Buddhism in the wider currents of Indian culture is perhaps most evident in the Śākta elements that are present in the iconography, ritual motifs, and gender ideology. Tantric Buddhism and Śāktism (goddess-worship) share an emphasis upon female deities and women as embodiments of female divinity.[23] Both movements display a tendency to see the universe as generated by female creativity, a recognition of femaleness as ontologically primary and maleness as derivative and dependent, and a deference to women in social and ritual contexts. Tantric Buddhist texts include passages of a genre that is sometimes termed "praise of women" (*strīprasaṃśa*), in which the virtues of femaleness are proclaimed. These passages have no direct precedent in earlier Buddhist literature but echo passages in Hindu Tantric and Śākta texts, revealing their proximity to the Śākta cultural realm. Tantric Buddhist and Śākta texts have parallel passages urging respect of women and extending threats and punishments to those who would transgress this inviolable command.[24] Tantric Buddhists also share with Hindu Tantrics a practice of worship of women (*strīpūjā*, also known as "secret worship," or *guhyapūjā*).[25] The theoretical basis of this Buddhist and Hindu practice is the belief that women are embodiments of goddesses and that worship of women is a form of devotion explicitly required by female deities.[26]

These features can best be understood with reference to contemporaneous Tantric and Śākta movements rather than by appeal to factors internal to Buddhism. The judgment of André Padoux, a world-renowned authority on Hindu Tantra, that "as a whole, *śākta* ideology is

. . . fundamentally inherent to Tantrism,"[27] could apply equally to Buddhist Tantra. The confluence of Buddhism and Śāktism is such that Tantric Buddhism could properly be called "Śākta Buddhism."

---

Until several decades ago it was customary for scholars to identify the Pāla period as a time of decadence and decline for Buddhism due to the rise of Tantra. However, more judicious reflection has recognized that in the Pāla domains of northeastern India, and farther west and south as well, Buddhism flourished, in large part because of the creativity of the evolving Tantric movement. The viability of Buddhism in India was reflected in its institutional strength, artistic and literary productivity, growth within and beyond India, and high cultural visibility. International expansion and missionary activity attested to the vigor of the Buddhist faith during this period, as such famous missionaries as Śāntarakṣita, Padmasaṃbhava, Amoghavajra, Vajrabodhi, Subhākarasiṃha, and Atīśa exported Buddhism to Central, East, and Southeast Asia, often by royal invitation. Buddhist pilgrimage centers like Bodh Gaya, Śrāvastī, and Kuśinagara attracted scholars, artists, and religious seekers to India from throughout Asia.

Buddhist artistic creation and conception reached a zenith during the Pāla period, which was a golden age of Buddhist art. Tantric works of art and literature were commissioned on a lavish scale. The impressive artistic remains of this period represent only a fraction of what was originally produced, since works of more ephemeral materials (wood, cloth, stucco, and clay) have long since succumbed to the elements. This artistic legacy includes the elaborate monastic architecture of the period, which gave way either to torch and sword or to time and climate. The level of artistry was so high that artists, craftsmen, and iconographers throughout the Buddhist world turned to India for inspiration. The far-flung survival of Pāla artistic influence throughout Asia provides concrete evidence in pigment and stone of the appeal and strength of Pāla Buddhist culture.[28]

Buddhist literature flourished during this period, making Pāla India an international intellectual mecca as well. Buddhist authors and communities produced enduring classics of philosophy and ethics, notable plays and poetry, and thousands of works of the emerging Tantric genre.[29] Many of these works were lost when Muslims burned the monastic libraries in the thirteenth century, but fortunately large numbers of Buddhist texts had been imported by Tibet, China, and other countries throughout Asia and translated from Sanskrit into a number of languages, preserving them outside the country of their origin. Thus, rather than undergoing a period of decline, Buddhism attained one of its highest cultural expressions during the Pāla period.

Tantric Buddhism was one of the vital religious forces within Pāla India. Pāla period culture was not an abstract, monolithic entity from which Tantric Buddhism diverged, against which Tantric circles launched a minor protest, or from which the Tantrics withdrew in countercultural isolation. Rather, Pāla society was a dynamic and pluralistic environment for cultural creativity and diversity of which Tantric Buddhism was an integral part. Instead of approaching Pāla culture as something definable apart from its Tantric elements, it is important to document the Tantric movements as one of the major currents of Pāla culture. Similarly, the role of women in Tantric Buddhism is not a minor footnote or discordant chord against the symphonic backdrop of "Indian culture" but a central feature of one of the most brilliant flowerings of Indian civilization.

## CHAPTER THREE

# Women in Tantric Theory

## *POWERFUL AND AUSPICIOUS*

> The Buddhas command that you must serve
> A delightful woman who will uphold you.
> A man who violates this is foolish and
> Will not attain enlightenment.
>
> —*Caṇḍamahāroṣaṇa Tantra*[1]

THE RELIGIOUS LIVES of women unfold within a matrix of beliefs about women's capacities and the nature and value of femaleness. Beliefs and attitudes shaping women's self-perception—such as the symbolic content and interpretation of their religious practices—are just as important as material objects they wield and physical actions they perform. Beliefs about women are readily accessible in Tantric literature, particularly in biographical works and in the *yoginī-tantra* texts. These beliefs occur in the form of explicitly stated doctrines, terms for female practitioners, classifications of women, narrative accounts of women, and descriptions of interactions between women and men. Tantric texts articulate a profound and appreciative metaphysical understanding of female embodiment. Tantric works depict spiritually independent and powerful women who inspired awe and dependence and demanded respect and obeisance. Consistent with these depictions, Tantric texts are remarkably free of the condemnations of women that blemish so much religious literature. There are no pronouncements of women's inferiority or religious incapacity. Conspicuously absent are portraits of submissive, oppressed women and depictions of abusive, exploitative relationships. The texts do not seek to legitimize or justify male authority or superiority, nor do they suggest that women should not practice, teach, or assume leadership in Tantric circles.

Since views of women are easily accessible in Tantric literature, scholarly inattention to them cannot be attributed to their obscurity. The positive views of women have not readily been perceived or accepted by Western scholars because they defy the expectations of most Western interpreters regarding gender relations. Indian scholars, Tantric teachers, and Western initiates like Sir John Woodroffe and Lilian

Silburn acknowledge the stature of women in Tantra, but this irreducible feature of the classical Tantric worldview has eluded most scholarly interpreters, particularly Buddhologists seeking to locate it strictly within a Buddhist frame of reference, an approach that fails to reckon with the Śākta orientation of this movement.

In the absence of explicitly negative attitudes or misogynistic condemnations of women, scholars have taken the discernible emphasis upon women as evidence in itself that the Tantric texts express only male views and interests:

> All these tantric texts . . . have clearly been produced primarily for the benefit of male practitioners. . . . Thus despite the eulogies of woman in the tantras and her high symbolic status, the whole theory and practice is given for the benefit of males.[2]

> We must . . . recognize a persistent androcentric focus even in the elaboration of this feminine ideal. . . . Any valorization of the feminine is primarily of benefit to the male practitioner.[3]

> The texts invariably proceed from and reflect the viewpoint of male practitioners. . . . This is not solely a matter of stylistic conventions in a patriarchal society but may also reflect tantra's greater resonance for the male psyche and physiology in Indian culture.[4]

The linchpin of this twist of androcentric interpretation seems to be that because women are so often the subject of the discussion, this must be a sign of male authorship and evidence that women functioned only as the objects and ancillaries of men. The unstated premise seems to be that if women are present in a text, it must a priori be as objects of male subjectivity. By this arbitrary leap of logic, although the *tantras* express positive views of femaleness and urge religious cooperation between women and men, the content of the texts is irrelevant to their interpretation.

My hypothesis regarding the authorship and gender perspective of the Tantric texts is quite different. Although the *tantras* are gynocentric texts in which women are often the subjects of the discussion, it does not follow that women were the impassive objects of male observation or subjugation. I argue that since these texts were not created by men in isolation from women, they do not express exclusively male views. These views grew out of communal exploration and practice and proceed from the insights of *both women and men*. Indeed, many of the insights contained in Tantric writings can only find their source in practices done by women and men together. The texts openly present Tantra as a religious path on which the lives of women and men are closely intertwined. I contend that the extensive descriptions of the interactions and shared practices of women and men are in themselves sufficient evidence that the *yoginī-tantras* are the products of circles consisting of both women and men. Therefore, I include women among the creators of the *tantras* and conclude that the texts reflect the views and interests of women as well as those of men.

Reading texts as repositories of the insights of both men and women, rather than approaching them as texts written solely by and for men, opens new avenues of interpretation. Passages on women can be examined for potential evidence of how women viewed and experienced their own lives. This hermeneutical approach raises the possibility that women helped to create and at times dictated the categories within which men viewed them, the terms on which men approached them, and the conditions under which they would accept male companionship. Therefore, instead of foreclosing on Tantric texts as irremediably male creations and dismissing women as the lowly "objects" of these texts, this volume looks afresh at the texts in order to explore their actual content—-the kinds of women and gender relationships they actually portray and the ideal kinds of partnerships they envision.

## NUMINOUS, SKY-BORNE WOMEN

The female figures that appear in Tantric literature are portrayed therein primarily as religious aspirants in their own right. These strikingly independent women at times take a proud, condescending stance toward men and at others cooperate with men in dynamic religious partnerships. When they join forces with men, the women become spiritual allies and esteemed teachers, mystical companions, and bestowers of magical powers and enlightenment. Men are portrayed not as dominators of women but as supplicants, lovers, and spiritual sons and brothers. The texts do not define women in relation to men, but they do define male Tantrics as men with a specific relationship to women. A woman did not need male approval to participate or advance in Tantric circles; however, a man's progress in Tantra is marked by stages in his relationships with women. The proper homage to women is a prerequisite to his enlightenment.

Since women are their indispensable allies in the Tantric quest, male practitioners must seek them out and court their favor. According to the *Cakrasaṃvara-tantra*:

> My female messengers are everywhere;
> They bestow all the spiritual attainments
> By gazing, touching, kissing, and embracing.

The most excellent place for yogis is
Wherever there is a gathering of yoginis;
There all the magical powers will be attained
By all those blissful ones.[5]

Because this is a path upon which they must cooperate with women, men may travel afar to find their female counterparts, in order to undertake the practices that increase bliss:

Enjoyment and magical powers are attained
At places where female adepts (*ḍākinīs*) reside.
There you should stay, recite mantras,
Feast, and frolic together.[6]

These passages exemplify the playful and celebratory ambience of the *tantras*. The spirit of carefree joyousness and festivity surrounding the companionship of men and women is the antithesis of the ponderous mood of male domination attributed to this literature.

Preliminary evidence of the status and roles of women in Tantric circles can be found in their iconography and the terms used to designate them. In art, the spiritual stature of female Tantrics is conveyed by their characteristic insignia, such as delicate jewelry fashioned from flowers or carved bone and a crown of skulls or flowers. The women either strike joyous dance poses or sit firmly in a stable yoga posture displaying symbolic hand gestures (*mudrā*). They may sit on an antelope skin or have a lower garment made of tiger skin, both prerogatives of expert meditators. The women often carry a skull-bowl (*kapāla*) in which to drink and serve their sacraments and bliss-bestowing nectar. In the other hand yoginis typically wield a knife with an ornately carved handle and a curving, crescent-shaped blade. This small knife is not a physical weapon but a ritual implement and a meditative tool for destroying illusion, negativity, and all self-centered responses to life. A female Tantric may imagine that she grinds and chops negative appearances and distills the pure, blissful essence of the energy, which she proffers to her sisters and disciples in a shining skull-cup.

The terms used to designate female Tantrics are all honorific titles denoting their religious seriousness and meditative attainments. Foremost among the terms are yogini, *ḍākinī*, messenger, and heroine. "Yogini" means a female practitioner of yoga or ritual arts, a female being with magical powers, or a type of female deity.[7] The term *ḍākinī* eludes precise definition but is translatable as "sky-walker," "woman who flies," or "female sky-dancer," highlighting the flights of spiritual insight, ecstasy, and freedom from worldliness granted by realization of emptiness (figure 1).[8] Female Tantrics are sometimes called "female messengers" (*dūtī*) because they deliver success in all endeavors, both transworldly and mundane.[9] "Heroine" (*vīrā*) denotes a courageous woman who has undertaken the challenges of the Tantric path, with its primal psychological explorations and radical departures from the conventional.[10] Another term found in early works is "knowledge-holder" (*vidyādhārinī*), meaning a woman who possesses knowledge of magic, ritual, and meditation techniques.

Some of the terms—particularly "yogini" and *ḍākinī*—have a dual connotation of humanity and divinity, because the Tantric way of thinking posits a spectrum of gradations rather than a clear-cut distinction between the human and the divine. Advancement in Tantric practice brings supernatural powers and realization of innate divinity. Women who progressed on this path were revered and held in awe for their special abilities, and the fruitful ambiguity of these terms allows their use to designate a woman at any point along the spectrum, from neophyte status to a woman blazing with the glory of full enlightenment.

## RESPECT AND HONOR

The most salient feature of Tantric literature in regard to women is an uncompromising attitude of respect and homage. This respect is sometimes urged with impassioned conviction, as in the following passage from the *Caṇḍamahāroṣaṇa-tantra,* a major Tantric scripture of the *yoginī-tantra* class:

> One should honor women.
> Women are heaven, women are truth,
> Women are the supreme fire of transformation.
> Women are Buddha, women are religious community,
> Women are the perfection of wisdom.[11]

One of the earliest expressions of this concept can be found in a work by Lakṣmīṅkarā, one of the founding mothers of Tantric Buddhism. In a treatise entitled *Realization of Nonduality,* Lakṣmīṅkarā argues for this respect on the grounds that women are embodiments of female deity:

> One must not denigrate women,
> In whatever social class they are born,
> For they are Lady Perfection of Wisdom,
> Embodied in the phenomenal realm.[12]

The "Lady Wisdom" to whom Lakṣmīṅkarā refers is a goddess of early Mahāyāna origin. Also known as Prajñāpāramitā and Mother of All

Buddhas, this female deity embodies the highest truth and continues to be honored in Tantra. The affirmation of women as embodiments of female deity was a new theme for Buddhism but one that was also seen in Śākta and Hindu Tantric texts of the same period. It appears that women like Lakṣmīṅkarā took the initiative in embracing these Śākta values and integrating them into the Buddhist path. Linking human women and female deities provided an unassailable affirmation of femaleness.

In the same text, Lakṣmīṅkarā goes far beyond the simple requirement of respect and demands worship of women. Her advocacy of this practice is interesting in view of the antinomian tenor of her text. Throughout the work, Lakṣmīṅkarā insists that external restraints are not binding upon a Tantric practitioner, who can eat and do whatever she likes and go wherever she chooses. Although Lakṣmīṅkarā dispenses with the necessity of fasting, pilgrimage, mantra recitation, devotional practices, and ritual performance, she imposes a firm requirement upon male practitioners:

> One who knows this yoga should always worship,
> By the method of wisdom and skillful means,
> Mother, sister, daughter, and niece.
> He should always worship women
> With his powerful scepter of wisdom,
> Even crippled women, artisans, and women of the lowest class.[13]

Thus, according to Lakṣmīṅkarā, a man's response to a woman's divinity should range from respect to ritual worship. A yogi worthy of the name "should always worship women"—not only the female relatives of whom he is fond but women toward whom he might be unfavorably disposed. By promoting the worship of women (*yoṣitpūjā*, or *strīpūjā*), Lakṣmīṅkarā did not introduce a new ritual form but endorsed a practice that was already present in her cultural milieu, as seen in non-Buddhist sects of the period.[14] Her promotion of the worship of women is particularly remarkable for the fact that it occurs in a text devoted to the realization of nonduality. Clearly gender was not one of the dualisms Lakṣmīṅkarā wanted to deemphasize or eliminate. She left gender dualism firmly in place and taught the appropriate relationship between the sexes, which is to be enacted concretely as ritual worship of women.

As expressed by Lakṣmīṅkarā, the metaphysical basis of respect for women in Tantric Buddhist theory is the tenet that women are embodiments of the great goddesses of Tantric Buddhism. The identification of human women and goddesses is often voiced by a female deity. For instance, in the *Caṇḍamahāroṣaṇa-tantra*, Vajrayoginī repeatedly states that she reveals herself in and through women. She claims that all forms of female embodiment—including supernatural beings, women of all castes and forms of livelihood, female relatives, and female animals—participate in her divinity and announces:

> Wherever in the world a female body is seen,
> That should be recognized as my holy body.[15]

Vajrayoginī insists that all women and female beings in the universe are her embodiments (*rūpa*), or manifestations, and thus should be respected, honored, and served without exception.[16]

Respect for women was enjoined upon both men and women, although it has different implications for their respective development. For women, the relationship with Vajrayoginī is one of identity. Women must discover the divine female essence within themselves. This should inspire self-respect, confidence, and the "divine pride" that is necessary to traverse the Tantric path.[17] Divine pride, or remembering one's ultimate identity as a deity, is qualitatively different from arrogance, for it is not motivated by a sense of deficiency or compensatory self-aggrandizement. This pride is an antidote to self-doubt and discouragement and an expression of the pure Tantric view. When a woman reclaims her divine identity, she does not need to seek outer sources of approval, for a bottomless reservoir of self-esteem emanates from the depths of her own being.

In the *Caṇḍamahāroṣaṇa-tantra*, which addresses this theme, the female Buddha Vajrayoginī (also called Dveṣavajrī, or "Diamond of Hatred," in the text) reveals her metaphysical link with women and expresses her special concern for them. She announces that she is fully immersed in emptiness and bliss, and thus on some level is formless, but that she appears in bodily form "for the benefit of women who do not know that I exist in the bodies of all women."[18] Vajrayoginī takes form so that women, seeing enlightenment in female form, will recognize their innate divinity and potential for enlightenment:

> When [a woman] meditates on my form,
> If supreme pride in her innate divinity arises,
> She will not be stained by sin,
> Even if she kills a hundred Hindu priests. . . .
> Even if she is pitiless, fickle, and irascible
> And considers taking life for profit,
> That yogini will remain stainless.[19]

Significantly, this vehement defense of women is placed in the mouth of a female deity. She reminds her devotees that her gender is a trait she shares with human women. This revelation clearly had the potential to ennoble women, because of the obvious implication that femaleness cannot be a liability for a human being if it is not a liability for a Buddha. On the contrary, since the female Buddha is present within all women, all women partake of her divinity. This doctrine could encourage women to recognize their inner strength and spiritual self-sufficiency. Having a female divine exemplar helped women to deconstruct their unenlightened self and recover an enlightened identity in a way that did not devalue femaleness.[20] Further, having a divine counterpart is essential for Tantric practice, so this metaphysical position effectively kept the doors of Tantra open to women. The presence of female Buddhas in the iconography of enlightenment affirms that a woman can attain Buddhahood in her present lifetime, in her present female body.



While a woman's relationship with Vajrayoginī is one of identity, for a man it is primarily one of devotion that he must extend to women as her living representatives. Devotion to goddesses like Vajrayoginī should be expressed as respect for women, while respect for women provides a way of measuring devotion to a goddess. In the same Tantric scripture, the female Buddha helps men improve their attitudes toward women by dictating what a man should contemplate and recite in the presence of his female companion:

> Women alone are the givers of life,
> The auspicious bestowers of true bliss
> Throughout the three worlds.
>
> . . . . . . . . . . . . .
>
> When one speaks of the virtues of women,
> They surpass those of all living beings.
> Wherever one finds tenderness or protectiveness,
> It is in the minds of women.
> They provide sustenance to friend and stranger alike.
> A woman who is like that
> Is glorious Vajrayoginī herself.[21]

For men, meditating on women as embodiments of Vajrayoginī and transferring their reverence for Vajrayoginī to all women was a way to remedy their ordinary views of women and purify their vision. This process was not an arbitrary exercise in deconstruction of social conditioning, but a means of perceiving women accurately—as embodiments of female divinity, inherently divine and sacred in essence. Meditation should lead to direct vision:

> A man should meditate upon his female companion
> As an embodiment of your [Vajrayoginī's] form,
> Until intense practice produces
> Clear, direct vision.[22]

One of the things that distinguished a male Tantric and marked his religious progress was his ability to see women as divine. We see many examples of this kind of hierophany in Tantric narratives. For example, the adept Urgyanpa met a courtesan's daughter who had the power, through her blessing, to purify his mind of lingering neurotic and negative tendencies. She accomplished this while serving him a bowl of curry. This mental purification enabled Urgyanpa to see the young woman in her true form, as Vajrayoginī.[23] Thus, a scene that to ordinary vision might appear to be a low-caste woman serving food to a man was in actuality the glorious Vajrayoginī dispensing a blessing, and a person of pure vision would be able to perceive the reality of the situation. In another example, the yogi Tilopa had unsuccessfully sought someone to guide him in meditation on the female Buddha Tārā. As the account is told by Tāranātha, Tilopa went to Uḍḍiyāna, a place famous for its female Tantrics, and met a dark green woman with the characteristics of a *ḍākinī*. He displayed the secret signals that male Tantrics are supposed to use when approaching yoginis, and she welcomed him with the answering signs. When he asked her for religious guidance, the woman revealed herself to him in the form of Tārā and poured her blessings into Tilopa's mind, thereby giving him the initiation he had sought.[24]

For a reader outside this tradition, it might seem that these divinized women must have been visionary apparitions or figments of imagination—not human at all—but according to this tradition an illumined person can manifest the presence and appearance of deity. Full identification with deity is one of the goals of Tantric practice, whereas the ability to perceive deity is one of the fruits of spiritual progress. Therefore, Tilopa's vision was purified to the extent that he could recognize the innate divinity of a human woman and discern in her the presence and spirit of Buddha Tārā. Urgyanpa similarly came to realize that his companion was an embodiment of the female Buddha Vajrayoginī.

The doctrine of the divinity of all women provided a test case for purity of vision, as seen in the following account of two yogis who were on pilgrimage together in northern India. They had both made significant progress in meditation and gained some magical powers, and they were going to pay homage and meditate at some holy sites. One day they happened upon two women tending their animals on a hillside. Because the men's vision was not fully purified, they simply saw two women at their lowly labors, but could not see beyond their ordinary perceptions to the marvelous scene that unfolded before them: "At the foot of the hill, holy Tārā sat giving Buddhist teachings to the *nāgas*, but they saw only an old woman tending a big herd of cows. When they reached the middle of the hill, the goddess Bhṛkuṭī was preaching Buddhism to a group of *āsuras* and *yakṣas*, but they saw a girl tending a big herd of goats and sheep."[25] The nonhuman serpentine creatures (*nāgas*), malevolent spirits (*āsuras*), and treasure-guardians (*yakṣas*) to whom these women were preaching were also invisible to ordinary vision. One of the yogis, Buddhaśānti, became suspicious. Because he was on pilgrimage, he expected that everything he encountered should be full of import, and therefore he mistrusted his ordinary perceptions of these hill women. He prayed to Tārā with contrition, and she rewarded his timely apology with a gift of miraculous powers. His fellow pilgrim was not alert to the situation and missed an opportunity for spiritual progress.[26]

The Tantric Buddhist valuation of the female gender shares the basic orientation of the goddess-worshipping, or Śākta, strand of Hinduism, with its emphasis upon the divinity and worship of women. Hindu Tantra and Śākta texts also argue for respect for women as representatives or embodiments of the goddess. When Vajrayoginī says that she is embodied in all women and demands respect for women on this basis, she echoes similar passages in Śākta texts.[27] Consistent with its Hindu counterparts, Tantric Buddhism displays the conviction that all the powers of the universe flow through and from women. This affirmation of femaleness is a radical departure from the neutrality of Mahāyāna nondualism and clearly derives from the Śākta view of women as possessors of a special spiritual potency and as vessels and channels of the energy (*śakti*) that gives rise to life and well-being on all levels.

This Śākta theme is seen in the following passage from the *Cakrasaṃvara-tantra*, which likens women to the earth (*bhūmi*, Tib. *sa* or *sa-gzhi*), making conscious reference to the metaphorical meaning of earth as both source and foundation. "Foundation" in this context means something that has the power to produce something that was not previously present, just as the earth generates new life and then supports everything that lives upon it. In Tantric sources a female companion, a spiritual guide, the mind, and anything else that is a generative source and support of spiritual progress is said to be an earthlike foundation. It is in this sense that a man's association with a female counterpart can be the foundation of his religious life:

> A vow-possessing woman is like the earth—
> She is the wealth of the hero who loves [her].
> Making her his foundation, [like] the earth,
> The yogi of Cakrasaṃvara worships [her].[28]

This Buddhist passage would equally be at home in a Śākta text, insofar as it honors both women and the earth as sources of life, energy, and physical and spiritual well-being.[29]

Commenting on this analogy between a yogini and the earth, the *Pearl Rosary*, an eleventh-century Tibetan Cakrasaṃvara commentary, states: "Having recognized a yogini who will delight and transmit energy and power (*adhiṣṭhāna*) to him, and feeling passionately attracted to her, if the male aspirant does not worship that yogini, she will not bless the yogi, and spiritual attainments will not arise."[30] According to the *Pearl Rosary*, a yogini possesses the spiritual qualities herself and thus can offer spiritual sustenance, just as the earth yields life-giving sustenance. A man's attainment of enlightened qualities is dependent upon his association with a female companion who possesses them.[31] Just as a goddess blesses and benefits her devotees, and just as *śakti* vivifies all biological, cultural, and religious life, so a woman channels this life force, or spiritual energy, to her consort-devotee. A woman is no more depleted by providing this religious nourishment than is a mother by nursing a child or a candle flame by lighting many lamps.

Contrary to what is suggested in Western sources, this energy is not something that a man can extract or steal from a woman at will. The woman chooses when and on whom to bestow her blessing. Her ability to enhance a man's spiritual development depends upon her innate divinity as awakened and brought to fruition by her own religious practices, which include envisioning herself in the form of various goddesses and imaginatively investing herself with their appearance, ornaments, tender and wrathful expressions, and supernatural powers for liberating beings. By conferring energy and power upon a man—"blessing" or "empowering" him (*adhiṣṭhāna*)—she is not thereby depriving herself but rather sharing her energy voluntarily with a man who has won her favor by meeting various requirements that she may impose, such as displaying ritual etiquette, using secret signs, and making offerings and gestures of obeisance.

The etiquette that a man should display includes "behavior of the left."[32] Texts that are classified as *yoginī-tantras*, or "mother-*tantras*," commend this formal show of deference. As the name indicates, this system of esoteric etiquette requires that a man focus on the left side in all his interactions with women: when walking with a woman, staying to her left and taking the first step with the left foot; when circumambulating her, doing so in a counterclockwise fashion; using his left hand to make the secret signs; making offerings and feeding her with his left hand; and embracing her with his left arm.[33] This stylized behavior is a way for a yogi to show respect for a yogini and let her know that he is part of the Tantric in-group. Tsongkhapa comments that "the sign of a Tantric yogi is to perform all activities on the left,"[34] explains that he should do so because it pleases yoginis, and elaborates upon what is entailed:

> Many female messengers, that is, *ḍākinīs*, are pleased by all the activities of the left. Set about doing those activities. By doing what is agreeable to them, namely, activities of the left, their minds will be gladdened.[35]

> When a man sees a woman, he should circumambulate her three times from the left [i.e., counterclockwise] with his hands on his head and make obeisance to her three times, saying, "You are my mother, I am your son. Until enlightenment, I will be nurtured by the milk that arises from your breasts, which are the limbs of enlightenment." Pay homage thus.[36]

According to the *Cakrasaṃvara-tantra*, another *yoginī-tantra* vow requires that a man who is fortunate enough to have found a powerful woman who is richly endowed with spiritual qualities should not leave her side for the duration of the Tantric quest.[37]

In addition to the activities of the left, men are required to use secret signs in their initial approach to yoginis. The signs include hand signals and a syllabic code (*chommā*, sometimes called "*ḍākinī*-language") that would enable Tantrics who didn't speak the same language to communicate with one another. Tsongkhapa explains that the purpose of the esoteric codes goes beyond communication and includes the establishment of rapport: "Through these signs, the hero, that is, brother, and sister will attain an understanding, meaning that the minds of the *ḍākinī* and the male aspirant will achieve intimate rapport. . . . These are the symbols of accomplished yoginis, the symbols of the female messengers who wield the spiritual accomplishments."[38] Several chapters of the *Cakrasaṃvara-tantra* give code phrases, gestures, and body language used to convey essential messages such as "I'm hungry," "have some meat," "assemble in the *maṇḍala*," "remain in the forest," and "stay with me."[39] The same text also describes the vocabulary of facial expressions that a yogini might use to communicate her moods, especially her pleasure and displeasure.[40]

Thus, although respect for women is the cornerstone of Tantric gender relations, it has different implications for women and men. This philosophy challenges a woman to recognize her own divinity, while it requires a man to purify his vision, approach women with deferential behavior such as activities of the left, and use the secret codes the women imposed on them. By virtue of these divergent, but complementary, patterns of training, the relationship between a man and a woman is delineated as a relationship between a devotee and a deity. The terms used to express the requisite attitudes and behavior of a man toward his female companion are drawn from the vocabulary of devotion. They include reliance and dependence upon her as his religious refuge (*niśraya*, *āśraya*), honor and service (*sevā*), reverence and devotion (*bhakti*, *śraddhā*), devotional servitude (*upāsanā*, *upacāra*), and giving gifts (*dāna*), as well as ritual worship (*pūjā*).[41] The woman may also see her male partner as a deity in certain ritual contexts, but his divinity does not carry the same symbolic weight. She is not required to respond to his divinity with any special deference, respect, or supplication or to render him service in the same way that he is required to serve her.

This relationship also parallels human-divine relationships insofar as the deity is the benefactor and the human devotee is the beneficiary. Although the deity may derive some gratification from the relationship, the devotee has much more to gain than does the sovereign object of devotion. What supplicants ultimately want from their deity is supreme deliverance, or liberation, and this is what male Tantrics seek to gain from their relationships with spiritual women. The texts reiterate that a man cannot gain enlightenment without respecting women and allying himself with a woman.[42] Although it may be tempting to interpret this ritual worship as evidence that men were exploiting women in an attempt to make spiritual progress at their expense, this interpretation ignores the overarching context of a devotional and hierarchical relationship patterned after, and expressed in terms of, the human-divine relationship between a devotee and a goddess. The woman's beneficence is a gracious, yet voluntary, response to her devotee's supplication and devotion, homage and worship.

## CONSEQUENCES OF DISRESPECT

Unconditional respect for women was so integral to the Tantric ethos that men who failed to take seriously this aspect of Tantra were severely criticized and rebuked. Men were instructed regarding what behaviors and attitudes toward women were to be cultivated and which were inconsistent with the Tantric worldview. Male practitioners were warned to dispense with any denigrating attitudes they might have about women and admonished that these were incompatible with the Tantric path. The special commitments of a Tantric initiate include, as the culminating vow, a pledge never to disparage or belittle women.[43]

In a chapter entitled "Praise of Women," the *Caṇḍamahāroṣaṇa-tantra* argues in the strongest possible terms against the denigration or ascetical avoidance of women:

> Even if you fear bondage and death thereby,
> Withstand all that.
> On this path, women must not be abandoned!
>
> . . . . . . . .

Free from trickery, arrogance, and shame,
Always helping with whatever is needed,
The real bestowers of the spiritual attainments,
They should be honored with all one's possessions.[44]

One must not disparage women . . .
One should speak with pleasant words
And give a woman what she wants.
Having worshipped with one's belongings,
Accordingly one should not despise her.
Never abandon women!
Heed the Buddha's words!
If you do otherwise,
That transgression will land you in hell![45]

Male Tantrics who fail to render the respect and devotion that women deserve can expect to be rewarded not with full enlightenment but with spiritual regress and even a terrible punishment. Tsongkhapa warns of the dire consequences of disrespect in his Cakrasaṃvara commentary:

If one who aspires to enlightenment
Generates anger toward a female messenger,
The merit accumulated over ten million eons
Will be destroyed in an instant.[46]

According to the *Caṇḍamahāroṣaṇa-tantra*, a man could kill one hundred Hindu priests and not be stained by sin, but criticizing or disparaging a woman will send him to hell.[47] This aspect of Tantric Buddhism has a strong Śākta resonance, for Śākta texts similarly threaten severe punishments for even the mildest criticism or show of disrespect toward women.[48] A passage from the *Kaulāvalīnirṇaya* epitomizes this sentiment:

One should not strike a woman,
Even with a flower,
Even if she commits one hundred misdeeds![49]

Vajrayoginī evinces little patience with those who belittle women and pronounces hyperbolic curses on those who think they can scale the Tantric peaks while disparaging women:

Chattering fools . . . who disparage women out of hostility,
Will by that evil action remain constantly tortured
For three eons in the fathomless Raudra hell,
Wailing as their bodies burn in many fires.[50]

Caṇḍamahāroṣaṇa, Vajrayoginī's consort in this text, has as his general function the subduing of the evildoers of the world, but among them he singles out those who transgress against women. He assures her that he keeps his sword and noose at the ready as he scouts for men who fail to pay homage to women (figure 5), so he can slash the scoundrels to pieces:

FIGURE 5. Caṇḍamahāroṣaṇa, defender of women, with Dveṣavajrī

Mother, daughter, sister, niece,
and any other female relative, as well as
a female musician, Brāhman, sweeper,
dancer, washerwoman, and prostitute;
holy woman, yoginī, and ascetic as well . . .
these he should serve in the proper way
without making any distinction.
If he makes a distinction,
Caṇḍamahāroṣaṇa will be provoked
and slay the practitioner,
throw him into Avici Hell,
and threaten him with sword and noose.
Nor will he obtain Success in this world or the next.[51]

Clearly, classical texts of the Tantric tradition take respectful attitudes and proper behavior toward women quite seriously. Tantric biographies bolster these doctrines with narrative accounts of what can happen to a man who shows disrespect for a woman, even a woman of seemingly unsavory character. The corpus of Tantric biographies includes many stories of hapless yogis who advertently or inadvertently disparaged women. One tells how the yogi Maitrīpa went deep into the Śrīparvata mountains of southern India in search of Śavari, a famous Tantric guru. When Maitrīpa found him, the guru was sitting with two female companions (figure 6). Women of the forest, they had long, matted hair, skirts woven of bark and leaves, and hunting gear slung over their shoulders. Freshly killed game lay at their feet, and they were picking lice from the guru's hair. When Maitrīpa saw this scene, he couldn't suppress a sneer at the women as he wondered what a spiritual master was doing in such distasteful company.

Unbeknownst to Maitrīpa, the women were the Tantric adepts Padmalocanā ("Lotus-Eyes") and Jñānalocanā ("Wisdom-Eyes"). Soon the women began tutoring Maitrīpa in the very Tantric wisdom he had come to seek. *Ḍākinīs* have a special talent for removing obstacles to omniscience with a swift, decisive stroke of the sword of nondual wisdom, and these huntresses were superlative *ḍākinīs*. When Maitrīpa was walking in the forest, he saw one of the ladies shoot a wild pig. As his mind was reeling with shock, she delivered her unerring message:

Shooting the arrow of clear understanding,
I slay the boar of ignorance—
Now eat the meat of nonduality!

Then she shot a deer and sang:

FIGURE 6. Padmalocanā, Jñānalocanā, and Śavari

> Shooting the arrow of ultimate experience,
> I slay the deer of subject-object—
> Now eat the meat of nonduality![52]

Her real target had been the dualistic judgments that were preventing Maitrīpa from attaining enlightenment. When he realized that they were spiritually more advanced than he was, Maitrīpa accepted the women as his gurus, but his recognition came too late, and there was a penalty. Since he had insulting thoughts about them and did not pay homage to them at the first meeting, his life span was shortened, and he did not attain enlightenment during that lifetime.[53] Maitrīpa was punished for failure to pay homage to his gurus, but the deeper implication of the story is that the reason he failed is that he was not alert to the possibility that women—female hunters, no less—might become his gurus. Thus, a show of disrespect for women turned out to be one of the most decisive, and disastrous, acts of his religious career.

Such encounters are not unusual in the Tantric corpus. The yogi Kāṇha similarly failed to recognize a mere woman as a Tantric guru. His guru had sent him in search of someone who could transmit a particular teaching to him, and even though Kāṇha was forewarned that the teacher he sought was a woman, he could not bring himself to believe that it was the one to whose door the guru's directions led him, namely, a peasant living in a forlorn, isolated cottage. Skeptical that it could be her, Kāṇha set out again, but another day of travel simply brought him back to the same cottage. Still unconvinced, he went through the process a third time, which finally persuaded him that she was the spiritual teacher he sought. When his vision was purified he saw her in her true form, as a female Buddha sitting on an ornate throne in a mansion. Kāṇha returned to his guru with the requested teaching, but the guru was not pleased. He remonstrated that Kāṇha had missed the real purpose of the visit. If only he had been able to approach the *ḍākinī* without any mental reservations, he would have gained complete enlightenment. His prejudice had sabotaged him.[54]

In another case, Abhayākaragupta, a scholar who took great pride in his learning, was given several opportunities to recognize Vajrayoginī in her human manifestations. Because he had a strong devotion to the female Buddha in his former lives, in this lifetime she arranged meetings that were spaced years apart, giving him time to grow in wisdom in the meantime. In the first encounter, when he was still a Hindu of the priestly class, before he had even become a Buddhist, an outcaste woman came to his door and asked him to make love with her. He said he couldn't even touch her, much less make love with her, or he would be defiled. The scholar chased her away, fearing for his reputation if someone saw him talking to her at his doorway. Before she left, she advised him to go to Magadha and take Tantric Buddhist initiation, but he did not rush to follow her advice. In the second encounter, sometime after he had taken Buddhist monastic vows, a young girl offered him some raw meat, saying the animal had been killed especially for him.

He was repulsed by this offer, and accepting the meat would have violated his monastic vows, so he refused. In the third encounter, which took place when Abhayākaragupta was well into his Tantric apprenticeship, his guru's female attendant, the woman who usually brought him his water, came to his meditation cell with meat and alcohol and invited him to join her in the performance of a Tantric feast. When he hesitated, she ordered him to do so, perhaps hoping that her insistence would apprise him of the seriousness of what was transpiring. Oblivious, the scholar declined once again. The woman upbraided him that despite his extensive knowledge of Tantric teachings he had missed the import of her offer. She told him that he had missed his chance to attain spiritual perfection during that lifetime, since he had thrice rejected the emissaries of Vajrayoginī.[55]

This account implies that Vajrayoginī herself was testing Abhayākaragupta by appearing to him in the form of women whose spiritual authority he would tend to reject, such as a low-caste woman and an attendant. This could mean either that the female Buddha sent magical emanations of herself or that she inspired the women to act in this way on her behalf. In either case, Vajrayoginī's tests were designed to challenge the scholar to recognize women as her embodiments and as bearers of spiritual authority. As a Tantric practitioner, Abhayākaragupta had come to revere Vajrayoginī, but when he failed to extend his devotion to her to her human manifestations, the divine yogini was very displeased. His penalty was the postponement of his enlightenment to another lifetime.

The point of these stories is not that these men harbored blatant prejudice against women. The discrimination motivating their behavior in each case could well have been quite subtle. As Tantrics, they would have been familiar with the prescribed attitudes toward women, but because of lingering reservations or simply because they had not fully internalized these teachings, these men were betrayed by their lack of pure vision regarding women. In this tradition, to see women as they truly are is to see them as replete with the power and presence of female divinities. In the living tradition of Tibetan Buddhism today, there are those whose monastic orientation requires them to abstain from the kinds of intimacy described in the *tantras* and sometimes causes them to develop compensatory fear and hatred of women. However, there have always been and continue to be many within the tradition—lay people and monastics alike—who take the Tantric teachings on gender very seriously. This contingent of practitioners believes that recognizing the innate divinity of women and treating women accordingly is crucial to their religious progress.

## CLASSIFICATIONS OF WOMEN

The *tantras* of the *yoginī-tantra* class devote considerable attention to the classification of women.[56] The practice is loosely patterned after classification schemes found in secular Indian erotic literature, although the Tantrics adapted the categories to reflect their own religious aims and values.[57] While the secular works emphasize the beauty and agreeableness of the woman, the purpose of the Tantric schemes is to match a temperamentally suited yogi and yogini for the purpose of a fruitful spiritual collaboration. Spiritual compatibility is expressed in terms of membership in the same Buddha family, or Buddha lineage (*kula*). Men study the characteristics of women of different Buddha families in order to learn what colors they prefer to wear, their bodily types, and their behavioral and psychological traits. Tsongkhapa even recommended study and contemplation of the classifications of women for his monastic followers on the grounds that "even if one is not fortunate enough to be able to practice with a woman in this lifetime, one will create mental habits for future lifetimes when one is able to do so."[58]

The classificatory descriptions of women provide evidence of the women that one might find in Tantric circles, in terms of characteristics that they either actually possessed or ideally should possess. Although the emphasis upon classification of women in Tantric literature may seem to attest to the subordination of women in these circles, the kinds of traits that recur would argue against that conclusion. To give an example, one chapter of the *Cakrasaṃvara-tantra* describes women of various Buddha families. The first type sounds pleasantly mild-mannered. She has a peaceful temperament, an affectionate countenance, and a picture of a lotus in her house. One could argue that such a woman might be an easy target for a predatory yogi. Yet as the list progresses, the women become increasingly vigorous and strong-willed. In turn, we find women who always speak truthfully and are proud of their strength; women whose minds are powerful and energetic; women who delight in shrewish behavior and speak boastfully; women who are fearless, revel in their own ferocity, and like to eat meat and frequent cemeteries; and women who derive pleasure from the fact that they are untamable.[59] These do not sound like the kinds of women who could easily be manipulated or coerced. Instead of being told to look for women who are meek, gullible, and defenseless, as one might expect if the men's intentions were the recruitment of passive victims, one finds women who not only are strong but are aware of their power and enjoy it, for they are "proud of their strength," "delight in shrewish behavior," and "derive pleasure from the fact that they are untamable."

Another example of the types of women that characterize Tantric literature, and thus presumably Tantric circles, can be found in a chapter of the *Cakrasaṃvara-tantra* that divides yoginis into four types. The first type cannot be prevented from speaking the truth and always takes delight in the Buddhist teachings. The second type is haughty, wealthy, and domineering and loves to hear news of deaths in battle. The third type is moody, angers at the slightest provocation, likes to argue, and is very proud. The fourth type has an unpleasant expression and imperfect features and is exceedingly arrogant.[60] None of these women sounds like a promising candidate for effortless seduction. Thus, when one looks at the actual content of the classifications, where one might expect to find an emphasis upon docility and subservience, one finds instead that the female counterparts of the yogis are likely to be ferocious, domineering, and untamable. There is a complete absence of submissiveness. These sound like formidable women by any standards.

The kinds of places to which yoginis were attracted also suggest a boldness of temperament. In addition to cremation grounds and forests, their haunts included caves, crossroads, riverbanks, abandoned houses, theater and pleasure districts, and goddess temples. Yoginis apparently frequented beautiful wilderness areas and desolate spots where their meditations and ritual activities would be undisturbed. A woman who would travel alone or even in a group to such places would have to be hearty, intrepid, and adventuresome.

To help the men recognize their female counterparts, Tantric texts also describe general signs of yoginis, such as a reddish or bluish tint to the skin, sidelong glances, an unusual hairline or skin markings, laughter one moment and weeping the next, and forthright, aggressive behavior. Men were warned that yoginis can be very intimidating at the first meeting. Yoginis may try to repel an approaching hero with frightening cries and wrathful guise, as a test of his bravery and discernment. The *Cakrasaṃvara-tantra* promises:

> If the hero isn't frightened,
> The *ḍākinīs* will take him by the left hand and
> Carry him to their own place.
> Then the *ḍākinīs* will cavort with that person, and
> That place will become like paradise.[61]

Armed with knowledge of these habits and signs, a man increased his chances of recognizing a potentially numinous encounter, as in the case of Atīśa:

> He once met a naked woman wearing a necklace of bones and skulls. She herself looked like a skeleton, laughing at one moment and weeping at the next. Atīśa . . . felt that she perhaps had some esoteric instructions to impart, so he mentally bowed down to her and asked if he could receive religious instruction from her.
>
> "If you want religious teachings you will have to come to eastern Bengal," she said, and departed.
>
> Atīśa followed her until she reached a great cremation ground. There she suddenly turned back and asked Atīśa, "How did you guess that I had some special religious instruction to impart? Do I look like I have any?"
>
> "Yes," replied Atīśa, "you certainly do!"
>
> Pleased with him, she initiated him.[62]

Recognizing her by her bone ornaments and laughter and tears, and not diverted by her unconventional appearance, Atīśa was rewarded by an enlightening encounter. He remained in Uḍḍiyāna for three years, living among the yoginis there.[63]

The indomitable women that appear in Tantric classification schemes populate the biographical literature as well. Without exception, the women of Tantric biographies are outspoken and uninhibited. They appear to be unrestrained either by social conventions or psychological reticence. There is no hint of deference to male authority or concession of male superiority. Rather, the women openly and without hesitation rebuke men whom they find to be spiritually errant. The pages of the Tantric biographies are enlivened by their memorable ripostes as they shatter male self-complacency. We have only to think of the insouciant reply of the Arrow-making Yogini to Saraha when he tried to make small talk with her. She coolly informed him: "The Buddha's teaching can only be known through actions and symbols, not words and texts."[64] Later, Saraha entered a deep meditative state while his female companion was preparing some radish curry. He remained in trance for many years, but his first act upon awakening was to ask for the curry, a display of attachment that unleashed her criticism. She told him that clearly he needed additional meditation, so he announced that he would go into the mountains to meditate in solitude. Provoked by his quietistic attitude, she admonished that it would be pointless for him to isolate himself in the mountains, since physical solitude would avail him of nothing if he did not abandon conceptual thought.[65] Her rebuke occasioned his final spiritual awakening and is now immortalized in one of his verses: "Do not sit at home, do not go to the forest. But recognize mind wherever you are."[66]

Stories like these illustrate the audacious expression of infallible observations for which Tantric yoginis are famous. Luipa, too, received his decisive lesson in the form of an insult from a woman. Luipa, a yogi of princely birth, had been practicing Tantric meditation for many years and considered himself to be above reproach when he ran into a yogini tavern-owner. With her clairvoyant vision, she perceived a small but obdurate knot of royal pride in his heart, despite his many years of renunciation. Instead of giving him something from the menu, she served him a bowl of moldy leftovers. Luipa threw the bowl into the street in disgust and shouted, "How dare you serve garbage to a yogi?" She shot back, "How can an epicure attain enlightenment?" Stung by the accuracy of her riposte, he saw where to direct his efforts in order to scale the final peak of enlightenment. He took up residence on a riverbank and began to live on fish entrails discarded by the fishermen. Through this practice, Luipa attained a state of continual bliss in which the fish entrails tasted just like ambrosial nectar.[67]

In another instance, a very poor yogi, Kantali, lived by the side of a road and made a meager living by scavenging rags and piecing them into patchwork cloth. When he stabbed his finger one day while sewing, he lost his equanimity and cried out in pain. A yogini who was strolling by saw an opportunity to help someone who was trapped by the illusion of selfhood, as evidenced by his self-cherishing behavior. She told him that he had been caught in a cycle of suffering for many lifetimes and asked if he was ready to change. Her confident delivery of this psychological observation inspired his faith, so Kantali asked what he could do to break the cycle. The yogini challenged that she didn't know if he had the fortitude to follow her. He assured her that he was willing to do whatever was necessary. She became his guru and directed his path to enlightenment, from the visualization of deities through the subtle inner yogas and ultimate realization of the nature of mind.[68]

When she saw that her disciple was having trouble meditating upon deities while he was sewing, the wandering yogini offered her assistance in the form of a spontaneous song:

> Envision the rags you pick and stitch as empty space.
> See your needle as mindfulness and knowledge.
> Thread this needle with compassion
> And stitch new clothing for all the sentient beings of the three realms.[69]

Her song opened the floodgate of infinite compassion in his heart, and the surge of freedom and exhilaration made him laugh and shout, "Look at the wonderful cloth this yogi has sewn!"[70] Passers-by thought the dust-covered wretch by the side of the road had gone mad and marveled that the madman had a companion—a woman in rags who was laughing just as hard as he was. These are just a few characteristic examples to show that the astute and indomitable women who appear in Tantric literature cannot accurately be characterized as passive or victimized sex-objects.

## MOTHERS, SISTERS, AND DAUGHTERS

Another classification of women appears in Tantric literature in the form of references to female relatives. Most shocking to early scholars of Tantra were passages urging the necessity of making love with one's mother, sister, and daughter, such as the following passage from the *Guhyasamāja-tantra*:

> One who unites with mother, sister, and daughter
> Will attain the extensive perfections and truth
> At the pinnacle of the Mahāyāna.[71]

These controversial images, whose shock value was intentional, communicate the distinctive vision of relationships in Tantric circles. Outsiders would be offended by these images, but insiders would understand their symbolism. In place of biological families, Tantric adherents formed voluntary and tightly knit groups bound by secret initiations and pledges. Primary allegiance shifted from biological kin to a religious family with a shared worldview and common aspirations. Thus, Tantrics defined themselves as family members in relation to one another, as in the following passage from the *Cakrasaṃvara-tantra*:

> Stay only with female messengers:
> Mothers, sisters, daughters, and wife.
> Practice in a circle, like this,
> And not in any other way.[72]

Male Tantrics were seen in parallel terms:

> If a man can recognize *ḍākinīs*
> Who maintain their Tantric vows,
> They will instantly regard him as a
> Brother, father, or husband.[73]

These kinship terms inspired a range of exegeses. A widely accepted interpretation is that the female companion of one's guru is like a mother, a female disciple of the same guru is a sister, one's own disciple is a daughter, and a man's female companion is his wife or consort.[74] Similarly, for a woman, the male disciple of the same guru is a brother, a male disciple is a son, and a male companion is a husband or consort. The mother also has a more general significance as the mother of liberation and spiritual life. In accordance with the gynocentric perspective of these texts, the vulva is honored as both the gateway to life and the citadel of Buddhahood. The male practitioner is directed to contemplate the womb of his partner and realize that this organ has been his passageway to numerous rebirths and now becomes a threshold to enlightenment.[75] This is one sense in which a man may unite with his "mother"—the mother of his liberation.

Although statements about union between family members have an air of antinomian bravado, they refer primarily to the religious lineages created by Tantric affiliations and the necessity of familial loyalty among secret compatriots. They underscore that Tantric disciplines involving sexual union should be undertaken only with Tantric insiders—people who share the same initiations, vows, and training.

## DANCERS, COURTESANS, AND LOW-CASTE WOMEN

Dancers, courtesans, and a range of low-caste women such as washerwomen, weavers, barmaids, hunters, fisherwomen, artisans, and even outcastes figure prominently in Tantric biographies, poetry, and ritual manuals. The presence of this group of women in the literature has been cited as evidence of the exploitation of women in Tantric circles. The explanation generally proffered by Western scholars is that women of these classes were ignorant, promiscuous, and sexually available to male Tantrics who needed them for Tantric practices involving sexual union:

> Practical considerations also necessitated the use [*sic*] of low-caste women. . . . outcaste girls [*sic*] were more promiscuous, uninhibited by Manu's laws.[76]

> They appear there because women of these castes had been employed [*sic*] and presumably still were employed whenever "fools" actually performed these rites.[77]

> The role played by girls [*sic*] of low caste and courtesans in the tantric "orgies" (*cakra*, the tantric wheel) is well known. The more depraved and debauched the woman, the more fit she is for the rite.[78]

This line of speculation attributes the presence of such women in Tantric circles to their usefulness to men and social vulnerability to sexual predation.

A slightly more genteel theory regarding the low-caste women in Tantric sources is the suggestion that associating with these women provided men with an opportunity to overcome their class prejudice.

Mingling with a social inferior—a woman of low caste—might force a male practitioner to abandon class pride and concerns about ritual pollution:

> When the Indian initiate belonged to a twice-born caste there is obvious motive for the Guru to employ [*sic*] an outcaste woman in the initiation rite; destruction of social conditioning, reduction of pride and cultivation of the wisdom of equality may result from such an association.[79]

According to an influential version of this theory, since low-caste women occupy the bottom of the social hierarchy, their elevation in Tantric practice and symbolism brings about religious insight by an inversion, or *coincidentia oppositorum*, of what is low in the social sphere and exalted in the religious sphere:

> It is the symbolism of the "washerwoman" and the "courtesan" that is of chief significance, and we must reckon with the fact that, in accordance with the tantric doctrines of the identity of opposites, the "noblest and most precious" is hidden precisely in the "basest and most common."[80]

Proponents of these theories do not suggest what the women themselves might gain from this arrangement, since it would appear that they were simply being "employed" to serve as an instrument of male purposes.

These explanations for the presence of low-caste women in Tantric circles are untenable for a number of reasons. They focus on superficial characteristics of the women and extrinsic reasons for their participation in Tantric rituals. When a man sought a spiritual companion, we are to believe that he chose a woman on the basis of her caste rather than because of an intrinsic reason such as whether she was a Tantric practitioner like himself. The *yoginī-tantras* always advocate intrinsic reasons for the choice of religious companion. The foremost requirement is that she be a Tantric initiate who has kept her vows. Also important are her religious training, level of spiritual insight, and knowledge of rituals, yoga, and meditation.[81] When the man in question had a higher caste background or was a monk, often the man sacrificed a great deal—social position, the prestige of monastic status, wealth, reputation, even in a few cases a throne—for the sake of a long-term, openly displayed relationship with such a woman. It seems unlikely that a man would sacrifice so much for the sake of an ignorant, promiscuous woman devoid of intelligence, refinement, and religious endowments. High-caste women of royal and priestly backgrounds were also known to relinquish their caste status in order to take a low-caste consort, although in those cases no one suggests that it is because the men were socially disadvantaged, promiscuous, gullible, or stupid.

These theories founder on a fundamental misunderstanding of the cultural roles of these women in Indian society. The hypothesis of "Tantric inversions" to explain the presence of low-caste women has been critiqued on ethnographic grounds by Frédérique Marglin, who argues that although women of low caste, such as dancers, courtesans, and washerwomen, may occupy a low rung in the social hierarchy, this does not exhaust their social meaning. These classes of women are traditionally attributed with powers of fertility and auspiciousness in Indian culture.[82] The presence of these women in the Tantric context cannot be attributable to a structural opposition or "reversal of values" because Tantra explicitly rejects social hierarchies in the interests of a pursuit of power. The female power (*śakti*) of birth, growth, and religious transformation does not correlate with the dualistic hierarchical principles ordering society.[83] This power of transformation (*adhiṣṭhāna* in the Buddhist context) cannot be gained either by adhering to social hierarchies or by overturning and transgressing them. This power supersedes and transcends hierarchy because its efficacy does not depend upon the social status of the beneficiary. By virtue of their occupations low-caste women possess and embody transformative power, or female energy. As a tradition that is preoccupied with power and locates that power in women, it is natural that Tantra would attract and welcome women who already have or seek to cultivate a sense of confidence, strength, and spiritual power.

Another reason that these theories fail to account fully for the presence of low-caste women in Tantric circles is that they do not consider the subjectivity and intrinsic motivations of the women themselves. This is a serious omission for a theory that seeks to shed light on the gender dynamics of a movement that clearly attracted and held the loyalty of large numbers of women. Their elevated status in a realm of cultural meaning that values spiritual power above ritual purity would naturally make Tantric movements attractive to such women. The fact that their power is acknowledged and celebrated in this tradition could only encourage their participation. Women of these classes often had a relatively high degree of financial independence and freedom of action and movement in Indian society. Tantric Buddhism would be appealing to such women by virtue of an absence of either a gender-based hierarchy or a class-based one that would exclude them or limit their participation. Their internal sense of power and autonomy would be mirrored and magnified by the Tantric philosophy of gender. Further, these women would be unencumbered by caste strictures that would inhibit their own participation.[84] Their social background meant that these women were free to make an independent choice of religious affiliation and male partner and to adopt the often unconventional life-style of a Tantric yogini.

Interpretations that stress extrinsic reasons for the participation of low-caste women also ignore the relevance of the social backgrounds of these women to the Tantric enterprise. The emphasis upon the lower castes showed that Tantric wisdom was not limited to a particular social class, either high or low. The emphasis of the *tantras* upon low-caste women and low castes in general is a complex motif that finds philosophical justification in the Mahāyāna ontology that everything is pure and equal in value, but it also carries a message that Tantric wisdom should be sought from any social class, for low-caste people are no less likely than others to possess and transmit such teachings and initiations. Women from those backgrounds had their own religious insights to bring to bear on the Tantric enterprise precisely because of their varied backgrounds. Low-caste women came to Tantra not as blank slates but with skills and cultural knowledge that were directly applicable to Tantric methodologies. Dancers brought bodily discipline, knowledge of sacred gesture and movement, and techniques for embodying deity. Courtesans brought erotic skills and sophistication. Wine-makers and wine-sellers brought a background in the distillation of alcohol so important to the Tantric sacraments. Ḍombs brought familiarity with the cremation grounds where Tantric feasts often took place. Tribal people brought skills like the fashioning of bone ornaments and musical instruments, the ritual use of skulls, magical arts, mantra recitation, worship of goddesses, and ritual techniques for embodying forth and communicating with spirits and deities.

The social classes to which the low-caste women belonged were classes from which Buddhism and the other classical traditions were receiving infusions of cultural energy during this period. The melding of Buddhist soteriology with archaic religious practices and symbols is part the genius of the *tantras*. By emphasizing these classes, Tantric Buddhism points to the quarters of society from which it received many of its distinctive ritual and iconographic elements. By highlighting women of those classes, it is possible that Buddhist sources are pointing to their own roots.

When all of these factors are considered, it becomes clear that the presence of low-caste women in the Tantric movement is much more complex than a matter of sexual availability. These women were possessors of spiritual power and funds of cultural knowledge. They could find in Tantric Buddhism a sphere of participation in which they would not have to sacrifice their autonomy, initiative, or personal strength.

They were free to undertake Tantric disciplines as serious practitioners in their own right. Their forthright aggressiveness would serve them well in Tantric circles, and instead of being pressed into the service of male compatriots, they could enforce the requirement that men respect and honor them.

## THE DANCER AND THE KING

The usual interpretations of Tantric Buddhist women in general and low-caste women in particular crudely simplify their religious lives and misrepresent the kinds of intimacy envisioned in the *tantras*. An example of the religious career of a low-caste female Tantric may help to clarify the interpretive issues at stake here. In this case a king gave up his throne to join destinies with a dancer. She is Ḍombīyoginī, while the king is known to history only as Ḍombīpa and Ḍombīheruka, names he received by virtue of his association with her. When their story opens, the king, a ruler in Assam, was already an advanced Tantric practitioner under the guidance of the guru Virūpa. The king was approaching readiness for some of the advanced yogic practices that are undertaken with a partner, and the imminent arrival of his karmically ordained female companion was revealed to him in a vision. They first met when she came to the palace with her parents, as part of a troupe of singers and dancers who had come to perform at court. She was twelve years old at that time and possessed an unworldly temperament and aptitude for spiritual training. The king offered a large sum from his treasury, namely, an amount of gold equal to her weight, to induce the dancer's family to allow her to remain with him.

The presence of Ḍombīyoginī in the palace remained a secret for twelve years, until the king's subjects discovered their relationship. After being driven from the kingdom, the couple secluded themselves in a wilderness hermitage and meditated in retreat for another twelve years. The fortunes of the kingdom declined so much during the ruler's absence that his contrite subjects decided to invite him back. When the ministers went into the forest to summon him, they saw the dancer floating on the surface of the lake on a lotus leaf. Clearly both the dancer and the king had made progress during their retreat. They mounted a tigress and rode her into town, brandishing a poisonous snake as a whip, demonstrating their mystical attainments (figure 7). Ḍombīyoginī and the king later transformed into Nairātmyā and Hevajra, one of the Buddha couples upon whom they had been meditating, and the king declined to take back his kingdom after all, having discovered more sublime pastimes.[85]

FIGURE 7. Ḍombīyoginī and Ḍombīpa riding a tigress

The usual interpretation of their partnership of more than twenty years is that the king was exploiting the dancer, who was useful to him because she provided him with an opportunity to overcome his caste prejudice.[86] However, according to the story itself Ḍombīyoginī's distinguishing characteristics were not her availability or caste, or even the fact that she was classically beautiful by Indian standards. Rather, it was such personal qualities as spiritual sensitivity that made the king recognize in her his destined companion. She was not simply a low-caste person who was socially marginal and hence "available" for his practices, nor was she an ignorant and unrefined person. As a dancer qualified to perform at court she was someone with an extensive artistic background. By the age of twelve she would already have undergone years of training, since dance instruction begins at a very young age, particularly in a family of dancers. Therefore, Ḍombīyoginī was an educated, cultured, and refined person with a high level of self-mastery from years of rigorous physical discipline. It was mainly because of these qualities that the king recognized in the dancer a potential Tantric companion. The king's payment to her family was a token of his sincerity and regard for the daughter and thus a sign of how well he would care for her. The king was not purchasing her but rather compensating her parents for the loss of her future earnings. The king removed her from her former life and family, but he did not expect her to give up more than he was willing to sacrifice. They both had to sever ties with their former way of life in order to embark on a new path of life together.

It is hard to maintain that the dancer was "exploited" by the king when they remained together for more than twenty years. During this time she received extensive Buddhist training in preparation for the yogic practice of Tantric union, which, as Ḍombīheruka himself states in his treatise on the subject, "is not for beginners."[87] For the first twelve years he remained in the palace and may or may not have seen much of the dancer, but over time they became close enough that, given a choice between his low-caste companion and his kingdom, the king chose her—and, by implication, the enlightenment they would win together. Their mutual reliance is seen in their willingness to venture into the wilderness together, entrusting their physical survival and spiritual destiny to one another. For the second twelve years, beginning when she was twenty-four, they were sole companions in the wilderness, a situation demanding exceptional rapport, interdependence, and a shared dedication to their religious ideals. By this time, Ḍombīyoginī had many years to practice meditation and reach a level of expertise comparable to that of her consort so they could pursue the higher yogic practices together. The dancer and the king needed one another to enter the visionary realm of Tantra. They shared the hardships and illuminations of the spiritual quest as peers.

Ḍombīyoginī's progress in meditation was manifested by her displays of magical powers, such as walking on water (figure 8) and mastery of the four gazes. Tāranātha also reports that she composed songs

FIGURE 8. Ḍombīyoginī dancing on lake

of realization (*vajra*-songs), most of which are lost to us.[88] One of her songs has fortuitously survived in a collection of Tantric songs preserved in Nepal. The song takes as its theme her ability to walk on water, a supernatural ability demonstrating the dancer's understanding of emptiness. The song finds her in the center of a lake meditating upon a Buddha couple, the female Buddha Vajrayoginī and her male consort Cakrasaṃvara:

> On the lake, Ḍombīyoginī becomes two.
> How can they sit in the middle of the lake?
> The two of them sport in a palace of enlightenment,
> Dancing in the sphere of phenomena,
> In a land of stainless purity.
> Naturally, beauteously, they rest calmly
> On Buddha knowledge.
>
> Vajrayoginī appears in four forms
> And traverses the world.
> The one with a boar's head, Vajravārāhī,
> Embraces (her lover).
> She sits on a four-cornered *maṇḍala*, bestowing compassion.
> Sometimes in one form, sometimes in another,
> She embraces the blue-faced lord.[89]

The lake is where Ḍombīyoginī drew water when she was on her wilderness retreat, but the lake is also a metaphor for the world, which is either a realm of suffering or a realm of bliss depending upon how one looks at it. The dancer's purity of vision enables her to play with phenomena without sinking under the weight of ponderous aspects of conventional reality like the laws of physics and force of gravity. In the first half of the song, Ḍombīyoginī visualizes a Buddha couple in union. She imagines herself to be Vajrayoginī, who manifests in different forms in order to meet the needs of living beings throughout the world. When she embraces her partner, whom she envisions as a blue Heruka Buddha, the dancer playfully imagines herself first in one form and then in another, alternating among the four divine yoginis of the innermost Cakrasaṃvara *maṇḍala*. Their union, although exquisitely blissful, is ultimately undertaken out of compassion for the world. The sacred communion of male and female Buddha generates waves of bliss and harmony that turn the world into a *maṇḍala* and showers forth a rain of nectar that satisfies the spiritual hunger in the hearts of living beings everywhere.

Ḍombīyoginī's song, a ray of visionary splendor streaming from her mind, attests to the highly polished luster of her spirit. This lone surviving song bears witness to the riches that have been lost, although some of her verses may have been pseudonymously attributed to Ḍombīpa.[90] The song also demonstrates that the dancer had immersed herself in the aesthetic universe of Tantra and fully understood and mastered the yoga of Tantric union.

The example of Ḍombīyoginī suggests how misguided Western assessments of low-caste women have been. Western interpretations stress her supposedly debased nature; however, the Tantric narrative depicts her not as lowly or ignoble but as a beautiful and artistically gifted yogini. The long-awaited spiritual companion of the king made significant progress herself and eventually became a religious teacher and enlightened poet. After Ḍombīheruka died, Ḍombīyoginī, who was at least in her thirties by that time, taught independently as a Tantric guru. She gave initiation and secret oral instructions regarding the subtleties of the esoteric yogas, and two Hevajra lineages are traced from or through her.[91]

This careful reading of the account of a low-caste Tantric yogini shows that promiscuity did not figure in her story, and it is unlikely that the king needed to spend twenty years with her in order to overcome his caste prejudice. Rather, we see a serious, long-term, committed partnership devoted to the emancipation of both persons. Ḍombīyoginī was practicing and advancing throughout the course of their relationship, as seen by her career as a guru. The dancer was not being exploited; she was pursuing enlightenment—and she attained it.

## TANTRIC GENDER IDEOLOGY: A GYNOCENTRIC BALANCE

Indian Tantric Buddhism is distinctive among Buddhist subtraditions in its understandings of femaleness. Attempts to interpret it as a movement that differs from other Buddhist schools only in methodology will miss this essential feature. The Tantric philosophy of gender emerged at a time of great creativity and change within Buddhism, and attitudes toward women were uppermost in the minds of the reformers. Rita Gross has convincingly argued that an egalitarian vision has blazed at the core of Buddhism throughout its history, although this vision has been obscured and denied in various ways over the centuries.[92] Theravāda Buddhism has a nondiscriminatory doctrinal foundation overlaid by negative assessments of female embodiment and by male monastic denunciations of women.[93] Mahāyāna teaches the irrelevance of gender as a false dualism but also condones expressions of misogyny. Tantric Buddhism renewed the perennial Buddhist effort to maintain an egalitarian philosophy by offering a new strategy. In place of Mahāyāna neutrality in regard to gender dualism, Tantra highlights gender polarities. In this gendered discourse, the female pole receives more emphasis than the male. Technically men are considered to be of equal metaphysical status and value, but in the empirical realms of image and ritual women receive more explicit affirmation.

The mainstay of this affirmation is an elaboration of the principle that women are embodiments of female deity. Women are seen as earthly, or bodily, manifestations of goddesses, and this identity is reinforced by the patterning of male-female relationships upon the relationship between a devotee and a deity. The man's divinity is an accepted premise of Tantric metaphysics, but it is not given the same range of concrete expressions as the woman's divinity in this gynocentric context.

Identification with divine female role models gave women an unassailable basis for self-confidence, namely, the "divine pride" that comes from awakening one's innate divinity. The presence of divine female exemplars who openly rejoice in their femaleness, free from shame and fear, seems to have empowered women to speak the truth fearlessly, to be physically and mentally adventurous, and to be argumentative and aggressive when it suited them. In the Tantric biographies, women freely and without apology reprimand men who need to be recalled to a direct vision of reality, by challenging his prejudices, shattering a cherished illusion, or puncturing an inflated self-image. Women's sense of freedom from male authority in this movement was reinforced by the fact that women were not dependent upon male approval for religious advancement either in theory or in practice. There was no male clerical body to bar their way and no promise of metaphysical gain by submission to male authority. Women could pursue Tantric apprenticeship on their own initiative. They needed only to be accepted by a guru, and that guru might be male or female.

Tantric Buddhist women's absence of fear and submissiveness is consistent with the nature of Tantric partnerships. The women did not need to seek relationships with men in order to gain self-approval, maintain their social respectability, or uphold the moral order. Psychologically this freed a woman to undertake relationships solely for her own enlightenment. Unlike arranged marriages, Tantric relationships were voluntary. Their basis was a passionate commitment to the same religious goals and ideals. A woman sought companionship for one reason: to achieve the religious ideals of complementarity and harmony that could be perfected in such a relationship. The woman's spirituality could nurture that of a man, but this was not the focus of her religious life, which was her own enlightenment.

This gynocentric arrangement set the women's and men's spiritual growth on different but parallel paths. On a complementary course of development, men acknowledge their interdependence with women. While a woman becomes more confident and self-reliant, a man becomes more capable of relationship as he comes to realize that a woman can support and enhance his religious life as a side effect of her own self-cultivation. Training themselves to see women as female Buddhas gave men a chance to deconstruct unenlightened thought patterns, most notably gender pride and prejudice. In a Tantric relationship, the man's concrete behavior—his symbolic, ritual, and stylized expressions of obeisance—acknowledge that he will not attempt to dominate the woman or enlist her energies in support of his spiritual growth at the expense of her own. The man's show of homage signals that he is willing to enter a relationship that will not be centered upon his ego or his needs but rather will be dedicated to their mutual enlightenment. Her needs will not be subordinated to his, nor will his to hers; their intimacy is to be an interweaving. In fact, the word *tantra* is derived from the verbal root *tan*, meaning "to weave." Many things are interwoven on the Tantric path, including the lives of men and women.

In the intricate equilibrium of this arrangement, the balance of esteem is nonetheless tipped toward the women. Tantric texts specify what a man has to do to appeal to, please, and merit the attention of a woman, but there are no corresponding requirements that a woman must fulfill. Further, there are numerous instances of men seeking female acceptance and approval, but no corresponding motif in the life stories of women. Since women do not need to take any special measures to meet the approval of men, the women in Tantric biographical literature display the blithe indifference to male approval and occasional condescension that one might expect in such an arrangement.

This gynocentrism probably helped to establish psychological parity between men and women. Although it may appear that women were dominant in this arrangement, it seems that the surface imbalance helped to ensure the deeper harmony of the sexes that is celebrated by the Buddha couples of Tantric iconography. The purpose of this dynamic was not female domination of the male for its own sake but the creation of partnerships devoted to the realization of ultimate truth. This type of companionship precluded that either partner should be deflected from her or his path to enlightenment by fulfillment of the other person's unenlightened ego needs. Therefore, the men's training offered a process of refinement and sensitization that rendered the men more capable of undergoing self-transformation in the context of an intimate relationship.

I contend that in Tantric Buddhism a balance is achieved in practice by privileging the female in theory, to counteract an erosion or total loss of the balance by even the slightest male strategy of appropriation. Tipping the balance of esteem in favor of the woman could serve as an expedient to prevent the female gender—and human women—from being submerged or suppressed. In Mahāyāna thought, the equal treatment of the two genders, although liberative and egalitarian in intent, meant that even a minor male gesture toward expropriation resulted in a loss of gender equality. In Tantric Buddhism, the gynocentric philosophy provided a preventive and corrective counterweight against male attempts to elevate themselves at the expense of women. Women had the incontrovertible authority of scripture and enlightened precedent at their disposal to counteract male attempts to devalue or displace them. This gender ideology armed women against individual male attempts to gain psychological ascendence or religious authority over them and against collective male attempts to dispossess them of the religious movement the women had worked to create. Insofar as men have been successful in disenfranchising women (for example, in certain institutional settings in Tibet), these doctrines survive from the early centuries of the movement to indict them. There is nothing ambiguous in the Buddha's pronouncement: "On this path, women must not be abandoned!"[94]

When we consider who might have initiated this gynocentric, yet balanced, configuration of gender relations, it seems possible that women were the agents of change. Men have rarely of their own accord created movements or authored philosophies in which women were explicitly privileged and from which women unambiguously benefit. Therefore, I do not presume that the respect and homage to women so central to the Tantric worldview was a magnanimous gesture on the part of male Tantrics or a courtesy that men spontaneously extended to women. It seems far more likely that the men's attitudes and behavior resulted from female leadership in forging this ethos. I suggest that women communicated their self-understanding and requirements to men, shaping the men's attitudes, behavior, and writings. Women would also tend to select as companions men who would mirror their own sense of dignity and empowerment, and this selection process could well have been a factor in determining the constituency of Tantric circles and formation of Tantric partnerships.

Clearly, it would be in women's interests to configure men's development in this way. Any progress that a man made on this path would be of immediate benefit to his female partner and associates. A man who underwent this kind of cultivation would be a better companion and lover than a man schooled in misogyny, convinced of his superiority and divinely ordained right to dominate women. Such a man could relate to a proud, sensitive yogini with a well-defined sense of personal power, and he would be a good companion for a woman who might be intolerant of male pretensions and coercions by virtue of her temperament, background, or concern about their toll upon her spiritual progress. Women's obvious benefit from this arrangement is another reason I suggest that women guided men in fashioning this cooperative, radically liberating vision of spiritual partnership. In response to the initiative of the Tantric yoginis, the yogis respected women in order to bring their own vision into alignment with the ontological reality of women's divinity and to become capable of the kind of relationships required for success on the Tantric path.

---

This chapter begins to delineate the cultural realm in which Tantric Buddhist women have pursued their religious lives. Tantric teachings present positive understandings of female embodiment, while explicit rules for behavior toward women encourage the concrete expression of respect in social and ritual interactions. The doctrines presented in this chapter do not represent intellectual strategies to suppress, subordinate, or exclude women. Women were not laboring against condemnatory attitudes, an ideology of male dominance, or the obsessional loathing of female sexuality that one sometimes finds in male ascetical texts. The Tantric doctrines affirm women in their religious aspirations while depriving male dominance of theoretical justification.

Instead of authorizing either sex to dominate the other, Tantric teachings enjoin close affiliation between women and men in the pursuit of spiritual excellence. Although individual practitioners might fail to attain these ideals, they were put forward as guiding principles that come increasingly into play on the approach to enlightenment. These ideals were pursued, and at times they were achieved in reality. The shared odyssey or "tale of liberation" of Ḍombīyoginī and Ḍombīpa epitomizes the couples who sought and attained the crowning achievement of liberation through spiritual companionship.

Women enjoyed psychological parity in a delicate, but tenable gynocentric balance in which they were the ones who were sought, supplicated, and pleased. A woman could exact certain forms of homage, communication, and obeisance before she would accept a male disciple or partner, and this gave the man an opportunity to demonstrate his seriousness of purpose in approaching her. This dynamic explicitly places their relationship in the context of their pursuit of enlightenment. Their egos will be relinquished in this relationship, and his suppliant behavior frees her to relinquish her own ego rather than serve his.

This gender ideology configured men's and women's spiritual development in complementary ways so that they could serve as ideal companions in a relationship dedicated to their mutual liberation. Respect for women was a touchstone of a man's spiritual progress, and the man's reform was necessary for the cooperative practices and higher octave of intimacy envisioned in the *tantras*. Women, on the other hand, cultivated the psychological independence that would enable them to maintain parity in relationship. In sum, Tantric teachings supported women in their spiritual aspirations and exhorted men to honor the women in their midst. Further, Tantric classification schemes and biographical vignettes portray the kinds of bold, forthright women who were likely to inspire awe, admiration, and allegiance. The triumphal tone of this material suggests that the men's respect was not a gratuitous or grudging concession but genuine admiration for the talent, energy, and passion for enlightenment of their female companions and teachers.

CHAPTER FOUR

# Women in Tantric Circles

## *ADEPTS AND EXPERTS*

TANTRIC YOGIS AND YOGINIS assembled in a network of pilgrimage sites throughout India, where they met other Tantrics, practiced their outer and inner yogas, and staged elaborate rituals. In this open and freewheeling religious setting, there were no formal barriers to the participation of women. Tantric sources express no prohibition of women's full participation alongside men or assumption of leadership and authority over men. Although there were no formal restrictions upon women's participation, modern scholars of Tantric Buddhism have placed the men in a brightly lit foreground and relegated the women who practiced alongside them to a shadowy background. Historical studies, with few exceptions, have claimed that women were an anomaly in Tantric circles and did not share the aspirations, training, and attainments of male practitioners but simply provided ritual assistance to them.

This claim flies in the face of extensive evidence that women were present and fully participated in Tantric circles as a matter of course. For example, Kāṇha had an equal number of male and female students, and his foremost disciple was a woman.[1] Pha-dam-pa sangs-rgyas had a large number of women among his fifty-four teachers and had twenty-four female students who attained enlightenment.[2] Two of the four most accomplished disciples of Jñānamitra were women.[3] One of the two best disciples of Śāntigupta was a woman, Dinakarā.[4] When the princess Śrīsukhā became a Tantric guru, hundreds of women in her retinue became her disciples and became accomplished yoginis.[5] The adept Bodhivajra, one of Kāṇha's disciples, reportedly had hundreds of yoginis among his disciples.[6] Among the students of the adept Nāropa, reportedly two hundred men and one thousand women attained complete enlightenment.[7] A majority of the eighty male "great adepts" (*mahāsiddha*) of India had female companions. Scores of yoginis held the Tantric feasts to which men like Kāṇha, Atīśa, Kamalaśīla, and rGod-tshang-pa were admitted. When yogis like Luipa, Nāropa, and Kantali were on the verge of a momentous spiritual breakthrough, women in their immediate vicinity came forward to deliver the decisive lessons and then continue on their carefree way.

What were the religious practices of these women? What were their attainments? On the basis of biographical compendia, lineage histories, textual colophons, songs of praise, scattered references to women, and writings by women, a pattern of women's religious practices can be discerned. Other studies may dismiss the type of evidence that I present here as reports of imaginary episodes or figures, reducing the references to women to literary flourishes or flights of imagination rather than accept them as statements with the same historiographic value as equivalent statements about men. My study gives equal weight to adjacent statements about men and women and allows the evidence of women to coalesce into a meaningful pattern.

## CHALLENGING ANDROCENTRIC READINGS

The interpretation of Tantric Buddhism that highlights men and marginalizes and tokenizes women is accomplished in part by an androcentric reading of Tantric sources. All sources describing what Tantric practitioners believe, practice, and accomplish are arbitrarily assumed to apply only to men unless women are specifically mentioned, without inquiring into whether the texts' creators intended their generic language to be male-exclusive or gender-inclusive. There are several logical and linguistic problems with the androcentric approach.[8] The logical problem is that the assumption represents a circular and hence invalid argument:

PREMISE: Tantric texts don't generally refer to women.
CONCLUSION: Women are not the referents of statements in Tantric texts.

The circularity of this argument, in which the conclusion simply restates the premise, shows how historical assumptions about women are already projected onto the written sources before self-conscious and deliberate interpretation has even begun.[9]

Linguistic problems with the androcentric readings stem in part from varying grammatical and compositional rules governing the original Sanskrit sources and their Tibetan translations. The Sanskrit language, which is always inflected for gender and number, uses a masculine plural noun whenever a group includes men, even if women are also present. Therefore, the Sanskrit term *sādhakāḥ* (masc. nom. pl.), meaning "practitioners," is a generic construction, nonspecific regarding the gender(s) of persons intended. It would be used to refer to a group including both male and female practitioners as well as to one consisting only of male practitioners. Whether one interprets such generic constructions, which pervade Tantric texts, as referring just to men or to men *and* women will depend upon one's historical understanding of the tradition and not upon the grammar of the original sources.

A related compositional problem is that when Sanskrit *tantras* were translated into Tibetan, the Tibetans generally rendered Sanskrit *ślokas* into seven-syllable or nine-syllable lines. Sometimes prefixes and plural and case endings were dropped to shorten a line, at times obscuring the intended number and gender of the original. For instance, the Sanskrit word *mantrinaḥ* (masc. nom. pl.), meaning "mantra practitioners," potentially meaning both male and female practitioners, is properly rendered in Tibetan as *sngags-pa-rnams*, but to meet the numerical requirements of a line it might be shortened to *sngags-pa*, a singular form, or even at times to the single syllable *sngags*. It is natural to translate the shortened form as a singular noun, as "Tantric practitioner," which in English is appropriately gender neutral, although many readers will "read" it as male. However, such shortened forms will also at times be translated as "yogi," which takes on an even stronger masculine specificity, or even, when a pronoun is called for, as "he."[10] Similarly the Sanskrit word *yoginī*, properly rendered into Tibetan as *rnal-'byor-ma*, is frequently shortened to *rnal-'byor*, losing its feminine ending, and is then translated into English as "yogi." A comparison with the Sanskrit original (if one is available) or consultation with variant Tibetan translations can retrieve the intended gender, but to date it has been customary to accept such linguistic constructs as evidence of the male specificity of Tantric texts and male exclusivity of Tantric circles. The end result of this process of linguistic and cultural translation is the complete obliteration of the women who were an integral part of the movement.

Androcentric readings also seize upon the issue of the proportional representation of women in some of the major sources. A standard type of document relating to this period is the compendium of short sketches of the eighty-four *mahāsiddhas*, or "great adepts," whose legendary careers marked the fluorescence of Tantric Buddhism in medieval India. An important early and widely used work of this genre is the *Caturaśītisiddha-pravṛtti* of Abhayadatta (twelfth century). There is a relatively small amount of information about women in this and parallel works, and only four of the standard set of eighty-four great adepts are female. This has been accepted as an accurate indication of women's proportional representation in Tantric circles,[11] but it is well established that numerical representation in historical sources does not correlate with numerical presence or historical importance.[12] Further, if we examine their biographies and iconography, about sixty of the male *mahāsiddhas* had female Tantric companions. Some of the women who are not mentioned by name in this work are known from other sources.

For instance, the adept Śavari is often portrayed with two women who are merely mentioned in passing in his biography (figure 6). However, their names and teaching activities are known from other sources, and some of their songs have been preserved.[13] When Maitrīpa came to study with Śavari, the women, Padmalocanā and Jñānalocanā, became his gurus as well, and they delivered some of his most critical lessons, including the culminating revelation of the nature of his own mind.[14]

That certain women are merely mentioned in Abhayadatta's work, sometimes not even by name, does not indicate their lack of importance in the Tantric movement; rather, it reflects the genre and rhetorical purposes of the text. Since Abhayadatta's compendium provides information that is useful to historians, scholars have tended to approach it as a historical work; however, Abhayadatta composed it primarily as a didactic work. The hagiographical accounts are of uniform length, and it is clear that the author was not trying to include everything that he knew but simply to give the highlights of the careers of the great adepts, with just enough detail to provide an intelligible narrative structure. Additional information, popular stories, and anecdotes about the adepts were probably widely circulated in his day, and it may have seemed unnecessary to supply mundane details about such lofty and famous figures—such as the names of all their teachers, compatriots, and students. These tales were meant primarily to instruct and inspire other Tantric practitioners, and additional details would be provided as oral commentary in the instructional setting. Therefore, Abhayadatta's work should not be read as a detailed photograph of a particular segment of Buddhist history but as a pastiche of a milieu of Buddhist practice. It indicates the types of practices that were pursued and the varying life patterns of Tantric practitioners, but it does not necessarily provide a reliable basis for compiling statistics.

We can contrast the didactic purposes of Abhayadatta's work with the lineage histories compiled by Jo-nang Tāranātha (seventeenth century), who includes more information, evaluates differing sources, and sometimes quotes conflicting accounts and weighs their relative merits.[15] Tāranātha was deliberately writing religious history, whereas Abhayadatta was not. Accordingly, much more information about women is available in Tāranātha's accounts, since he often includes the names of teachers, compatriots, and students.

Androcentric selectivity is seen in the way that Abhayadatta's work is consulted for numerical evidence of women in Tantric circles while Tāranātha's work, in which women have a much higher rate of representation, is not. The fact that more than half the gendered references in the *yoginī-tantras* refer to women is taken not as evidence of the predominance of women in Tantric circles but as evidence of male authorship and preoccupation with the opposite sex. Thus, the androcentric criteria applied to Tantric texts are simply modified so that a conclusion of male dominance can be reached regardless of the content of a given text. Further, criteria have been applied to written sources that would never be applied to other types of evidence. A historian is often like an archaeologist, sifting among ruins for artifacts and potsherds of evidence. Concluding that a 5 percent rate of explicit references to women correlates with a 5 percent rate of women in the movement is like saying that if two potsherds are found at an archaeological site it is because originally there were not many pots in that locale or that if two building foundations survived, then originally there must have been very few buildings. Further, claiming that women's lives were not recorded because they were not worth recording is like claiming that the potsherds and ancient monuments that have survived are those that "deserved" to survive by virtue of their intrinsic historical importance. This line of argument is equally absurd when applied to archaeological materials or to written sources. In written history as in archaeology, whatever evidence has fortuitously survived must be pieced together into a composite portrait that accounts for all the evidence and weaves it into a coherent whole.

When the information about women in the different genres of Tantric literature is juxtaposed, it becomes clear that women's lives and teaching careers were no less interesting or historically consequential to Tantric Buddhism than those of their male counterparts. It is possible to discover the pattern of women's participation in Tantric circles by documenting their knowledge and expertise in such areas as magic and ritual, Tantric feasts, visualization of deities and *maṇḍalas*, inner yogas, attainment of enlightenment, and assumption of the role of guru.

## MAGIC AND RITUAL

Magic, ritual, and supernatural powers are integral to Tantric Buddhism as methods to convert people and demonstrate mastery over phenomenal reality. Claims of supernatural powers and expertise in magical arts may seem dubious to modern Western readers, but within the Tantric Buddhist context they are accepted as evidence of spiritual attainments. Magical abilities represent the ability to wield the deities' energies[16] and to penetrate beyond the apparent solidity of so-called material objects to their indeterminate fluidity, which makes them malleable by ritual acts. Effective ritual performance requires yogic mastery of the body and elements (earth, air, fire, water, space). This mastery can then be wielded to control weather, perform healings, ripen crops, and deliver religious lessons. In view of the centrality of ritual and magical abilities to Tantric practice, women's accomplishments in this area serve as tangible evidence of their progress in Tantric methodologies.

Surviving stories about female Tantrics feature their magical and ritual attainments. Many of the women in question were gurus, and their magical powers were related by their disciples as evidence of their religious mastery. The guru Dinakarā had diligently practiced Buddhism since the age of thirteen, progressing from the Vinaya and Mahāyāna teachings to Tantric studies. Among her many accomplishments, she was an expert in ritual gazes (the ability to control people, animals, and objects with her stare), which she used to convert a meddlesome non-Buddhist yogi and on another occasion to rebuke a yogi who boasted of powers he did not possess. Dinakarā also possessed the power of flight and other supernatural talents (*siddhis*).[17] Ḍombīyoginī, another guru, was renowned for her mastery of the ritual gazes and the four types of ritual activities (peaceful, prospering, conquering, destroying) as well as for her ability to walk on water (figure 8).[18] The sister gurus Mekhalā and Kanakhalā mastered the gazes and the ability to pass through solid objects. They possessed the ability to transport objects, which they used on the huts of some Hindu yogis who were heckling them, relocating them to a safer distance.[19] Gaṅgādharā, a princess who became famous as a teacher of Khyung-po rnal-'byor and spiritual companion of Maitrīpa, was also famous for the efficacy of her ritual gazes. She preferred to dwell in the forest and could transform her body into many shapes. Once she turned herself into a wolf and accepted ritual offerings in that form.[20]

To give more examples of women's attainment of magical powers, Bandhe, the foremost disciple of Kāṇha, was clairvoyant, could become invisible, had mastered the ritual gazes, and had the power of fleet-footedness, the ability to traverse vast distances in a matter of minutes. She converted an entire kingdom in Assam with her magical powers, first conjuring rain to quench a raging fire and then using mantras and bodily transformations to ward off an attack by Hindu (Vaiṣṇava) Tantrics, disrupt their temple worship, and wreak havoc until the people converted and supplicated her.[21] Jalahari, another of Kāṇha's disciples, could transport rice, soup, and beer out of people's kitchens and into her skull-bowl. Once her bowl was full she did not eat the food but nourished herself by inhaling its essence.[22] When Jatijālā's consort, Buddhaśrījñāna (a former monk, also known as Jñānapāda), was ready to undertake a *mahāmudrā* retreat, she taught him the ritual arts of propitiating Jambhala, the god of wealth, so that he would have the resources to sustain himself on retreat.[23] Eight female disciples of

Lokapradīpa (eleventh century) in South India attained the supernatural power of remaining eternally youthful.[24] Ālokī and Duḥśīlā, two courtesans who were disciples of the same forest-dwelling yogi, were also well known for their magical powers.[25] One yogini, whose name is lost to us, gained the power of becoming invisible by reciting Tārā mantras in a cremation ground for one month and rubbing cremation ashes on her eyelids.[26] The renowned yogini Menakā, whose realization was "vast as the sky," had mastered the four ritual gazes and could walk on water without sinking.[27] Kangkanā, one of Kāṇha's close disciples, could render herself invisible and amused herself by moving fruit from one tree to another,[28] while the female companion of Kukkuṭipa had the talent of turning herself into a hen.[29]

Magic and ritual require detailed esoteric knowledge of ritual substances, actions, and recitations, in addition to contemplative preparation. Women wrote instructions on the use of mantras and rituals to accomplish specific ends, documenting their ritual expertise. The Severed-Headed Vajrayoginī manuals written by Lakṣmīṅkarā[30] and Mañjuśrī manuals written by Yaśodattā and Yaśobhadrā[31] include instructions for the recitation of mantras for the accomplishment of specific and in some cases quite ambitious aims, such as shaking a city, subjugating a king, or even, with the maximum of five hundred thousand recitations, accomplishing anything one desires.[32]

The writings of Siddharājñī are particularly rich in ritual detail. She developed a comprehensive ritual, meditative, and yogic system for the practice of the Buddha of Infinite Life (Amitāyus) and wrote practice manuals on the related deities Hayagrīva and Avalokiteśvara. Her Hayagrīva manual includes instructions on how to consecrate a sculpted dough offering (*bali*, Tib. *gtor-ma*) representing inner bodily substances and innate enlightened qualities and how to use the ritual sculpture to remove the obstacles of one's disciples.[33] The ritual knowledge of Siddharājñī is amply displayed in her practice manual on an esoteric form of Avalokiteśvara.[34] This work describes the creation of a complex offering *maṇḍala*, the preparation of medicinal pellets and Tantric sacraments, the proper dismantling of the ritual substances, and a fire offering of the subjugation category. She wrote another text on how to perform a fire offering at the end of an Amitāyus retreat.[35] Her authority in this area is acknowledged by three of the four major Tibetan Buddhist sects.

These numerous examples, which necessarily represent a fraction of the actual cases, clearly demonstrate that women were not simply providing ritual assistance to men but were acquiring magical powers and ritual talents in their own right. Although Tantric literature offers only passing glimpses of women's (and men's) magical powers, these glimpses reveal a religious landscape in which women roamed freely and stepped lightly across the threshold between the world of ordinary reality and the realm of magic wherein thoughts are real, appearances are symbolic, and objects mirror the creative capacities of the mind. Through Tantric practice a woman comes to see the creativity of her mind at work in whatever she experiences in the so-called external world. Ḍākinī Shining Lion celebrated the magic that reigns in the realm of wisdom:

> I do not look at that, I look at myself.
> I am vast primordial wisdom,
> That is my magical creation—
> Nondual knowing is inconceivable![36]

## TANTRIC FEASTS

Tantric feasts, or communal assemblies (*gaṇacakra* and *cakrapūjā*),[37] are among the paradigmatic Tantric practices. The feast is an esoteric ritual that unfolds in many stages. The sacred space for the ceremony is demarcated by geometric designs drawn on the ground with powdered pigments, and an elaborate array of offerings and foods are laid out. The participants don special insignia like bone ornaments and crowns and use musical instruments of archaic design—such as skull-drums, thighbone trumpets, and conch horns—for inducing heightened awareness. Practitioners sit in a circle and partake of sacramental meat and wine served in skull-cups. The feasts also provide an occasion for the exchange of ritual lore, the ritual worship of women (*strīpūjā*), and the performance of sexual yogas.[38] The feast culminates in the performance of Tantric dances and music that must never be disclosed to outsiders. The revelers may also improvise "songs of realization" (*caryāgīti*) to express their heightened clarity and blissful raptures in spontaneous verse.

The feasts are the rituals to which it has been claimed that women were "admitted" when their "services" were required by male practitioners.[39] However, there is abundant evidence that women themselves staged feasts independently of men. At least two collections of "songs of realization" in the Tibetan Buddhist canon are anthologies of songs sung at all-female feast assemblies. One collection commemorates a feast held in Bihar at the Śītavana cremation ground, one of the favored sites for Tantric assemblies, and was attended by thirty-five "exalted ladies who have realized ultimate reality" (*dhātvīśvarī*).[40] A feast held by *ḍākinīs* at the Aṭṭahāsa cremation ground occasioned another anthology in the Tibetan canon.[41] There is also evidence that women presided over Tantric feasts and staged them alongside men. For instance, when Kāṇha's numerous yogi and yogini students held a feast, a woman—Bandhe, Kāṇha's foremost disciple—presided over the assembly.[42]

Tantric literature typically describes feasts staged solely by women or by equal numbers of men and women. The literature does not describe feasts performed solely by men, nor does it suggest that women were admitted to the feasts under male auspices.[43] I have not encountered an instance of a feast staged by men into which a woman was inducted or admitted, but I have often seen descriptions of the reverse. Tantric literature records numerous instances wherein yogis gain admittance to an assembly of yoginis. Inclusion in a yogini feast is seen as a high honor for a male practitioner. In the classic scenario, a yogi unexpectedly finds himself in the presence of a convocation of yoginis, perhaps in the depths of a forest, a deserted temple, or a cremation ground. He seeks entry to their assembly circle and feasts with them, receives initiation from them, and obtains magical lore and Tantric teachings in their midst.

One Tantric practitioner, a Tibetan on pilgrimage to India, reported how he fortuitously discovered a yogini assembly while on pilgrimage to a goddess temple (possibly Jvālāmukhī) in the foothills of northern India.[44] At nightfall he saw many women enter the temple courtyard bearing flowers and preparations for a feast. Their nocturnal ritual preparations and their crowns, elaborate jewelry, and rainbow-colored dresses signaled to him that they were yoginis. Aware of the danger should he anger them by intruding, but emboldened by determination not to let such a rare opportunity pass, he forced his way past the gate guardianess, evading her blow, and entered their presence. The presiding yogini permitted him to join them. He enjoyed the women's songs and dances, partook of the feast, and recorded the event in his travel diary as the high point of his religious quest.[45]

The motif of yogini feasts and assemblies is pervasive in this literature. Kāṇha was ordered by his guru Jālandhari to attend a yogini feast and get an apron made of bone from one of the yoginis he would meet there. Kāṇha did find the yogini at the feast and obtained the apron from her, but he retied the knots connecting the carved bone pieces, dissipating the blessings and magical potency the yogini had woven into the garment.[46] Before he became a monk, Atīśa, one of the founders of Tibetan Buddhism, spent three years in Uḍḍiyāna, where he performed Tantric feasts with yoginis and heard many *ḍākinī*-songs.[47] Luipa attended a feast held by *ḍākinīs* in a cremation ground in Uḍḍiyāna and received a Vajravārāhī initiation in their midst.[48] Several collections of songs in the Tibetan canon consist of songs sung to yogis who had the good fortune to attend a yogini assembly. Among these are a series of songs sung to Kamalaśīla at a Tantric feast staged by the yogini Mahāsukhāsiddhī ("Adept of Great Bliss") at a cremation ground in Uḍḍiyāna. The opening portion explains that the *ḍākinīs* were pleased with Kamalaśīla and composed symbolic songs to celebrate his wisdom.[49]

Tantric scriptures also present communal feasting as a ritual that is staged and presided over by women. For example, the motif of a man attending an otherwise all-female feast assembly occurs in the *Hevajra-tantra*. A significant portion of the work focuses on how to locate yogini feast assemblies and gain admittance to them. If a man uses the proper secret signs to communicate with yoginis, they may admit him to their assembly, as the text relates: "If [the yoginis] show garlands in their hands, they are indicating that you should gather there. Motioning with their garlands means, 'O holder of Tantric vows, stay and take part in this assembly.' At that place of assembly, he should remain in the sacred circle and do all that the yoginis command."[50] In this description of a Tantric feast the women sit in a circle and preside over the ritual while the yogi, who embodies Hevajra (a male Buddha), sits in the center. This pattern mirrors the *maṇḍala* iconography of the *Hevajra-tantra* itself. After the yogi and yoginis eat the sacramental foods, the yogi worships the assembled women and by honoring them attains spiritual perfection in their company.[51]

Instead of a practice to which women might on occasion hope to be admitted, the feast in its classical form appears to be a ritual performed either exclusively by women or communally by men and women as a matter of course. Women gathering in circles to feast, perform rituals, teach, and inspire one another constitutes a practice that also appears in the secular literature of the period. Such a nocturnal gathering of women was termed a "circle of yoginis" (*yoginī-cakra*, *yogeśvarī-cakra*, or *yogini-maṇḍala*), "gathering of yoginis" (*yoginī-gaṇa*), "congregation of yoginis" (*yoginī-melaka* or *yoginī-saṃvara*), and "assembly of dakinis" (*ḍākinī-saṃvara*),[52] all terms that indicate women gathering in circles, the same motif that appears in Buddhist Tantric literature.

The descriptions of feast assemblies in secular Sanskrit works also resemble those found in Buddhist Tantric works. The *Rājataraṅgiṇī* describes an assembly witnessed by the yogi Iśāna. He had fallen asleep in a forest near a cremation ground when he was awakened at midnight by an enchanting, unearthly scent. Iśāna crept forward with sword drawn until he caught sight of the yogini assembly. The yoginis played cymbals, bells, and tambourines and danced within a halo of light and a cloud of incense. The spiritual revelers were intoxicated and sported with a skeleton, pretending that it was their lover. This account resembles Tantric ones, except that the assembly disbanded when the interloper was discovered,[53] whereas the Tantric texts generally report of yogis being admitted to yogini feasts. This parallel invites deeper investigation, for it suggests that women assembling in nonhierarchical circles may have been a non-Buddhist practice that Tantric Buddhists adopted, memorialized in their literature, and replicated in their ritual and iconography.

## ENVISIONING DEITIES AND MAṆḌALAS

One of the main goals of Tantric Buddhist practice is to realize the innate perfection of the world by visualizing the world as a celestial mansion (*maṇḍala*) and all beings as divine. The deities that are envisioned represent aesthetic patterns of enlightened energy and liberating activity. For instance, the savioress Tārā, whose emerald green complexion evokes the healing coolness of medicinal forests, sits on her lotus with one foot stretched forward so that she can leap into action at any moment.[54] This female Buddha represents the quality of liberation that maternally protects the supplicant from every spiritual and worldly danger, while her serene yet joyful smile is an invitation to spiritual well-being (figure 9). Vajrayoginī, a coral red female Buddha who dances in a ring of fire, represents enlightened wisdom as untamable clarity and freedom.

It is clear from various biographical accounts, lineage histories, and women's own writings that women practiced the visualization of deities and *maṇḍalas*. A woman's practice of visualization was generally recorded only when a woman perfected and then taught a given practice, especially to a disciple who subsequently became famous. For example, it is recorded that Kumudarā taught the visualization technique of Black Bhairava, a fierce Tantric Buddha, to Dam-pa-skor.[55] Dinakarā perfected the visualization of Vajrayoginī and Heruka and could evoke their image before her very eyes whenever she wished.[56] Ḍombīyoginī taught Durjayacandra and other disciples how to envision Nairātmyā and Heruka.[57] Śrīsukhā taught Padmavajra the visualization of Guhyasamāja.[58]

Women also wrote instruction manuals on how to visualize beatific and wrathful deities, male and female deities, and *maṇḍalas* of the most esoteric Buddha couples. For example, the lay women Yaśodattā and Yaśobhadrā wrote manuals on the visualization of Mañjuśrī, a bodhisattva of wisdom.[59] Vajraḍākinī wrote instructions for visualizing Vāgīśvara, a form of Mañjuśrī.[60] Vajravatī wrote practice manuals on

FIGURE 9. Buddha Tārā

Pīṭheśvarī, a form of Tārā in which she appears as wrathful and red and presides over a *maṇḍala* of yoginis in the sacred place of Uḍḍiyāna. Lakṣmīṅkarā gave instructions for a severed-headed form of Vajrayoginī, while two of her disciples, the sisters Mekhalā and Kanakhalā, formulated the inner yoga associated with this distinctive female Buddha. In some cases, their instructions and innovations form the basis of transmission lineages that have survived to the present day.[61]

These accomplished women are not token women who stormed the bastions of Tantra and scaled its heights, because the available names do not constitute a comprehensive list of female practitioners. Each recorded example represents a far larger number of serious female practitioners, because for every woman who reaches the summit there are many who strive but never reach the peak and others who reach the peak unseen and unsung.

## INNER YOGAS AND PERFECTION STAGE

After the "creation stage" or "development stage" (*utpattikrama*) of visualizing deities and *maṇḍalas*, Tantric practitioners graduate to the "perfection stage" or "completion stage" (*saṃpannakrama*), a spectrum of inner yogas involving subtle veins and drops that a Tantric meditator envisions within her body in order to attain rarefied states of blissful awareness. Energies are circulated within the body in order to purify the "psychic body" or *vajra*-body (*vajradeha*), a subtle but nonetheless tangible body that registers changes in vitality, temperature, and a range of subtle sensations for which the *tantras* have developed a specialized vocabulary. The *vajra*-body is called an "adamantine body" or "diamond body" because the inner yogas accomplish complete physical, mental, and emotional purification and uncover a level of being that is as radiant and flawless as a highly polished diamond. The inner yogas untie the knots created by habitually negative and self-referential responses to life, clearing the inner channels for an unobstructed flow of energy and power. This clearing of the inner channels is believed to render the body increasingly refined and immaterial, replacing the gross matter with particles of light until it becomes a gossamer but nonetheless visible "rainbow body." It was said of Bandhe that she perfected the inner heat, untied all the knots in her psychic channels, could spend six months in a single meditation session, and attained a rainbow body.[62]

The inner yogas could be practiced without a human partner if necessity demanded, although the classical pattern of Tantra calls for practice with a partner at certain stages and for certain rituals.[63] In any case, knowledge of the inner yogas is integral to the practice of the sexual yogas, which involve subtle exchanges of energy and a mutual resonance between the psychic bodies of the two partners. The inner yogas bring about an increase in the sensitivity of the partners so that they can detect delicate shifts, movements, and exchanges of energy. Therefore, evidence of women's knowledge in this area refutes the widespread claim that women were unskilled, unknowledgeable assistants who did not or could not benefit from such practices.

Evidence of women's knowledge of the inner yogas includes women's extant writings on the subject. Among these, we find Siddharājñī's instructions for the perfection stage yogas of her Buddha of Infinite Life (Amitāyus) and Lord Who Dances on a Lotus practices, which are discussed here in the next chapter. Several texts in the Tibetan canons record the epigrammatic oral precepts (*upadeśa*) of Niguma on the subject.[64] Another example is a long text on the perfection stage written by Lakṣmī the Great of Kashmir (i.e., Bhikṣuṇī Lakṣmī).[65] This detailed work is a technical analysis of the five stages (*pañcakrama*) of the Guhyasamāja perfection stage. Among other works on inner yogas by women, we find a manual on the perfection stage yoga of Severed-Headed Vajrayoginī by the sisters Mekhalā and Kanakhalā.[66] Jalahari, a disciple of Kāṇha, mastered the inner heat yoga and guided "countless" disciples during a teaching career of many years. She is reported to have written a manual on the perfection stage entitled *A Series of Paintings*, which seems not to have survived. When she died, her body dissolved into a rainbow, final proof of her yogic attainments.[67] Perhaps a woman should have the last word on the inner yogas. Vajravatī, who designed a practice of Wrathful Red Tārā especially for women, claimed the inner yogas as the indisputable preserve of women. She defines them as "the practice of yoginis."[68]

## REALIZATION AND ENLIGHTENMENT

At the end of the elaborate rituals, visualizations, and inner yogas of Tantric Buddhism, the final states of realization come like a fresh wind sweeping through an empty sky. The ultimate achievement, after all the complex visualizations, is a divine simplicity, an ability to be spontaneously and fully present to each moment of awareness in a state of pristine clarity. Many Tantric Buddhist women attained enlightenment. Their accounts of the enlightened state can be found in the form of Tantric songs, spontaneous celebrations of enlightened awareness that are sung or spoken in poetic form and recorded by someone present.[69] Some songs are straightforward and descriptive, some use engaging metaphors, and others take recourse to enigmatic or paradoxical expressions.

In Tantric Buddhist literature in India, the term *mahāmudrā* is used to refer to the ultimate, enlightened state of mind.[70] It is a natural state that is fully present during each moment of awareness but adds no conceptual or emotional overlay that would obscure the clarity of the next moment of awareness. Niguma, the legendary founder of the Shangs-pa lineage, wrote (or recited) several short works on *mahāmudrā*. Her essay entitled *"Mahāmudrā" as Spontaneous Liberation* alternates between description and instruction as she conveys how to remain in this state of alert relaxation:

> Don't do anything whatsoever with the mind—
> Abide in an authentic, natural state.
> One's own mind, unwavering, is reality.
> The key is to meditate like this without wavering;
> Experience the great [reality] beyond extremes.
>
> . . . . . . . . . . . . . . . . . . . .
>
> In a pellucid ocean,
> Bubbles arise and dissolve again.
> Just so, thoughts are no different from ultimate reality,
> So don't find fault; remain at ease.
> Whatever arises, whatever occurs,
> Don't grasp—release it on the spot.
> Appearances, sounds, and objects are one's own mind;
> There's nothing except mind.
> Mind is beyond the extremes of birth and death.
> The nature of mind, awareness,
> Uses the objects of the five senses, but
> Does not wander from reality.
>
> . . . . . . . . . . . . . .
>
> In the state of cosmic equilibrium
> There is nothing to abandon or practice,
> No meditation or post-meditation period.[71]

Niguma portrays a state of alert mental repose. She emphasizes that although the mind does not engage in deliberate thought, *mahāmudrā* is not a blank state. The five senses continue to register their objects, and thoughts continue to bubble up spontaneously like foam on waves and then dissolve just as readily. It is possible to remain in this state as long as one does not attempt to grasp the ongoing stream of experience in any way. To release a thought or sensation "on the spot" means to allow it to remain just as it is, since it is going to last only for a fleeting moment, without grasping it by judging, accepting, fearing, rejecting, or desiring. The process could be likened to relaxing on a riverbank and watching a fish leap out of the water, sparkle for a moment in the sunlight, then dive back in a graceful arc. There is no need to engage in a mental dialogue about the merits and demerits of the fish, emotionally react to the fish, or jump into the water to try to catch the fish. Once the fish is out of sight, it should also be out of mind. Hence her instruction "don't do anything whatsoever with the mind."

Niguma suggests that by shifting the attention from the momentary products of the mind to the mind itself, which doesn't come into existence or pass away, it is possible to gain a vantage point from which to watch the parade of passing sensations. A woman who attains this state undergoes no transition between formal meditation sessions and daily life, for the heightened clarity that is sought through meditation has become an integral part of ongoing, everyday consciousness.

The "songs of realization" that yoginis sang at their Tantric feasts represent a banquet of poetic expressions of the enlightened state. Many of the songs were sung at Tantric feasts held by women, either attended entirely by women or occasionally with one man present. One collection hails from a feast held at the Śītavana cremation ground in Bihar, one of the famous sites for Tantric assemblies. According to the colophon, a yogini whose name means Blissful Corpse-Eater hosted the feast, which was attended by thirty-five spiritually advanced women (*dhātvīśvarī*, i.e., "queens of space," or illustrious ladies who have realized ultimate reality). After the external offerings to deity, Blissful Corpse-Eater distributed sacramental grape wine to the participants and requested each woman present to sing a song of realization expressing her insights into ultimate reality.[72] It is easy to imagine this twilight scene, set in the rolling hills of Bihar, silhouetted by a sky glowing with the rose and violet tones of sunset and ornamented by a crescent moon. The women, intoxicated by spiritual ecstasy, regaled one another with spontaneous songs of deep spiritual insight.

A similar scene probably unfolded at a feast held by *ḍākinīs* at the Aṭṭahāsa cremation ground, which occasioned another anthology in the Tibetan canon. This assembly of yoginis hosted twenty-one highly realized ladies, who offered their songs of realization in the form of metaphorical and paradoxical "*ḍākinī*-symbols" (*ḍākinī-nimitta*).[73] Refreshingly vivid and brief, these songs offer a taste of the enlightened insights and realizations of these women.

At one of the feasts, a *ḍākinī* named Kambalā sang a song that distills centuries of metaphysical inquiry:

> KYE HO! Wonderful!
> Lotus pollen wakes up in the heart's center—
> The bright flower is free from mud.
> Where do the color and fragrance come from?
> Why accept or reject them?[74]

Her song expresses a Mahāyāna philosophical doctrine in imagery that is poetic yet intellectually precise. She invokes the concept of *tathāgatagarbha*, the doctrine that a pure seed of Buddhahood resides in the heart of every being, by likening the heart to a lotus and the Buddhahood within to the pollen in its center. In the Tantric view, sense experience and emotions have a blissful and pristine lucidity when they first arise, but this is quickly overshadowed by the assignment of labels and judgments that obscure the blissful clarity at the heart of experience. The clarity of Buddhahood is always present, unstained by thoughts and emotions, just as a lotus flower is unstained by the mud that nourishes its roots. Thoughts and emotions are the colors and fragrance of the mind; there is no reason to accept or reject them—their mysterious, momentary existence should simply be appreciated. There is no need to prevent thoughts from arising or to direct them with a formal meditative discipline. By the time a woman reaches the *mahāmudrā* level of practice, many meditative disciplines have been practiced and mastered. Now is the time for directly experiencing the true nature of the mind.

Many of the women's songs of enlightenment express the illusory nature of the world of experience. A poem by a woman named Blissful Diamond discloses that the world does not really exist as one experiences it at all:

> KYE HO! Wonderful!
> Whatever you see or hear,
> Think or feel—the myriad things,
> Are only reflections
> In the clear wisdom of the mind—
> Empty, they don't exist at all![75]

Blissful Diamond likens the world of experience to the reflections in a mirror. Although a myriad of objects and people appear in a mirror, they do not exist within the mirror. Similarly, the world of everyday experience is actually a reflected world unfolding in the theater of the mind; the cast, props, and plot are determined by a woman's sense organs, temperament, linguistic categories, and cultural background. An enlightened woman's mind becomes a clear mirror of wisdom, accurately reflecting whatever appears. Its very clarity dissolves the dualism of "mind in here" and separate, concretely reifiable "things out there."

If objects do not inhabit a definitively external world, where do the captivating illusions unfold? A song by Tree-Leaf Woman addresses this question:

> Who speaks the sound of an echo?
> Who paints the image in a mirror?
> Where are the spectacles in a dream?
> Nowhere at all—
> That's the nature of mind![76]

Her verse draws attention to the difficulty of pinpointing the source and locus of the phenomenal world. Even the mind is not the creator or location of experience, for it is no more an independent generator of experience than the external world. No single thing or person produces the sound of an echo or paints the images in a mirror. They arise through a complex interplay of causes, and enlightened insight brings an awareness of this delicate, subtle web of interdependence.

Realizing the illusory nature of everything one perceives is a powerful solvent of attachment, just as a woman, upon awakening, no longer feels attachment to objects in a dream. She doesn't take out insurance on jewels acquired in a dream, run for water to put out a fire that blazed in a dream, or spend the day raking leaves that fell in a dream. She realizes that they are not ultimately real. Similarly, when a woman recognizes that the objects of waking consciousness are simply the products of individual and collective imagination, she becomes less absorbed in them. She comes to appreciate an innate perfection that lies beyond the dualism of acceptance and rejection, as Victorious-Minded Woman sang:

> Kye ho! Wonderful!
> Emptiness, with the artistry of awareness,
> Creates magical shows that are unborn, yet appear.
> Don't accept or reject what is perfect as it is—
> I can't find a reason to tamper with that![77]

Another woman uses the metaphor of clouds in the sky to describe how thoughts arise without affecting the underlying clarity of mind:

> Kye ho! Wonderful!
> Magical displays arise in the sky
> Through the dynamism of the sky itself,
> Arising spontaneously as transformations of sky—
> Don't find any faults in that![78]

It is natural for thoughts to arise, just as it is natural for clouds to coalesce in the sky. The sky represents a space within which things can arise, but it is not an active causal agent in itself. Therefore, anything that arises in the sky, from clouds and rainbows to the magical apparitions that fill the life stories of Tantric adepts, must be said to be rootless, lacking an ultimate cause or basis. Clouds, rainbows, and thoughts arise from and dissolve back into something that in itself does not intrinsically exist. There is no purpose in accepting and rejecting things that have such an ephemeral, spontaneous, insubstantial existence.

A poem by a *ḍākinī* named Wings of Breath expresses how all things arise and dissolve in a mysterious, inconceivable way:

> Kye ho! Wonderful!
> All things are baseless, like a dream.

Appearing to arise contingently, like a reflected image,
Spontaneously arising and disappearing, like bubbles,
Vast and root-free, like the sky![79]

Her poem echoes the classical analyses of the Madhyamaka philosophers Nāgārjuna and Candrakīrti, who demonstrated the logical impossibility of causal agency, existence, and nonexistence. The *ḍākinī* joins these philosophers in pointing to a mode of being that is ultimately inexpressible and inconceivable, beyond the logical extremes of existence and nonexistence.[80] Reminiscent of these analyses is the song of Ḍākinī Lion-Face:

KYE HO! Wonderful!
You may say "existence," but you can't grasp it!
You may say "nonexistence," but many things appear!
It is beyond the sky of "existence" and "nonexistence"—
I know it but cannot point to it![81]

Many of the women's songs provide instructions for *mahāmudrā* practice while acknowledging the paradoxical nature of what is in essence an "effortless effort." As one woman imparted, "the nature of the path is that you cannot traverse it."[82] That is, the highest form of meditation consists of exerting no effort and imposing nothing upon experience. A song by Corpse-Raising Woman insists upon the one-pointed attentiveness of this state but also maintains that it is not a meditation in the usual sense:

Don't become distracted, but don't meditate;
To practice like this is skillfulness.
When myriad experiences leave not a trace, how great!
To practice like this is liberation![83]

She says "don't meditate" because this state is beyond meditation, a "path of no meditation." It requires a relaxed openness to whatever arises in the field of awareness. At this stage, there is no formal meditation practice to implement, because everyday life becomes the arena of ongoing spiritual revelation. Now "everything—everything!—is the path of liberation."[84]

A woman who attains this level of realization discovers reality to be innately complete and fulfilling. Her experience of its perfection is spontaneous and no longer requires effort:

KYE HO! Wonderful!
Great fresh awareness is the supreme path.
No need to walk—it's the ground of suchness;
No need to practice—it's effortlessly accomplished.
AHA! Those who practice yoga are fortunate indeed![85]

Buddhist philosophy teaches that everything is empty, or devoid of intrinsic reality. This is as true of the world that is experienced as it is of the putative self that undergoes the experiences. In the *mahāmudrā* stage, this philosophical principle is experientially verified. Recognition of the mutual emptiness of self and other releases experience into a dance of energy, a sparkling, incandescent display of light and color, sound and awareness, that shimmers momentarily like a magician's illusion in the open space created by the simultaneous dissolution of self and other:

> KYE HO! Wonderful!
> Recognize the magical show of appearances
> As reflections of your own thoughts.
> Know your own mind as empty by nature—
> No need to seek elsewhere for the bliss of reality![86]

This woman's song draws attention to the primacy of the mind in shaping experience, giving voice to one of the central insights of Yogācāra philosophy, namely, that the quality of a woman's awareness determines the quality of her experience. In the exalted state of *mahāmudrā* awareness, sensory experiences attain a translucent, jewellike quality. For a woman who is awakened, the play of sense experience adorns the state of pure awareness. No longer a source of suffering, such experiences become a bedazzling magical show, a source of bliss:

> KYE HO! Wonderful!
> Whatever appears is *mahāmudrā*,
> Ornamented by the objects of the five senses.
> You cannot enter or leave your natural state—
> Run on the plain of great bliss![87]

Some women emphasize its naturalness and the need to remain loose and relaxed in this state in order not to interfere with spontaneous clarity, whereas others celebrate the exhilarating sense of freedom from the prison of ego. One woman likens her freedom to celestial flight:

> When you see what cannot be seen,
> Your mind becomes innately free—reality!
> Leave the stallion, the wind, behind—
> The rider, the mind, will soar in the sky![88]

This soaring quality eludes any attempt at conceptual formulation, just as, in one woman's words, "a bird flying in the sky doesn't touch anything."[89] Other women revel in the inexpressible blissfulness of this state of awareness in their songs:

KYE HO! Wonderful!
When someone experiences reality,
The whole sky cannot contain her bliss.
Can you express that? Then speak!
I have seen what is utterly invisible![90]

Some women simply marvel at the indescribability of enlightenment:

KYE HO! Wonderful!
This spontaneous stream of great ecstatic wisdom—
Without realization, one cannot describe it;
After realization, why speak?
Taste it and you're struck dumb, speechless![91]

Since the awakened state is indescribable, a mystic must resort to metaphors. The following song uses a series of images to suggest a panoramic vantage point that encompasses and subsumes every other experience and point of view:

HUM! Having reached the top of Mount Meru
One sees the lesser peaks in every direction.
By harnessing a thoroughbred
One can run to any border.
A bee gathers the essences of many flowers
And blends them into a single flavor . . .
A vision encompassing all of space
Destroys craving for a partial view.[92]

Niguma held that the blissful state of *mahāmudrā* is inherently altruistic and naturally gives rise to compassionate acts and liberative activities:

When one attains realization,
Everything is spontaneously accomplished.
One fulfills all the hopes and desires of living beings,
Like a wish-granting gem.[93]

As in classical Mahāyāna, compassionate activity proceeds with an awareness of the emptiness of the teacher, the pupil, and the teachings. The yogini Ekavajrā offered a song on this theme:

In the volume of skylike emptiness,
Write with letters of pure awareness and wisdom.
Impart instructions for many diverse methods—
Proclaim the teachings in a stream that's unceasing![94]

When a woman understands the illusory nature of all phenomena, even compassionate acts take on the quality of magical displays. An enlightened being employs the magically illusory quality of existence and becomes a master magician to liberate living beings:

> In the changeless adamantine sky,
> Miraculous vignettes flash in dynamic array.
> They benefit diverse living beings,
> Then dissolve in the sky of spontaneous freedom![95]

The recognition of the illusory nature of liberative activities is not a distinctively Tantric insight. The theme of enlightened master as magician has a long history in the Mahāyāna tradition, as seen in the *Vimalakīrtinirdeśa-sūtra*, wherein the layman Vimalakīrti conjured magical displays and illusions to dazzle, disorient, and then deepen the wisdom of his audience.[96] An advanced bodhisattva can literally play with reality, producing illusions, creating universes ("Buddha-lands"), and generating as many bodies as there are atoms in the universe in order to liberate sentient beings.

*Mahāmudrā* seems to be a blissful state of natural clarity, but it opens the door to a realm of magical fluidity. A wild, playful, unpredictable quality erupts when experience is released from its predetermined patterns. As a state of freedom from the moorings of conventional awareness, *mahāmudrā* becomes a level of awareness in which anything is possible. Many of the women's songs celebrate the entry into the realm of utter freedom and unlimited possibility with startlingly incongruous images.[97] By presenting seemingly nonsensical questions and statements, a woman can point to a realm of experience wherein ordinary laws of logic and nature do not hold sway:

> HUM! What do you think when you cry out in surprise?
> What can distract you when you stare in amazement?
> How can the sky be polished?
> What does a butterlamp think?
> The track of a water-bubble can't be found.
> Upon waking, dream-thoughts evaporate.
> . . . . . . . . . . . . . . . . .
> Who does the mother of a dead child love?
> Which of the six flavors is the taste of water?
> What is the speech of a mute woman?[98]

Direct questions that are impossible to answer assault the listener's sense of reason. It is difficult to exegete such poems, and any attempt to do so will miss the point, because the images are meant to be impenetrable and the questions unanswerable from the standpoint of ordinary logic.[99] The lines of these songs create moments of stunned surprise and disorientation that give a foretaste of nondual, nonconceptual clarity.

These poems are situated in a wider current of Indian mystical poetry that employs enigmatic imagery, absurdities, and startling reversals to evoke the enlightened state.[100] This genre of paradoxical imagery is seen in the following song by Lakṣmīṅkarā:

Lay your head on a block of butter and chop—
Break the blade of the axe!
The woodcutter laughs!
A frog swallows an elephant!

It's amazing, Mekhalā,
Do not doubt.
If it confounds you, adept,
Drop concepts now!

My teacher didn't tell me,
I didn't understand—
Flowers blossomed in the sky!

It's marvelous, Mekhalā,
Have no doubt!
If you're incredulous, adept,
Drop your doubts!

A barren woman gives birth!
A chair dances!
Because cotton is expensive,
The naked weep!

. . . . . . . .

Amazing! An elephant sits on a throne
Held up by two bees!
Incredible! The sightless lead,
The mute speak!

. . . . . . . .

Amazing! A mouse chases a cat!
An elephant flees from a crazy donkey!

It's marvelous, Mekhalā,
Do not doubt!
If you're stunned, adept,
Drop your doubts!

Amazing! A hungry monkey eats rocks!
Wonderful! The experience of the mind—
Who can express it?[101]

Lakṣmīṅkarā addresses her song to Mekhalā, one of the female disciples who recorded the song, and to a disciple who is adept at the inner yoga of making the wind enter the central channel.[102] The enlightened poet offered this song to help her disciples cut off conceptual thought and usher them into nondual states of awareness. By posing unbelievable images and impossible scenarios, like a chair dancing and a monkey eating rocks, Lakṣmīṅkarā dramatizes the inability of logic to enter this experiential realm. It would appear from the reports of these women that philosophers and meditators enter the realm of *mahāmudrā* and emerge as magicians, as comedians, and above all as poets of enlightenment.

## WOMEN AS GURUS

Since women mastered every level of Tantric Buddhist practice and realization, it follows that women would assume roles of leadership and authority as enlightened teachers and initiating gurus. In this unrestrictive religious setting, there were no institutional barriers to the leadership of women, such as a priestly hierarchy of clerics seeking to exclude women from their ranks, wealth, and prestige. Religious authority was based on personal realization and timely displays of supernatural powers or religious insight. These qualifications represented no disadvantage for women. For the duration of the movement in India, women claimed authority and undertook religious guidance of others on the same basis as men—their wisdom, magical powers, and religious expertise.

Many female gurus figure in Tantric literature as wandering teachers who appear on the scene to deliver a timely lesson and then continue on their wandering way. Others settled in one place where disciples could seek them out. Most of the women discussed in the preceding sections were qualified to act as gurus, and many of them did. Although in most cases we have little information about their guidance of disciples (which is also true of most of the male gurus), their very presence in the literature generally attests to the repute of their teaching activities.

Women were free to develop unique teaching styles that suited their temperament, expressed their special insights, and met the needs of their disciples. For example, there is the case of Kumudarā, who treated her disciple with a mother's fondness:

> Little son, fearful of life and death,
> You struggled hard for the truth.
> How wonderful!
> Therefore, I will give you the diamondlike Tantric vehicle
> That is not worldly and is free from error.
> Meditate on that, my child![103]

She then exercised a guru's prerogative to tailor the training to the disciple and conferred initiation upon her spiritual son by placing her foot on his head.

A dramatic example of a self-styled female guru is the case of a yogini who lived in the village of Yambu (probably Kathmandu) in Nepal, a northern outpost of Tantric Buddhism. She didn't use many words, but she didn't need to. She chose to give initiations rather than teachings, and her unorthodox initiations had the power to immerse the recipient in a deep state of bliss and wisdom. Her disciple Rwa-ru-can took his friend Dam-pa-skor to meet her in the little temple where she lived on offerings or garbage—whatever came her way. Her life-style and demeanor proclaimed her transcendence of worldly conventions. When the yogis found her, she was sitting naked on a statue of a reclining Buddha. Her pose fully revealed her breasts and sexual organ, and she was smiling triumphantly, free of embarrassment or shame. Apparently her behavior sufficiently impressed Dam-pa-skor, for he asked her for religious teachings. Rwa-ru-can explained that she preferred to give initiations and recounted how she had initiated him by throwing a handful of dirt at him. Attracted by her freedom, he had decided to apprentice himself to her. The yogini ordered him to give away all his possessions and property and return to her, so he gave away everything he owned and returned for further instruction. She then gave him another initiation by spitting on the palm of his hand and placing her hand on his head, which plunged him into a deeply concentrated state. Rwa-ru-can praised the efficacy of her unorthodox method: "Now I have no need of precepts—by these methods she has liberated me!"[104] Her unorthodox initiation, reinforced by her own startlingly unconventional appearance and iconoclastic behavior, was highly effective in evoking in him the meditative realizations he had long sought.

A very advanced form of initiation, which occurs after a disciple has completed a substantial course of meditation, is a direct revelation of the nature of mind itself, sometimes called a "direct pointing" to the nature of mind.[105] This form of initiation does not conform to any particular pattern but is devised for each disciple as the occasion arises. The teacher reveals the nature of mind in a spontaneous and direct manner, through words, gestures, symbols, or songs of realization. This revelation is regarded as a direct mind-to-mind transmission because the guru embodies the meaning of the words, making them a living reality for her disciple.

We find a number of women giving this ultimate form of initiation. For instance, a yogini revealed to Saraha the nature of his own mind.[106] Padmalocanā and Jñānalocanā revealed the nature of his mind to

Maitrīpa.[107] Gaṅgābhadrī was one of the ten gurus who introduced Dam-pa sangs-rgyas (eleventh century) to the nature of his own mind.[108] Other yoginis who gave him direct teachings on the nature of mind included Kumuḍā, Lakṣmī, Padmapādā, Cintā, Sukhākarā, Sukhāsiddhī, Śabarī, Vimalā, and Vṛkṣaparṇī.[109] It is implicit that, if they were able to help others realize the nature of their minds, these women had fully realized the nature of their own minds.

---

There was no area of Tantric Buddhism in which women did not participate and attain mastery, including magical techniques and incantations, the performance of rituals, the visualization of deities and *maṇḍalas,* advanced techniques of inner yoga, and the loftier realms of pure contemplation and philosophical reflection. It is natural that their expertise would find expression in teaching activities and acknowledged authority as initiating gurus. Tantric literature does not treat these women's practices, accomplishments, and teaching activities as in any way unusual or exceptional for women. There is no evidence of external constraints upon women's activities as gurus, such as pronouncements that women should not teach, give initiations, or exercise the other forms of authority involved in being a guru. When women's liberating activities are reported, they are treated as if they were a matter of course. Unless texts specify that it was anomalous or remarkable for a women to perform a certain practice or attain a certain accomplishment, there is no basis for a historian to tokenize the women heralded in this literature by claiming that it was. Therefore, this overview of women's practices in Tantric Buddhism can serve as a guide for interpreting the activities of women whose religious practices are not specified in the literature.

Since Tantric Buddhism was a movement in which women participated on every level, claims that women simply served as ritual assistants are false. The evidence offered here refutes the contention that these women were languishing in the shadows, hoping to be allowed to attend a ritual. Women were not uninterested parties who happened to be in the vicinity when a ritual was staged and were somehow induced to attend. In this analysis, Tantric Buddhism does not conform to its usual portrayal as a movement of male ascetics and savants who strenuously avoided and excluded women except when they abducted ignorant, defenseless women for the purposes of sexual exploitation. There is nothing in these reports to indicate that women were acting as ritual accessories to men or that they were "sluts," mere "means," "alien objects," "passive counterparts," or "ritual assistants." Rather, the female Tantrics were full co-religionists of the male Tantrics, performing the same array of practices and winning the same supernatural powers and accomplishments, including the ultimate attainment—enlightenment itself.

It appears that, like the emerging Bhakti and Hindu Tantric movements of the same period, Tantric Buddhism could boast an absence of barriers to women's participation and progress. These movements offered vital new alternatives to established priestly, monastic, and ascetical traditions. One finds women of all castes and outcastes, artisans, and tribal people among their ranks and leadership. These socially inclusive movements in turn were vitalized by an influx of new religious insights, symbols, and practices. Formerly excluded persons were not simply "permitted" to participate but actually provided much of the impetus and creativity generating the exciting new developments. In view of the fact that women participated in every aspect of Tantric Buddhist practice and achieved the magical powers and meditative attainments promised through these methods, and in view of women's prominence in various teaching and leadership roles, it would follow that women helped to shape the emerging movement. This issue is addressed in the next chapter.

CHAPTER FIVE

# Women in Tantric History

## *FOUNDERS AND PIONEERS*

TANTRIC BUDDHISM offers an array of methods for cultivating the mind and refining the heart. These methods include deities to contemplate and worship, colorful and dramatic rituals, sacred art and movement, and subtle yogic practices for transforming worldly passions into rarefied states of bliss and enlightened awareness. These techniques arose in Pāla period India (eighth through twelfth centuries) as new deities, practices, and teachings were introduced by highly accomplished Tantric masters. The new teachings were seen not as products of individual creativity but as revelations of truths that exist on another level of reality and can be discovered through meditative trance, dream journey, and visionary encounter.

The appearance of innovative new teachings was not problematic, because Mahāyāna had long before posited a level of meditative concentration in which it is possible to perceive Buddhas and receive additional teachings from them. According to an important early Mahāyāna scripture, persons who attain this level of meditative awareness will:

> become pure in mind, and see the Buddhas. . . . They will apprehend . . . the Buddhas sitting and expounding the True Dharma. . . . for them no other object will arise except the Buddhas and likewise the supreme Dharma. For those who are so endowed, no other sight or sound will be apprehended as objects, apart from the teaching of many Buddhas.[1]

According to Mahāyāna thought, Buddhist truths (or Dharma) will always be accessible to persons of sufficient visionary attainment. As promised in another Mahāyāna scripture, Buddhist teachings "have been concealed in mountains, at the base of mountains, and in trees. . . . For those whose minds are perfected, even if the Buddha is not present, the Dharma will appear from the sky, walls and trees."[2] As masters taught their students what had been revealed to them, some of their religious innovations became the basis of religious lineages that flourished in India and later were transmitted to Nepal and Tibet, forming the core of Himalayan Buddhism as it has survived to the present day.

The social marginality and loose organization of the Tantric movement in medieval India enabled women to participate freely in the revelation process. In the absence of formal barriers to their participation, women had the same access to visionary experience and religious authority as men. Women gained religious experience through their practice of meditation and subtle yogas, and they wielded authority on the basis of that experience rather than through ordination or clerical office. As a result of their unrestricted participation, women helped to create Tantric Buddhism, handing down doctrines, rituals, meditations, and yogic practices that remain prominent in the contemporary practice of Nepalese and Tibetan Buddhism.[3]

Many of the contributions of women blended so seamlessly into the tapestry of Tantric Buddhism that it will never be possible to link each specific practice and doctrine with a specific woman. This has allowed historians erroneously to claim that the tradition was developed by and for men without the insights or contributions of women. However, some women's contributions can be identified with a high degree of specificity and certitude. Evidence of their pioneering activity survives in the form of their extant writings, their presence in lineage histories, and biographical narratives describing their lives and teaching careers. It can be shown that women introduced new deities and new methods of meditating upon previously introduced deities, such as the Buddha of Infinite Life (Amitāyus) and esoteric Avalokiteśvara practices introduced by Siddharājñī and the Cakrasaṃvara healing *maṇḍala* stemming from Niguma. Women introduced rituals that are now featured in the Tibetan Buddhist ritual year, such as the long-life initiation taught by Siddharājñī and the Avalokiteśvara fasting ritual taught by Bhikṣuṇī Lakṣmī. Women also introduced female deities that enjoyed particular prominence among women, such as the Wrathful Red Tārā practice introduced by Vajravatī and the Severed-Headed Vajrayoginī practice taught by Lakṣmīṅkarā, Mekhalā, and Kanakhalā. Except for Wrathful Red Tārā, whose survival I have not yet documented, all these deities and related practices survive to the present day. Additional women who figured in the founding of this movement are the women who appear in the annals of Tantric Buddhism as the teachers and gurus—in fact, the spiritual mothers—of the men who have been celebrated as the founders of the movement.

## VAJRAVATĪ AND WRATHFUL RED TĀRĀ, A FEMALE BUDDHA

The spiritual biography of Vajravatī is told in a text by another female adept, Lakṣmīṅkarā, who describes a group of enlightened masters who appear to be part of her immediate circle. According to

Lakṣmīṅkarā's account, Vajravatī Brāhmaṇī, a woman of the Hindu priestly caste in Uḍḍiyāna, was known for her scrupulous maintenance of ritual purity through ablutions and observance of caste rules. Ānandavajra, a Tantric Buddhist guru of the weaver caste, heard of the young woman's reputation and intuited that she was destined to become his disciple. His own guru had been a woman, so he had no doubts about the ability of a woman to attain enlightenment. However, he would have to cross a caste barrier to approach the girl, since caste laws require that a low-caste person avoid contact with members of the priestly class in order not to risk defiling them.

When Ānandavajra sensed that the time was ripe to convert Vajravatī, he approached her on the riverbank where she performed her ritual bathing. Confronting Vajravatī's preoccupation with purity, Ānandavajra urged her not to waste her time attempting to purify herself externally with water, but to purify herself internally with the water of Buddha-wisdom:

> If you believe that you purify by bathing,
> Then even fishermen attain that goal—
> They're in the water day and night!
> How can that be so?[4]

Impressed by his composure as he violated caste law to address her, and stirred by his argument, the girl asked how she might purify her inner self. The guru instructed her to "bathe by the effortless method" of meditating directly on the inherent purity of all experience. He offered a spontaneous song to inspire her:

> O priestly girl! In the pure expanse of sky
> Pure clouds arise and then dissolve.
> Just so, in the river of purity, pure fish arise.
> Thus, priestly girl, look at your own mind!
> Enter the beginningless sphere of all Buddhas,
> Bathe in the water of wisdom—
> Remove all impurities of belief in a self![5]

His song instantly awakened Vajravatī to the purity of her own mind. After attaining perfect insight, Vajravatī decided to remain in Uḍḍiyāna to guide other members—especially women—of the priestly class, "who were stained by the belief in a self," just as she had been.[6] In her instruction of other women, Vajravatī emphasized that true purity is the ability to recognize all things as equal in essence. She urged her disciples to cease to discriminate among foods, companions, and activities on the basis of conventional social distinctions. This realization is the diamondlike wisdom after which Vajravatī is named.

The name Vajravatī, translatable as "Diamondlike Woman," denotes a woman whose mind is faultless as a diamond, or a woman who has realized the nature of reality. Vajravatī indicated that her teachings were revelations by stating that "this religious teaching on the nature of reality, which is difficult to understand, is expressed with the adamantine words of secret Tantra."[7] The "secret Tantra" to which she refers appears not to be a specific text,[8] but rather the Tantric teachings as a body of truths, some of which have been recorded and some not. These truths exist on another level of reality and can be discovered by persons of vision and mystical attainment, who may then put them into writing. If they were already written in a form that was accessible to others, there would be little need to record them anew. Although Vajravatī says that she is drawing on meditation instructions that were "written,"[9] this doesn't necessarily mean that they were written by a human hand, for there are any number of ways that such instructions might be "written." For instance, they could have been written in *ḍākinī* language on the eddies of a flowing river or the leaves of a tree, a tiny scroll of paper or a precious amulet of lapis lazuli. Such forms of writing are symbolic codes that must be deciphered by a visionary like Vajravatī.[10] It is in light of this belief that Vajravatī assures her audience that her teachings are not a product of her own imagination or intellect but rather the object of her illumined vision.

Vajravatī addresses her teachings to "yoginis" and "yoginis and their good friends,"[11] presumably indicating that a man might join the feast if he were a "good friend" of one of the yoginis. Vajravatī describes the suitable candidate for this practice as a yogini who aspires to perform the ten virtuous activities, express her power of compassion by giving many gifts, and accomplish the four pure merits.[12] The four pure merits are attained by constructing a Buddhist commemorative mound (*stūpa*) where none formerly existed, offering a garden to the religious community, healing a schism in the community, and cultivating infinite love, compassion, sympathetic joy, and equanimity. Clearly Vajravatī expected her students to be women of lofty aspiration.

When Vajravatī further specifies her intended audience, she disqualifies those who have insufficient devotion, fail to give initiation offerings (*dīkṣā*) to the guru, or exhibit an angry or agitated state of mind. However, Vajravatī adds an unusual qualification. She states that the guru should not teach this practice to "sons," that is, male disciples. Rather, the practice is intended specifically for "daughters," or female disciples, of the priestly caste in Uḍḍiyāna. This teaching is to be given to women who have attained adamantine speech—the ability, like her own, to give voice to profound truths:

> Those [to whom this teaching] should not be given
> Are those who lack faith, are inferior,

Don't give offerings, are attached, or are angry.
Also not to those who are agitated,
Not to disciples, and not to sons.

The teacher should give this method to others—
To human daughters in priestly places
Who hail from Uḍḍiyāna in the north,
Those multitudes of yoginis
Who have attained adamantine speech.[13]

It is not surprising that Vajravatī would want her female peers to receive the Buddhist teachings. Sharing their cultural background, she had an insight into what meditations would be most effective for them. If this meditation was restricted to women or especially associated with women, that might explain why it seems not to have survived as a transmission lineage in the monasteries of Tibet, beyond its inclusion in the canonical writings.[14] However, whether or not it was restricted to women,[15] it is clear that this practice was originally taught by a female guru to her female students.[16]

Vajravatī revealed a form of Tārā in which the female Buddha appears as red and wrathful, with many arms, dancing in a ring of flames. This form of Tārā is known as Pīṭheśvarī, meaning "Sovereign Mistress of the Great Sacred Place."[17] The "sacred place" in question is Uḍḍiyāna, one of the strongholds of Tantric Buddhism, in northwestern India.[18] Pīṭheśvarī is one of several female deities associated with Uḍḍiyāna.[19] This region gained fame as a "land of *ḍākinīs*" and thus as an ideal place to learn and practice Tantra because of all the female practitioners and teachers there.[20] That reputation is supported by the example of Vajravatī, a woman who introduced a meditation to be practiced primarily by women in Uḍḍiyāna.

The presence of female Buddhas in Tantric iconography is not generally acknowledged in Western scholarship, but Vajravatī presents Wrathful Red Tārā (Pīṭheśvarī) unambiguously as a Buddha, referring to her as Buddha Tārā:

Envision the Buddhas of the ten directions
In the form of Tārā. . . .
They purify all beings with rays of wisdom light,
Establishing them as Buddhas.
From now until complete enlightenment, pray
Quickly to become Buddha Tārā.[21]

Various kinds of settings are recommended for the practice, including cremation grounds, mountain retreats, red-light districts, any place frequented by yoginis, or near a "worldly *ḍākinī*," an enlightened woman who has not yet ascended to transcendent spheres.[22] A woman prepares mentally for this practice by viewing all beings as ethereal and ephemeral, like a magical illusion or fairy castles in the air, and by envisioning everything animate and inanimate as the dazzling body of Buddha Tārā.[23]

These preliminaries having been accomplished, a woman should proceed to imagine herself as Wrathful Red Tārā:

> On a many-colored lotus, sun, and deer skin,
> One [becomes] a woman with the body of holy Tārā . . .
> Standing with one leg outstretched and one drawn up . . .
> Ornamented with human bones,
> With loosely flowing hair,
> Three red eyes, and a resplendent body.[24]

This form of Tārā has four faces and eight arms:

> With red, blue, and green slightly angry faces and
> A heroic, peaceful, yellow head on top,
> With the five-wisdom crown and a garland of heads,
> Adorned by all the ornaments,
> Holding a scepter (*vajra*), sword, blue lotus, and jewel,
> Skull, staff, bell, and skull-drum (*ḍamaru*).
> The fruit of blissful wisdom arises.
> Wearing a tiger skin, in a dancing pose,
> Poised on a many-colored lotus and moon,
> Compassionately angry,
> With three red eyes looking to the left . . .
> In the middle of an assembly of excellent yoginis.[25]

Bliss is the source of Wrathful Red Tārā's power. One of her epithets in the text is Ānandasukheśvarī, or "Glorious Queen of Bliss and Joy."[26] Her bliss is symbolized and heightened by her Tantric implements, such as her skull-drum, mystical staff, and Tantric scepter. As the Buddha in the center of the *maṇḍala*, her enlightened energy and ecstasy envelop the assembly in a cloud of bliss. Her retinue of twenty-four divine yoginis consists of eight wrathful goddesses in the eight directions, six red and six green goddesses in the next tier, and four door guardianesses in the directional colors who are ornamented by snakes and trampling the Māras. Like Red Tārā, the goddesses of her retinue appear ferocious but are blissful, wise, and tender beneath their ferocity.[27]

In the course of the practice, all levels of reality are envisioned in turn as the yogini *maṇḍala* of Wrathful Red Tārā. A *maṇḍala* is an aesthetic blueprint, or template, for the apotheosis of reality on every level: terrestrially, bodily, ritually, and ultimately. Geographically, the twenty-four goddesses correspond to twenty-four sacred places of Tantric pilgrimage, so the *maṇḍala* presents a "sacred geography" of the Indian subcontinent, with a female Buddha at Uḍḍiyāna in the center, enveloping the earth in a cloud of bliss. Somatically, the meditator envisions her body as containing the entire world, with its subterranean, earthly, and celestial spheres. She then mentally arrays the divine yoginis within that world, thereby turning her body into a yogini *maṇḍala*. The geography of this inner world corresponds to the twenty-four sacred places on earth where goddesses and yoginis dwell.

Ritually, the iconography of the *maṇḍala* of yoginis reproduces an assembly of yoginis staging a communal feast. In a feast assembly (*gaṇacakra*), everything is treated as intrinsically pure and nothing is forbidden. Therefore, the motif of feasting with yoginis symbolizes the enlightened view of reality, the realization that everything is inherently pure. Recalling the instruction of her low-caste guru to concentrate on inner purity, Vajravatī uses the yogini feast image to teach her students to see everything as pure and to comport themselves as if dwelling in a sacred realm. Vajravatī teaches that this impartiality is a "stable truth," an ultimate view that transcends mere social conventions:

> The meditators are the yoginis and their good friends.
> Always act, [disregarding] what should and should not be eaten,
> What should and should not be drunk, and
> Who is and is not a suitable sexual partner.
> These sacred circles of assembled yoginis
> Are unstained by sin, a stable truth, beyond partiality.[28]

Vajravatī assures her students that this ultimate view places them beyond the "sin" that would be ascribed to them by socially sanctioned caste laws. To the extent that a woman has purified her vision, she will realize that she lives in a sacred realm in the midst of a circle of yoginis. She will disport herself accordingly, relishing sense experience as a luscious banquet savored by the yoginis and the venturesome men who befriend them.

The all-female iconography of the Wrathful Red Tārā *maṇḍala* also has a historical resonance, for the female Buddha surrounded by her retinue of yoginis presents a divine counterpart of female teachers like Vajravatī in Uḍḍiyāna, surrounded by their circles of female disciples. Thus, the practice that Vajravatī introduced enables us to picture what some of the women of Uḍḍiyāna practiced together in their Tantric circles.

## NIGUMA AND A CAKRASAṂVARA HEALING MAṆḌALA

Niguma, a legendary yogini of the eleventh century, is one of the most historically elusive of the female founders of Tantric Buddhist practices. Although she is associated with the adept Nāropa as his companion or sister, the yogi who claims the most extensive contact with her and who transmitted her teachings saw her only in visions and dreams. Thus, the figure of Niguma is shrouded in visionary mists.

Niguma is the lineage founder of a specialized meditation that is designed for the healing of illness through visualizing Vajrayoginī and Cakrasaṃvara in sacred union. The iconography of the visualization is a five-deity *maṇḍala* of Cakrasaṃvara.[29] The practice represents a very advanced method even within the most esoteric class of teachings, because it compresses the entire Tantric path into a powerfully streamlined technique. In the hands of an expert meditator, such a practice brings swift results.

Niguma's Cakrasaṃvara imagery functions as a healing *maṇḍala* because it focuses directly upon removing disease and its causes, along with more subtle impediments to enlightenment. The meditator creates the healing image, or *maṇḍala*, three times: a white version at the crown of the head, a red version at the throat, and a blue version at the heart. Each location becomes the site of a process of internal combustion that removes all defilements of body, speech, and mind preventing the attainment of Buddhahood. In each re-creation of the *maṇḍala*, the deities stand on a horizontal flaming wheel. The wheel has sharp edges and rotates, turning into a blazing, spinning knife that chops and burns diseases, defilements, demons, and negative forces of every kind. The meditator reinforces the mental imagery by reciting a continuous stream of mantras that revolve like wheels, burn like fire, flow like water, and rush like a mighty wind.[30]

The meditator begins by filling her body with nectar. As the male and female Buddha on the uppermost wheel unite, the elixir (*bodhicitta*) of their union flows down, entering the aperture of the meditator's crown and filling her body with purifying, healing ambrosia:

> Having made the secret offering (of sexual union)
> And the natural offering (of enlightened awareness),
> The union of the divine couple
> Produces white elixir with a reddish glow.
> The stream enters the crown of one's head.
> The four (goddesses on) the wheel
> Unite with their *khatvāṅgas* [staffs symbolizing male consorts].
> Streams of elixir flow from their secret places
> And, coming together in (the meditator's) crown,
> Flow down into the four places (head, throat, heart, and navel),
> Purifying the impediments to enlightenment.[31]

Each *maṇḍala* targets a different set of bodily and mental ills, which are chopped by the flaming wheels, incinerated by mountains of fire, and dispersed by winds of wisdom.[32] In order to heal the environment as well, the meditator sends out hooked light rays and gathers negative forces to be consumed in the inner fire. In the following passage, Niguma portrays the red wheel at the throat:

In the center is Cakrasaṃvara in sacred union (*yab-yum*),
The color of a red lotus,
Ornamented by bones and fresh and dry skulls,
With a swaying dance movement.
The goddesses in the four directions
Hold curved knives and skull-cups;
They're red and hold mystical staffs.
There is a RAM on the spokes, as before.
The wisdom fire burns; please the deities with offerings.
From the place of union of the male and female sovereigns of the *maṇḍala*,
A stream of red elixir of union arises.
Imagine that as purifying
All sources of disease and defilements
By filling one from the throat downward.
Do the heart-mantras as before,
[Like] a stream of water, wheel, bonfire, and wind.[33]

The drama heightens as Niguma proceeds to the blue wheel at the heart:

The heart-wheel is blue.
In the heart is a BRUṂ, blue in color.
Envision the wheel as strong and sharp . . .
HŪṂ's and diamond scepters (*vajras*) radiate out and return.
Envision blue Saṃvara and red female partner
As wrathful in nature and accompanied by attendants.
On the spokes, dark blue flames blaze.
The divine male and divine female unite . . .
Spiritual ecstasy increases;
HŪṂ! PHAṬ! and laughter resound like a thousand thunders.
The elixir of union, blue in color,
Fills the body from the heart downward,
Purifying causes of disease and mental defilements.
Particularly evil spirits and anger
Are sliced by the wheel,
Burned by the bonfire of wisdom, and
Dispersed by winds of wisdom.
A torrential stream of elixir
Washes away obscurations like a mountain of ashes.[34]

The graphic and dynamic imagery of this healing meditation lends it a strong aesthetic appeal, which may be one reason it has survived as a transmission lineage to the present day. Niguma's text on how to confer initiation into this practice is also preserved.[35] The practice survives in the Sa-skya "Compendium of Tantras"[36] and in the Shangs-pa lineage currently held by several Karma bKa'-brgyud masters.[37] Niguma is reputed to have given teachings on other major Tantric deities, like Guhyasamāja, Hevajra, and Mahāmāyā, but only the instructions for the Hevajra initiation survive in written form.[38] Niguma is also renowned for her teaching on the "stages of the path of magical illusion," her formulation of advanced meditations for realizing the illusory nature of all phenomena, up to and including the attainment of Buddhahood, which she teaches is the supreme illusion but an illusion nonetheless.[39]

## LAKṢMĪṄKARĀ AND SEVERED-HEADED VAJRAYOGINĪ

The life story of Lakṣmīṅkarā describes the kind of heroic journey that is often required of those who seek ultimate truths. She was born into a privileged position as a princess and enjoyed a good education and a life of luxury in the palace. As a child, she spent carefree days dallying in the royal gardens with her maidservants and young companions, playing with peacocks and parrots, weaving flower garlands, and bathing in lotus ponds. Her life was idyllic until she was betrothed to the king of Ceylon as part of a political alliance. She traveled to Ceylon with a lavish dowry, and at the outset the trip seemed like an adventure. The princess watched excitedly when her fiancé came to meet her, but her heart sank when she saw his weapons and hunting gear. He had even brought the carcasses and skins of deer he had killed as a tribute.

Lakṣmīṅkarā resolved that she wouldn't marry a pitiless hunter, even if doing so would make her a queen. Regarding marriage to him as a fate worse than death, Lakṣmīṅkarā gave away her possessions, secluded herself in a room, and threw things at anyone who tried to approach her. Finally she ran away, without regard for her safety or welfare. In a leave-taking much like that of Śākyamuni Buddha, she took off her fine silks and jewels. The princess unbound her hair, which was perfumed with sandalwood oil and braided with jasmine flowers, and never again braided it or tied it back. In place of clothing, Lakṣmīṅkarā rubbed ashes on her body. She talked incoherently, pretending to be mad. Since she was eminently unmarriageable and also an embarrassment in this condition, the wedding was cancelled.

Lakṣmīṅkarā escaped to a cremation ground, hoping to evade any hunting parties that might come in search for her. Anyone who caught sight of the princess there barely recognized her, for the ashes gave her skin a blue tint and she was clothed only in her long hair, which was caked with dirt, leaves, and twigs. Lakṣmīṅkarā put her solitude to good use and spent many months plumbing the depths of meditation in complete seclusion.

Lakṣmīṅkarā's story dramatizes the lengths to which a mystic must sometimes go in order to sever the attachments that prevent full immersion into the egoless state. Lakṣmīṅkarā had already received religious training and practiced meditation before she left her palace, but the sojourn in the wilderness catapulted her into a realm of visionary experience in which she could see and communicate directly with Buddhas and bodhisattvas. The Buddhas themselves gave her religious instruction. The female Buddha Vajrayoginī appeared to Lakṣmīṅkarā in a distinctive form that became the basis of a widespread meditation practice. When Lakṣmīṅkarā came out of seclusion, she attracted a circle of disciples, several of whom subsequently became quite famous. Her former fiancé even converted to Buddhism and asked her to be his guru, but she assigned one of her low-caste disciples to be his guru instead.[40]

The female deity whose practice Lakṣmīṅkarā introduced is Severed-Headed Vajrayoginī.[41] Severed-Headed Vajrayoginī has a yellow body, a dynamic dancing pose, and long black hair streaming behind her. The meditator identifies with her and envisions her as raising a sword, cutting off her own head, and triumphally waving it aloft. Three streams of blood spout from her body at the neck and flow into the mouth of her own severed head and the mouths of two yoginis at her sides. The yoginis are green Vajravarṇanī (or Vajrapraṇavā) on her left and yellow Vajravairocanī on her right. The divine yoginis are naked and have loosely flowing hair (figure 10).

In her texts, Lakṣmīṅkarā instructs the practitioner to practice this in a secluded place, as she did, and to imitate the deity, with hair loosely flowing and "clothed with the sky," that is, naked. The place for offerings is a ritually drawn triangle, an ancient Indian (and indeed worldwide) symbol of female life-giving powers and ontological primacy. This cosmic cervix is to be drawn with vermillion, the menstrual blood of the earth, deepening the female resonances of the ritual and meditation.

Lakṣmīṅkarā taught the practice of Vajrayoginī on the basis of the way this deity appeared to her in a vision. It seems fitting that a female deity would reveal herself in her severed-headed form to a female mystic, for who but a woman would immediately appreciate this viscerally

FIGURE 10. Severed-Headed Vajrayoginī

direct symbol of spiritual nourishment, in which streams of life-giving liquid flow from a woman's body. Although the image refers on one level to biological nourishment, on another level it locates the source of spiritual life and sustenance in a woman's body. It affirms that a woman can tap a never-ending stream of energy within herself and choose to direct that energy to her own liberation and the liberation of her disciples. Severed-Headed Vajrayoginī locates the power to rejuvenate, replenish, and restore herself in a woman's own body, as well as her ability to nourish others without sacrificing her own needs or spiritual development.

Another level of symbolism of the female Buddha who beheads herself is the need to cut off dualistic thinking at the root if a woman is to reach a level of direct knowing beyond conceptual dualities. As a way to inspire her disciples, Lakṣmīṅkarā composed songs to usher them into the nondual state. One of the songs was recorded by two of her female disciples.[42] Lakṣmīṅkarā's association with the Severed-Headed Vajrayoginī practice is reflected in the occasional portrayal of the former princess with a curved knife or sword in one hand and a head in the other.[43]

Lakṣmīṅkarā transmitted the practice to several female disciples and to the male disciple Virūpa, who transmitted it to Nepal and Tibet. Virūpa wrote a Severed-Headed Vajrayoginī practice manual that he says is "based on the secret oral instructions of the yogini and should be kept secret."[44] Although he does not mention her by name, the "yogini" is clearly Lakṣmīṅkarā, the woman from whom he learned the practice.[45] Lakṣmīṅkarā's transmission of this practice then passed through Virūpa, traversed Nepal, and reached Tibet, where it was popular for several centuries.[46] Lineal descendants of the practice are still maintained by the 'Bri-gung bKa'-brgyud sect[47] and by the Sa-skya school of Tibetan Buddhism, which traces its origins to Virūpa.[48] Although Virūpa's reputation eclipsed that of Lakṣmīṅkarā over the centuries,[49] this practice nonetheless had a founding mother.

## MEKHALĀ, KANAKHALĀ, AND SEVERED-HEADED VAJRAYOGINĪ INNER YOGA

Mekhalā and Kanakhalā were sisters who both undertook Tantric practice and attained enlightenment together. They devised the authoritative version of the inner yogas of Severed-Headed Vajrayoginī. Lakṣmīṅkarā had introduced meditation on this deity, but perhaps because of their special expertise it fell to the sisters to provide a definitive formulation of the inner yoga.

According to their biography, the sisters were betrothed to a pair of brothers, but when the sisters became the object of gossip and undeserved criticism by their neighbors, the doubt cast upon their character caused their fiancés' family to break the engagements. Disgraced and embarrassed, the sisters considered leaving their village, but Mekhalā, the elder, realized that their problems would follow them wherever they went. When the Tantric guru Kāṇha visited their village they confided their misery to him, and he prescribed the Severed-Headed Vajrayoginī practice for them. The meditative disciplines gave them a sense of purpose and increasing inner freedom in the midst of their unhappy circumstances, and they devoted themselves to the practice for the next twelve years.

After twelve years the sisters sought out Kāṇha in his hermitage. When he asked them for an offering, they asked him what he would like. The guru pretended not to recognize them and asked for their heads as proof of their gratitude. They dutifully cut off their heads, and he promptly restored them. Kāṇha confirmed their high level of realization, declaring that they were now fully qualified to act as gurus.[50] He praised them:

> Behold! Two great yoginis
> Have attained excellence and bliss!
> Your own peace and happiness is the lesser path—
> Live to benefit others.[51]

Mekhalā and Kanakhalā are usually portrayed with swords, either dancing with the swords held aloft or in the act of cutting off their heads (figure 11). By cutting off their heads they demonstrated that they had severed their egos with the sword of wisdom.[52] One interpreter suggests that the sisters beheaded themselves to show that they had conquered the "self-centered conceit" and "vanity" that characteristically afflict women;[53] however, nothing in their story indicates that the sisters were vain. To become the object of unjust accusation is something that could befall anyone, male or female, and the guru gave them the Buddhist teachings as a remedy not for specifically feminine weaknesses but for the core of human suffering, namely, attachment to an illusory self.

The sisters' iconography also refers to their mastery of the practice of Severed-Headed Vajrayoginī. Portraying someone with attributes of a deity shows that she has fully identified with that deity through meditation. Portraying the sisters in a manner that likens them to this form of Vajrayoginī—naked, with flowing hair, and with swords or flaying knives in the act of cutting off their heads—expresses their identification with the female Buddha and the successful awakening of their divine potentialities.

According to their biography, the sister adepts learned this meditation from Kāṇha. Kāṇha probably learned the practice from his guru, Jālandhari, who was a disciple of Lakṣmīṅkarā, the acknowledged originator of the practice.[54] It is also likely that the sisters received instruction in the practice directly from Lakṣmīṅkarā, since they traveled in the same circles. Their acquaintance with Lakṣmīṅkarā is evidenced by the fact that she addressed a "song of realization" to them.[55] In any case, it is clear that the sisters were closely associated with the introduction of the Severed-Headed Vajrayoginī practice[56] and that they had mastered the perfection stage sufficiently to formulate the inner yogas that culminate the practice.

The sisters' text, entitled *Oral Instructions on the Three Whirling Crosses*, is not a *sādhana*, or a liturgical manual to be recited while performing the practice, but rather provides details that would be helpful to someone learning the practice.[57] Since the text is called "oral instructions" (*upadeśa*), it may have been recorded by their disciples. The orig-

FIGURE 11. Sister adepts Mekhalā and Kanakhalā

inal audience of these teachings would have been advanced practitioners of Tantric meditation. Only someone embarking upon the inner yogic practice of this deity would find these teachings relevant and be able to put them into practice.

According to the instructions of Mekhalā and Kanakhalā, this inner yoga re-creates the iconography of the three deities within the meditator's body. In the basic visualization, Vajrayoginī has cut off her own head, and two streams of blood issue from the severed neck and flow into the mouths of the attendant yoginis at her sides, Vajravarṇanī (or Vajrapraṇavā) on her left and Vajravairocanī on her right (figure 10). In the inner yoga practice, the central vein, or *avadhūtī*, that traverses the body vertically is assimilated to Vajrayoginī, while the two subsidiary veins (*lalanā* on the left and *rasanā* on the right) become the accompanying goddesses. The meditator, identifying with the central yogini, imagines that she cuts off her head and then seals the three veins with whirling crosses, thereby keeping the psychic energy (*prāṇa*) circulating within the body. A random and outward motion of this energy characterizes an unenlightened mind, whereas increasing control and centralization of the energy signals progress toward enlightenment.

Concentrating the energy into small points, or drops, helps the meditator direct the energy at will:

> Having ignited the fire of wisdom, one's body,
> From the throat to the soles of the feet,
> Dissolves in stages into the sphere of reality (*dharmadhātu*).
>
> Concentrate the mind on the point of equanimity,
> Which is not found by analysis, is not a material thing, and
> Is free from all objective characteristics.
> If you don't meditate like this, no matter what else you do
> You won't realize what is innate (*sahaja*)
> And will wander in worldliness (*saṁsāra*).
>
> Rising from that point,
> Magically create yourself as the Severed-Headed Goddess,
> Then envision the letter HRIṂ at your navel.
> The wind rises where the three channels meet.
> Dissolve HRI into three drops:
> Dissolve the I into a drop of wind,
> The HA into a drop of semen, and
> The RAṂ into a drop of blood—
> In short, blue, white, and red [drops], respectively.
> [If] they don't rise, push them upward with the wind.
>
> When [the drops] move in the hollow channels
> Of Severed-Headed Vajrayoginī,
> Envision [them] as rising four finger-widths.
> The left one spins counterclockwise, the right one clockwise.
> The central drop, burning, dissolves.[58]

At this point in the practice, the exhalation of the two attendant goddesses transfers energy from the subsidiary channels to the central channel, which is the goal of all inner yogas. Once the energy is concentrated in the central channel, nondualistic and nonconceptual states of mind arise spontaneously:

> The two goddesses exhale, which makes
> The left and right drops dissolve into the middle one.
> By inhaling that [drop] downward,
> Envision it dissolving into the HŪṂ at the heart.
> That [HŪṂ] is clear and stainless,
> A nondual drop of intrinsic awareness,
> Free from all happiness and suffering—
> Pure awareness that is emptied of worldly appearances.

How wonderful! Practice yoga—
You will attain nondual wisdom![59]

This passage moves quickly through a highly technical exercise in creative imagination. The process of inner combustion culminates in nondual states of pure, objectless meditation, the most advanced level of meditation practice.

The yoga of Mekhalā and Kanakhalā survives as precious evidence of one of the practices—perhaps the major practice—that the sisters mastered and transmitted as Tantric gurus. It also stands as evidence that their self-beheading iconography represents not their conquest of feminine vanity but their triumph over the self-centeredness at the root of all suffering and their role in developing a distinctive inner yoga.

## SIDDHARĀJÑĪ AND THE BUDDHA OF INFINITE LIFE

Siddharājñī herself is virtually hidden from historical view, although her influence on Tantric Buddhism is tangible and widespread. Siddharājñī, a twelfth-century yogini from Uḍḍiyāna in northwestern India,[60] pioneered a comprehensive ritual, meditative, and yogic system of Amitāyus, the Buddha of Infinite Life. Her teachings on this deity have remained authoritative to the present day for three of the four schools of Tibetan Buddhism.[61]

The visibility of Siddharājñī's influence is due to the frequent performance of her long-life ceremony (Tib. *tshe-dbang*, technically a long-life initiation) as a public ritual for conferring long life. Since everyone desires longevity, rituals devoted to the Buddha of Infinite Life are a frequent occurrence in the Tibetan ritual year, bringing together lay and monastic adherents. The ritual holds an annual position in the ritual calendar (the full moon of the tenth lunar month) and can also be performed at a donor's request on any astrologically auspicious day. The donation would generally have to be a relatively large one, since these elaborate rituals include extensive offerings and the preparation of mounds of medicinal pellets that are distributed after the ceremony. A donor might sponsor the ritual for someone who was ill or to ensure long life for the entire family.[62] However, the staging of the ritual benefits the entire community, because anyone can attend and partake of the consecrated medicines, to absorb the blessings generated during the ritual.

The long-life ritual is also performed at the beginning of Mani Rimdu dance performances, which are performed at New Year celebrations and on other occasions. The religious purpose of the dance is to exorcise negative influences and increase positive ones. Although the dance has several components, its name (Tib. *ma-ni ril-sgrub*) contains a reference to the long-life pellets (Tib. *ril*) distributed at the long-life ceremony, reflecting its centrality to the dance.[63] A nineteenth-century observer in Tibet reported that long-life ceremonies were in such high demand that they were performed weekly at the larger monasteries,[64] and a contemporary anthropologist observed the performance of a long-life ceremony at the close of a fasting ritual.[65] Because of its frequency and public nature, several scholars have witnessed and described the ritual.[66] In addition to these public rituals for communal well-being, the meditations and yogas associated with the Buddha of Infinite Life are performed by monastics, yogis, and yoginis. Thus, between the public rituals and private meditations, the Buddha of Infinite Life is quite important in Tibetan Buddhism.

Siddharājñī's biography is contained within the biography of Rechungpa (1084–1161), the disciple who transmitted her teachings to Tibet.[67] A separate and more complete biography of Siddharājñī may come to light, and indeed it would be unusual if no such biography existed, since the preservation of biographies and lineage histories proceed in tandem in Tibet and she is the foremother of the major gSar-ma Amitāyus lineages.[68] Siddharājñī is a rather elusive figure in Rechungpa's biography, for the work does not provide information about her family background or religious training but rather concentrates on Rechungpa's meetings with her and the Tantric teachings he received from her.[69] The details included are those that convey the spiritual greatness of Rechungpa's guru; therefore, although this account pays tribute to Siddharājñī, she does not really come alive in the telling, since it is Rechungpa's liberation tale, not hers.

Rechungpa went to India and received teachings from many masters, but Western historical works do not as a rule mention his female teacher.[70] According to Rechungpa's biography, he was in India studying under the master Tiphupa when a yogi prophesied his imminent death. Traumatized, he rushed to Tiphupa and said he didn't want to die before he had fulfilled Milarepa's command that he bring more Buddhist teachings from India to Tibet. Satisfied regarding Rechungpa's motivation, Tiphupa sent him to Siddharājñī, the living authority on longevity practices. When Rechungpa first set eyes on Siddharājñī, her presence was so powerful that his hair stood on end. Devotion so overwhelmed him that he trembled, wept, threw himself on the ground at her feet, and placed her feet on his head in a gesture of supreme respect.

Siddharājñī was strict with her disciple. She granted Rechungpa an initiation and taught him one of her methods on the condition that he practice it for seven days without sleeping. This averted his impending death and earned him further instruction and teachings, which he later took to Tibet. Siddharājñī prophesied that Rechungpa would live to twice his present age, to the ripe old age of eighty-eight. In gratitude for the guidance he had received from Siddharājñī and Tiphupa, Rechungpa offered his gurus a generous measure of gold and a song of praise. At a Tantric feast on the eve of his departure for Tibet, the Queen of Adepts gave her spiritual son some parting advice, prophesies of his activities in Tibet, and whispered transmissions (*karṇatantra*, i.e., very secret oral instructions), then bade him return to Tibet and benefit living beings there. She gave him a *ḍākinī* skull from Uḍḍiyāna and bone ornaments as a gift for Milarepa.[71]

The esteem in which Siddharājñī was held is clear from a song of praise offered by Tiphupa, wherein he compares and even equates her with a number of female deities, a way of expressing that she embodies the enlightened presence of those deities:

> Vajravārāhī incarnate,
> Female Victor Pāṇḍaravāsinī,
> Mother who gives birth to all Buddhas,
> Homage to Siddharājñī!
>
> . . . . . . . . . . .
>
> You have the thirty-two signs of a Buddha.
> White with a red luster,
> An enchantingly beautiful woman,
> Your rainbow body is brilliant as a diamond.
>
> Bliss-bestowing woman with every excellence,
> Wearing jewels and six ornaments of bone,
> You hold a curved knife and skull-cup full of nectar
> And wear a diadem with silk ribbons.
>
> In the middle of an ocean of female enlighteners (*ḍākinīs*),
> In a crystal meditation bower,
> On a throne of gold, silver, turquoise, coral, and pearls,[72]
> You are our only mother, Siddharājñī![73]

Tiphupa expresses Siddharājñī's enlightenment by calling her Vajravārāhī, a female Buddha, and celebrating her possession of the thirty-two bodily signs of a Buddha. The "meditation bower" (*gandhakuṭī*) in which she sits is a canopy built to welcome and honor a Buddha.[74] A rainbow body (Tib. *'ja'-lus*), the quintessential Tantric attainment, refers to the rainbowlike translucence and beauty of enlightened being that shines forth when all mental and emotional impurities have been removed without a trace.

Tiphupa's song next describes Siddharājñī's meditative journeys through the visionary landscape of Tantric Buddhism, meeting enlightened beings and receiving teachings and initiations directly from them, an ability possessed only by the greatest masters:

> You looked upon the faces of all the long-life deities
> And received the long-life empowerment
> And instructions for practice.
> A Tantric knowledge-holder,
> You mastered the spiritual attainment of longevity.
> . . . . . . . . . . . . . . . . . . . . . . . .
> Having gone to Akaniṣṭha heaven and
> Met Vajradhara in his visionary experience form,
> Completed the four Tantric initiations, and
> Realized the four unexcelled bodies of enlightenment,
> You are known as [the female Buddha] Vajravārāhī,
> Surrounded by your assembly, an ocean of Victors . . .
> Having met Cakrasaṃvara,
> Heard the Tantric Vajrayāna teachings,
> And obtained the supreme Tantric accomplishments,
> You are known as Vajrayoginī,
> Surrounded by the heroes and sky-dancers of the three realms.[75]
> . . . . . . . . . . . . . . . . . . . . . . . . . . . . . . . .
> Having met Ḍākinī Siṃhamukhā,
> Heard the secret explanation of supreme bliss, and
> Perfected the four spiritual activities,[76]
> You are called Cremation-Ground Corpse-Eater,
> Surrounded by many bears, jackals, tigers, and
> Leopards—emanations of *ḍākinīs*.[77]

After she met the Buddha of Infinite Life face-to-face, the attainment for which she is most known and the basis of her authority concerning this Buddha, the Queen of Siddhas met Vajradhara in Akaniṣṭha heaven and received the Tantric initiations from him, achieving equality with the female Buddha Vajravārāhī. She met Cakrasaṃvara, received Tantric teachings from him, and identified fully with Vajrayoginī. From the lion-faced female deity Siṃhamukhā (figure 4), she heard the secret exposition of supreme bliss. In the course of her meditative journeys she met the deities Avalokiteśvara and Hayagrīva and on the basis of these meetings wrote manuals for their contemplation as well. Tiphupa's song also celebrates Siddharājñī's completion of pilgrimages to the eight great cremation grounds and twenty-four Tantric *pīṭhas*, where she received key secret oral instructions from the *ḍākinīs* there.[78] This account does not describe her personality or spiritual struggles before attaining enlightenment, but it does express the basis of her authority as a founder of an important body of practices.

The writings about Siddharājñī communicate the awe in which she was held by those who knew her. Her own writings detail the religious practices she introduced, providing tangible evidence of her ritual expertise and philosophical background. One of her works is a manual instructing Tantric gurus how to create an Amitāyus *maṇḍala*, prepare and consecrate the initiation flasks, and administer the initiation.[79] Before performing an initiation, a guru must invoke the energies embodied by the deity in order to transmit the divine energy, power, and blessings to the initiates. Accordingly, Siddharājñī's initiation manual describes how to achieve identification with the deity through mantra recitation and self-consecration (*svādhiṣṭhāna*). The gSar-ma schools of Tibetan Buddhism and their branches all use her system for the Buddha of Infinite Life initiation. The liturgies in current use are later, shortened versions of Siddharājñī's detailed system. These later texts generally open with a prayer to the lineage masters through which the transmission has come, starting with the female founder of the practice. Her mediation between the divine and human realms is the basis of the authenticity of the subsequent transmission lineages.

In addition to this initiation text addressed to gurus, Siddharājñī wrote a meditation manual on contemplation of the Buddha of Infinite Life that covers the outer, inner, secret, and natural levels of meditation.[80] During the outer stage the meditator learns to picture the deity in vivid detail. The inner stage practice requires that the meditator envision her own body as a *maṇḍala* and imagine deities at different points within her body. The secret level consists of inner yogic practices involving psychic heat, winds, and veins to generate bliss. The final stage is a recovery of the natural state of the mind, purified of delusion. It is a complex series of meditations, and the practice manuals in current use are generally abbreviated versions written by later masters of the various schools, whereas the type of detail found in Siddharājñī's text is imparted orally and in commentaries.[81] As an adjunct to the system, Siddharājñī wrote a manual on Hayagrīva ("Horse-neck"), a wrathful but nonetheless compassionate protective deity associated with the Buddha of Infinite Life. Her Hayagrīva manual includes instructions on how to consecrate a sculpted flour offering and use it to remove the obstacles of the officiant's disciples.[82] Completing the Amitāyus system, she wrote a text on the fire offering performed at the end of an Amitāyus retreat.[83]

In Tantric Buddhism, a vision of deity is a measure of spiritual mastery and basis for religious authority. The authoritativeness of Siddharājñī's teachings derives from her visionary encounters with

Amitāyus. The yogini met the Buddha of Infinite Life face-to-face and received the long-life teachings and initiations directly from him. Subsequently, she taught her disciples and their spiritual descendents how to approach and experience this Buddha. In one version of her standard portrayal, Siddharājñī's posture and iconography reflect her association with the Buddha of Infinite Life. She displays a meditative pose and holds the same life-bestowing vase as Amitāyus (figure 12). In addition, she wears the insignia of a Tantric yogini: a tiger skin as a lower garment, bone ornaments combined with jewelry, and skulls atop her crown. In another version of her iconography, the Queen of Siddhas is shown as a dancing *ḍākinī* with billowing scarves and bone ornaments, a crescent-bladed knife, and a skull-cup brimming with the nectar of immortality, her gift to her spiritual descendents.

Although her long-life ceremony and Amitāyus practice lineages are eminently visible in Tibetan Buddhist culture, Siddharājñī herself is not. The Tibetan term for her system, or transmission, of Amitāyus is sGrub-pa'i rgyal-mo'i lugs, but in the commonly used abbreviation (sGrub-rgyal-lugs), the feminine ending (*-mo*) is one of the syllables that is dropped, concealing from all but the intelligentsia the true identity—and gender—of the founder of the system. Awareness of this fact would require a deeper historical knowledge than most followers of any tradition possess. Therefore, although the Buddha of Infinite Life teachings of Siddharājñī are prominent in Tibetan Buddhism, many are not aware that the initiation they receive, the practices they perform, and the public rituals they stage and attend are based on the revelations and teachings of a woman.

## SIDDHARĀJÑĪ AND THE LORD WHO DANCES ON A LOTUS

Siddharājñī also pioneered an esoteric form of Avalokiteśvara that is used by the three New (gSar-ma) Schools of Tibetan Buddhism. This form is Padmanarteśvara, or "Lord Who Dances on a Lotus."[84] Currently he is more commonly known as Jinasāgara, meaning "Ocean of Victorious Ones."[85] The exoteric forms of Avalokiteśvara—such as the thousand-armed form transmitted by Bhikṣuṇī Lakṣmī and the four-armed, seated form associated with Atīśa—are commonly depicted in every medium of Tibetan art and widely and publicly taught. This highly esoteric form of Avalokiteśvara is rarely encountered in art or general literature; it is customarily reserved for Tantric initiates and requires extensive instruction in intricate ritual and yogic practices. Traditionally an image of Padmanarteśvara would be unveiled during an initiation and could subsequently be owned and used by someone

FIGURE 12. Siddharājñī holding vase of immortality

performing the practice, although this is slowly changing in the present atmosphere of increasing openness regarding Tantric images.[86]

There are several forms of the Lord Who Dances on a Lotus, distinguished by such iconographic features as number of hands, hand implements, sitting or dancing posture, and the presence or absence of a female consort.[87] The red, four-armed form delineated by Siddharājñī is practiced by the Karma bKa'-brgyud, Sa-skya, and dGe-lugs sects of Tibetan Buddhism.[88] Padmanarteśvara appears in union with Guhyajñānā, and they are seated on their lotus. Guhyajñānā is red and has four arms that hold a skull-bowl, flaying knife, sword of wisdom, and Tantric staff (*khatvāṅga*). The lord and lady may be portrayed with four arms each, representing an earlier stage of the visualization, or two arms each, representing the secret practice. They are surrounded by five divine couples who display the colors and emblems of the five Buddha families.[89] These are only a few of the many deities envisioned in the course of this complex meditation.

Siddharājñī's text follows a sequence of outer, inner, secret, and truly secret stages of the practice.[90] Consecrated medicines prepared by Tantric masters are an important part of the outer rituals, since ingesting these medicines is one way for participants to absorb the long-life blessings generated during the rites. After delineating the ritual implements, consecrated medicines, sacraments, and offerings to be arrayed, Siddharājñī describes Padmanarteśvara, Guhyajñānā, and their retinue as the meditator is to envision them. The inner practice involves imagining the deities at different points within the body, then dissolving them into radiant energy and spreading the warmth and light throughout the body to accomplish mental and emotional purification. The meditator ignites a fire in the lower abdomen, and the flame melts the deities above it. Siddharājñī explains how all illusions and impurities are burned away by this inner flame:

> The deities at the secret place burn;
> The chiefs of the four *cakras* also burn completely.
> The fire, having touched the A at the navel,
> Burns [the A] and touches the HAṂ [at the crown],
> Whereby a stream of elixir drips, filling the four *cakras*,
> [Whose] deities burn, increasing their great bliss.
> All the Buddhas of the three times,
> Living beings, love, hatred, and so forth . . .
> Become inseparable from the breath and are condensed and absorbed.
> The fire burns away impurities.
> In a state of emptiness and deep compassion,
> The natural mind doesn't do anything.
> [In] the authentic state of nonconceptual clarity,
> Maintain stainless intrinsic awareness.
> Hold the breath and purify oneself of all biases [of dualistic thought].[91]

To this rarefied state of inner combustion Siddharājñī adds a culminating stage of "truly secret practice" in which philosophical insights are applied to the results of the preceding yogic processes, effecting the subtlest stages of purification. The Queen of Adepts describes the metaphysical insights that scale the final peaks of meditative attainment:

> Don't look for an outer place of solitude;
> The body itself is a divine mansion (*maṇḍala*).
> Don't look elsewhere for the deity;
> The mind itself, unborn and unperishing,
> Is the family Buddha and guru.
> Not realizing this, one has disturbing emotions and ignorance;
> Realizing this is liberation and great compassion.
> One's profusion of thoughts . . .
> Are the thousand Buddhas.
> Violent, angry hatred is baseless;
> This realization is Hayagrīva.
> Desires that strike so swiftly have no root;
> This realization is Guhyajñānā.
> The legion of proud emotions, freed from self-cherishing,
> Become the heroes.
> Jealousy is like a tornado; when hope and fear are abolished,
> That is the heroines.
> . . . . . . . . .
> The delusion of not realizing the nature of mind
> Is entrapment in worldliness;
> Realizing that is blissful liberation.
> Deity forms are the creativity of one's own mind;
> If you grasp [deities] as material things, this is delusion;
> Deities are also the mind itself,
> Clearly manifesting in the expanse of unconditioned reality.
> . . . . . . . . . . . . . . . . . . . . . . .
> Whatever is spoken or heard is an echo of the inexpressible.
> This primordially pure awareness
> Abides in reality from the beginning.
> When that is shown [by the guru] and one recognizes it,
> One realizes the sphere of ultimate reality.
> That is known as Buddhahood.[92]

Siddharājñī's detailed description of how Buddhahood can be attained shows that women attained the ultimate goal of this tradition. This evidence would remain valid even if this work were only attributed to her, because such writings would not be ascribed to a woman unless there were living exemplars who rendered such an attribution believable—and necessary.[93]

## BHIKṢUṆĪ LAKṢMĪ AND AVALOKITEŚVARA FASTING PRACTICE

Unlike some of the other founding mothers, Bhikṣuṇī Lakṣmī has attained the stature of a culture hero. She introduced a vastly popular ascetical discipline for lay people that continues to be important for Tibetan Buddhism in all its geographical locations and among followers of all the sects. One cannot live in a Tibetan Buddhist community for very long without hearing about individuals or, more often, large groups undertaking the fasting ritual of Bhikṣuṇī Lakṣmī. Works of art depicting her meditating at the feet of Avalokiteśvara will be encountered in Tibetan homes and temples. Bhikṣuṇī Lakṣmī is better known than some of the other female founders perhaps because her practice is less esoteric and hence more public and also because she is often put forward as an exemplar when her practice is imparted.

Bhikṣuṇī Lakṣmī (Tib. dGe-slong-ma dPal-mo), a Kashmiri princess of the late tenth or eleventh century,[94] forged this widespread fasting practice out of her experiences of life-threatening illness, devastating rejection by her religious community, and healing hierophany. Young Lakṣmī was endowed with a sensitive and sympathetic temperament, and when she discovered that animals—such as lambs, of which she was particularly fond—are slaughtered for food, she was so horrified that she resolved to cut her ties with worldly life. Overcoming the opposition of her parents, the princess became a fully ordained nun (*bhikṣuṇī*) and then apprenticed herself to a Tantric guru. Lakṣmī became extremely skilled at logical debate, so her guru ordered her to debate the leading philosophers and Tantric scholars of the day. When she defeated one after another, Lakṣmī was installed as abbess of a monastery and held this position for many years, until she contracted leprosy. The monks then drove her out and ruthlessly abandoned their abbess to die in the forest—according to one version of the story because they suspected her of having a miscarriage.[95]

Too ill even to walk, Lakṣmī crawled into a cave and collapsed there, using her waning strength to call upon Avalokiteśvara, the bodhisattva of compassion. Avalokiteśvara responded to her prayers and appeared to her in a dazzling white, thousand-armed form, proffering the vessel of liquid that fulfills every thirst and need of sentient beings. In one version of the story he poured clear water through her entire body, instantly curing her of leprosy;[96] in another version, he gave her some medicinal pellets and her symptoms disappeared after three days.[97]

After her miraculous healing, the revelations continued. The abbess flew with Avalokiteśvara to a celestial realm, where she danced amidst the clouds with beautiful *ḍākinīs*. As the culmination of her visionary journey, the bodhisattva of compassion revealed a fasting practice to her and instructed her to teach it to everyone—including lay people—as a powerful method of merit-accumulation and purification. Meanwhile, the abbess's personal attendant assumed that she had died in the forest and came looking for her bones. Bhikṣuṇī Lakṣmī emerged from the cave fully restored to health and reported all that had happened. The attendant advised that they should return to the monastery and impart the fasting practice to the monks. Still upset about her treatment there, she retorted, "That monastery? I wouldn't even go there to pee!" Compassion prevailed, however, and the two women went to the monastery and taught the newly revealed practice, which was accepted by those who still felt devotion to their abbess and rejected by those who had turned against her. The two women then set out traveling and taught the newly revealed fasting practice in India and Tibet.[98]

The Kashmiri nun's fasting practice (*upoṣaṇa*, Tib. *smyung-gnas*, pronounced nyu nay) became an important discipline for monks, nuns, and lay people alike. It is practiced throughout the Himalayan region and wherever Tibetan Buddhism has spread, including America, Europe, Taiwan, and other outposts of the Tibetan diaspora, by Tibetans as well as Buddhist converts in these countries. It is a key event in the Tibetan Buddhist ritual year and, in addition to its annual performance during the sixth lunar month, can be undertaken at any time. So important is it in the ritual life of the Nepalese Sherpas that Sherry Ortner devotes a chapter of her ethnographic study of these Himalayan Buddhists to the fasting ritual.[99] She ascribes to the fasting ritual a unique role in Sherpa religious life because it is solely concerned with salvation rather than worldly benefits and because it directly appeals to a major divinity rather than a local god or intermediate guardian figure.[100] Ortner also judges the fasting ritual to be the "most orthodox" of Sherpa rituals, embodying classical Buddhist ideals of asceticism, renunciation, merit-making, and intensive efforts toward personal liberation.[101] She observes that *smyung-gnas* is the major opportunity for merit-accumulation in Sherpa life and concludes that, for the Sherpas, the fasting ritual is the "most dramatic and meritorious" way to express and deepen religious commitment.[102]

The core of the fasting practice is a total fast from food and drink, accompanied by prostrations, prayers, and mantra recitation.[103] The laity may also shave their heads, go barefoot, and avoid leather products.[104] It is a chance for lay people to undergo the rigors of monasticism and for monastics to undergo a period of intensified renunciation. The usual length of the ritual is between two and four days, although consecutive sessions may be undertaken, in some cases for several months.[105] The end of the ritual and return to ordinary life is marked by a feast.

Since Śākyamuni Buddha nearly died from a prolonged fast prior to his enlightenment, fasting was not initially an integral part of Buddhist practice; however, fasting eventually found its way into the repertoire of Mahāyāna piety. In the seventh century, the Chinese pilgrim Hsuan Tsang reported a practice of fasting in front of a famous statue of Avalokiteśvara in order to attain a vision of the bodhisattva. The statue in question was located in a convent or monastery in Kashmir.[106] Therefore, this kind of religious observance—combining austerity and visualization—may have been in the background of Bhikṣuṇī Lakṣmī's healing vision of Avalokiteśvara, but her fasting practice is not simply an adoption of a Mahāyāna practice. In addition to classical Mahāyāna *anusmṛti* meditation, which cultivates a vision of deity, Bhikṣuṇī Lakṣmī's system includes the identification of the meditator with Avalokiteśvara in a characteristically Tantric process of envisioning oneself as a deity (*atmotpatti*).[107] If similar practices did flourish previously in Kashmir, Bhikṣuṇī Lakṣmī provided a vital connecting link between an ascetical, devotional stream of Mahāyāna Buddhism in Kashmir and the gulf waters of Tibetan Buddhism into which all the rivers of Indian Buddhism flowed.

The fasting ritual introduced by Bhikṣuṇī Lakṣmī is practiced by all the schools of Tibetan Buddhism. The prominence of two of her early successors—Rin-chen bzang-po and Atīśa—as founders of Tibetan Buddhism helped to ensure the survival of the practice in Tibet. Bhikṣuṇī Lakṣmī wrote an instruction manual for the visualization, but other manuals offering slightly different liturgies for the same core practice have been written over the centuries, as is the case for any active tradition in Tibet. The major meditation texts in current use include the *bKra shis kun khyab* ("All-Pervading Auspiciousness"), written by mKhan-chen bKra-shis Od-zer;[108] the *sDig sgrib rnam sbyong* ("Washing Away Sins and Defilements"), compiled by Zhu-chen Tshul-khrims Rin-chen;[109] and a manual by the Fifth Dalai Lama.[110]

Bhikṣuṇī Lakṣmī wrote a hymn of praise that is particularly treasured and is recited for many hours each day during the ritual as an accompaniment to the prostrations, regardless of whose liturgy is used. Her poetic descriptions of Avalokiteśvara sparkle with the vividness of her visionary encounter, invoking a sense of intimate familiarity with the deity's appearance. One hears echoes of her palace education in the metaphors she uses to convey the effulgence and otherworldly beauty of her healing vision:

Your face shines with full moon splendor;
Your eyes, like lotus petals, are exquisitely tapered.
Fragrant and white as a snowy conch shell,
You hold a glistening rosary of immaculate pearls.
You are adorned by the beauteous blush of dawn;
Like a lotus lake, your hands exude nectar.
Youthful one, white as an autumn cloud,
Many jewels cascade from your shoulders.
The palms of your hands are tender and fresh as delicate leaves. . . .
Your navel is soft as a lotus petal.
. . . . . . . . . . . . . . . . . . . . .
Source of eternal bliss, you cure old age and sickness.[111]

One can easily imagine how this hymn would create a devotional mood and help worshippers call the compassionate lord vividly to mind. With her own experience of Avalokiteśvara's dramatic response to prayer fresh in her mind, Bhikṣuṇī Lakṣmī promises that "anyone, man or woman," who rises at dawn and recites these "sublime praises" while contemplating the greatness of Avalokiteśvara will be able to accomplish his or her aims in this and future lives.[112] Perhaps in reference to the *Lotus Sūtra* passage that the bodhisattva appears in female form when to do so meets a need,[113] she praises Avalokiteśvara for sometimes manifesting as a woman:

Moonlike mother of Buddhas,
Whose form is that of a beautiful goddess. . . .
Empty by nature, you [emerge] from emptiness
In the form of a woman
And tame living beings thereby.[114]

The form in which Avalokiteśvara appeared to the Kashmiri abbess is one of the most widely depicted of Tibetan Buddhist icons. As a tremendously beloved deity and major focus of religious aspiration, this form of Avalokiteśvara is often encountered in Tibetan scroll paintings, statuary, and temple frescoes. He can be recognized by his eleven heads, thousand arms, and identifying attributes in his eight major hands: a rosary, Dharma-wheel, and gesture of giving (*varada-mudrā*) in his right hands; a golden lotus, bow and arrow, and initiation vessel in his left hands; and a pair of hands in *añjalī-mudrā* cupping the wish-granting gem of enlightenment at his heart. The colors of the heads, the hand positions and implements, and the significance of the hand attributes are described in her meditation manual and other writings.[115] This form of Avalokiteśvara, when accompanied by subsidiary figures,

FIGURE 13. Avalokiteśvara (left) and Bhikṣuṇī Lakṣmī in cave (right)

is named after Bhikṣuṇī Lakṣmī in formal iconographic compendia, although her role in popularizing the image is not widely known.[116] Nonetheless, as his foremost devotee, the Kashmiri abbess is sometimes portrayed meditating beatifically at his feet. Mirroring his gesture, she cups a wish-fulfilling jewel at her heart (figure 13), symbolizing her intimate communion with the bodhisattva of compassion and her role as pioneer of the divinely revealed fasting practice.

## THE MOTHERS OF THE "FOUNDING FATHERS"

Certain male figures recur in the sectarian annals, religious biographies, and historical works of India and Tibet as the founders of Tantric Buddhism, while the names of equally glorious foremothers, such as those introduced here in the previous section, do not shine with the same luster as those of their male counterparts and in some cases have nearly been forgotten altogether—save for sufficient evidence for a historian to rediscover them. The acknowledged "founders" are those who have been identified as such in retrospect by their historical successors. Their names are enshrined in lineage histories, colophons, and hagiographical works.[117] The most prominent forefathers include

Saraha, Kāṇha, Virūpa, Luipa, Tilopa, Kambala, Maitrīpa, Padmavajra, and, for the rNying-ma sect, Padmasaṃbhava.

Very little of a genuinely factual or historical nature is known about any of the founding figures. The available hagiographical materials present numerous problems of identity, chronology, and dating.[118] Thus, one may never know, for example, during the life of which Pāla dynast Saraha lived,[119] or if the figure "Saraha" is in fact a composite figure, or if he was a single person whose biography has been augmented by popular stories about the exploits of Tantric yogis or embellished by the storyteller's art. However, the quasi-legendary nature of the source materials does not deter the present inquiry, because the purpose of this section is to investigate the history of the tradition *as it understands and presents itself*. The material regarding female founders has the same historiographical value as the information about male founders. It is equally true of the male and female figures in Tantric literature that if a given person does not correspond to a historical personage, he or she nonetheless represents a type of figure found in Tantric circles or a composite figure around whom the deeds and escapades of several people have constellated.

In accordance with my hypothesis that women contributed to the development of Tantric Buddhist practices, theory, and iconography, the present work investigates the biographies of various founding figures to determine whether any of them had female teachers or, secondarily, female companions who might have worked closely with them in developing their Tantric teachings. My method is what in crime fiction is called *cherchez la femme*, the principle that when one is looking for the cause or root of something one should "search for the woman." The purpose of this exercise is to question the current portrait of the Tantric movement as strictly and exclusively a male cultural creation by exploring whether women may be found at its roots.

One of the towering founding fathers of Tantric Buddhism is the adept Saraha, a former priest and scholar. Saraha's Tantric songs (*dohā*) are prized as the authoritative source of *mahāmudrā* tradition and its characteristic expression in epigrammatic, poetic form.[120] Saraha also heads the transmission lineage of the *Cakrasaṃvara-tantra*[121] and is identified by Tāranātha as the founder of *anuttara-yoga tantra*.[122] Formerly known as the Hindu priest Rahula, Saraha showed great intelligence from a young age and applied himself seriously to his studies, memorizing the Vedas and mastering many other subjects before he converted to Buddhism and became a monk. Saraha's life took a decisive turn when he allowed some girls to convince him to drink beer, in violation of his monastic vows. When he was reeling in a drunken euphoria, a bodhisattva appeared to him and directed him to seek out a mystically talented arrow-making woman who lived in the city, promising that many people would benefit from their meeting.

Convinced of the authenticity of this message, Saraha ventured into the marketplace. Among the arrow-makers he spotted a woman who was making arrows with a deliberateness and finesse that bespoke deep meditative concentration. Wholly focused upon her task, she never looked up or became distracted as she cut the arrow-shaft, inserted the arrowhead, affixed the feathers, and checked the arrow for straightness (figure 14). Saraha tried to break the ice with a trivial question but, not one for trivialities, her first words to him were, "The Buddha's meaning can be known through symbols and actions, not through words and books."[123] Instantly realizing that he had found a worthy teacher, Saraha put off the monastic robes and devoted himself to his yogini guru. The arrow-maker accepted Saraha as her disciple and Tantric companion. According to Tāranātha, she taught him the meaning of things as they are and enabled him to see reality as it is.[124] Saraha became renowned for giving voice to his spiritual insights in verses characterized by the piquant, pithy mode of expression in which the Arrow-making Yogini had instructed him.

The yogini taught Saraha that there is a mode of companionship that is not based on ordinary attachment. His wonderment at her enlightened presence knew no bounds:

> This yogini's action is peerless.
> She consumes the house-holder, and
> Enlightened spontaneity shines forth.
>
> Beyond passion and absence of passion,
> Seated beside her own, her mind destroyed,
> Thus I have seen the yogini.
>
> One eats and drinks and
> Thinks what occurs to thought.
> It is beyond the mind and inconceivable,
> This wonder of the yogini.
>
> Here sun and moon lose their distinction,
> In her the triple world is formed.
> Perfecter of thought and unity of enlightened spontaneity—
> O know this yogini.[125]

Having become an ardent devotee of the arrow-making woman, the former priest and monk lived out his days in a mountain retreat with his guru and partner, earning his living by making arrows. Saraha took the name of his female companion's caste and adopted a Tantric life-

FIGURE 14. Arrow-making Yogini, Saraha's guru

style that included feasting in cremation grounds. When he was criticized for his conspicuously improper behavior, Saraha vindicated himself by expressing his mystical attainments in poetic form (*dohā*) and by displaying supernatural powers, a favored means of deflecting public criticism in medieval India.[126] It turns out that in the case of Saraha, clearly one of the greatest founding figures in the history of Tantric Buddhism, the founding father himself had a spiritual mother, an arrow-maker who, despite her low caste and menial occupation, was a woman of spiritual refinement, profundity, and enlightening capabilities.

Ghaṇṭapa, Luipa, and Kāṇha are regarded as the main founding fathers of the Cakrasaṃvara tradition. They mastered its practice and generated authoritative commentaries and meditation systems.[127] However, when we inquire into the forebears of these founders, we find that Ghaṇṭapa received two Cakrasaṃvara initiations: one from Dārika and one from Sahajayoginīcintā, a woman.[128] Sahajayoginīcintā was a philosopher who nonetheless made her living by herding swine. From her, Ghaṇṭapa also received highly esoteric instructions on how to achieve liberation through ecstasy.[129] After receiving these instructions in Uḍḍiyāna, he proceeded east to Orissa and spent many years there living in a forest and practicing with his spiritual companion, a courtesan's daughter with whom he had a karmic relationship of several lifetimes.[130] Therefore, one of the Ghaṇṭapa's initiating gurus and major teachers on this advanced topic in the Tantric curriculum was a woman.

Luipa's biography does not say from whom he received the Cakrasaṃvara initiation, but most of the teachers his biographies mention are women: the *ḍākinīs* from whom he received instruction in Bodh Gaya, the women in Uḍḍiyāna who staged the feast at which he received Vajravārāhī initiation,[131] and the *ḍākinī* innkeeper whose criticism sent him to the riverbank to develop nondual awareness by living on fish entrails. Luipa even received his name from women, the fisherwomen who observed him eating fish guts by the riverbank.[132] Luipa is also reported to have received initiation from Śavari.[133] Since Śavari had two female gurus, Padmalocanā and Jñānalocanā, who taught conjointly with him (as seen in the biography of Maitrīpa), it is likely that Luipa received the combined instruction of these mountain-dwelling masters. Thus, according to the traditional accounts, it is clear that the founders Ghaṇṭapa and Luipa also had female teachers.

Kāṇha's main guru was Jālandhari, who had received Tantric instruction from the female adept Lakṣmīṅkarā as well as from Kambala (discussed below).[134] In addition to his importance in the Cakrasaṃvara system, Kāṇha is credited with bringing to light the *Saṃpuṭatilaka-tantra*, a short Tantric work of the most esoteric class. However, his biography shows that he attained it from someone else. Kāṇha's teacher, Jālandhari, had sent him in search of a *ḍākinī* named Bhadri in order to obtain the sacred text and teachings from her. Kāṇha found a woman living in a ramshackle hut and did not believe her when she told him she was Bhadri, so he resumed his search. Two more days of searching brought him back to her doorstep, at which point he realized his mistake and prostrated at her feet, requesting the text and initiation. Bhadri foresaw that many people would benefit if she granted Kāṇha's request, so she gave him the initiation, instructions, and clarifications of fine points regarding practice. Although Kāṇha's vision had been obscured when he first met her, seeing only an ordinary woman in a run-down hut and assuming that she could not be the religious teacher he sought, his vision was purified by this encounter. Thus, when Bhadri conferred the initiation he saw the hut as a mansion and the woman's seat as a magnificent throne.[135] Once again, the "founding father" had a spiritual mother.

Kambala, a *mahāsiddha* from Orissa, is another important founding father who imparted Cakrasaṃvara teachings and other key teachings, like the *Hevajra-tantra*, to the originary circles of Tantric Buddhism.[136] Kambala's spiritual mother was also his biological mother, who was a Tantric *ḍākinī*. She oversaw his entire religious career, urging him first to abdicate his throne and become a monk, then to leave the monastery and retire to the forest, and finally to give up his monk's robes and become a Tantric yogi. She herself gave her son the Cakrasaṃvara initiation and teachings,[137] and thus it can reasonably be assumed that his two works on the subject reflect the teachings of his guru—his mother.[138] The teachings Kambala received from his mother were in turn imparted to Indrabhūti,[139] whose many texts on the Cakrasaṃvara system may also be expected to reflect the influence of her teachings, although seamlessly and anonymously woven into the Tantric fabric. In light of the original descent of this initiation and teaching from a woman, it seems fair to ask *whose* teachings are represented in these texts. Are they men's teachings or a woman's teachings? When a woman's teachings are present in a text, male authorship—that is, a man's name in the colophon—cannot in itself be accepted as prima facie evidence that the text represents solely a male cultural creation, as is so often claimed of Tantric texts.

Padmavajra is another major founding father of Tantric Buddhism and is especially renowned as an "author" of the *Hevajra-tantra*—that is, one who discovered or wrote down this revealed text—a distinction he shares with Kambala.[140] Padmavajra was a reputable scholar and skilled public speaker in Uḍḍiyāna when he went to seek out Anaṅgavajra, a pig-herding Tantric guru. When Padmavajra reached Anaṅgavajra's farm, he became totally fascinated by a woman he saw there. She approached her chores with meditative concentration, and her gestures were graceful and bespoke great spiritual depth. She accepted Padmavajra as her disciple and gave him teachings on how to attain spiritual bliss through the expression of passion.[141] Their daughter accepted Padmavajra as her spiritual companion and returned to the capital with him, where their relationship earned them notoriety, while their Tantric practices gained them magical powers and enlightenment.[142] Again, in the career of a "founding father" we find the presence of a spiritual mother.

Virūpa, an adept whose idea of religious discipline was to meditate in a tavern over a dozen glasses of wine, is important as the Indian forefather of the Sa-skya school of Tibetan Buddhism, with its distinctive Path and Fruit (Tib. *lam-'bras*) formulation of the religious path beginning with Mahāyāna philosophy and culminating in Tantric teachings on the *Hevajra-tantra*. According to the official Sa-skya telling of his biography, he received his Tantric teachings and initiations directly from the blue female Buddha Nairātmyā, and no human guru is mentioned.[143] Yet according to the *Blue Annals*, Virūpa also received at least one initiation from a human guru, for he was initiated into the practice of Severed-Headed Vajrayoginī by its founder, Lakṣmīṅkarā, and then transmitted the practice to his own disciples, who spread it to Nepal and Tibet.[144] Thus, in the case of Virūpa, too, we find a spiritual mother.

Tilopa (late tenth through early eleventh centuries) is a founder of the bKa'-brgyud schools, along with Nāropa and Maitrīpa. These Indian founding fathers transmitted their teachings to the Tibetan masters Marpa, Milarepa, and sGam-po-pa before the school divided into the various bKa'-brgyud lineages. Tilopa's early spiritual journey was entirely directed by a woman who converted him to Buddhism, advised him to study Buddhist scripture and philosophy, and decided with which gurus he should study (Saryapa and Matāṅgi), finally taking it upon herself to give him the *Cakrasaṃvara-tantra* initiation and teachings.[145] This *ḍākinī* continued to oversee Tilopa's development as he left the monastery, studied with additional gurus, and did Tantric disciplines in a cremation ground. When she perceived that Tilopa was ripe for complete enlightenment, she sent him to a town in Bengal to find a woman named Barima, ordering Tilopa to work for Barima when he found her.[146] Barima was a spiritually advanced bodhisattva and *ḍākinī* who lived as a courtesan in order to liberate sentient beings.[147] The entire town was saturated with her spiritual presence and provided the optimum environment for the final stages of Tilopa's journey to enlightenment, as he worked as a sesame-pounder by day and as a servant to the courtesan by night.[148]

Tilopa's realizations later were reinforced by direct visions of the Buddha Vajradhara and a transcendent (i.e., enlightened and disembodied) *ḍākinī*,[149] but we can see from his biography the indispensable role played by female spiritual advisors and teachers. Another important woman in Tilopa's life who is not mentioned in the bKa'-brgyud version of his biography, but is emphasized in Tāranātha's account, was his spiritual companion, the sesame-pounding woman. Because he broke his celibacy vows, Tilopa was expelled from the monasteries and adopted her profession, for which he received his name, meaning "sesame-pounder."[150] According to Tāranātha's account, the couple traveled and taught together, singing songs that filled their listeners with wonder at the spiritual depths of life. When some Bengali villagers doubted the religious credentials of the obviously low-caste religious wanderers, Tilopa and the sesame-pounding woman allayed their doubts by rising into the sky above them and hovering there, pounding sesame seeds and singing.[151] It is impossible to interpret Tilopa's career without reference to the guidance of his numerous spiritual mothers.

Maitrīpa, along with Tilopa and Nāropa, was one of the Indian founding fathers of the bKa'-brgyud lineages.[152] When Maitrīpa found his guru Śavari and paid homage to him, Maitrīpa displayed a condescending attitude toward the two women who were with Śavari. They were tribal women and huntresses, and thus Maitrīpa regarded them as his inferiors and doubted that a guru should have such uncouth companions. Unbeknownst to Maitrīpa, the women, Padmalocanā and Jñānalocanā, were gurus who acted in concert with Śavari. Later, the huntress-gurus displayed symbolic actions and sang spiritual verses that helped him cut through the dualistic tendencies of his mind.[153] Gaṅgādharā, Maitrīpa's female companion, was also influential later in his life. She was a guru in her own right, and the famed Khyung-po rnal-'byor was one of her students.[154] Although Gaṅgādharā had enjoyed a pampered upbringing in a palace, after becoming a Tantric yogini she preferred to dwell in the forest. She had such magical powers as the ritual gazes and the ability to transform her body into many shapes, including that of a wolf.[155] Thus, the life of the founding father Maitrīpa was entwined with those of several female gurus. His religious understanding and teachings developed in the context of his apprenticeship to and relationships with these women.

When one inquires into the lives of the male "founders" of Tantric Buddhism in India, one finds that many of them were instructed and initiated by women. Official lineage histories are selective compilations that do not necessarily give a complete account of the original "founders" of a particular practice. One principle of their selectivity is clearly gender. One reads of men of noteworthy attainments, but when one looks more deeply at the history one realizes that these men were surrounded and trained by women. Although men are celebrated in the biographical anthologies, their religious lives are embedded in a female matrix that determines and even defines their lives. Thus, it is clear that exclusively male transmission lineages do not necessarily indicate an exclusively male religious community, an absence of highly accomplished women, or an absence of female teachers, even as gurus of the male founders themselves.

Although it is commonly held that Tantric Buddhism was created only by men, such as Saraha, Kāṇha, Virūpa, Luipa, Tilopa, Padmavajra, Kambala, Maitrīpa, and Ghaṇṭapa, evidence reveals that it was created by women like Vajravatī, Lakṣmīṅkarā, Mekhalā, Kanakhalā, Siddharājñī, Padmalocanā, Jñānalocanā, Kambala's mother, Gaṅgādharā, the Arrow-making Yogini, Tilopa's lifelong female mentor, *and their students.* A question of origins is always a hard one to answer, but based on the available evidence—namely, the tradition's own legendary sources of its origins and founders—the trail does not end at the male founders but rather leads to a deeper stratum, to their female teachers: their mothers, female companions, and gurus. The identity of the women's teachers poses another question regarding the historical origins of the movement, but the fact remains that the historical trail runs cold not at the so-called male founders but at their female mentors and gurus.

In view of the evidence that women played a crucial role in instructing the "founding fathers" of Tantric Buddhism, the movement can no longer be regarded as an exclusively male cultural creation that took shape without the insights and contributions of women. The available evidence demonstrates that Tantric Buddhism was not created by men and does not solely express male insights and interests. This is not surprising when one considers that male Tantrics distinguished themselves from other Mahāyāna Buddhists precisely by apprenticing themselves to women and sharing their religious lives with women. For a man, pursuing the Tantric path often meant leaving the monastery at the behest of a woman possessing Tantric knowledge or for the purpose of companionship with a female practitioner. Men pursued their religious quest in the midst of female gurus and highly accomplished yoginis who were in no way seen or treated as their subordinates or inferiors. Tantric histories do not record the sovereign accomplishments of remarkable, solitary men but the progress and teachings of men who accepted the religious authority of women. Men may have been the fruit of the Tantric vine, but women were the root, stalk, leaves, and flowers.

---

Women helped to create Tantric Buddhism by introducing new meditations and practices and by adding their insights to the evolving ethos of the movement. Some women, like the female founders discussed in this chapter, can be restored to their rightful place in the historical canon as founding mothers of Tantric Buddhism. In addition, there are the women—many of whose names are lost to us—who taught the men who are now honored as the great founding fathers of the tradition. However, women's contributions to this movement were too numerous and pervasive for it ever to be possible fully to identify them all. If the unofficial, undocumented instances of participation and patronage were included, the influence of women would be incalculable indeed.

The historical search for the women of Tantric Buddhist history is far from finished. Additional founding mothers and practices introduced by women will continue to be discovered. Nonetheless, many women's contributions will never be recognized as such. Their "anonymous" and authorless contributions may never be counted. The lack of a female gender marker in some names can obscure forever the gender of the author of a given text. When a woman's name has no gender specificity and there is no corroborating evidence of her gender, her contributions may not be identifiable as a woman's.[156] The anonymity and pseudonymity of many texts in the Tibetan canon may also obscure instances of female authorship. However, Buddhist scholarship eventually will benefit from approaches and lines of inquiry already well under way in other fields. For example, new hermeneutical strategies will uncover more texts by women, as in the case of the development of more gender-conscious hermeneutical strategies for determining the authorship of early Christian writings.[157] In any case, Tantric theory as a whole should equitably be seen as the product of both women and men. Women's teachings and points of view are represented in texts produced by their male students and compatriots as well as in the sacred texts issuing from the Tantric circles of which women were an integral part.

Although historians have glorified the men of Tantric Buddhism and effaced the women, Tantric Buddhism in India was characterized by the close association and cooperation of women and men who traveled, meditated, and explored the religious life together as esteemed peers. Women taught other women independently of men and male authority, and men readily apprenticed themselves to women. Women and men shared their insights, discoveries, and experiences with one another, and Tantric Buddhism was the fruit of their shared explorations. One of the results of this remarkable collaboration and male acceptance of female guidance was a distinctive religious discipline that women and men can perform together to achieve their mutual goal of enlightenment. This sexual yoga is the topic of the next chapter.

CHAPTER SIX

# Women in Tantric Relationships

## *INTIMACY AS A PATH TO ENLIGHTENMENT*

Love, enjoyed by the ignorant,
Becomes bondage.
That very same love, tasted by one with
understanding,
Brings liberation.
. . . . . . . .
Enjoy all the pleasures of love fearlessly,
For the sake of liberation.
—*Cittaviśuddhiprakaraṇa*[1]

TANTRIC BUDDHISM is unique among Buddhist subtraditions in its acceptance of the body and sense experience as sources of knowledge and power. Tantric Buddhists eulogized the body as an "abode of bliss" and boldly affirmed that desire, sexuality, and pleasure can be embraced on the path to enlightenment. In keeping with this life-affirming orientation, the movement upheld the possibility of liberating relationships between men and women. The male and female founders of the movement developed cooperative yogic methods that men and women can perform together in order to transform the ardor of their intimacy and passion into blissful, enlightened states of awareness.

The emphasis upon intimacy between women and men has perennially been one of the most fascinating, controversial, and misunderstood aspects of the tradition.[2] In the nineteenth century and throughout much of the twentieth century, Tantric practices met with general reprehension and censure, whereas currently it is customary for writers on the topic to defend their religious seriousness.[3] However, this defense is generally made only on behalf of male practitioners. The former impugnment of the women stands unchallenged and is reinforced either by excluding them from the discussion or by offhand assertions of their marginal participation in the rites. This judgment reflects different attitudes toward male and female sexuality on the part of many Western interpreters. Although the practices themselves are enjoying increasing acceptance and appreciation, the women who performed them are still maligned as promiscuous, low-caste unfortunates or prostitutes who have come under the thrall of virile and admirable male Tantrics.

The continuing denigration of the women who perform these practices evidences a misapprehension of the practices themselves. This misunderstanding is the view that Tantric union consists of outer ritual acts lacking meditative, affective, or aesthetic intimacy between the partners who perform it. Agehananda Bharati voices this judgment:

> Most admirers of tantrism think it has something to do with a profound commitment of an interpersonal kind, with profound esoteric love between a male and female, or sophisticated erotic emotions, or an improved or perfectable sex life. . . . Unfortunately, there's no such thing in tantrism. . . . It is quite mechanistic.[4]

In this prevalent view, Tantric union requires the presence of two bodies but yogic abilities on the part of only one of the participants—the man; there is no necessity of an inner psychic attunement between the two partners. This impoverished mechanistic reduction of the practice prescribes a limited, purely physical role for women. Thus, the scholarly condescension toward the women hinges upon the belief that Tantric union consists solely in physical actions.

While persons outside the tradition tend to be preoccupied with the outer form of the rituals, the tradition itself is primarily concerned with the subjective and contemplative components that animate them and are considered essential to their efficacious performance.[5] As a blending of content and form, Tantric union resists description in purely physical terms. The answer to the question of whether Tantric union was designed to be one in which men made spiritual progress at the expense of women must primarily be sought in the content rather than the outer form of the rituals. That is, what is the requisite attitude toward a partner in Tantric union? What competence is required for the yoga of union, and is this competence required of both participants? Are the experiences sought through ritual union compatible with contempt and exploitation? Is the basis of Tantric bliss the physical body of a partner or the meditative and yogic abilities the partner brings to bear and the refinement of awareness that the partner inspires? Are both the woman and the man intended to benefit from the practice?

Fortunately, it is not necessary simply to conjecture about the content of the yoga of union in order to answer these questions. Primary texts of the *yoginī-tantra* and *mahāyoga-tantra* class and their Indian and Tibetan written and oral commentaries provide enough evidence on which to base a fuller understanding of the religious dimensions of the practice.[6] Tantric union is commended and praised as well as metaphorically and allusively portrayed in such classical *yoginī-tantra* texts as the *Cakrasaṃvara, Hevajra,* and *Caṇḍamahāroṣaṇa tantras.*[7] In addition to the examination of these classical sources, there are some Western assumptions that must be set aside if Tantric Buddhism is to be understood in light of its own categories and values.

## TANTRIC UNION: CENTERPIECE OF THE TANTRIC PARADIGM

Tantric union is a central, distinguishing feature of the most esoteric and advanced class of Tantric Buddhism. The Sanskrit term that refers to the genre of yogic practices done with a partner is *karmamudrā*. Tantric union is not a single practice, but a category of practices enacted in several contexts, such as wisdom initiation (*prajñābhiṣeka*), the secret feast offering (*guhyapūjā*), and a radical Tantric life-style that expresses nondual wisdom in everyday life.[8] In this work, the terms "Tantric union," "yoga of union," and "sexual yogas" refer to these practices as a group, whereas specific forms to be discussed are worship of the female partner and the inner fire offering.

Tantric union is an essential feature of the Tantric tradition in its classical formulation. The paradigmatic works teach that the blissful, contemplative yoga of sexual union is necessary for attaining full enlightenment. The indispensability of Tantric union is clear from an opening announcement in the *Cakrasaṃvara-tantra*:

> The aspirant should strive for spiritual attainments
> With the mantra and consort
> Found on the secret path.
> The secret path without a consort
> Will not grant perfection to beings.
> Thus, attain enlightenment
> By applying oneself most diligently
> To the activities of erotic play.[9]

Presenting Tantric union as a necessary condition for realization, the text proclaims that practicing Tantra without a partner is as useless as churning water to make butter: "For example, if someone who wants butter churns water, however diligently, fresh butter will not be produced."[10] The choice of analogy is deliberate, for Tantric union is sometimes called the "method of churning" and "union of the churner and the churned."

The *Caṇḍamahāroṣaṇa-tantra*, another major *yoginī-tantra*, addresses the apparent discrepancy between the Buddha's ascetical lifestyle and his later advocacy of Tantric union as a path to enlightenment. The text, spoken by Śākyamuni in a Tantric manifestation, explains:

The wise son of Queen Māyā
Gave up eight thousand royal ladies, then
Walked on the banks of the Nairañjanā River,
Proclaimed the attainment of Buddhahood,
And there defeated Māra.
That (whole ascetical display) was solely to benefit others.[11]

Here the Buddha announces that his renunciation of life in the palace was staged for the benefit of people who would be inspired by that kind of detachment and be attracted thereby to undertake a spiritual discipline.

This account places more importance upon what Śākyamuni did before he left the palace and attributes his attainment of enlightenment to the bliss that he experienced with his wife, Gopā:

Along with Gopā, he experienced bliss.
By uniting the diamond scepter and lotus,
He attained the fruit of bliss.
Buddhahood is obtained from bliss, and
Apart from women there will not be bliss.[12]

According to this account it was the bliss of sexual union that enabled Śākyamuni to attain enlightenment. For this reason, Tantric iconography includes the motif of Śākyamuni Buddha and Gopā embracing one another in *maithuna*, or sacred union undertaken for the sake of enlightenment (figure 15).

Following this surprising disclosure regarding the enlightenment of Śākyamuni, the text proceeds to argue against asceticism and celibacy:

The practice of Caṇḍamahāroṣaṇa
Will not be accomplished by asceticism.
As long as the mind is not purified,
One is fruitless and bound by chains of ignorance.
One who, possessing desire, represses desire,
Is living a lie. Whoever lies sins and
Because of that sin will go to hell.[13]

The Buddha discloses that torturing oneself with self-denial will not yield the supreme victory of Buddhahood:

Therefore, one who desires Buddhahood
Should practice what is to be practiced.
To renounce the sense objects
Is to torture oneself by asceticism—don't do it!
When you see form, look!
Similarly, listen to sounds,

FIGURE 15. Gopā and Śākyamuni in sacred union

> Inhale scents,
> Taste delicious flavors,
> Feel textures.
> Use the objects of the five senses—
> You will quickly attain supreme Buddhahood!
> . . . . . . . . . . . . . . . . . . . . . .
> Take refuge in the vulva of an esteemed woman
> To attain the rank of Caṇḍamahāroṣaṇa.[14]

If the senses and sexuality do not represent obstacles to enlightenment, then one might wonder why the Buddha previously taught renunciation. He anticipates this question and replies:

When I teach avoidance of sexual union,
That is so that weak worldly beings will abandon it.
I teach whatever will mature worldly beings.
One and all will become Buddhas
By the dance of the magical displays of a Victorious One,
By various diverse methods.
In all the discourses and Abhidharma texts,
Women are disparaged,
Spoken for the sake of disciples of various capacities—
The real truth is taught secretly.[15]

The text reveals that the Buddha's teachings on celibacy were devised for people who would not benefit by a teaching on Tantric union or might even be harmed by it.

The female interlocutor of the text, a Tantric form of the wife of Śākyamuni and of the Mahāyāna goddess Prajñāpāramitā, proceeds to question Caṇḍamahāroṣaṇa:

"Why do the early disciples and others slander women?"
The Lord answered:
"That is common to the early disciples and others
Who live in the realm of desire,
Not knowing the path of liberation
That relies on women and bestows everything."[16]

Here the Tantric Buddha makes it clear that he considers the early disciples (*śrāvakas*) and other renunciants to be persons of lesser understanding: "The minds of these men of inferior faith don't know reality."[17] Because people of "inferior faith" will not understand or benefit from teachings on sexual practices as a path of liberation, he hides it carefully and teaches the real truth secretly, saving the highest teaching for the rare person of superior faith and diligence who desires to attain Buddhahood quickly.[18]

Clearly, the disparagement of women is an inferior teaching that is to be abandoned as one moves up the hierarchy of teachings. The Buddha explains that just as people who live near saffron do not place a high value on it, for they do not recognize its worth, so the disciples of the lesser vehicles do not appreciate the jewel of sexuality, because it is so close at hand.[19] Such disciples renounce their own desires and in the process denigrate women and sexuality, unwittingly alienating themselves from the very source of Buddhahood.

In addition to the classical scriptures, Tibetan sources on supreme yoga practice (termed *anuttara-yoga* in the Tibetan context) uphold the requirement of union with a human partner for the attainment of Buddhahood. Tsongkhapa softened the implication of its absolute necessity but conceded that it is "extremely difficult" to attain liberation without a partner.[20] Elsewhere he stated that the most highly qualified practitioner should practice with a human partner, while a less qualified one should practice with an imaginary one. Buddhist literature perennially has stressed the importance of spiritual friends whose companionship undergirds the journey to enlightenment.[21] In a dialogue recorded in the Pāli canon, a disciple asked the Buddha if it were indeed true that a spiritual friend is half of the spiritual life, to which the Buddha replied that it was not true, for a spiritual friend is the whole of the religious life. Tsongkhapa invoked this concept to explain the role of a female partner: "A female companion is the basis of the accomplishment of liberation. Spiritual friends are women who are like-minded companions of the yogis."[22] The intimate association of a like-minded woman makes all the difference in a man's spiritual life. Propelled by her inspiring friendship, his progress will be swift indeed.[23]

Following the orthodox views of Tsongkhapa, the founder of their sect, dGe-lugs-pas generally acknowledge the indispensability of the yoga of union to the achievement of Buddhahood.[24] Modern dGe-lugs exponents who maintain its necessity include Lama Yeshe, who explains the role of this practice in self-transformation: "There is a certain point in the mastery of the completion stage when physically embracing a consort is *necessary* for bringing all the pervading energy winds into the central channel, a prerequisite for opening the heart centre completely and experiencing the profoundest level of clear light."[25] The dGe-lugs scholar Geshe Kelsang Gyatso similarly holds that practice with a human partner is necessary for attaining enlightenment during the present lifetime.[26] Gyatso therefore maintains that practice with a human partner, or *karmamudrā*, is intended for a more highly qualified person, while practice with an imagined partner, or *jñānamudrā*, is intended for those who are less qualified.[27] Tsongkhapa's own life epitomizes his sect's most deeply held views on this subject. dGe-lugs-pas believe that Tsongkhapa, qualified for enlightenment though he was, postponed full enlightenment during his lifetime in order to maintain his monastic vows and thus set a good example for his followers and lay the groundwork of his monastic reform. Thus, Tsongkhapa deferred complete enlightenment until he could unite with a partner in the realm of visionary experience that arises after the death of the physical body.[28]

Meditation in union with a human partner is deemed to offer a significant advantage over solitary meditation. The addition of the partner's energy heightens the intensity and power of the meditation. The combination of their energies adds the quality and quantity of each partner's energy to that of the other, thus accelerating the inner yoga practices of each. Tantric Buddhist yoga hinges on the belief that negative emotional and cognitive patterns become lodged in the psychic body in the form of knots and blocks in the subtle psychic channels (*nāḍī*). The purpose of the inner yogas is to "untie the knots" (*nāḍīgranthi-nirmocana*) and bring all the energy that is released by this process into the central channel (*avadhūtī*) that traverses the body vertically. This energy can then be used to untangle the karmic knots, clear the pathway of the central channel, ignite the inner fire of *caṇḍālī* (Tib. *gtum-mo*), and kindle the lights that dawn in inner awareness as the central channel is cleared. The inner breaths or winds move through the central channel more forcefully during meditation in union with a partner. The added force helps to unravel the final and most intransigent knots—those at the heart.[29] For this reason, practice with a partner is believed to make it possible to open the heart fully at the most profound level, freeing it from all knots, constrictions, and obscurations created by false views and self-cherishing emotions.[30] This is the technical explanation for the ultimate necessity of Tantric sexual yoga, although it has a range of other purposes and applications.

The relationship between Tantric consorts can at times be volatile, as the contents of psychic excavation are dredged to conscious awareness. The yogi and yogini will be aware of the source of these powerful emotions and the need to transmute them as they arise, instead of responding to their appearance as an occasion to generate more negativity and create more karmic knots. Ultimately, since the heart is the site of the deepest fears, hatreds, and self-centered distortions of reality, the openness, mutual transparency, and total trust required by the yoga of union make it an ideal discipline to bring the negative emotions to awareness and transform their poison into the ambrosia of enlightened awareness.

## UNION WITH AN IMAGINED PARTNER

Although Tantric union is an integral part of the Tantric paradigm in its classical formulation, divergent statements in popular and scholarly works, by those inside and outside the tradition, create confusion regarding the role of union with a human partner (*karmamudrā*) in the Tantric repertoire. One can find the claim that enacting union symbolically with an imagined partner is preferable to union with a human partner. For instance, the First Dalai Lama wrote that superior practitioners will practice with an imagined partner, while "those of dull capacity, not having the strength or purity of mind, must rely upon *karma-mudra* [a human partner] until they gain the experience of great bliss."[31] In this view, a physical, human partner is a concession for less able meditators who cannot accomplish the practice mentally with an imaginary, or visualized, consort (*jñānamudrā*). At first glance, one does not know whether such statements are monkish denigrations of intimacy with members of the opposite sex or references to different levels of practice and understanding, particularly since one also encounters statements in the same literature to the effect that practice with a human partner is superior to practice with a visualized partner.

The wisdom initiation (*prajñābhiṣekha*) in its classical form required union with a human partner, as a vestige of its descent from coronation rituals.[32] However, as this initiation has evolved and been transmitted in a monastic context in Tibet, physical union is generally considered inappropriate for most novices, because of either constraint by monastic vows, a reason cited by Atīśa,[33] or a lack of sufficient yogic expertise, as adduced by Tsongkhapa's disciple mKhas-grub-rje.[34] Neither Atīśa nor mKhas-grub-rje denied that union with a human partner occurs in the classical form of the ritual.

Thus, in the case of wisdom initiation as it is currently performed, it has become standard for a person of lesser qualifications to unite with an imagined partner, while the initiating guru or a more advanced practitioner would be qualified to unite with a human partner, in keeping with the original design of the ritual.[35] An imagined partner is also preferable for a person who is just beginning the inner yogas and has not yet mastered the elaborate visualizations and other yogic processes necessary for Tantric union, specifically, the ability to make the currents of inner energy (*prāṇa*) enter, abide, and dissolve in the central channel of the psychic body.[36] Thus, statements that prescribe symbolic union with an imagined partner may refer to early parts of the perfection stage, in which the aspirant is learning practices that will later be deepened with a human partner. In other cases, statements that subordinate the human partner to an imagined partner simply reflect the necessity for monk-scholars to defend celibacy in the face of the obvious advocacy of yogic union with a human partner in the Indian *tantras*.

Although there are circumstances in which practice with a human partner is impracticable or inadvisable, there is a consensus within the tradition that union with a human partner is necessary for traversing the final perfection stages and attaining ultimate liberation. This position is maintained even by the most strictly monastic sect, the dGe-lugs sect, precisely because of this sect's conservative desire to maintain an orthodox view consistent with classical Indian sources and practices.

## TANTRIC UNION AND TANTRIC METAPHOR

One of the ways in which Tantric union has been concealed from open view is through the use of oblique, metaphorical language. A given passage in a Tantric text does not have one single intended meaning but a spectrum of meanings that unfold as a person traverses the visionary path of meditative experiences they describe.[37] The intentional ambiguity of Tantric language is invoked as a teacher guides a disciple into the twilight depths of the symbolic language. The more obvious or literal meaning of a passage is generally the one intended for a person at an earlier stage or of lesser aptitude.[38] For a more advanced practitioner who has already gained precise intellectual understanding, the teacher may use the same text to loosen the disciple's grasp on consensus reality and plumb new levels of experience and psychological insight. At these deeper levels, language is used not to enhance conceptual clarity so much as to dissolve previous certitudes and, in the vulnerable moment of disorientation, introduce potent symbols capable of remodeling the disciple's psychological reality into increasingly blissful, compassionate, wise forms of subjectivity.[39]

Since the Tantric path has identifiable stages, the potential meanings of a given passage are not infinite but rather correspond in a systematic way to progressive stages of Tantric practice. These stages are set out in Indian and Tibetan exegetical systems. Hermeneutical categories that emerged first in Guhyasamāja interpretation (the classical source being the *Pradīpoddyotana*) provide the basic parameters of Tantric exegesis, in which sexual yoga falls within the third of four levels of exposition, the "secret" level. This secret level is intended to "illuminate the nature of passion" or "reveal the truth of passion" (*rāgadharmaprakāśanam*) for practitioners of the inner yogas.[40]

Since references to sexual union have an assigned place in the levels of interpretation, they are not merely one of several contested meanings of a given passage but an ever-present possibility of meaning that will be invoked for those at the appropriate stage of practice. This level of meaning can be present whether or not a given passage uses obvious or recognizable sexual imagery. Giuseppe Tucci wrote of the sexual imagery of the *tantras* that "it is not always easy to separate the two interpretations and distinguish the real from the allegorical sense."[41] However, the distinction between a "real" and "allegorical" sense does not apply in this context, for the tradition itself considers that any given scriptural passage will have a range of valid meanings corresponding to different levels of practice.

To give a simple example of the metaphorical nature of Tantric language, the texts often refer to the union of a lotus and *vajra*, or diamond scepter. Clearly, "lotus" and *vajra* are metaphors, not literal terms. One is not meant to bring together a flower and a scepter, but something denoted by those terms. Depending upon the level of interpretation, uniting the lotus and *vajra* can mean uniting wisdom and compassion, or bliss and emptiness, within the practitioner's psyche, or bringing together the female and male organs in physical union, or a number of other things that must be combined on the path to enlightenment. Interpreters outside the tradition may attempt to settle upon a final reading; however, multiple meanings are intended simultaneously, and the language cannot validly be reduced to a single level of meaning, as is implied when some authors offer a misleadingly tidy "key" to Tantric terminology.[42] The possibility of more abstract meanings has led to some doubt regarding whether the texts ever refer to physical union or whether motifs like lotus and *vajra* always refer to psychic processes and attributes; however, for the tradition itself, Tantric union is one of the established levels at which texts consistently are interpreted, as their "hidden" or "secret" meaning.

Since Tantric language is irreducibly multivalent, passages that obviously refer to Tantric union can also communicate a range of other meanings, whereas images that seem on the surface to be unrelated to Tantric union can become the basis for intricate and elaborate analyses of the yoga of union. To give an example of the application of this hermeneutical principle, the first chapter of the *Cakrasaṃvara-tantra* instructs practitioners:

> Draw the *maṇḍala* on a mountain,
> In a medicinal valley or forest,
> Near the bank of a large river,
> Or in a primordial cremation ground.[43]

This passage would seem to be a straightforward statement about the best locations for Tantric practice, but Tsongkhapa analyzes the passage as a description of a female Tantric:

> Because her great bliss is imperturbable,
> She is a mountain.
> Because lesser beings cannot fathom her profundity,
> She is a forest.
> Because her cavern is filled with nectar,
> She is a cave.
> Because her union of wisdom and skill is deep,
> She is a riverbank.

Because she [knows] the natural state beyond birth and death,
She is primordial.
Because she is the object of great bliss,
Her activity is natural.
Because she burns the views of early disciples and solitary
achievers in the fire of great passion,
She is a cremation ground.[44]

Although the passage in the root-*tantra* seems straightforward enough to be easily comprehended without commentary, Tsongkhapa interpreted the passage allegorically in reference to Tantric union. As the location of Tantric practice, the *maṇḍala* has many levels of reference. The *maṇḍala* can be a diagram for ritual practice that is drawn with colored powder or rendered in painted or sculpted form, and it can also be a circle of yogis and yoginis who have assembled for Tantric practice. As the psychically enclosed, sanctified space in which enlightenment unfolds, the *maṇḍala* can also refer to the vulva of the female consort or the drop of sexual fluid held at the tip of the phallus of the male consort.[45] These bodily *maṇḍalas* are also sites for ritual practice, because they are "locations" for traversing the higher reaches of the perfection stages, the threshold of Buddhahood. Thus, another "place" for a man to do Tantric practice is in union with the kind of woman Tsongkhapa describes.

Another example from the *Cakrasaṃvara-tantra* shows the complex layers of meaning that can be condensed into a metaphor for Tantric union:

Hearken to what is taught in this *tantra*
Of unexcelled yoga:
Knowledge of the sacred rite of union,
Combined with contemplation and mantra recitation,
According to the way of
The true union of the churner and the churned.[46]

The image of the "churner and the churned" is a common Tantric metaphor for sexual union. Tsongkhapa, drawing on a range of Indian sources,[47] explains that churning the female partner with the diamond scepter is the efficient cause of the nectar of Buddhahood. Tsongkhapa argues that just as fire is kindled by rubbing two sticks together, bliss is generated by churning. This bliss in turn becomes the basis of enlightenment when it is combined with a realization of emptiness.[48] The image of churning also refers to the Hindu Purāṇic myth wherein gods and demons churn the cosmic ocean of milk to extract its nectar. The goddess Śakti is produced from this process, and her sexual fluids become the immortality-bestowing nectar the gods are seeking.[49] Thus, churning the yogic partner, which stimulates the flow of her nectar, mirrors the stirring of the cosmic ocean for its potent, liberating nectar. Churning also connotes the circulation of the yogic energy as it surges within the psychic channels and then rises in the central channel.[50] Thus, the metaphor of churning, which appears to be a simple physical analogy, resonates richly with various nuances of Tantric union.

Multiple interpretations reflect the complex intentionality of the original text. Tantric exegetes attempt not to settle upon a definitive meaning but rather to accumulate and juxtapose layers of interpretation that deepen and enrich an image until every encounter with it evokes a symphonic chord of philosophical, aesthetic, and mythic overtones that are dynamically called into play in the experiential context of religious instruction, by a master aiming the teaching at a particular disciple. Modern interpreters, no less than Tibetan heirs of the tradition, must consult layers of written and oral commentary in order to discover the patterns of interpretation that have been applied. Any discussion of Tantric union therefore requires that a range of commentaries be consulted, as well as the original *tantras* themselves. The commentaries show that the physiological, yogic, and aesthetic dimensions of Tantric union are ever-present possibilities of meaning.

## UNION AS WORSHIP OF THE FEMALE PARTNER

The Tantric Buddhist yoga of union is often termed "worship of women" or "worship of the female partner."[51] Because of its esoteric nature, this practice is sometimes called "secret worship" and also "great worship."[52] Buddhologist Louis de la Vallée Poussin declared "worship of women" to be the "most conspicuous topic" of Tantric Buddhism,[53] attesting to the importance of this theme in Tantric literature. In the role of worshipper, the man makes a series of offerings and symbolic and concrete expressions of subordinate status. The culmination of the worship is an offering of sexual pleasure that assists the woman in her yogic practices, spiritual cultivation, and transformation of passion into divine ecstasy.

The Buddhist practice of ritual union as a form of worship has Hindu parallels.[54] Since Buddhism shares the worship of women with Hindu Tantra, this genre of practice can be seen as part of a broader cultural stream rather than as an isolated strand of historical development that is interpretable solely in light of Buddhist doctrines and categories.

The point of departure of this worship is the recognition of one's partner as divine, or inherently enlightened. The following passage from the *Caṇḍamahāroṣaṇa-tantra* expresses this theme:

> The man [sees] the woman as a goddess,
> The woman [sees] the man as a god.
> By joining the diamond scepter and lotus,
> They should make offerings to each other.
> There is no worship apart from this.[55]

Seeing one's partner as divine is the key to this form of worship. Having seen one's partner as a god or goddess, one naturally feels a sense of devotion. At this point there is no need for elaborate instructions, as love play spontaneously becomes the sport of deities. Every gesture becomes an act of worship, every sigh and word of love becomes a prayer, and gazing into the lover's eyes becomes a one-pointed meditation.

Although the man and woman recognize one another's divinity, implying complete reciprocity, the man is required to respond to the woman's divinity with numerous expressions of devotion, physical acts of homage, and a reverential, suppliant attitude. For the woman, to see the man as a Buddha is simply part of her yoga, or training of perception. For the man, to see the woman as divine is part of a full devotional complex in which he makes offerings of gifts and traditional tokens of reverence, such as lamps, incense, flowers, clothes, ornaments, and perfume, which he should apply to her with his own hands.[56] The same passage continues with directions for how the man should worship the woman:

> Then the yogi lovingly
> Makes a *maṇḍala* in front [of himself],
> And the woman enters that.
> As the embodiment of Perfection of Wisdom,
> He continuously worships [her] with flowers,
> Incense, butter lamps, and other articles.
> After uniting the five *maṇḍalas*,[57]
> He should prostrate to her,
> Circumambulate [her] clockwise, and
> Worship the ardently passionate yogini.[58]
> The man worships the woman in that way,
> With a mind full of reverence.[59]

Prostrations and circumambulation are traditional ways of showing respect in India. The text also exhorts that the man's mind, as well as his actions, should be "full of reverence."

For a man practicing the worship of women, expressions of reverence are not limited to the ritual setting but permeate daily life. In general, a man "should speak with pleasant words and give a woman what she wants."[60] The text directs that after ritual union and between sessions of practice, the man should prostrate to the woman, rub her feet, cook for her, feed her, and wait until she has eaten to partake of her leftovers.[61] A relationship in which a man prepares the food and eats only after the woman is a dramatic form of service and nurturance in Indian culture. It is also an expression of subordination in a hierarchical relationship. Touching and massaging the woman's feet is another way of showing his humility and subordinate status. Further, a man should regard every substance discharged by a woman's body as pure and should be willing to touch and ingest it. For instance, he should be willing to sip sexual fluid and menstrual blood from her vulva and to lick any part of her body if requested to do so.[62] The following statement becomes his prayer of aspiration:

> I must practice devotion to women
> Until I realize the essence of enlightenment.[63]

In this worship, the relationship between the man and the woman parallels the relationship between a male devotee and a goddess. This theme is elaborated in the *Caṇḍamahāroṣaṇa-tantra*, wherein the Buddha Vajrayoginī demands homage in the form of worship of women. In a lengthy passage, Vajrayoginī pronounces that all women and female beings in the universe are her embodiments (*rūpa*) and thus should be honored and served.[64] When Caṇḍamahāroṣaṇa asks her how a yogi should honor Her Holiness, Vajrayoginī replies that he should make offerings to her by worshipping women:

> He should continuously worship Vajrayoginī
> With flowers, incense, and clothes and
> Honor her with speeches and ornate expressions,
> With palms pressed together.
> He should gaze, touch, and contemplate [her]
> And behave consistently with his speech.
> Kissing and embracing, he should always worship Vajrayoginī,
> Physically if he can, or mentally and verbally if he cannot.
> The aspirant who satisfies me wins the supreme attainment.
> I am identical to the bodies of all women, and
> There is no way that I can be worshipped
> Except by the worship of women (*strīpūjā*).
>
> . . . . . . . . . . . . . . . . . . . . .
>
> Visualizing that she is fully my embodiment,
> He should make love to his woman.

> Because of uniting the diamond scepter and lotus,
> I will grant enlightenment.[65]

Vajrayoginī also insists that sexual pleasure and satisfaction should be part of her worship. This method of worshipping the female partner is sometimes expressed as worshipping the female organ. The female organ is referred to directly as a vulva (*bhaga, yoni*) or metaphorically as a lotus (*padma*). The outer opening of the sexual organ resembles the petals of a lotus, while the vulva and cervix are like the heart of the flower. This formal similarity, as well as the fact that the lotus is a Buddhist symbol of purity and enlightenment, makes this magnificent flower a natural symbol for the vulva. The *Cakrasaṃvara-tantra* instructs that "a skillful one worships the yogini's stainless lotus of light."[66] Vajrayoginī promises her approval and blessings to a man who worships her in this way:

> Aho! I will bestow supreme success
> On one who ritually worships my lotus,
> Bearer of all bliss.
> A wise one unites patiently,
> Doing the requisite activities in the lotus.[67]

In the *Caṇḍamahāroṣaṇa-tantra*, Vajrayoginī describes how this Tantric worship is to proceed. A yogi and yogini should seclude themselves in a hermitage to practice together. After gazing at each other and attaining single-minded concentration, the woman should address the man, affirming that he is her son and husband, brother and father, and claiming that for seven generations he has been her servant and slave, purchased by her and owned by her. He in turn should fall at her feet, press his palms together in a gesture of reverence, and declare his devotion and humble servitude to her, asking her to grace him with a loving glance. She will then draw him to her and kiss him, direct his mouth to between her thighs, and embrace and pinch him playfully.[68] She guides him in how to make the offering of pleasure to her:

> Constantly take refuge at my feet, my dear . . .
> Be gracious, beloved, and
> Give me pleasure with your diamond scepter.
> Look at my three-petaled lotus,
> Its center adorned with a stamen.
> It is a Buddha paradise, adorned with a red Buddha,
> A cosmic mother who bestows
> Bliss and tranquility on the passionate.
> Abandon all conceptual thought and
> Unite with my reclining form;

Place my feet upon your shoulders and
Look me up and down.
Make the fully awakened scepter
Enter the opening in the center of the lotus.
Move a hundred, thousand, hundred thousand times
In my three-petaled lotus
Of swollen flesh.
Placing one's scepter there, offer pleasure to her mind.
Wind, inner wind—my lotus is the unexcelled!
Aroused by the tip of the diamond scepter,
It is red like a *bandhūka* flower.[69]

In this *yoginī-tantra* passage, a female Buddha demands pleasure for her embodiments, human women. The passage reflects what can be called a "female gaze," or gynocentric perspective, for it describes embodiment and erotic experience from a female point of view. The female Buddha alternates between referring to the woman in the third person, as someone else, and in the first person, equating the woman with herself. This identification is an important part of the man's—and woman's—contemplation process when performing the yoga of union. Instructions specify that the man should be free from lust and maintain a clear, nonconceptual state of mind. He is instructed not to end the worship until the woman is fully satisfied. Only then is he allowed to pause to revive himself with food and wine—after serving the woman and letting her eat first, of course![70] Selfish pleasure-seeking is out of the question for him, for he must serve and please his goddess.

Toward this salutary end, various *tantras* describe the talents that a Tantric yogi should develop, requiring that he employ an array of erotic techniques paralleling those described in the secular *ars amoris*, or *kāmaśāstra*.[71] The *Caṇḍamahāroṣaṇa-tantra* describes a number of oral techniques and provides a catalog of sexual positions to be used, such as the "swing-rocking" position, in which the partners interlace their arms like braids of hair and rock slowly, and the "thigh-rubbing" position, in which the woman places the soles of her feet on the base of the man's thighs.[72] "Reverse union," in which the man is supine and the woman takes the more active role, is particularly recommended.[73] Although this repertoire is enjoined upon the man, the woman's knowledgeability is also implicit in these descriptions. From the extensive lists, one would imagine that Tantric couples might enjoy a sexual virtuosity equaling that of the amorous couples *in flagrante delecto* adorning Indian temple towers.[74] The mood of exuberant delight, graceful sensuousness, and reciprocity that characterizes the sculpted couples also suffuses the literary descriptions in the Tantric texts, which exult in an open and unashamed affirmation of sensuality in a religious context.

The intimate offering of sexual pleasure, appropriately called the "secret offering," or "secret worship,"[75] proceeds in stages. One of the goals of erotic play is to stimulate the flow of the woman's sexual fluid, the female equivalent of the man's seminal fluid. This process is described with poetic delicacy in the *Hevajra-tantra*:

> In a forest, a secluded place, or even in your own home,
> A knowledgeable yogi should continually worship
> A superlative female consort who has disrobed.
> Having kissed and embraced, stroke the vulva.
> The tip of the man, pressing (or kissing),
> Drinks sweet nectar from the lips below.
> The possessor of the scepter should with his hands steadily do
> Activities that produce the musk of desire . . .
> Again and again unite by means of the diamond scepter,
> Looking her up and down.
> Thus one attains extensive spiritual perfections and
> Becomes the equal of all Buddhas.[76]

The passage describes how the tip of the phallus distills nectar from the corolla of the woman's lotus, likening it to a mouth that sips sweet wine from a lotus flower. The Sanskrit original has many shades of poetic nuance. The male organ is indicated by such terms as "diamond scepter" (*vajra*) and "nose" or "tip" (*nāsikā*). The contact that stimulates the woman to produce her generative fluid means to "taste" and "enjoy," while the term for "drinking" also means "kissing" and "distilling," drawing upon the similarity among kissing, distilling nectar from a *soma* press, and distilling an intoxicating beverage.

The same term (*śukra*) is used for the male and female sexual fluids, although the usual translation of the term into English as "semen" has led to widespread misunderstanding that only a male fluid is designated.[77] The woman's fluid is called by other terms as well, such as *madhu*, meaning something sweet, like honey, nectar, or wine.[78] Another term is "flower water," or "self-arisen flower water."[79] Because the flow of the nectar of her lotus accompanies her experiences of bliss and heightened awareness, the fluid is also called "musk of desire," or "musk of intoxication," referring to intoxication by pleasure.[80]

Tantric union requires a mixing of sexual fluids, for the purpose of spiritual illumination rather than procreation. The man and woman mingle and then absorb some of their combined fluids, a mixture that is generally referred to as a blend of white drops and red drops, or of camphor and red sandalwood. There is a common misconception that the red element contributed by the woman is menstrual blood, but this is not the case.[81] The term "red" refers to the endocrinal content of the female sexual fluid rather than its color.[82] The yogic practice of mixing the white and red fluids is expressed poetically by Babhaha, one of the Tantric adepts who pursued enlightenment in the company of a woman also seeking enlightenment:

> In the sacred citadel of the vulva of
> A superlative, skillful partner,
> Do the practice of mixing white seed
> With her ocean of red seed.
> Then absorb, raise, and spread the nectar, for
> A stream of ecstasy such as you've never known.
> Then for pleasure surpassing pleasure,
> Realize that as inseparable from emptiness.[83]

The sexual fluids are considered to possess a special potency for nourishing the psychic or yogic anatomy. Therefore, the yogi and yogini visualize that they reabsorb and spread the bliss-giving nectar through the body. Tsongkhapa praises the essence of the sexual fluid as the nectar that confers the omniscience of Buddhahood.[84] The *Caṇḍamahāroṣaṇa-tantra* eulogizes: "This is the best diet, eaten by all Buddhas."[85]

Although the man and woman both perform this yogic process (seen in Hindu Tantra and yoga as well),[86] "mixing their essences," the *tantras* (both Hindu and Buddhist) place somewhat more emphasis upon the man's absorption of female fluids. The *Hevajra-tantra* says that spiritual women, or women belonging to the five Buddha families, are "bestowers of *siddhi*, and their sexual fluid is adamantine, so worshipping them, a yogin drinks it."[87] Extracting the essence of the female fluid is considered to provide the most rarefied kind of nourishment, the birth of great bliss.[88] The *Hevajra-tantra* instructs the man to vow to continue to absorb the female essences in all future lives, until enlightenment is reached.[89] The emphasis on the male absorption of the female essence is one of the features that distinguishes this from ordinary sexual union.[90] Indologists Frédérique Marglin and Wendy O'Flaherty have noted that the Tantric pattern, in which the female fluids are deliberately absorbed by the male, is a reversal of ordinary conjugal union, in which it is primarily the woman who absorbs the male fluid.[91] The gathering of the female fluids by the man, found in the Hindu Śākta Tantric complex as well, is a sign of the affinity between Tantric Buddhism and the Śākta stream of Indian religiosity. O'Flaherty suggests that this expresses the relative status of male and female within the ritual, for it signals the power flowing from the female to the male.[92]

Although the male absorption of female fluid is explicitly mentioned, it is clear that a mingling and exchange of fluids is intended. The man also uses the "substance of himself" to make an offering to the female partner: "One should make offerings to the woman of one's Buddha lineage by using the substances of oneself and offering to her."[93] This "offering substance of oneself" refers to the most intimate yogic aspect of the ritual.

Thus, in worship of the female partner, the offering substance is the man himself, which includes his respect and adoration, his own body in the form of the pleasure that he gives her, the sexual fluids that he blends with hers, the breath that he mingles with hers, and the subtle energies that are exchanged and circulated through both, making possible types of experiences that neither can attain on his or her own.

## THE INNER YOGA OF THE YOGINI

The worship of the female partner includes an offering of the sexual pleasure necessary for her Tantric contemplation. The offering of pleasure is not an end in itself but a point of departure for an advanced Tantric yoga that uses the bliss of union as a basis for meditation. This intimate worship is in essence the man's offering of the yogic experiences that this makes possible for the woman. The specific yogic process she seeks to master is to concentrate the inner breath, or wind, at a spot near the base of her spine and then to inject the winds into the central channel and hold them there, traversing her body vertically.

In the visualization that supports this yoga, the inner anatomy of a woman's sexual organ is seen as a *maṇḍala,* the jeweled palace at the center of a Buddha-land. This palace has no set dimensions, for it is a "measureless mansion" on the visionary plane of experience.[94] The center of the *maṇḍala* radiates out from the cervix, or innermost point of the vulva, but the size of the envisioned *maṇḍala* will vary depending upon the purpose of the meditation. At times the *maṇḍala* will be imagined as expanding beyond the woman's body, to embrace the world and all living beings in the perfection of the celestial environment. For some practices the yogini arrays a Buddha couple and their divine entourage within the mansion according to the iconography of the *maṇḍala* upon which she is meditating. Regardless of the precise meditation, the purity, bliss, and wisdom that coalesce into the *maṇḍala* emanate from the central point, the cervix, which is where the woman focuses her attention for this meditation.

The yogini's "secret place," in Tantric parlance, is sometimes referred to as Crowface. Crowface (Kākāsyā) is the name of a female deity, one of the eight door guardianesses of the Cakrasaṃvara *maṇḍala*. These eight goddesses share their names with eight main veins radiating from the vaginal nerve center, according to the Indian understanding of female anatomy that is reflected in the Tantric texts.[95] The use of deity names for these veins conflates the vulva and the *maṇḍala* in this symbolic realm.[96] To "enter the *maṇḍala*" at this stage means that a woman brings her meditative awareness to the place where enlightenment will unfold.

In order to help the woman focus her attention on the inner *maṇḍala*, the man makes a subtle offering: "With the finger, that is, the diamond scepter, move the earth, that is, the veins of the base—the lotus, and after waking up the veins, bind the diamond scepter. In other words, unite in the practice that binds the two veins inseparably."[97] The man assists the woman in her inner yoga practice by moving the veins in the lotus and "waking them up," drawing the woman's attention to the lower end of the central channel, helping her to concentrate energy at the point where the energy will be drawn into the central channel.[98] Stimulating that nexus of veins helps her unify all her sensations and concentrate her attention at a point near the lower opening of the central channel. The man must be careful to incite arousal without detracting from her mindfulness, a challenge to his erotic and yogic virtuosity. A woman who is skilled at this process can draw the inner wind, or breath, into the central channel at that time.

This is the point at which the addition of the partner's energy is crucial. This exchange of energy is initiated by the joining of the "tips" of the sexual organs of the Tantric partners, sometimes expressed as "joining the tips of the thumb and ring finger" or "kissing." As Tsongkhapa explains, "the tip of the secret place of the male partner is the lower opening of the central channel (*avadhūtī*), the tip of the secret place of the female partner is called Crowface, and the two veins kiss."[99] The central channel of the man terminates at the outermost tip of the sexual organ whereas that of the woman terminates at the innermost tip of the vulva, and the two points are brought into contact during sexual union. The joining of the veins occasions the mingling of the red and white essences, and this in turn facilitates a delicate yet tangible exchange and circulation of energy between the two partners. The yogi and yogini direct their now-combined energy in specific ways to produce subtle states of bliss and insight.

When a woman's nectar begins to flow and blends with that of the man, the woman is said to be "intoxicated" by the "elixir of union." This intoxication provides the bliss that is central to Tantric contemplation:

> The mantra-practitioner becomes intoxicated by liquor, which means he has a female partner who belongs to a Buddha lineage (*kulikā*), knows mantra, and is intoxicated by sap. . . . This means practice with the great quality-possessing woman and she will become intoxicated by the sap of the elixir of union as it descends.
>
> Because of this, all the Buddhas will assemble in a *maṇḍala* in the aspirant's body, and likewise all the female divinities will assemble in a *maṇḍala* in the body of the great lineage consort, whom one visualizes as Sparśavajrī.
>
> Worship that woman.[100]

Whether or not the "intoxicating" mixture of red and white drops is literally reabsorbed, the visualization draws the bliss wherever the drops are imagined to spread. The woman eventually focuses this process upon the central channel. She "inhales" this wind, or energy, into the central channel and raises it to the crown of her head, then "exhales," or lets the energy descend again, imagining the drops of nectar streaming up and down the central channel.[101] In the words of a famous yogini:

> From the crown of the head, on a moon-pedestal,
> The five nectars overflow and shower down.
> Stabilize that and visualize the letter OṂ.
> Doing yoga in this manner continuously,
> Make [the nectar] fall and rise—
> This is the practice of yoginis![102]

The yogini revels in the intoxication of the sensations spreading through her body. She delights in the many nuances and flavors of bliss and joy, savoring sublime sensations that make her feel that she is soaring, or "enjoying the sky" in Tantric terms.[103]

As delectable as these unearthly pleasures may be, they are but the basis for more rarefied states of mind to follow. Their attainment signals the time to meditate upon emptiness. Thus, the secret offering, or "churning union," makes possible and now gives way to the "real offering" of the union of bliss and emptiness, the final stage of the yoga of union. At this stage, the yogini (and yogi) must relinquish attachment to the pleasure and meditate that everything, including their bliss, is devoid of intrinsic reality. In the midst of intense desire, it is necessary to renounce desire by seeing it as dualistic grasping for something that ultimately does not exist. At this point it may be helpful to imagine oneself as a thirsty person pursuing a mirage in the sky. Ordinary bliss can never bring ultimate realization, just as a mirage can not quench thirst. Analyzing that the object of the bliss is no more real than a mirage in the sky may help to dissolve attachment into the expanse of skylike awareness.[104]

The *Pearl Rosary*, an early Sa-skya commentary, recapitulates the steps by which a woman uses worship by a man as a basis for her inner yoga. She accepts the man's series of pleasurable offerings and uses the enjoyment of each stage to enter a deeper state of meditative concentration, turning her attention inward as he makes increasingly intimate offerings. The first stage is the offering of what pleases the senses, such as perfume, food, drink, loving words, beautiful cloth, and sacramental meat and wine. In yogic terminology, these offerings are made at the "nine doors" of the body (eyes, ears, nostrils, mouth, lower openings), that is, the doors that admit sense pleasures. When her outer senses are satisfied, the woman naturally withdraws her attention from them to receive the next level of offering, which is sexual pleasure. The man inflames and incites the passion that will fuel her meditation and then directs the offering specifically to her secret *cakra*. He stimulates the veins, or nerves, of the vulva to generate bliss and drops of nectar. The partners may envision the veins as deities receiving offerings. This visualization can become quite elaborate as the yogi and yogini imagine the deities accepting and enjoying the ambrosial nectar showered upon them by the Buddha couple in the center. For example, in one method of visualizing the Cakrasaṃvara *maṇḍala* superimposed upon the vulva, the twenty-four hero-and-heroine couples are visualized on twenty-four veins, or nerves, imbibing the nectar as the fare of their Tantric feast.[105]

Now that the woman's attention is completely withdrawn from the outer senses and from worldly appearances, it is time for the supreme offering. The supreme offering occurs at the central channel of her body, the *avadhūtī*. The woman uses this offering to bring her winds and drops into the central channel and stabilize them there.[106] This offering is the pouring of the yogi's rarefied energy into her own, which kindles and intensifies her experience of the joys, insights, and luminosity that arise within the central channel. Because this is the offering that enables the woman to traverse the final passes of the path to enlightenment, "this is the quintessential worship of a woman."[107]

A woman must have considerable mindfulness and meditative ability to make use of this series of offerings. It is very easy for this worship to cause a loss of mindfulness and increase desire and attachment. It is important for the woman to understand emptiness and preferably to have tasted the realization of emptiness beforehand, so she can combine it with bliss at this time. As she applies her understanding of emptiness to this experience, the inner wind in the central channel becomes a "wisdom wind" that is a vehicle of nondualistic Buddha-perception. A mind that is permeated by bliss, yet aware of emptiness, will replace the ordinary mode of sense experience.[108] Free from thoughts and dualistic grasping, desire and attachment, the yogi and yogini meditate with complete clarity of mind. At this level, the woman experiences the primordial nature of her own mind as vast, unobstructed awareness. She realizes that everything, including her mind, is clear, pure, and spacious, like the sky.[109] This is the "real offering."[110]

## INNER FIRE OFFERING

A Tantric feast (*gaṇacakra*) includes a series of offerings made by an assembly of yogis and yoginis. The "outer offerings" (*bāhyapūjā*) are shared in common with other forms of Buddhism and include the pleasing sights, scents, and sounds of food, flowers, incense, butter lamps, dance, and music. The outer offerings are followed by specifically Tantric offerings.[111] These "inner offerings" feature alcohol, five kinds of meat (dog, horse, cow, elephant, human), and "five nectars" (semen, blood, brain, urine, feces). Tantric Buddhists also perform a fire offering (Tib. *sbyin-bsregs*) that is patterned after Hindu fire sacrifices (*homa, agnihotra,* or *yajña*).

Hindu fire sacrifices include a complex ritual of Vedic derivation, which retains a vital role in Brāhmaṇic Hindu worship, as well as interiorized yogic and meditative versions of the sacrifice. Upaniṣadic literature puts forward the human life span, digestion, breathing, and mystical contemplation as interiorized fire sacrifices.[112] According to the *Bṛhadāraṇyaka Upaniṣad*, sexual union also constitutes a fire sacrifice, as performed by the creator god Prajāpati upon creating woman:

> Having created her, he worshipped her sexual organ;
> Therefore, a woman's vulva should be worshipped.
> He stretched forth from himself a stone for pressing nectar
> [i.e., causing a woman's sexual fluid to flow]
> And impregnated her with that.
> Her lap is the sacrificial altar;
> Her hair, the sacrificial grass;
> Her skin, the *soma* press;
> The labia of the vulva, the fire in the middle.
>
> . . . . . . . . . . . . . . . . . . .
>
> Many mortals . . . go forth from this world . . . without merit,
> Namely, those who practice sexual union without knowing this.[113]

The basic pattern of the sacrifice is the offering of something less refined (solid, liquid, or composite) into a cosmic receptacle—epitomized by the *yoni* (vulva or womb)—that transforms it into a simpler, more concentrated, or more advanced state,[114] whether it be digestion rendering complex food into simpler particles or wisdom rendering dualistic thoughts and perceptions into enlightenment. Adhering to this pattern, Tantric Buddhism participates in the broader stream of Indian religiosity rather than following a uniquely Buddhist program of thought and practice. Like the Hindu tradition with its outer and inner fire sacrifices, Tantric Buddhism also developed numerous versions of the fire sacrifice. The outer fire offering is seen as an occasion for accomplishing the four types of ritual activities: peaceful, prospering, conquering, and destroying.[115] The inner fire offering is an advanced yogic practice that a woman and man perform together while engaged in yogic union.

When spiritual consorts practice sexual yoga—for instance, at a Tantric feast—they make a "secret offering" by offering the bliss and pleasure of their union to the deities of the *maṇḍala* and to all beings in the universe.[116] As this process is presented in the Cakrasaṃvara system, an inner fire offering can be performed at this time.[117]

The inner fire offering is a specific visualization for combining the bliss generated by passionate union with meditation upon emptiness. In this process, ordinary consensus reality is first sacrificed, or renounced, by envisioning all beings in the universe as arrayed in a palace of enlightened awareness (*maṇḍala*), enjoying their bliss and wisdom as divine beings. Then the yogic partners offer the *maṇḍala* itself, dissolving its outermost rings and proceeding inward, finally reaching the Buddha couple in the center, which is identified with the woman and man performing the meditation:

> Envision the beings of the three realms [subterranean, terrestrial, celestial] as the *maṇḍala* and all of them as enjoying great bliss. Having experienced bliss, the heroes and heroines of the three outer realms dissolve into the eight great cremation grounds, and the cremation grounds dissolve into the measureless mansion, which dissolves into the four [innermost yoginis], Khandaroha and so forth. These [four then] dissolve, entering the left nostrils of the four faces [of Heruka Cakrasaṃvara]. Then, having entered the central channel between the eyebrows, the elixir descends, pervading the four *cakras*. Then oneself and Vajravārāhī melt in great bliss.[118]

Next the yogi and yogini themselves enter into the sacrifice. At the place where the tips of their sexual organs touch, or "kiss" in Tantric metaphor, the drops of sexual fluid that have gathered there mix and intermingle, creating the ultimate libation. Details sufficient to perform the practice cannot be found in a text, but in its general outline the drops of sexual fluid (called "red" in the case of the woman and "white" in the case of the man, referring not to their color but to their respective concentration of female and male endocrinal elements) intermingle and melt, inaugurating each partner's successful gathering of the inner winds into the central psychic channel (*avadhūtī*). The exact location of the inner hearth may differ in different yoga systems, although a consensus places it at the navel, where it is imagined as a short "A" that is ablaze.[119] Regardless of where the inner hearth is visualized, the real fire is understood to be the higher form of consciousness that devours any lesser forms that are fed into it or sacrificed for its sake.

In the Buddhist understanding the fire sacrifice means subjecting all phenomena and experiences to the realization of emptiness. On the yogic dimension, the philosophical principle of emptiness is conflated with the central channel of the body and the inner fire. These are interrelated because they simultaneously accomplish the transition to nonconceptuality, or the cessation of dualistic thought. As Kambala observed, the "fire" that removes all impurities of thought can be equated with the central channel,[120] because the cessation of dualistic thought and gathering of inner wind into the central channel occur simultaneously. Into this sacrificial fire of blazing wisdom the constituent elements of the universe, in their fundamental forms as the four elements and five sense faculties and their respective objects (sound, tangibility, form, flavor, smell), are offered as metaphorical meat and blood.[121] As bliss increases and all traces of attachment are abandoned, the fire of the play of spontaneous awareness (*sahaja*) burns brighter. The goal is the complete combustion of all dualistic thought and habitual tendencies accumulated over centuries of lifetimes. Since this is not an instantaneous process but requires prolonged and gradual effort, many sessions of practice will be required.[122] Initially, coarser aspects of the personality and delusory beliefs will be offered into the fire. Eventually, increasingly subtle forms of conceptuality and attachment will be offered.

Just as the Hindu Upaniṣads make mystical contemplation the ultimate fire sacrifice, the *Cakrasaṃvara-tantra* makes the nondual states of wisdom the real fire offering, culminating in full illumination by the flame of wisdom. As Tsongkhapa states, "the burning of conceptual thought is the true meaning of the fire offering—in other words, dissolution into clear light."[123]

The inner fire offering outlined herein, based upon the Cakrasaṃvara system, recapitulates both Vedic and Upaniṣadic fire sacrifice in their basic pattern. Despite its similarity to Hindu rituals, the Buddhist inner fire offering has a distinct soteriology, for it requires another step beyond total renunciation and illumination by the fire of wisdom, namely, expressing the compassion generated by the warmth of the fire of wisdom. Having dissolved the entire universe and all concepts and dualistic modes of perception and entered into clear light, higher mental states and expressions of imagination and altruism become possible. After the universe is offered into the inner fire and dissolved, the yogini and yogi re-envision the *maṇḍala*, but this time in a subtler state of mind. According to Tsongkhapa, when the *maṇḍala* is created again, it "arises from the mere mind-wind of clear light."[124] This process of envisioning is qualitatively different from previous ones, because formerly the mind-wind was laden with dust and dirt, whereas now it is like a clear wind. This *maṇḍala*, complete with all the details of a jeweled mansion, is to be "created the size of a mere atom or particle of dust on a white lotus in the heart of the deity [the real deity, *jñānasattva*] . . . blissful in essence, radiating garlands of pulsating light-rays, emanating the bodies of different Buddhas."[125] Thus, after everything ordinary has been offered into the sacrificial fire of bliss, inner heat, and wisdom, the world of ordinary appearances is replaced by the artistry of enlightened imagination, creating the gossamer, rainbowlike divine bodies that are the goal of Tantric practice.[126]

As descriptions of the inner fire offering make clear, both yogi and yogini perform the same visualization and proceed through its steps together, attuning their minds to one another and combining their energies for their shared journey. By virtue of the close attunement of their minds and bodies and the exchange of thought, breath, and fluid that is taking place between them, one person's success at a certain stage can precipitate this process in the other through a sympathetic resonance between them.[127] Their intimate communion makes it possible for the consorts to transmit mental-bodily states to one another and to complete this process in harmony and in unison.

## INTIMACY AND TANTRIC UNION

Intimacy is achieved in Tantric union through the creation of a shared aesthetic and visionary universe. During yogic union, every aspect of the practice serves to transform ordinary awareness into enlightened vision. For instance, the man cultivates pure vision by seeing the woman as a deity, her sexual organ as the throne of enlightenment, and her sexual fluid as divine nectar. The poetic and symbolic terms for sexual anatomy and for the stages of union shape the attitudes, meditations, and experience of both a woman and a man engaging in these disciplines. The use of a specialized esoteric vocabulary serves at once to hide references from noninitiates and to create intimacy between yogic partners.

Although it has been suggested that the symbolism distances the partners and renders their interaction more abstract,[128] the realm of visionary experience into which the partners venture together requires and deepens intimacy. The Tantric language may serve to distance the practice from conventional, "profane" sexuality, but it does not distance the partners from each other. Because they interpret their practice within the same symbolic framework, the esoteric language ushers them into a universe of shared meaning wherein their communion can partake of the dignity and gracefulness of deities, without a tinge of worldliness. The symbolic language thus guards the communicative and religious content of the ritual.

In order to embark upon this journey of intimacy, the partners create a separate, hermetically sealed world that is invisible to humans and gods, as described in the *Cakrasaṃvara-tantra*:

> Worship the naked Tantric consort;
> By this very activity, one will be fully liberated.
> Clothed like that [i.e., naked] or otherwise
> [i.e., with a tiger skin and bone ornaments]
> Don't be touched by desires!
> Unloosen one's hair
> And commence all the activities.
> With the root mantra and others,
> Bind the borders and,
> Unseen by the assemblies of gods and spirits,
> Worship.[129]

The yogi and yogini seal off their experiential universe by "binding the borders," that is, by enclosing themselves in an iridescent, bubblelike sphere of crisscrossed diamond scepters. Tsongkhapa explains that in order to prevent obstacles to this practice, they intone the root mantra and visualize a protective tent, canopy, lattice of arrows, and net of flames, thus rendering the ritual invisible even to gods with their supernatural vision, much less to human beings.[130] This barrier—an impenetrable force field between the ordinary world and the realm of visionary experience—protects the sacred space from invasion by negative influences, as well as from the curious eyes of men and gods.

Because Tantric union involves passion and intimacy without neurotic attachment, its higher octave of passion is sometimes called "great passion" (*mahārāga*).[131] This passion is free from desire, ordinary lust, and the taint of aggrandizing ego. There is a degree of detachment insofar as the relationship is intended to dissolve the ego, but there is an ineluctable element of intimacy as well, since subtle unifications of perception and interfusions of fluids and breaths are an integral part of the practice. The self (or nonself, as it were) that enters into this practice is an unboundaried, nonessentialist (i.e., selfless, according to Buddhist metaphysics), dynamically fluidic one that can be permeated by the energy, breath, and mind of another person. The yoga of union is predicated precisely upon this ability to be infused by the energy and mental states of another person.

What is sought in the yoga of union is a quality of *relationship* into which each partner enters fully in order that both may be liberated simultaneously. This level of intimacy is not easily achieved. Therefore, often a man and a woman would forge a lifelong spiritual partnership. In other cases a male and female Tantric would go into retreat and practice together for a year or two to accomplish specific religious goals together. When the breath, fluids, and subtle energies of the yogic partners penetrate and circulate within one another, they produce experiences that otherwise are extremely difficult to generate through solitary meditation. The texts describe a complex spiritual interdependence, with an emphasis upon the dependence of the man upon the woman and his efforts to supplicate, please, and worship her. Their interdependence reaches fruition as they combine their energies to create a *maṇḍala* palace spun of bliss and emptiness. Thus, the female and male partners in union both literally and figuratively are ensconced within a *maṇḍala* generated from and infused by their bliss and wisdom, which radiates from the most intimate point of their physical union. They use the energies and fluids circulating through one another's bodies to become enlightened beings in the center of that *maṇḍala*.

## WOMEN'S COMPETENCE FOR TANTRIC UNION

The area in which female Tantrics have been most impugned is in their supposed lack of qualifications for the practice of the sexual yogas. Women's competence, knowledgeability, and independent initiative are consistently denied in most studies as a stated or unstated corollary of the belief that women were hangers-on who were drafted into Tantric rituals at the behest of yogis who needed them for their own ends. Thus, the only qualification with which women have been credited is sexual availability.

Mircea Eliade stated the currently accepted position quite clearly when he opined that "the more depraved and debauched the woman, the more fit she is for the rite."[132] In actuality, promiscuity and sexual availability, the main qualifications cited in Western literature, are not explicitly mentioned in Tantric literature as desired qualities in either women or men; however, there are related qualities that are required for both men and women aspiring to Tantric practice. Tantra is a path that uses passion as a basis for self-transformation through ecstatic beatitude. Therefore, passion (*rāga*) and desire, specifically amorous or sexual desire (*kāma*), are essential for both male and female Tantrics. As the *Caṇḍamahāroṣaṇa-tantra* proclaims, "There is no greater sin than dispassion, no greater virtue than pleasure."[133] If passion is to be transformed, the yogi and yogini must both possess this erotic sensitivity, capacity, and appetite, preferably in abundance. Passion alone does not suffice, however, for discipline and proper motivation are also essential. Tantric texts agree that the sexual yoga for transforming passion to divine ecstasy should be performed in a state of meditative awareness that is free from lust, ordinary attachment, and conceptual thought. This presumes both a passionate temperament and tangible progress toward cultivating a pure heart and clear mind. The passion of such a person is sometimes eulogized as "great passion" (*mahārāga*).

From the intimate nature of Tantric union as described above, it is apparent that the meditative training and spiritual refinement of the partner with whom the practices are performed are consummately important. Preparation and discipline are also required because the sexual practices involve advanced inner yogas, and these presume extensive preparation. Male practitioners are instructed not to choose a partner who is "ignorant and lustful," as is stated in the *Cakrasaṃvara-tantra*: "Don't approach those who are ignorant and lustful. Liberation is loving a female messenger (a qualified female practitioner). . . . Don't stay with inferior partners, and don't serve them."[134] Tsongkhapa glosses this, "Do not unite with those who are ignorant and possess desire, only female messengers who are vow-possessing women; not others, especially women who have ordinary attachment."[135] Tsongkhapa comments on this passage:

> If a woman lacks the messenger signs and superlative qualities, that is an inferior lotus. Do not stay with that one, because she is full of negative qualities. Make an offering and show some respect, but don't practice [with her].
>
> According to Kambala, "To one who possesses the characteristics of a female messenger, offer food, drink, and other things, and don't limit it to that or be stinting. Unite with her."
>
> Bliss is gathered by passion. Therefore, unite profusely. One attains [realization] by virtue of being passionate; otherwise, spiritual ecstasy will not arise.[136]

Although most of the qualifications for Tantric union apply to both men and women, texts sometimes specify the qualifications of female Tantrics. For instance, in his Cakrasaṃvara commentary, Tsongkhapa states that a man should seek a female companion who is pure and who knows many hand gestures (*mudrā*) and sacred chants (*mantra*).[137] She should be someone who pursues enlightenment with the same passionate intensity that he does: "The supreme female counterpart of that practitioner . . . should be diligent and not lazy and should have a passion to practice and attain the spiritual attainments. Having found one like that, unite with her, do all the associated ritual activities, and enjoy the pleasure of intense passion."[138] Elsewhere in the same work, summarizing his Indian sources, Tsongkhapa explains that a man should look for a woman with the three excellences (of body, speech, and mind), signs of having attained enlightened awareness (*mahāmudrā*), and a divine body, that is, the ability to envision herself as a deity and confidence in her intrinsic divinity.[139] The woman should be spiritually disciplined and replete with virtuous qualities.[140] Tsongkhapa cites the *Herukābhyudaya* to the effect that the man and woman must both be fully qualified and that mistakes in Tantric union will result in a sojourn in hell. If both partners "are not fully qualified, the penalties will be extremely great."[141]

Tantric texts sometimes refer to three types of female consort: best, middling, and lesser. Varying interpretations of the three categories can be found, and Tsongkhapa reviews these definitions in his Cakrasaṃvara commentary. One is that the best type of *ḍākinī* is one whose awareness is so transcendentally lofty that her mind is free from worldly thoughts and flows in a natural and spontaneous stream, a level of attainment known as *sahaja* realization, or "enlightened spontaneity." The second type is the class of yoginis who are born in Tantric sacred places and watch over them, blessing, guiding, and teaching whoever seeks them there. The third type consists of accomplished yoginis who have received initiation and are skilled at Tantric visualization.[142] Clearly, all three types—even the so-called lesser type—represent highly accomplished women. None of them represents a concession to be made in the absence of a qualified female partner.

It is essential that both partners be qualified for the practice of the yoga of union. The sensitivity, skill at visualization, and religious training of both partners must be brought to bear upon this shared endeavor. The quality and intensity of the experiences depend upon the yogic expertise of both partners and their ability to achieve a subtle attunement to one another and to enter and stabilize progressive meditative states together. Therefore, in addition to the Tantric commitment and training of each person, profound compatibility with each other is critical.[143] The partners become saturated with one another's energy at the deepest levels of being. They consciously absorb one another's energy and then deliberately direct that energy through their yogic anatomy, into the subtle nerve-centers (*cakras*) along the central pathway (*avadhūtī*). This energy carries the quality of the partner's emotions, consciousness, and karmic traces. Therefore, at this level the partners permeate one another's being and literally merge their karma and blend their spiritual destinies. This is one of the reasons that Tantric union is designated as *karmamudrā* practice.

In view of the intricate interfusion, commingling, and communion that Tantric union involves, the need for compatibility is even stronger than it would be in the case of an ordinary marriage. In ordinary Indian marriages, questions of caste (*jati*) and lineage (*gotra*) are foremost. This concept is reinterpreted in the Tantric context as the need for a man to find a *kulikā* (Tib. *rigs-ldan-ma*), a term that can be translated equally well as "suitable partner" or "kinswoman," a woman of his own lineage. Lineage in this context means Buddha family (*kula*) or spiritual type and includes qualities like temperament, psychological traits, and religious propensities. It is not true, as one Western author has written, that "the tradition defines the 'superior consort' in physical terms."[144] Physical attractiveness and traits are not intrinsically important, although bodily signs may provide evidence of a woman's spiritual lineage and capacities. There is not a single ideal physical or mental type to which a Tantric partner is expected to conform, as might be found in secular systems like the *kāmaśāstra*.[145] Irascible, argumentative, and proud personalities are featured, as well as serene, gentle ones. The important qualifications are discipline, dedication, and the fulfillment of demanding Tantric requirements.

The Cakrasaṃvara system emphasizes that a female practitioner of the yoga of union should be one who keeps the Tantric vows or "commitments" (*samaya*). Thus, an appropriate female partner is often specified as a "possessor of vows," a "vow-holder," or a "nonbreaker" of vows.[146] The *Cakrasaṃvara-tantra* exhorts that "the yogi must be diligent in upholding vows and practice with a vow-holding woman of his Buddha lineage."[147] This assures that the spiritual companions are committed to the same practices and goals. Tsongkhapa comments, "When one sees a yogini who keeps the Tantric vows, eat and feast and make meat-offerings and . . . make all sorts of offerings. Do not give offerings to those who aren't keeping the vows."[148] This seemingly simple qualification is actually quite comprehensive, because the vows comprise a spectrum of attitudes, speech, and behavior.[149] For example, many of the vows require that a woman maintain a pure Tantric view, which means seeing everything as intrinsically pure and avoiding conventional views based on ordinary dualities. Consistency of Tantric view requires vigilance and meditative stability on the part of the woman, and her speech and behavior should outwardly reflect her purity of vision. Thus, maintaining the vows is not merely a formality but requires a high level of commitment, diligence, and attentiveness.

Most qualifications of sexual yoga practitioners are the same for women and men. They include acceptance as a disciple by a guru, initiation, and keeping Tantric vows of loyalty, secrecy, and purity of vision. Tsongkhapa, basing his views on his extensive study of Indian sources and consultation with living exponents of the tradition, maintains that the qualifications of both partners are equally important. In his commentary on the six yogas of Nāropa, he summarizes the qualifications for practice with a human partner (*karmamudrā*) that are given in the *Herukābhyudaya*, an Indian source:

> Oneself and the yogic partner should both be knowledgeable, have attained pure initiation, skillfully maintain the root and branch Tantric vows, be skilled in the methods of *maṇḍala* practice, be well disciplined by meditating throughout four daily sessions, be acquainted with the sixty-four arts taught in the secular treatises on love (*kāmaśāstra*), clearly understand the doctrine of emptiness, recognize the stages of the four joys and the arising of *sahaja* wisdom, and have the power of retaining the sexual fluids within.
>
> As for those who lack more than a modicum of the qualifications stated in the *tantras* and authentic treatises of the great adepts and claim that their superficial oral instructions are profound, and then practice accordingly, this is very terrible and opens the door to the lower realms.[150]

Recognizing the stringency of these requirements, Tsongkhapa reiterated that if one is not qualified for a human partner, one should imagine or visualize a partner (*jñānamudrā*). Once again, it is the more qualified person who can become, and unite with, a human partner.

Tantric Buddhist sources assume that women engage in self-cultivation. Female practitioners described in Tantric works are not the notorious and benighted unfortunates postulated in Western scholarly works but rather qualified and knowledgeable women who are prepared to practice and reap the intended benefits. The texts testify that women as well as men developed their minds and bodies on the Tantric path by engaging in mental disciplines, learning stylized bodily movements (yoga and *mudrā*) for communication and self-transformation, and using their bliss and passion as a basis for attaining enlightenment through the sublime yoga of Tantric union.

## RECIPROCITY AND TANTRIC UNION

The existence of stringent requirements for Tantric practice in general and the yoga of union in particular has not entered into modern Western discussions of female practitioners, perhaps because of an assumption that women could not undergo the demanding training or attain the level of mastery required for serious progress on this path. If one accepts this premise, it would logically follow that since women would not embark on this path of their own accord, any woman who did participate must have done so at the behest and in the service of a qualified male Tantric. The widespread acceptance of this premise and conclusion makes it insufficient simply to defend the competence of female Tantrics on the basis of "evidence" from classical sources. Sources that contradict current historical views can easily be dismissed as anomalous doctrines that were never invoked in practice or as rhetorical statements that do not represent deeply held beliefs. No amount of "proof" can refute such a position.[151] One can only articulate the assumptions underlying the position and present an alternate interpretation, hoping to determine which one is more internally consistent and makes sense of a broader range of available evidence.

The practice of union, at least as it was originally designed, was not inherently meant to be an exploitative process from which one person—the man—derived unreciprocated benefit. By the time a practitioner had attained readiness for this practice, which is a highly esoteric inner yoga, he or she would be aware of the broader context in which the practice occurs. Practices preparatory to the sexual yogas include cultivating a sense of universal responsibility, maintaining compassionate motivation, and abandoning the illusion of a separate, isolated self. Thus, each partner would consider the implications of Tantric union not only for the other person but for the evolutionary progress of the entire human and natural environment, including the planetary and cosmic environment beyond. With this emphasis upon compassion and universal sensitivity, it would be impossible to ignore the well-being of the single person most directly involved. An intention to abuse or exploit someone as a deliberate part of the practice would be absurd in such a context. The process ultimately is reciprocal and is meant for the benefit of both, on many levels. Both partners should be similarly motivated and committed to Tantric practice, and both engage in the practice intending to progress toward enlightenment.

The language used to describe Tantric union is not a vocabulary of domination or exploitation. It is a language of symmetry, complementarity, and interdependence. For example, the terms used to describe male and female practitioners are commensurate and symmetrical, equally weighted in terms of the relative status of each party. A reader seeking clues to status will find that equally honorific terms for male and female Tantrics portray both the men and the women as serious aspirants. The man is a practitioner of yoga (*yogi*), reciter of mantra (*mantrin*), hero (*vīra*), or aspirant (*sādhaka*); the woman is a practitioner of yoga (*yoginī*), possessor of Tantric knowledge (*vidyā*), heroine (*vīrā*), or woman who realizes emptiness and dances in space (*ḍākinī*).

It is commonly held that Tantric texts always reflect a "male gaze," that is, a man's point of view. This is not the case. Sometimes the instructions for practice give directions to a man, describing his attitudes, ritual actions, and forms of worship. Sometimes the texts reflect a "female gaze," describing what services and obeisances a woman is to require of a man, what forms of homage she can demand, and embodiment and sexual union from a female perspective. A given text may favor one type of description or the other or alternate between the two. For instance, the *Caṇḍamahāroṣaṇa-tantra* gives a clearer view of the practice from the woman's angle of vision, while the *Cakrasaṃvara-tantra* addresses the man regarding what forms of homage to render to the woman. In neither case does one gaze truly dominate, because the descriptions make it easy to imagine the process from either perspective. The gaze, whether male or female, does not obliterate the presence or experience of the "other," because the "other" is fully present as the object of the gaze. One can imagine the man's behavior by watching it from the woman's perpective, and one can imagine a woman's experience of the respect and worship required of the man. Since the process being described is one that two people undergo together, both poles are implicitly and tangibly present and can easily be deduced from any description of it.

The relationship between Tantric partners is one of mutual aspiration, effort, and assistance. The two are equals, with neither one regarding the other as inferior or as an object or instrument to be manipulated for selfish purposes. These texts express a Buddhist program of deconstructing self in synchronicity with another person's deconstruction, followed by a re-creation of their subjective identities as a male and a female Buddha in union. When they are in peaceful form, they rest upon a lotus in quiescent beatitude; when they appear in wrathful form, they trample upon the corpses of the unenlightened selfhood they have conquered. The dissolution and apotheosis of the two partners is interdependent. Their appreciation, enjoyment, and intimate involvement with one another is captured in their rapt, blissful, contemplative gaze—the gaze of deities (figure 16).

FIGURE 16. Rapt, blissful gaze of divine couple

The reciprocity of Tantric union may be difficult to recognize for a Western reader who assumes that gender always means a power relation or relation of domination.[152] Tantric Buddhism represents a different cultural realm and a novel variation on gender relations.[153] The power that reigns in this realm of cultural meaning is not a power of domination, but a power of transformation and liberation. This nonhierarchical power is seen as a fluidic, dynamic property variously and momentarily inhering in persons, objects, places, symbols, and especially ritual activities meant to generate and channel power. In Tantric Buddhist ritual, power at times inheres in persons, most often in women. This is not a discourse that either assumes or constructs male power or male social or ritual dominance. Insofar as gender is linked to power in this realm of discourse, women intrinsically possess and channel the power of transformation. The reason for this is not directly explained, perhaps because it is implicit in the Śākta metaphysics that Buddhist Tantrics share. Men can tap into this power, and it can flow through the women to the men, but it cannot be taken or stolen from women. The texts give no indication that the men are contesting or competing with the power of women, seeking to deprive them of it and appropriate it for themselves. A man's relationship to this power is one of awe, receptivity, and dependence.

Because Tantric union is a practice involving reciprocity, not domination or coercion, Tantric texts expressly forbid a derogatory or disdainful attitude toward a female partner. The *Cakrasaṃvara-tantra* enjoins sincerity and pure motivation:

> The male aspirant, with all his possessions,
> Should worship the female partner.
> This worship is supreme, but
> If he is scornful, he will surely burn [in hell].
> One attains ultimate realization
> By the *tantras* of the yoginis.
> Thus, one who is diligent
> Should worship with complete sincerity.[154]

Failing to honor women, or disparaging them, could have a dire outcome. A man who would engage in this Tantric worship with a disrespectful or critical attitude will not enjoy the fruits of the practice but will suffer serious karmic penalties. A man's attitude must match his behavior. He should be loving and worship with a cheerful attitude. Mere outward obeisance without a reverent, willing attitude is not meritorious or efficacious. Tsongkhapa surveys a range of Indian sources and concludes: "Be very loving to them, as one would toward a mother, sister, daughter, or mate. . . . One should always worship with a cheerful mind. If one does this cursing and with a vulgar mind, that creates difficulties, and all the superlative qualities will be depleted."[155]

Tantric union has explicit intellectual, emotional, meditative, and visualizational content that cannot be circumvented. If the prescribed attitude is not present, the activity becomes ordinary sexuality masquerading as religion, a form of hypocrisy that can be spiritually disastrous. Acts undertaken in the wrong spirit can never bear spiritual fruit. In order to be transformative, a practice must be undertaken with the requisite content as well as the proper ritual form. The requisite content is reciprocity, intimacy, and mutual aspiration to attain enlightenment for the sake of all sentient beings.

---

I base this study mainly on Tantric texts written in Pāla period India (eighth through twelfth centuries C.E.), but these beliefs and practices have survived as a living tradition today. Tantric union was part of the classical formulation of Tantric Buddhism through at least the tenth century in India, at which point there is increasing evidence of a monastic appropriation of this tradition and a reinterpretation of Tantric symbols to be compatible with a celibate lifestyle. Because of the inherent incompatibility between the life-affirming Tantric ethos and monastic renunciation, attempts to synthesize the two paradigms continued well into the fifteenth century in Tibet, where it occupied the great monk-scholars of the Tibetan renaissance.

Although the energy of the Tantric tradition was diverted into the creation of patriarchal institutions, the practices and symbols described herein have survived in Tibet and throughout the Himalayan region. In my interviews, I found that not all Tibetan Buddhists know about this yogic discipline, but those who practice it do so with a spirit of ardent advocacy. This lineage of yogis and yoginis is not as highly visible as the monastic universities, but it is nonetheless vital and influential and has been a continuous source of charismatic teachers and leaders. Competition and mutual criticism between celibate and noncelibate factions have contributed to the dynamism and vitality of Tibetan Buddhism over the centuries.

Most Western scholars have interpreted this ancient and living tradition by projecting the models of gender and sexuality that preexist in their own minds, without reference to the tradition's own values. To continue to use a vocabulary of domination is to remain locked in this realm of discourse, losing sight of the fact that Tantric texts eloquently present a unique universe of visionary experience—a universe that bears little resemblance to the modern Western epistemologies and ontologies that have been invoked in its interpretation. The colors in this world cannot be perceived through a lens that reduces them all to a black-and-white pattern of manipulation and subjugation, or domination and submission. Tantra envisions a resplendent world of vivid color, choreographed movement, exquisite texture, and intimate gesture. This world of heightened experience is a jewel hidden within the ordinary world of self-enclosed, separate, habitually numb and insensate selves whose relationship to one another is routinized and self-referential at best, neurotic, addictive, and compulsive at worst. In the Tantric worldview, dominance and exploitation characterize the neurotic and addictive behavior pattern that must be abandoned if one is to recover the jewel—the natural, spontaneous ecstasy of being that emerges through the practice of Tantric union.

CHAPTER SEVEN

# Spontaneous Jewel-like Yogini on Passion and Enlightenment

TANTRIC BUDDHISM is a religious path upon which men and women can pursue enlightenment together, through a series of ritualized and choreographed expressions of intimacy that transform passion into divine ecstasy. Tantric union is designed to be a mutually liberative and transformative practice for both the woman and the man who perform it together. Men are required to honor and worship their female partners, while women, as embodiments of female divinities, accept this worship, a reciprocal exchange meant to refine the man's emotions and provide the woman with experiences useful to her pursuit of liberation. Buddhism already offered an array of techniques for the solitary and monastic pursuit of liberation. Tantra introduced a method that could be pursued in the context of intimacy with another person.

Tantra arose at a time when Buddhism was expanding the social inclusiveness of its constituency, teachings, and path to liberation. Monastic Buddhism was flourishing, but Tantra opened a new path for lay participation and initiative. Janice Willis has observed that women's status in Buddhism generally rises along with the status of the laity in general.[1] As women voiced their insights, their revelations and teachings helped to shape the theories and practices of the emerging movement. Practices that involve intimacy between women and men would most naturally evolve out of their combined insights and experiences.[2] It would be unlikely for such practices to have originated as a flight of imagination in the seclusion of a monk's cell. It follows that women's views would be present in the area of the tradition that most directly involves the mutual efforts and close cooperation of women and men.

Women were indeed among the early teachers of the sexual yogas. Evidence that women had expertise in this area includes numerous instances of women providing "secret oral instructions" (*upadeśa*) on the advanced inner yogas, or perfection stage practices, of Tantric union. We know, for instance, that Sahajayoginīcintā gave the esoteric teachings to Ghaṇṭapa and Padmavajra;[3] Śrīsukhā gave them to Padmavajra;[4] Lakṣmīṅkarā instructed Jālandhari;[5] Bhadri gave them to Kāṇha;[6] a yogini in Bengal taught Atīśa;[7] a prostitute's daughter taught

Urgyanpa;[8] and Samantabhadrī, Sukhāsiddhī, Kanaśrī, Gaṅgādharā, and Niguma instructed Khyung-po rnal-'byor.[9] Karopa received secret oral instructions from Lakṣmī the Great of Kashmir and received the initiation from another woman, Kumudarā,[10] while Buddhaśrījñāna (also known as Jñānapāda) received his advanced instruction from the yogini Guṇeru.[11] The great Tibetan scholar Tsongkhapa relied heavily on a number of men who had female teachers on the topic of Tantric union (*karmamudrā*), such as Kāṇha, Ghaṇṭapa, and Kambala.[12] Thus, even teachings found in classical Tibetan treatises on the subject, such as those of the monastic reformer Tsongkhapa, can be traced back directly, at only one remove, to women.

The secret oral instructions that these women gave included the inner yogas that form the basis of the sexual practices. Several of the accounts relate that after receiving the esoteric instructions, the yogi in question was accepted as a consort by a female Tantric and proceeded to practice with her, in some cases for several months and in others for many years. For example, after Buddhaśrījñāna received secret instructions from the yogini Guṇeru, he had a dream about where he could find his destined partner, the daughter of an outcaste (*caṇḍāla*) gatekeeper in Uḍḍiyāna. He went there and found Jatijālā as foretold, and they practiced together for eight months.[13] Ghaṇṭapa subsequently found a lifelong spiritual companion, a courtesan's daughter. Because of previous lifetimes they had spent together, they were destined to meet and to help one another attain enlightenment through Tantric union (figure 17). Together they attained enlightenment and manifested many miracles for the benefit and wonderment of others.[14] Atīśa's partner was the woman who had instructed him in the practice. Gaṅgādharā, one of Khyung-po rnal-'byor's teachers, was herself the spiritual companion and partner of Maitrīpa.[15]

These accounts show that women were acknowledged authorities on the very practices of which, according to current theories of Tantra, they were ignorant, unwitting victims. The women may not have recorded their views, but their male partners and students took care to record them and pass them on to their own students. Thus, women were the teachers of some of the men who are now consulted as the great authorities on the practice.

If women were sought out for their expertise on the inner yogas and Tantric union, it logically follows that women might have helped to create them. This would help to explain why a new practice appeared just as the tradition was opening to new voices and perspectives. It would also help to explain why this practice was not designed as a form of domination, manipulation, or coercion of women. Counting women among the creators of this practice has not been considered as a possibility by historians for reasons that have been discussed else-

FIGURE 17. Courtesan's daughter and Ghaṇṭapa enjoying enlightenment

where in this work, including the assumption that all Tantric texts were written by men and describe only the practices and experiences of men.[16] Alex Wayman suggested that "if women had been writing the books, the titles and contents would have diverged considerably,"[17] but the approach I am suggesting allows for the available texts to be read as the creations of both men and women.

Fortunately an important text on this topic by a woman has survived, making it possible to confirm women's contributions to the development of this distinctive yoga for passionate seekers. The text dates to the eighth century, relatively early in the historical emergence of these practices. When Tantric Buddhism was imported into Tibet, Tibetans accepted seven texts as the fundamental Tantric works, and several of the texts were by women, including the work to be discussed presently. Thus, this treatise is not simply an intriguing document of women's history but a pioneering and influential work of its period. It is intrinsically important as a major theoretical contribution on sexual union as a spiritual discipline. This text provides an excellent opportunity for exploring a woman's views on Tantric union.

The author of the work is Sahajayoginīcintā, whose name means "Spontaneous Jewellike Yogini." She was part of the core group of yogis and yoginis whose writings provided the theoretical foundations of the emerging Tantric movement.[18] The group centered on Princess Lakṣmīṅkarā, her brother Indrabhūti, her students Līlāvajra and Dārika, her associate and student Sahajayoginīcintā, and Sahajayoginīcintā's students Ḍombīheruka, Anaṅgavajra, and Padmavajra. Their works dominate the small group of Tantric treatises that have been preserved in Sanskrit, attesting to their signal historical importance.[19] Within this treasure trove there sparkles the gemlike treatise by Sahajayoginīcintā on liberation through ecstasy, entitled *Realization of Reality through Its Bodily Expressions* (Skt. *Vyaktabhāvānugata-tattvasiddhi*), in which she articulates the relationship between bodily pleasure and bliss and enlightenment.[20] Other Tantric texts take this relationship for granted, but it is rare to find a Buddhist text that approaches the subject in a detailed philosophical way. Sahajayoginīcintā elaborates a theory of how passion, or sexual desire, as a source of bodily bliss and pleasure, can provide a means to enlightenment by creating a bridge between ordinary experience and the higher octave of spiritual ecstasy. Her erudite, intellectually demanding composition draws on contemporary philosophy, psychology, biology, erotica, and meditative arts as well as her own experiences as a mystic and as a woman.

## THE TEACHINGS OF SPONTANEOUS JEWELLIKE YOGINI

Sahajayoginīcintā first presented this teaching to an assembly of women, as a revelation received in meditation. Although she drew upon a number of sources, including instructions on spiritual ecstasy, or "great bliss" (*mahāsukhā*), she received from the female guru Lakṣmīṅkarā,[21] the most immediate source of the teaching is revelation received in a deep meditative state called "indestructible cosmic concentration." The colophon describes how a group of yoginis, or female religious practitioners, gathered in northwestern India to hear her discourse:

> At the supremely great, adamantine place of Uḍḍiyāna, when glorious yoginis rich with the splendor of self-arising wisdom assembled, she entered the "indestructible cosmic concentration (*samādhi*)" that instantly confers the power-enriched energy of the truth of reality that is without error and arises from a realization of ultimate truth. The "Realization of Reality through Its Bodily Expressions," a honeyed stream rich with the glory of bliss, flowed forth from her blossoming lotus face without hesitancy.[22]

In Sahajayoginīcintā's religious milieu, authority derived from mystical attainment, and this colophon expresses the acceptance of her work as genuine revelation.[23]

Sahajayoginīcintā opens her text with an affirmation of gendered embodiment, both male and female. She immediately establishes that gender is an integral part of the path to enlightenment, since ecstasy is inseparable from embodiment and embodiment is inseparable from gender. Her first statement on the topic is a breathtakingly double-edged stroke that denies the ultimacy of gender—in a classical Mahāyāna move—and at the same time endows gender with metaphysical roots extending deep into ultimate reality, which is a more characteristically Tantric insight. She argues that the inner spirit may be nondual, or nongendered, but nonetheless:

> In order that one may realize one's inner self,
> Which is spontaneous (*sahaja*), naturally pure, and nondual,
> The inner self manifests here as man and woman.
> One's own self, creative by nature,
> Enacts reality through bodily expressions.[24]

Since the essential self, the innate and spontaneous or *sahaja* nature within, is inherently pure and nondual, it transcends the dualism of gender. At the same time, this inner self manifests as woman or man specifically to embody forth the nature of reality through bodily expressions (*vyaktabhāva*) and thereby provide a means to its realization.

Sahajayoginīcintā relates the idea of an inner self, or essence, to Tantric physiology, which posits a metaphysical element that is present throughout the genesis of a human being. She explains that at the moment of conception a spark of bliss unites with a drop of male and female generative fluid and forms a ball that is the kernel of a new being.[25] Thus, bliss is present at the inception of a human being and remains there, in the heart, throughout life.[26] The innermost self or spark of bliss manifests itself as, or creates a body that is, male or female to bodily enact and concretely express the nature of reality. This makes gender an expressive gesture of the blissful Buddha-nature within. Therefore, gender possesses a sufficient link with ultimacy to provide a bridge back to the ultimate.

Next Sahajayoginīcintā turns to the topic of the enlightened state, or Buddhahood. Tantric Buddhas are not celibate. Tantric iconography includes an image of enlightenment in the form of a male and female Buddha in sexual union (known as *maithuna* or *yab-yum* form). Such Buddhas are said to experience bliss and emptiness simultaneously, but beyond this the moods and activities of Buddha couples are generally left unstated. Sahajayoginīcintā describes Tantric Buddhahood in considerably more detail, adding experiential language and vivifying detail to her distinctive portrayal of a Buddha. In other contexts, a Buddha is hailed as a "conqueror of passion,"[27] whereas Sahajayoginīcintā portrays a Buddha as one who can feel and respond to passion:

> Seeing a delightful woman
> As enlightenment spontaneously appearing in embodied form,
> A Buddha gazes with passion and playfulness, and
> Desire for pleasure and bliss arises.[28]

A Tantric Buddha gazes amorously and feels desire. To the stimulus of a beautiful woman, a male Tantric Buddha responds with "passion and playfulness," not, as might be expected, with aversion or sublime indifference.

Since Tantric union is a process of *imitatio dei*, when human beings undertake this activity the woman envisions the man as a male Buddha, the man envisions the woman as a female Buddha, and the stages of lovemaking become Buddha deeds. At certain stages in this process one may visualize one's partner as a particular Buddha, such as a blue Heruka or red Vajrayoginī. In this method one visually superimposes upon one's partner a specific Buddha, by seeing the partner's skin as red or blue, picturing the body as translucent and luminous like a rainbow, and envisioning attributes like bone ornaments and silk ribbons. The purpose of this aesthetic exercise is to bring about an ontological revelation in which one sees one's partner as already a Buddha, as presently and continuously revealing a state of Buddhahood. It is essential that the woman and man see each other as a visible manifestation or embodiment of *sahaja*—pure enlightenment spontaneously expressing itself in embodied being. The former process develops imaginative creativity, the latter unveils metaphysical ultimacy.[29]

Since the woman (as well as the man) is a visible embodiment of *sahaja*, pure and enlightened in essence, their feelings of passion and desire have a transcendent aspect. Their mutual attraction ultimately is motivated by a religious impulse toward ecstasy and transcendence of the ordinary, dualistic mode of experience. Even a Buddha has such feelings, or at least can play at having such feelings for the sake of enlightenment:

> Then, uttering profound flirtations from the throat,
> The self, like a dancer, as if in a dream,
> Sports at the five natural kinds of erotic play.[30]

In Indian thought, play implies an innermost spiritual self or deity performing physical motions while remaining aware of transcending the body and its actions. Artistically, play implies the removed self-awareness of an actor performing a role or the self-recollection of a dancer performing graceful gestures and choreographed dance steps. Play also refers to erotic sport and enjoyment. The "five natural kinds of erotic play" probably refer to the enjoyment of the five sense objects.[31] Play is also a term that is used when spiritual discipline becomes light and effortless. Thus, the imagery of play poetically conveys the meditative concentration of Tantric partners, their identification with deities, and the choreographic quality of their intimacy. "Play" is an apt term for the contemplative yet amorous gestures of lovemaking as a religious discipline.

Sahajayoginīcintā describes the progress of this liberative play:

> Then with gentle and sincere speech
> He draws her to his heart.
> Rubbing her with thick perfume,
> He satisfies his mind by inhaling the lingering fragrance.
> Having experienced that and obtained
> Bliss and pleasure equal to a hundred vases of nectar,
> They embrace without hesitation,
> Enjoying the nuances of bliss.[32]

Each of the five senses is engaged and satisfied: sight by gazing, hearing by sweet words, smell by perfume, touch by rubbing with scent and embracing, and taste by kissing.

The female Buddha initiates union and assumes an active role:

> The female lover, gazing with desire,
> [Utters] sweet words like drops of honey.
> She unites with him,
> Moving the lotus
> That brings a rain of pleasure.[33]

In this woman's text, the metaphors of honey, flowers, and rainfall express a delicate, appreciative sensibility regarding female sexuality.

The active role of the woman in Sahajayoginīcintā's vision of sacred sexuality can also be seen in the artistic portrayal of Buddha couples, in which the male Buddha typically sits or stands firmly and calmly, tightly grasping his partner's waist, while the female Buddha dynamically embraces him, wrapping flexible limbs around his body, raising her face to kiss his lips, brandishing a skull-cup of nectar, and waving her curved knife aloft (figure 17).

As Sahajayoginīcintā's instructions continue, the bliss generated by passion becomes the basis of specific forms of meditative concentration and inner yogas.[34] She insists that both partners should maintain meditative alertness while performing activities that increase bliss:

> The innermost self, intent upon its purpose,
> Should remain mentally concentrated
> While engaging in the different styles of kissing
> For the sake of the singular taste,
> Engaging in all the specialities [of lovemaking],
> Like biting, piercing, and so forth.
> Then, having generated intense bliss,
> They scratch [each other]
> With their fingernails from time to time,
> Gently, to dispel delusion.[35]

The "innermost self," which has manifested as male or female, now rediscovers itself through bodily actions. A variety of kisses are to be known and tried, but the purpose is to attain the "singular taste" (*eka-rasa*) when every experience takes on the same emotional-aesthetic flavor of spiritual ecstasy. Having "generated intense bliss," the primary purpose of the activity, the partners must be careful not to succumb to its intoxication by becoming faint or mentally dull. To remind each other to maintain clarity and prevent a descent to drowsiness or ordinary passion, the lovers scratch each other with their fingernails. Sahajayoginīcintā's references to different types of kisses, methods of biting, styles of strokes, and techniques of scratching with the fingernails use categories from the secular arts of love, joining them to soteriological aims. If passion and spiritual ecstasy are two points along the same continuum, erotic sophistication can be made to serve contemplative ends.

Sahajayoginīcintā views this yoga of union as perfect for removing the subject-object dualism of ordinary experience. The loss of ego-boundaries during lovemaking ushers the partners into the nondual mode of experience:

> In stages, because of the taste of desire,
> One ceases to know who is the other and

What has happened to oneself.
The lovers experience an inexpressible bliss
They never experienced before.[36]

This merging of identities becomes the epitome of the nonduality wherein "subject" and "object" dissolve and fuse. Sexuality can be part of the path because erotic experience already contains the seeds of enlightened awareness: blissfulness, loss of ego boundaries, forgetfulness of self, and absence of subject-object dualism. Thus, passion and erotic pleasure bring the yogic partners to the threshold of desired religious states.

Sahajayoginīcintā's descriptions of Tantric union are celebratory, affirmative, and poetic. Her language bespeaks not aggression or manipulation but playfulness and reciprocity. Mutuality is essential to the meditative aim of the practice. The loss of a sense of separate selfhood occurs through a merging of identities and is predicated upon a unitary experience wherein, in her own words, "one ceases to know who is the other and what has happened to oneself." Through the dance of union the partners lose their individual subjectivity and discover psychic unity, or intersubjectivity. This nondual mode of experience becomes a basis for further yogic and meditative practices when the nondual awareness is stabilized, along with the bliss, by yogically disciplined partners.

Sahajayoginīcintā claims that sexual union provides a powerful basis for meditative stability by virtue of its natural one-pointedness. The numerous objects of the mind are replaced by one compellingly engaging object:

Both of them [the man and the woman]
Are bound by a stream of concepts
Born from and arising from the mind.
As long as they are united,
Their minds will not remember anything else;
They will be mindful only of pleasure.[37]

The verb for concentration (*smṛti*) is the same verb that is used when a Buddha or bodhisattva is the object of meditation. Here the bliss of union becomes the object of meditation:

Hissing passionately, both,
Undistracted by anything else,
Will attain abundant, unsurpassable pleasure
And increase that.
They awaken from the darkness of ignorance
By enjoying the wealth of the activities of bliss,
Then develop and increase bliss and pleasure.[38]

Sahajayoginīcintā explains that since this meditation has an object, or support (i.e., bodily desire and pleasure arising from the sense organs), it produces a conditional bliss that is dependent upon the senses. Nonetheless, this sensory, bodily bliss—"human pleasure"—supplies the dynamic motion that leads out of the mundane realm and into the transcendent sphere of experience:

> Human pleasure, with its identifiable characteristics,
> Is the very thing that,
> When its characteristics are removed,
> Turns into spiritual ecstasy,
> Free from conceptual thought,
> The very essence of self-arising wisdom.[39]

Once the dualism of self and other and all other identifiable characteristics are removed from it by an application of insight into emptiness, the bliss completes the movement into spiritual ecstasy.

Through the practice of this yoga, passion finally leads beyond itself, so the consorts eventually turn their attention inward and go beyond desires dependent on sense objects. One of the keynotes of Sahajayoginīcintā's teaching is that one taps this level of bliss not by avoiding sensual pleasure but by cultivating and channeling it. By immersing oneself deeply in the senses and sensation, one reaches an inner source of bliss so deeply satisfying that it suffuses the mind with perpetual satisfaction. Because it is the nature of the mind to seek the bliss from which it is born, the mind can finally rest, having found ultimate, unconditional bliss:

> Because the mind [carried by a subtle] wind
> Seeks its primordial essence of holy bliss,
> Being satisfied,
> The mind will not be distracted by other things—
> It rests in the radiant reality
> Whose essence is method and wisdom.[40]

The ultimate pleasure has no immediate cause, because it is the very nature of the mind—its "primordial essence" and "radiant reality." By following passion to its source, one lays bare the blissful core of the mind. This state of unconditional bliss is supremely satisfying. The senses no longer desire to wander in the desolate cities created by hunger and desire when they can be opulently entertained in palaces spun of bliss and luminosity, as the whole world acquires the same "taste," or emotional-aesthetic flavor (*ekarasa*):

> When one enters the palaces of the sense organs,
> Experiencing abundant delights,

This very world attains
The singular taste of spiritual ecstasy.[41]

This interior realization, a revolution (*paravṛtti*) of the partners' own minds, turns this world into paradise, a perfect Buddha-land, as every sensation, thought, and emotion becomes saturated with "holy bliss."

The ultimate state of experience is blissful, radiant, nondual, and infinitely wise. It is also inherently compassionate:

Holy bliss is stabilized by pleasure,
By supreme delight in bringing others happiness.[42]

The mind that turned within, resting in its ultimate nature, beyond subject and object, finding complete quiescence and joy therein, now turns outward again. The dynamism of concern for others impels an awakened woman back to participation in the world, to enter the city of the senses once again, not in search of personal satisfaction but in order to rescue those who are still lost and suffering.[43] It is impossible to remain inactive or to seek to avoid participation, for to do so would reify a dualistic quiescence.

Sahajayoginīcintā voices the question that weighs deeply upon a Buddhist practitioner committed to liberating sentient beings without number:

How is one to awaken the children
Whose inner brightness is obscured
By the burgeoning of beginningless karma?[44]

That is, from the standpoint of *sahaja*, which is natural and spontaneous, what basis can there be for motivated, volitional action? Sahajayoginīcintā explains that the knowledge attained through the body is now expressed through the body. An enlightened woman can engage in all the moods and behaviors that she formerly did, but now they will be spontaneous and liberative. The inner state of spiritual ecstasy naturally expresses itself in an unbroken stream of compassionate, liberative activities.[45] All bodily expressions become pure, dancelike, and sacred:

All bodily movements
Fashioned spontaneously from enlightened mind,
Pure in essence,
Become sacred gestures.
Whatever is spoken is sacred speech. . . .
Activities that are graceful, heroic, terrifying,
Compassionate, furious, and peaceful—
And passion, anger, pride, greed, and envy—
All these things without exception

Are the perfected forms
Of pure, self-illuminating wisdom.[46]

A simpler and more radical way of expressing this is that a woman with a pure mind can engage in any activity, and that activity will be pure.[47] States that are graceful, heroic, terrifying, passionate, or angry can be employed by an enlightened person to liberate someone who is predisposed to be liberated by that display.[48] Sahajayoginīcintā contends that any kind of behavior can serve on some occasion to instruct or inspire someone, be it laughter, weeping, sleepiness, wakefulness, stability, fickleness, playfulness, passionless solitude, foolishness, insatiability, dancing, singing gaily, gambling, bathing, being dirty, going naked, wealth, generosity, total poverty, laughing at Buddhist teachings, truthfulness, sinning, lying, speaking nonsense, or saying nothing at all.[49] Since everything is inherently pure, it would appear that an enlightened woman has considerable leeway in how to behave:

A skillful one
Who can use the wealth of all these things
As inherently pure
Has the great accomplishments of supreme Buddhahood
In the palm of her hand.[50]

Thus, according to Sahajayoginīcintā, gender, embodiment, the senses, and passion can be embraced on the spiritual path. The body participates in the path to enlightenment and then in the creative expression of enlightenment.

## SPONTANEOUS JEWELLIKE YOGINI, THE WOMAN

It is clear from her writing that Sahajayoginīcintā had received an excellent education and was trained in topics both religious and secular. As a woman, Sahajayoginīcintā might have received her education in any number of ways. Works from the period indicate that princesses, daughters of high officials and courtiers, girls of the nobility (*kṣatriya* class), and courtesans and dancers might receive training in Sanskrit language, composition, poetry, music, dance, and various sciences (*śāstra*),[51] including *kāmaśāstra*, or the science of love.[52] Although women of these groups were the ones most likely to receive an education, there is also evidence that a formal education was sometimes available to servants and low-caste women.[53]

Sahajayoginīcintā's background must be surmised from Tāranātha's reports of her occupations, her familiarity with court life and royalty, and the internal evidence of her text. Sahajayoginīcintā is said in Tāranātha's lineage histories to have engaged in selling wine and, later in life, herding swine. Earlier in life, when she was known as Vilasyavajrā, she was wineseller to the king, a position considerably higher than that of a common tavern owner. Tavern owners sold rice beer and local wines to a diverse and often unsavory clientele,[54] while Sahajayoginīcintā was a palace retainer entrusted with the serious charge of providing fine grape wines worthy of the royal palate. Wines of such quality would have to be imported from Arabia, Persia, and Kashmir.[55] Sahajayoginīcintā would have dealt with caravan traders, trading jewels and spices for the coveted wines, and was probably trained in ancillary business skills, such as accounting, gemology, and viniculture. In this capacity she would have frequented the palace and might even have lived there.[56] She was familiar enough with the king to know about his mortal fear of snakes. She confided this information to the guru Ḍombīheruka to help him convert the king. Further, according to the story, when Ḍombīheruka sent some snakes to the palace, Sahajayoginīcintā was on hand to tell his majesty where he could turn for help.[57]

A background in a noble or merchant family or as a retainer raised in the palace would be consistent with Sahajayoginīcintā's broad education and occupation, while a background as the daughter of a courtesan or dancer would also explain her access to the palace, associations with royalty, knowledge of erotic science, and references to art and dance.[58] Regarding her Buddhist eduction, at the beginning of her text Sahajayoginīcintā states that she spent many years of devoted service at the feet of her guru. This period of apprenticeship would have provided the opportunity for her to receive her Buddhist philosophical training in Abhidharma, Yogācāra, and Tantra.[59]

Sahajayoginīcintā was a learned and cultured person, capable of providing spiritual guidance from the philosophical fundamentals through advanced *yoginī-tantra* techniques. Nonetheless, she eventually left high society and moved to a small village with a low-caste consort, had a daughter, and lived by herding pigs. In this she resembles male adepts like Tilopa and Saraha, who subsisted by the lowly activities of oil-pressing and arrow-making, the occupations of their low-caste consorts, in spite of their scholarly accomplishments and ability to support themselves by scribal or educational work if they so chose. When she became a Tantric practitioner, the yogini chose a simpler and freer way of life unbounded by social constraints, for the activities, travels, and companions of a pig-herder are not likely to attract much attention or scrutiny from anyone—except perhaps someone looking for a Tantric guru!

Although Tāranātha reports that Sahajayoginīcintā was renowned as an expert on "supreme bliss," we have few anecdotes regarding her career as a guru. This is not unusual, even in the case of such a well-known figure, for Tantric narratives are regrettably brief. A surviving anecdote regarding Sahajayoginīcintā is quite telling. It relates to her disciple Padmavajra, one of the "founders" of Tantric Buddhism. Padmavajra served as priest to a king in Uḍḍiyāna and was proud of his scholarly accomplishments and his skill as a public speaker. On one occasion a wood-gathering woman attended one of his Buddhist lectures and alternately laughed and cried as he spoke. After the lecture she approached him and explained that she had laughed because she enjoyed his exquisite speaking style, but she had cried because he did not know what he was talking about. The wood-gatherer directed Padmavajra to seek out the guru Anaṅgavajra, a pig-herder in a squalid village to the north.

When Padmavajra found Anaṅgavajra he barely noticed the man, but he immediately became fascinated with the woman with whom the master lived. She gave her complete attention to every task, and her deep immersion in reality shone through every gesture. Her impeccable, graceful, dancelike movements deepened Padmavajra's spiritual understanding as he watched her perform her chores. He realized that watching her walk and move was more profound than listening to any discourse on Buddhist philosophy. The scholar begged Sahajayoginīcintā to accept him as her disciple, but she became furious and drove him away with a beating, asking how a low-caste woman like herself could be a guru. Not to be turned away, the scholar camped out in the pigsty. While he slept the pigs riffled through his bags and chewed on his books. The next morning when he discovered what had happened, he began shouting and stomping his feet. Sahajayoginīcintā was so impressed by this display of passion and anger that she agreed to accept him as a disciple: "Ah, so you are not perfect! Maybe you can learn something from me after all!" Padmavajra received initiation and instruction from Sahajayoginīcintā and her consort. Their daughter chose Padmavajra as her Tantric companion and returned with him to the palace, where Padmavajra resumed his official duties while the couple pursued Tantric practice in private, until discovery necessitated a display of magical powers on the part of both partners that succeeded in converting many people to the Tantric path.[60]

The versatility of her background and training is reflected in the discourse of the Spontaneous Jewellike Yogini from Uḍḍiyāna. Like the jewel that is her namesake, the illustrious yogini has many facets. She is a visionary revealer of Tantric teachings received in a deep meditative state. She is a skilled rhetorician who dazzles her audience with a sensuous and exuberant vision of Tantric sexuality. She is a skilled homileticist who motivates her audience to religious discipline, exhorting them that worldly pleasures are impermanent and ultimately unsatisfying. She is a subtle philosopher who spins and unravels the theoretical intricacies of her position. The women in her audience were rewarded for their attendance at her discourse by a striking and perhaps unique portrait of how a Buddha responds to passion, expresses love and desire, and engages in the transcendental pastime of erotic play.

Sahajayoginīcintā's work is critically important for an assessment of the knowledgeability of Tantric women, for Sahajayoginīcintā writes skillfully, authoritatively, and innovatively on a subject of which women have been considered to be ignorant, namely, the yoga of Tantric union. Further, the Spontaneous Jewellike Yogini was not unique among women in possessing this knowledge. She herself delivered this teaching to an assembly of women, and we can tell something about Sahajayoginīcintā's audience from the work. It is not primarily a beginner's lesson, for it refers in passing to many complex doctrines and advanced practices. Thus, the content of her text indicates that the women in her audience were not novices. Their advanced progress on the spiritual path is supported by their description as "glorious yoginis rich with the splendor of self-arising wisdom."[61] Sahajayoginīcintā also taught this teaching to male disciples such as Padmavajra and Ghaṇṭapa, who attained enlightenment by means of Tantric union and proceeded to become famous as "founders" of Tantric Buddhism.[62]

The fact that Sahajayoginīcintā's career took place in Uḍḍiyāna is also significant. Tantric literature presents Uḍḍiyāna as an ideal place to learn and practice Tantra because of the congregations of female Tantrics to be found there. Numerous famous male adepts like Padmasaṃbhava, Kambala, Anaṅgavajra, Līlāvajra, Luipa,[63] Tilopa,[64] Ghaṇṭapa,[65] Buddhaśrījñāna,[66] Gambhīravajra,[67] Padmavajra,[68] Atīśa, and rGod-tshang-pa went to Uḍḍiyāna and apprenticed themselves to female teachers there. More information is generally available about the yogis than about their female teachers, but Sahajayoginīcintā represents the type of woman they might have encountered there and provides an intriguing glimpse of the background, life pattern, and luminous wisdom that a female guru of Uḍḍiyāna might possess.

---

It has been claimed that women were ignorant of Tantric sexual yoga and were either exploited by men in their performance or were willing to participate because they were "witches" or "sluts." This claim must be revised in light of evidence that women originally taught and helped to design it. We even find the definitive foundational text on the subject to be of female authorship. Since women were teachers and experts on the sexual yogas, it is justifiable to suggest that women did not transmit teachings that they found unacceptable, offensive, or irrelevant to their religious aspirations. There were no external constraints upon them to do so, for in the Tantric context there is no higher authority than a guru, whose interpretations have supreme authority and validity for her disciples. In the role of guru, as living authorities on Tantric union, women were free to present the teachings in accordance with their own experiences and convictions. Thus, the women presumably taught and circulated the teachings on Tantric union in a form of which they approved. Some of the men who today are acknowledged by the tradition as authoritative formulators of the practices received the teachings from women. The male transmission of the teachings does not preclude their female origins.

Exploitation is inconsistent with the original design and purposes of Tantric union as it is presented in classical scriptural sources and in this influential teaching by a woman. Knowing the intended form and content of the practices can help to identify departures from them, as well as to identify social and cultural settings that favor their emergence. If exploitative dynamics were interjected at any point in the history of the tradition, as some have conjectured, it is important to investigate what social, institutional, and doctrinal configurations accomplished the abuse of women by means of a practice they originally helped to develop. Any degeneration that can be documented will have to be acknowledged as a betrayal of the original spirit of the practices as women designed them.[69] In any case, these teachings have been preserved in their classical form, and the practices have survived as a living tradition.

There may be Buddhist doctrines and practices that developed in the hothouse environment of a monastery, but the sexual yogas cannot lay claim to such a genesis. The sexual *sādhanā* provided a natural arena for the expression of women's interests and aspirations. Since women were among the early teachers and formulators of this genre of practice, it is reasonable to maintain that women did not create or view this practice as one in which they would be manipulated and exploited. It was conducive to women's enlightenment because women helped to design it. Educated women like Lakṣmīṅkarā and Sahajayoginīcintā, craftswomen like the Arrow-making Yogini, artistic women like Ḍombīyoginī, courtesans like the Tantric partner of Ghaṇṭapa, and female gurus like Gaṅgādharā all practiced the yoga of union as part of their own path to enlightenment.

CHAPTER EIGHT

# Conclusions

ORIGINALLY THE BUDDHA taught a life of renunciation and celibacy as the ideal pattern for pursuing enlightenment, yet in the Tantric movement in India we find people pursuing a different pattern. Saraha renounced his monastic vows in order to spend his life with an arrow-making woman. Tilopa, another great scholar, disrobed and married a sesame-pounder. Lakṣmīṅkarā turned down a royal marriage and took a low-caste man as her Tantric partner. Others never became monastics, and many who did eventually abandoned their vows in order to find a partner of the opposite sex, settle into a simple village life, make pilgrimages, and pursue their contemplative and yogic disciplines in the midst of all this bustle, liveliness, and passion. These seekers pursued a distinctive religious path that finds its most characteristic and nuanced expression in an intimate and sexual relationship. The presence of women alongside the men is not an afterthought or an optional feature; it is integral to the Tantric paradigm, prized by the movement as its ideal pattern. This pattern represents a lofty idealism, a belief that men and women together can create relationships that are nonexploitative, noncoercive, and mutually enlightening.

Tantric Buddhism shares its ethical and philosophical principles with Mahāyāna Buddhism, while the distinguishing features of the tradition occur in the area of symbol and ritual, most notably in the inclusion of intimacy and sexuality, gender and embodiment, as part of the path to liberation. Tantric studies were eventually integrated into the monastic curriculum in India and the monastic system in Tibet, but they were not easily transferable into a celibate, cenobitic context without considerable sublimation of the imagery and practices.[1] The Tantric beliefs and practices described in this work have lived on in the classical literature, the minds of great masters, and a thriving yogic and eremetical subculture.

## HISTORIOGRAPHIC ISSUES

Denials of the positive roles, status, and achievements of women in this movement have several points of departure. They would appear to be part of a trend identified by Veena Das in many fields of historical study: "The study of other cultures continues to be undertaken from the perspective of providing documentation of the universality of oppression against women."[2] The postulation of universal male dominance helps to legitimate current social arrangements by implying their inevitability and universality. This unconscious goal is a major obstacle to women's history.[3] A related factor is a reluctance to concede the potential diversity of cultural constructions of gender, gender relations, and sexuality. There is a built-in psychological resistance to acknowledging the existence of views at variance with one's own—a naiveté regarding the social constructedness of sexuality. This may help to account for the fact that the claims of Western scholars have consistently diverged from those of Indian scholars, Indian practitioners, and Western scholar-practitioners. Tantric views of gender and sexuality represent a distinctive variation among the world's traditions, and one way to avoid the implicit challenge of a dissonant voice is to recast its message into an exotic, orientalized version of one's own, which is what scholars have done when they "discover" in Tantra a medieval Indian mirror-reflection of their own denigration of women and exploitative model of sexuality. The attempts to mute the articulate voice of this tradition regarding its most treasured ideals betray the legacy of colonial contempt for the cultural values of other peoples.

This study has yielded results that differ from those of other studies because it proceeds from different assumptions and historiographic principles. One of the guiding assumptions is that, regardless of how men may view them, women experience and interpret their own lives as the *subjects* of their lives. How men may view women is not the primary concern of women's history, although men are sometimes the sole topic of works that purport to be histories of women. A women's history must seek to determine how women interpreted their own lives, areas in which they experienced authority and power, whether they shared men's views of women, whether they resisted male authority or contested for power, whether the men's sense of dominance was largely played out in the realms of imagination and literary production, and how social class and economic factors intersected with gender in the determination of status and social location.

This historiographic orientation has led me to seek evidence of what women practiced, believed, and experienced. Such a search depends to a degree upon the amount of evidence available about women and gender relations, but the outcome of such a search is equally dependent upon the theoretical assumptions of the historian. It is impossible simply to read texts for so-called raw data, since the presuppositions of the reader will predetermine what will be accepted as part of a meaningful pattern and what will be ignored as either anomalous or inconceivable.

What is inconceivable—what cannot be thought, due to an inadequate conceptuality—does not enter into one's universe of meaning or range of observations.

It is the inadequate conceptuality of much modern Tantric scholarship that has rendered the women of Tantra invisible and muted the passages that describe their experiences. When a Tantric passage describes a woman as her partner would see her, this is naturally taken by many scholars to mean that a male subject is constructing himself as a dominant, autonomous agent over, above, and in contrast to a female object that he is manipulating. Passages that describe what a woman is to visualize, say, or do are dismissed and ignored, because there is nothing in the interpretive strategy that would allow for the existence of such passages. As long as each passage of this type is discounted, multiple instances can never "accumulate" in the reader's mind sufficiently to suggest a different interpretation, change the regnant reading, or demand a reinterpretation.

Therefore, my study has "discovered" a different gender pattern by working with different theoretical assumptions. By assuming the subjectivity of women with regard to their own lives and their possession of intrinsic motivations for their actions, my approach to the sources has been different. For instance, in some cases I have worked with data—biographies, lineage histories, and scriptures—that have already been translated and interpreted by other scholars. The difference in my case has been that I have treated the references to women as information about *their* lives, rather than as place-markers in a blueprint for male domination. Instead of dismissing—or "tokenizing"—each example of a woman's activities or accomplishments as an anomaly or as evidence of women's subordination, I have accepted such examples as documents of women's history and have tried to weave or quilt those references together into a coherent pattern. On this basis I have been able to ascertain that women participated in every aspect of Tantric Buddhism. They were not relegated to the margins or to the lowermost rungs of religious progress but undertook the complete range of Tantric practices. I found no evidence of barriers to women's participation at any level, including the attainment of enlightenment and assumption of authority as gurus.

Women's full participation is consistent with the loose structure of Tantric circles. There was no clerical body or institutional structure to which women, or men, had to appeal to authorize their practice or authenticate their progress. The informal organizational structure was centered around individual teachers and their disciples. Thus, women embarked upon Tantric practice at their own initiative and were limited only by their own efforts and capacities. This egalitarian state of affairs is not unusual in India's yogic and ascetical movements, which are highly individualistic and in which all power of decision and interpretation rests with the guru, while religious progress depends upon the aptitude and diligence of the disciple.

A different interpretive approach, or historiographic perspective, opens new areas of research and information. My search for texts by women was prompted by the realization that women were active practitioners who made significant progress in Tantric practice. Previous assumptions of women's exclusion from this movement discouraged a search for women's writings, and it is even stated on occasion that none of the canonical texts were written by women.[4] Even when the existence of texts by women was recognized,[5] there was not a sufficient sense of their potential importance to motivate inquiry into their contents or historical significance. Other discoveries made in the course of my research inspired me to search more persistently for women's writings, learn to read the diverse genres represented among them, and do the research necessary to determine their historical influence.

This work has shown that women must be included among the creators of Tantric Buddhism. Women's innovations became the basis for transmission lineages that have continued to the present day, such as Siddharājñī's transmissions of the Buddha of Infinite Life and the Lord Who Dances on a Lotus, Niguma's Cakrasaṃvara healing *maṇḍala*, and Lakṣmīṅkarā's Severed-Headed Vajrayoginī. Some women's systems became the basis for prominent, well-known public rituals. A long stay in almost any Tibetan Buddhist community will afford an opportunity to witness a long-life ceremony based on Siddharājñī's system or the Avalokiteśvara fasting ritual introduced by Bhikṣuṇī Lakṣmī. The influence of these women's teachings was pervasive, affecting every sect, region, and religious institution of Tibetan Buddhism. Additional female founders have been and will continue to be discovered, but there are also numerous women whose contributions will never be recognized because they have blended seamlessly and anonymously into the fabric of the Tantric tradition.

Although parts of the historical record of women in Tantric Buddhism have been lost and erased, there is sufficient evidence to show that this was a movement in which women actively taught and freely introduced new practices, deities, and insights that they discovered in their meditations. This freedom was strong at the inception of the tradition in the seventh and eighth centuries, as seen in the careers of women like Lakṣmīṅkarā and Sahajayoginīcintā, and there is evidence of women's ongoing participation, creativity, and leadership through the eleventh and into the twelfth centuries, as exemplified by Siddharājñī and the female teachers of Atīśa (982–1054), Khyung-po rnal-

'byor (born 1086), and Pha-dam-pa Sangs-rgyas (died 1117). The evidence presented here suggests that women's participation and cultural creativity were not the result of a brief burst of egalitarianism at the beginning of the tradition but rather continued from the seventh through the twelfth centuries, up to the eclipse of the tradition in India.

In the cases of the Wrathful Red Tārā of Vajravatī, the Severed-Headed Vajrayoginī of Lakṣmīṅkarā, and Sahajayoginīcintā's teachings on passion and divine ecstasy, we have examples of women imparting their teachings to other women and at times addressing exclusively female audiences. There were no doubt other women who had large numbers of female students, women whose stories and teachings have not survived because their successors did not record their teachings or establish politically viable institutions to preserve and perpetuate their memory, and women whose teachings were absorbed and eventually claimed by other lineages.

Several factors supported the participation of women in this movement century after century. One factor can be found in Tantric doctrines, which provide explicit affirmations of femaleness and guides for behavior toward women. Terms like *ḍākinī,* "yogini," and "heroine," with their intimation of spiritual attainments and supernatural powers, help to create a numinous aura around women. Respect for women is an integral part of Tantric religiosity, not something that male practitioners could ignore or discard at will. The forms that respect and worship should take and the punishments for their violation are specified. There are guidelines for deferential, reverent behavior toward women and consequences for transgressions and expressions of disrespect. These affirmations of women were part of the appeal of this movement for women and strongly suggest the role of women in shaping the tradition.

There are no doctrinal barriers to women's complete participation in Tantric Buddhism. There are no pronouncements of women's disability, innate incapacity, or inferiority to men in the pursuance of enlightenment. The misogynist diatribes that figure in so many religious literatures have no place here. Therefore, any discrimination to which women may have been subjected in the long and varied history of this tradition cannot be attributed to Tantric doctrine but must be sought in cultural forces, institutional factors, and social patterns that have eclipsed the original vision. The full participation of women in Tantric Buddhism in medieval India is consistent with its loosely organized, itinerant pattern and marginality during that period. Although the movement came to enjoy royal patronage, widespread cultural influence, and international renown, it was not closely allied with centers of secular power and had amassed no fortunes or estates to motivate the kind of political struggles that emerged in Tibet and the Himalayan kingdoms.

One of the main symbols of enlightenment in Tantric Buddhism is that of a Buddha couple, or male and female Buddha in union. This *maithuna* symbol is an image of unity and blissful concord between the sexes, a state of equilibrium and interdependence. This symbol powerfully evokes a state of primordial wholeness and completeness of being. The perennial appeal of this motif is not that it commemorates a successful seduction or cosmic manipulation but rather that it offers a vision of authentic humanity in which women and men are restored to wholeness through a delicately balanced, joyous state of harmony. I would argue that the most tantalizing and evocative aspect of this symbol is its promise of an integration of aspects of life that are normally sundered: body and spirit, eros and transcendence, passion and beatitude.

When we turn from this exquisite aesthetic expression of interdependence and complementarity to the enactment of Tantric union in the human realm, we find that the sense of mutuality and ecstatic rapture carries over into the practice that is patterned after the union of deities. Passages that describe the yoga of union have a mood of joyousness, playfulness, and poetic delicacy. The spirit of domination and manipulation with which these practices have been attributed are nowhere present in the literary accounts, nor do they characterize the narratives in which Tantric partnerships are described. In these works the women generally emerge as forthright, assertive, and outspoken, while the men evince respect, admiration, and allegiance toward their female companions. Women and men both contribute their energies to the weaving of relationships that are characterized by cooperation, mutual reliance, and shared aspiration.

Although it is generally claimed that men were the serious practitioners of the Tantric sexual yogas and women were merely enlisted to participate because of the technical requirement of their presence, this study has documented that the classical *yoginī-tantra* sources written in Tantric circles present women as serious, genuine practitioners capable of spiritual perfection. The male and female partners are described in symmetrically honorific terms. Sometimes the practice is described from a female perspective and sometimes from a male perspective. Neither partner is described as seeking to dominate or manipulate the other, although women reserve the right of choice of consort, requiring that the men seek and await their approval.

This elaborate system is anchored in the spiritual interdependence of women and men and was not developed without the cooperation, participation, and insights of women. Many women can be found among the teachers of Tantric union. Some of their names are preserved because of the accomplishments and subsequent fame of their students, the acknowledged "founders" of Tantric Buddhism. A woman even wrote the charter text on the practice of sexual union as a religious discipline. The active role of women in helping to design the practice helps to explain the emphasis upon female initiative and upon mutuality and intersubjectivity, since men did not develop the practice independently with only their own benefit and interests in mind. Women attained a certain psychological advantage and authority in the Tantric movement because of its Śākta orientation, but they seem not to have used their power to dominate, devalue, or exclude men. Ultimately a mood of complementarity reigns in the *tantras*. Men and women enter this visionary world together.

## ICONOGRAPHIC ISSUES

The attempt to project a mood of male domination onto this movement becomes particularly convoluted when it contrives to explain away the passionate yoginis of Tantric iconography. These unrestrained damsels will dance blithely through raging flames, trample nonchalantly upon a corpse, or ride a tiger (figure 18). Turning them into meek, gullible victims of male seduction requires a special trick of metamorphosis. These ladies are known for their ability to change shape and adopt other forms, such as birds, jackals, and wolves. However, turning into weak, helpless victims would probably have been too much even for their magical powers.

When I first saw the female images in Tibetan scroll paintings, the exuberance and sense of power of these yoginis and *ḍākinīs* so impressed me that I spent many years searching for the historical women who might have inspired and been inspired by them. I was surprised to discover that scholars deny even a potential connection between these female images and actual women. Instead one finds elaborate explanations, generally along Jungian or Freudian lines, of how these images symbolize male psychic processes and development. The prevalent Jungian interpretation sees the female figures as anima figures, representing forces within the male psyche as they emerge to consciousness:

> She is all that is not incorporated in the conscious mental makeup of the individual and appears other-than and more-than himself.[6]

> The feminine sky-dancers or *ḍākinīs* are a powerful representation of the repressed feminine aspects of the male psyche.[7]

FIGURE 18. Yogini riding tiger

Also representing the Jungian line of interpretation, Nathan Katz analyzes the yoginis as symbols of forces operative within the male psyche as they emerge from the labyrinth of the subconscious to heal and integrate the conscious self.[8] Fokke Sierksma, offering a Freudian interpretation, says that the male adept, "obsessed by the aggressive Bad Mother, directs his mother symbols against his own ego so that he might die and be reborn."[9] Others claim that the female deities and *ḍākinīs* represent the inner wisdom (*prajñā*), inner heat, or transcendent consciousness of the Tantric yogi, or that they awaken the bliss and desire that are utilized in Tantric practices. Shashibhusan Dasgupta, an early historian of Tantric Buddhism, explicitly stated that the yogini figure "should not be confused with the woman of flesh and blood . . . she is but an internal force . . . residing in . . . different stages of yogic practice."[10] In order further to remove any possible connection or identification with women, one author recently stated that these female figures are not even really female.[11]

None of these views relate the female deities and figures to women, considering that they may have reflected men's views of women or women's views of themselves.[12] According to these interpreters, we are to believe that women never thought of themselves when they looked at these anatomically correct, naked female figures and that men never thought of women when they looked at them. Apparently it was clear to all of them that the images express the shape and drives of the male subconscious. However, on the basis of the present study we can return to the interpretation of those symbols and claim that, regardless of what else they might signify, they do bear a direct relationship to the women of Tantric Buddhism. I contend that these powerful images gained their credibility from human counterparts, while female Tantrics in turn found their spiritual aspirations mirrored in them. These female images are consistent with what this study has revealed regarding the attainments and contributions of the women of Tantric Buddhism. The artistic and historical records confront us with exuberant, passionate, enlightened women, unencumbered by patriarchal restraints upon their experience of ultimate reality and freedom.

## BUDDHOLOGICAL ISSUES

What we find in the Tantric practices and doctrines, as in Buddhism in general, is a strategy for deconstructing the unenlightened self, or ego. The interpretation of any Buddhist text as a strategy for constructing self is problematic at the outset, because that could not be the intended purpose of a Buddhist text or practice. If one avers that an exploitative, self-serving "self" or "selfhood" is being condoned by a whole genre of Buddhist texts, it becomes necessary to explain such a radical departure from central Buddhist values. Buddhism can coexist with oppressive social conditions, but the relationship between Buddhism and the institutional pattern or social setting needs to be explored in each case. In the case of Tantric Buddhism, the yoga of union provides a means for women and men to deconstruct their conventional selves *together*, or, in Tantric terms, to experience emptiness and bliss, neither of which is possible for an armored, boundaried, or selfishly motivated "self."

Any interpretation of Tantric Buddhism that denies this purpose of Tantric union—the purpose that drew Tantrics out of their monasteries and into intimate relationships—denies the radical intent of Tantra's religious vision, which is that *women and men can attain liberation together.*

Part of the Tantric methodology of deconstructing the ordinary self is to replace it with a divine self. In Tantric union, the self, as a deity, unites with a partner who is simultaneously conceived as a deity. To experience the divinity of the partner is the touchstone of Tantric vision. One cannot divinize oneself while abusing, degrading, or dehumanizing the other person, because the partners mirror each other. One of the attributes of a deity is to have an appropriate consort. A consort must by definition be an equal, and indeed, it does not befit a deity to unite with anything less than a deity. Thus, a Tantric practitioner cannot become a deity without an appropriate consort, who must also be a deity, and it is impossible to re-create oneself successfully as a blissful deity while retaining, much less cultivating, a condescending, contemptuous gaze. On the contrary, the gaze of a deity is one of tenderness, clarity, and passion (figure 16).

The claim that male Tantrics were ruthless seducers amounts to a contention that a major Buddhist tradition has functioned primarily as a tool of exploitation and oppression. In this view, Tantric Buddhism has served as a tool to construct and to solidify male selves as predatory, self-serving manipulators, acting under unchecked selfish motivations, while representing a social force of degredation, denigration, and suffering. This dramatic assertion cannot be allowed to pass unexamined, because if it were true then this entire form of Buddhism betrays the perennial goals at the heart of the tradition, namely, to alleviate suffering, serve as a force of liberation, and release people from the bondage of illusory separateness and selfhood. Even when one allows for pragmatic concessions to social, political, and economic conditions, the degree of corruption posited in the standard view of Tantra warrants more than a mention in passing and deserves less than immediate and universal acceptance by Buddhist historians.

The claim that Tantric Buddhism was solely a male creation is also problematic from another perspective. This claim reflects a model of Buddhist historiography that might be termed the model of independent existence (*svabhāva*), which sees Buddhism as an insular strand of development carried out by elite men in monasteries. This prevalent model may acknowledge the existence of "popular practices" and "folk traditions" but would not include them within the fold of Buddhism proper. This approach treats Buddhism as an impervious institution, insulated against the surrounding culture, contamination by other religions, popularization by folk practices, and corruption by the interests of women. A preferable model, which one could term a model of interdependent origination (*pratītyasamutpadā*), sees Buddhism as a dynamic stream that is constantly enriched by the insights of diverse peoples. In this model, Buddhism is a dynamically fluidic movement that has drawn on a range of sources and social groups and through this openness found the resources that enabled it to meet the needs of diverse people, as well as to gain viability in different cultural settings.

The presence of women and women's teachings, as well as affirmations of female energy and spiritual capacities, are distinctive features of Tantric religiosity. When one considers the historical position of Tantra, an influx of feminine elements and insights is consistent with the social inclusiveness of the movement and its receptivity to symbols, practices, and insights from new quarters. Monastic Buddhism had fostered an increasing emphasis upon philosophical dialectics, an elitist enterprise that is best pursued in a monastery and whose practitioners display a tendency to devalue other aspects of life, overemphasizing the role of intellect in gaining enlightenment and losing sight of the capacities and potentials inherent in the body, the senses, and the emotions. Tantra emerged as a corrective to this imbalance and as a witness to the fact that the mind alone does not provide sole access to knowledge. Passion and pleasure also represent primary sources of knowledge and power. Tantra represents an influx of precisely these elements and insights into Buddhism, and spiritual companionship between women and men is part of this constellation of ideals. The impetus to change may have come from pressures within Buddhism to expand its symbolic resources and social base, or the changes may have penetrated Buddhism from without. In either case, it is clear that insights from goddess-worshipping traditions, Śaivite sects, different social groups—-like dancers, courtesans, tribal peoples, and outcastes—and women inundated Buddhism at this time and provided the impetus for a stunning revitalization, launching several brilliant centuries of international expansion, florescence, and influence.

# Notes

## CHAPTER ONE

1. Notably, Mabel Bode, "Women Leaders of the Buddhist Reformation"; Isaline Horner, *Women under Primitive Buddhism*; Bimala Law, *Women in Buddhist Literature*; Hellmuth Hecker, *Buddhist Women at the Time of the Buddha*; Yuichi Kajiyama, "Women in Buddhism"; Renate Pitzer-Reyl, *Die Frau im frühen Buddhismus*; Janice Willis, "Nuns and Benefactresses"; and Susan Murcott, *The First Buddhist Women*.

2. Nancy Falk, "The Case of the Vanishing Nuns"; Chatsumarn Kabilsingh, *A Comparative Study of Bhikkhunī Pāṭimokkha*; and Karma Lekshe Tsomo, ed., *Sakyadhītā*.

3. Diana Paul, *Women in Buddhism*; and Paul Harrison, "Who Gets to Ride in the Great Vehicle?" pp. 73–74, 76–79, 86.

4. Reginald Ray, "Accomplished Women in Tantric Buddhism of Medieval India and Tibet"; and Kalu Rinpoche, "Women, *Siddhi*, and Dharma."

5. Most notably Janice Willis, "Tibetan *Ani*-s"; Karma Lekshe Tsomo, "Tibetan Nuns and Nunneries"; Sherry Ortner, "The Founding of the First Sherpa Nunnery, and the Problem of 'Women' as an Analytic Category"; and Hanna Havnevik, *Tibetan Buddhist Nuns*.

6. Most notably, Tarthang Tulku, trans., *Mother of Knowledge*; Keith Dowman, *Sky-Dancer*; Tsultrim Allione, *Women of Wisdom*; Rita Gross, "Yeshe Tsogyel"; and Adelheid Hermann-Pfandt, *Ḍākinīs*.

7. Work in this area has tended to conflate the roles of women—and similarly the interpretation of female imagery—in the radically different cultures of India and Tibet. This approach characterizes Fokke Sierksma, *Tibet's Terrifying Deities*; Anne Klein, "Primordial Purity and Everyday Life"; and José Ignacio Cabezón, "Mother Wisdom, Father Love."

8. Studies of women in Tibet have looked at religion only incidentally; e.g., Alexandra David-Neel, "Women of Tibet"; Matthias Hermanns, "The Status of Women in Tibet"; Siegbert Hummel, "Die Frauenreiche in Tibet"; Beatrice Miller, "Views of Women's Roles in Buddhist Tibet"; and Indra Majupuria, *Tibetan Women (Then and Now)*. The exception is studies of Tibetan nuns; see n. 5. Important new documentation of women and Tibetan Buddhism is currently being produced in the form of autobiographical literature.

9. The most disapproved texts were those of the *ma-rgyud*, or *yoginī-tantra*, category; see Samten Karmay, *The Great Perfection (rDzogs-chen)*, pp. 5–6. The *anuttara-yoga tantras* met a similar resistance in China, but with a different outcome; see Ch. Willemen, *The Chinese Hevajratantra*, pp. 10–11, 14–19, 23–29; and Jan Yün-hua, "Buddhist Relations between India and Sung China," pp. 136ff.

10. Consider, for example, the fascinating career of Gedün Chöpel. A brilliant, iconoclastic scholar, he became convinced that the path of passion is the essence of the Tantric teachings and forsook monasticism, seeking enlighten-

ment instead through the practice of sexual *sādhanā*. Although the knowledge required for this path was not immediately accessible to him, he re-created the path for himself on the basis of textual research and experimentation and then developed his own theoretical elaboration of the path; see Gedün Chöpel, *Tibetan Arts of Love*, trans. Jeffrey Hopkins.

11. Rita Gross, "Buddhism and Feminism," and Anne Klein, "Finding a Self." A summary of the progress of this dialogue is provided by Rita Nakashima Brock et al., eds., "The Questions That Won't Go Away," while the magnificent recent contribution by Rita Gross, *Buddhism after Patriarchy*, has raised this discussion to a new level of specificity and clarity and will set the terms of the dialogue for a long time to come.

12. E.g., Satindra Roy, "The Witches of Orissa," esp. pp. 185–86, 193; Charlotte Vaudeville, *Bārahmāsā in Indian Literatures*; Stella Kramrisch, "Unknown India," pp. 105–6; Doranne Jacobson and Susan Wadley, *Women in India*, pp. 128–31; Lindsey Harlan, *Religion and Rajput Women*; Frédérique Marglin, "Refining the Body"; Pupal Jayakar, *The Earth Mother*, pp. xvi–xvii; Julia Leslie, ed., *Roles and Rituals for Hindu Women*; Laxmi Tiwari, *The Splendor of Worship*; and Kathleen Erndl, *Victory to the Mother*, chap. 5. For a discussion of autonomous realms of women's religious knowledge and their implications for field research, see Peggy Brock, ed., *Women, Rites, and Sites*, and the useful bibliography therein.

13. Sir John Woodroffe, *Shakti and Shākta*, pp. 160–63, 505. Quoted in the same work, a Bengali reviewer praises Woodroffe: "He has understood in what light Hindus regard the *Tantra Shāstra* . . . He commenced his work with a Hindu's heart, with a Hindu's regard, and a Hindu's faith" (p. viii of "Some Press Notices" at the end of the book). Others who have expressed this view are Edward Dimock, *Place of the Hidden Moon*, pp. 98–102 (Dimock defers to Woodroffe's authority on this matter); S. C. Banerji, *Tantra in Bengal*, pp. 160–61; and Swami Satyananda Saraswati, *Kundalini Tantra*, p. 111.

14. Mark Dyczkowski, *The Canon of the Śaivāgama and the Kubjikā Tantras of the Western Kaula Tradition*, pp. 63–64; Lilian Silburn, *Kuṇḍalinī*, p. 158; and Sanjukta Gupta, "Women in the Śaiva/Śākta Ethos," pp. 208 and 208, n. 11.

15. See Narendra Nath Bhattacharyya, *The Indian Mother Goddess*, p. 291; Swami Saraswati, *Kundalini Tantra*, p. 111; and Lilian Silburn, *Kuṇḍalinī*, p. 158.

16. Debiprasad Chattopadhyaya, *Lokāyata*, pp. 277–80, 285; S. C. Banerji, *Tantra in Bengal*, p. 163; and Narendra Nath Bhattacharyya, *The Indian Mother Goddess*, pp. 291–93.

17. Bholanath Bhattacharya, "Some Aspects of the Esoteric Cults of Consort Worship in Bengal: A Field Survey Report II."

18. Lynn Denton, "Varieties of Hindu Female Asceticism," pp. 229–31. Denton reports that all the female ascetics (Tantric and non-Tantric) she interviewed were dedicated to their own liberation and had consciously rejected the role of upholding society and living for others.

19. Brajamadhava Bhattacharya, *The World of Tantra*, pp. 2–7, 34–44. Ramakrishna also received Tantric initiation and instruction from a female guru, and she was the first to recognize him as an *avatāra*; see Swami Nikhilananda, intro. to *The Gospel of Sri Ramakrishna*, pp. 18–20.

20. Lilian Silburn, *Kuṇḍalinī,* part 3, chaps. 4 and 5. This mutuality is also seen in the Aghori Vimalananda's description of his relationship with his Tantric partner; see Robert Svoboda, *Aghora,* pp. 291–94.

21. David Snellgrove, *Indo-Tibetan Buddhism,* p. 287.

22. Hanna Havnevik, *Tibetan Buddhist Nuns,* p. 35.

23. Kendra Smith, "Sex, Dependency, and Religion," p. 219.

24. Lee Siegel, "Bengal Blackie and the Sacred Slut," p. 57.

25. Shiníchi Tsuda, "'*Vajrayoṣidbhageṣu Vijahāra,*'" p. 607.

26. Lee Siegel, "Bengal Blackie and the Sacred Slut," p. 52.

27. Mircea Eliade, *Yoga: Immortality and Freedom,* p. 261, n. 204.

28. David Snellgrove, *Buddhist Himālaya,* p. 175.

29. June McDaniel, *The Madness of the Saints,* p. 171. Elsewhere in the same work, McDaniel states that "these female Sahajiyās were neither mystics nor madwomen, but were rather . . . ritual assistants for the male practitioners" (p. 175), and "the consort is strictly a ritual object, used to gain power" (p. 122; see p. 274 for similar comments).

30. Teun Goudriaan in Sanjukta Gupta et al., *Hindu Tantrism,* p. 33. This statement was cited by Douglas Brooks, *The Secret of the Three Cities,* pp. 25–26, even though Brooks observed the complexity of the roles of women in this Tantric movement during his own field research; cf. Douglas Brooks, "The Śrīvidyā School of Śākta Tantrism," pp. 354–58.

31. The noncelibate temple priestesses of the ancient Near East were similarly libeled. According to emerging research, the Near Eastern temple votaries, like the *devadāsīs,* were unmarried, bore children, and managed their own frequently considerable property. To their followers they were regarded as mediators of divinity, as their names signify (*qadesh,* or *qadishtu* in Akkadian, meaning "holy women" or "sacred women"), but they appear in Western literature as "ritual prostitutes" or "temple prostitutes." The Hebrew prophets denounced these priestesses, and their indignation continues to resonate in modern scholarly judgments; see Merlin Stone, *When God Was a Woman,* pp. xx, 156–58.

32. The pioneering ethnographic work on the *devadāsīs* is that of Frédérique Marglin, *Wives of the God-King.* The sacredness of the dust from their feet and the ground where they have danced in the Śākta realm of cultural meaning is discussed in detail by Frédérique Marglin, "Refining the Body," pp. 217–20, 226–28. For an analysis of the effects of British laws on the *devadāsī* tradition, see Amrit Srinivasan, "Reform or Conformity?"

33. Ashis Nandy, *The Intimate Enemy,* pp. 9–11, 36, 53–55, and *At the Edge of Psychology,* pp. 32–46. The actual and in many cases disastrous effects of colonialism on Indian women's lives, livelihood, and social and legal status are increasingly being recognized; see Kumkum Sangari and Sudesh Vaid, eds., *Recasting Women.*

34. Hans Küng, *Christianity and the World Religions,* pp. 414–15.

35. Herbert Guenther, in *The Tantric View of Life,* pp. 63–64, attributing the Western misunderstanding of Tantra to a Western preoccupation with control and domination. He criticizes the projection of "Western dominance psychology" upon Tantra by writers who "could not understand that the desire to

realize Being is not the same as the craving for power" (p. 64). Guenther also points out that a woman who is regarded as a slave or an oppressed, controlled object "cannot give the recognition sought for by the master as only a subject can do so" (p. 64). This points to the psychological inadequacy of a system in which women are mere things to be used. He says, rather, that "in order to find himself man needs the 'other' who is no intellectual abstraction, but part of himself, needed in order to be himself" (p. 67).

36. Trinh Minh-ha, in *Woman, Native, Other*, eloquently protests the way that the First World category of "universal male dominance" (espoused by feminist and nonfeminist alike) trivializes the experiences, dignity, social arrangements, and cultural creativity of many Third World women.

37. Shelly Errington in Jane Monnig Atkinson and Shelly Errington, eds., *Power and Difference*, p. 7; the bibliography of this volume is an excellent guide to literature on this subject.

38. The creation of the modern Western commodified self has majesterially been summarized by Frédérique Marglin, "Rationality, The Body, and the World." Michel Foucault argues that Western constructions of sexuality hinge upon commodity logic and power discourse; see *History of Sexuality*, vol. 1. The implications for sexuality of conceiving human relations as commodity relations are explored in Robin Schott, *Cognition and Eros*, pp. x–xi, 167–97.

39. Indologists have demonstrated the inadequacy of commodity logic for illuminating selfhood and interpersonal relations (including the sharing of bodily fluids, as in Tantra) in India. See McKim Marriott, "Hindu Transactions: Diversity without Dualism"; E. Valentine Daniel, *Fluid Signs*; and Gloria Raheja, *Poison in the Gift*.

40. The *Guhyasamāja-tantra*, a *mahāyoga-tantra*, also addresses these topics and repays an in-depth study on these themes.

41. See Herbert Guenther, *The Tantric View of Life*.

42. Gerda Lerner, "Placing Women in History"; Elisabeth Schüssler Fiorenza, "The 'Quilting' of Women's History"; and Joan Scott, *Gender and the Politics of History*, pp. 3–50.

43. Jane Lewis, "Women Lost and Found," p. 62.

44. Ibid., p. 59; Gerda Lerner, "Placing Women in History," pp. 361–62.

45. Elisabeth Schüssler Fiorenza, *In Memory of Her*, p. 86.

46. Elisabeth Schüssler Fiorenza, "The 'Quilting' of Women's History," p. 40, and *Bread Not Stone*, p. 111.

47. Elisabeth Schüssler Fiorenza, *Bread Not Stone*, p. 98.

48. For example, recent studies have shown that medieval Christian women's mystical writings reveal patterns of religious experience and symbolic interpretation that differ from those of their male counterparts; see Caroline Walker Bynum, *Holy Feast and Holy Fast*, pp. 24–28 and chap. 10; and Ulrike Wiethaus, "Sexuality, Gender, and the Body in Late Medieval Spirituality." In the study of Indian women, the groundbreaking work by Renuka Singh, *The Womb of Mind*, inaugurates inquiry into women's experiential lives in the form of women's interpretations of female religious symbols and figures, views of their own status, and sources of religious inspiration, shifting the focus away from "objective" measures of status, male attitudes toward women, and socie-

tal norms for female behavior. The women in her study demonstrate creativity, selectivity, and independence in the way they use religious motifs to interpret and enhance their lives. Another path-blazing work that treats Indian women as the subjects of their own lives rather than the objects of others is that of Indira Parikh and Pulin Garg, *Indian Women: An Inner Dialogue*.

49. For a highly useful overview of the potential range of evidence of women's history and the relative usefulness of different types of documents, see Bernadette Brooten, "Early Christian Women and Their Cultural Context."

50. Elisabeth Schüssler Fiorenza, "The 'Quilting' of Women's History," p. 40.

51. Many texts of potentially female authorship were omitted from this study pending more definite confirmation.

52. Douglas Brooks, *Secret of the Three Cities*, pp. 84–86, discusses the primacy of the "guru's power of discretionary action" in deciding who will receive Tantric teachings and provides an informative discussion of the range of possible considerations.

53. These five degrees of participation are formulated by James Spradley, *Participant Observation*, pp. 57–62. An even stronger case can be made for this in the case of attempting to understand a Buddhist practice or text, as recently articulated by C. W. Huntington, who argues that "we cannot expect *on our own terms* to engage in effortless conversation with . . . a seventh-century Sanskrit text. . . . It is necessary to invest some real energy in preparing to meet these distant texts, and for this project we must be willing from the very beginning to reassess what we most take for granted" (*The Emptiness of Emptiness*, p. 11).

54. I follow a Gadamerian hermeneutic in its insistence, in the process of aesthetic, historical, or textual-linguistic interpretation, upon a relationship that he calls a "primordial relation of belonging" (*Zugehörigkeit*), rather than the alienating distancing (*Verfremdung*) that is valued in the sciences; see Paul Ricouer, *Hermeneutics and the Human Sciences*, pp. 64–65. I also subscribe to the insight, now a commonplace in the sciences, that the subject and object are always implicated in each other. I agree with Heidegger that "to understand a text is not to find a lifeless sense which is contained therein, but to unfold the possibility of being indicated by the text" (Ricouer, p. 56).

## CHAPTER TWO

1. Following common practice, I refer to this tradition as Tantric Buddhism, meaning the tradition that finds its fullest expression in *tantra* texts, in contrast to Mahāyāna, which finds its fullest expression in *sūtra* texts. This term has the advantage of linking this form of Buddhism to non-Buddhist Tantric movements. Technically Tantric Buddhism is a branch of Mahāyāna. The tradition does not provide one definitive name for itself, variously using the terms Secret Mantra (*guhyamantra*, Tib. *gsang-sngags*), Mantra Vehicle (*mantrayāna*, Tib. *sngags kyi theg-pa*), and Adamantine (or Diamond) Vehicle (*vajrayāna*, Tib. *rdo-rje theg-pa*). I use the term "Tantric Buddhism" to refer to the Indian phase of the movement and to the Tantric paradigm as a whole, whereas I use "Tibetan Buddhism" to refer to developments that took place in Tibet and survived in the Tibetan Buddhist cultural sphere.

2. Translation by Thomas Watters as cited by Kanai Lal Hazra in *Buddhism in India as Described by the Chinese Pilgrims,* AD. *399–689,* p. 46.

3. J. Takakusu, trans., *A Record of the Buddhist Religion as Practised in India and the Malay Archipelago (*A.D. *671–695), by I-Tsing,* pp. 177–78.

4. Evidence for this can be found in the form of rules for how property was to be distributed when a monk or nun died; see Kanai Lal Hazra, *Buddhism in India as Described by the Chinese Pilgrims,* AD *399–689,* pp. 44–45.

5. The incident was reported by Hsuan Tsang; see ibid., p. 97.

6. Although Tantric teachings and meditations were incorporated, practices that were inconsistent with the monastic vows would result in expulsion if they were discovered. An overview of the curriculum and important scholars of this period can be found in R. C. Majumdar, ed., *The Age of Imperial Kanauj,* pp. 270–75; and Kanai Lal Hazra, *Buddhism in India as Described by the Chinese Pilgrims,* AD *399–689,* pp. 36–44.

7. This observation has been made by Giuseppe Tucci, "Animadversiones Indicae," pp. 157–58; Bholanath Bhattacharya, "Some Aspects of the Esoteric Cults of Consort Worship in Bengal," *Folklore* 18, no. 10 (October 1977): 318; and Debiprasad Chattopadhyaya, *Lokayāta,* p. 323.

8. This version of his statement occurs in oral traditions, whereas according to another version he announced, after uniting with the low-caste arrow-maker, that now he had become a true *brāhmaṇa,* or priest; see Herbert Guenther, *The Royal Song of Saraha,* p. 6.

9. Slightly amended version of translation by David Snellgrove in Edward Conze, ed., *Buddhist Texts through the Ages,* p. 226. For the delivery of this lesson by Saraha's female companion, see Sonam Tobgay Kazi, *Tibet House Museum,* p. 29; and James Robinson, trans., *Buddha's Lions,* p. 43. The companion is not specified as the arrow-maker in these accounts, but the narratives are sketchy enough to make this omission inconclusive.

10. Translation by Robert Thurman, *Holy Teaching of Vimalakīrti,* p. 66.

11. Lakṣmīṅkarā, *Lhan cig skyes grub kyi gzhung 'grel,* sDe-dge 2261, fol. 10a.6–10b.1. Indrabhūti gave her name simply as Sahajavajra, or Lhan-cig skyes-pa'i rdo-rje, which has no gender marker, so from Indrabhūti's account it is impossible to tell that he is referring to a woman; see Indrabhūti, *Lhan cig skyes grub,* sDe-dge 2260, fol. 1b.2. Lakṣmīṅkarā appended Chang-'tshong-ma, "Wine-Selling Woman," to the name, indicating the woman's gender and livelihood.

12. A phenomenological description of the five poisons and wisdoms can be found in Ngakpa Chögyam, *Rainbow of Liberated Energy,* pp. 55–105.

13. Terms for "female Buddha" include *tathāgatā* (Tib. *de-bzhin gshegs-ma*); *jinā* (Tib. *rgyal-mo*); the Tibetan term *sangs-rgyas-ma;* the title *sangs-rgyas,* or "Buddha," before the name of a female deity; and *bhagavatī* (Tib. *bcom-ldan 'das-ma*), a title generally but not exclusively used for Buddhas. Western works typically label female Buddhas simply as the "partner," "spouse," "wife," or "consort" of their male counterpart, even when the female deity appears alone.

14. *Bahudhātuka-sutta* 3.65; slightly amended version of translation by Martin Willson, *In Praise of Tārā,* p. 23. This position apparently took several centuries to evolve. Tracing its occurrence in Pāli and Chinese texts, Yuichi Kajiyama dates the denial of the possibility of a female Buddha to between the late third

and first century B.C.E.; see "Women in Buddhism," pp. 56–58. Kajiyama also discusses the Mahāyāna views in this article.

15. See Diana Paul, *Women in Buddhism*, chaps. 5–6; and Nancy Schuster, "Changing the Female Body." Future research may reveal a female Buddha in Mahāyāna. Denial of female Buddhas in some Mahāyāna quarters suggests a belief in female Buddhas in others.

16. Slightly amended version of translation by Janice Willis in "Nuns and Benefactresses," p. 69.

17. A helpful analysis of Mahāyāna views on gender and women can be found in Rita Gross, *Buddhism After Patriarchy*, chaps. 5, 12.

18. *Caṇḍamahāroṣaṇa-tantra*, sDe-dge 431, fol. 319b.4–5: *lha mo sgyu 'phrul sras nyid kyang / khro bo gtum po bdag nyid yin / sa 'tsho khyod nyid bcom ldan 'das / shes rab phar phyin bdag nyid ma / ji snyed pa yi bud med kun / khyod kyi tshig nyid 'dir 'dod do.*

19. The Tibetan term for "blood-drinker" is *khrag-'thung*. Tibetan terms for wrathful deities include *lha khro-bo, lha khro-mo*, and *yi-dam khro-ba'i zhal lugs*.

20. Sahajayoginīcintā, *dNgos po gsal ba'i rjes su 'gro ba'i de kho na nyid grub pa*, sDe-dge 2222, fol. 67a.3–4: *bya ba rnams 'di ltar sgeg pa dang / dpa' ba dang / 'jigs su rung pa byed pa dang / snying rje dang / rngam pa dang / zhi ba la sogs pa'i 'dod chags dang / zhe sdang dang / dregs pa dang / ser sna dang / phrag dog la sogs pa cung zad skyes pa de dag ma lus par rang bzhin dag pa'i ye shes kyi rnam pa yongs su rdzogs pa yin no*. Her text is discussed more fully here in chap. 7.

21. Christopher George, trans., *The Caṇḍamahāroṣaṇa Tantra*, p. 66.

22. See David Snellgrove, *Indo-Tibetan Buddhism*, pp. 153–58, 294; Alexis Sanderson, "Śaivism and the Tantric Traditions," pp. 678–79, and "Vajrayana." The story of the origins of the *Cakrasaṃvara-tantra* strongly suggests the rapprochement with Hindu systems; see Bu-ston, *bDe mchog spyi rnam don gsal*. Since many of the Buddhist, Śaivite, and Śākta developments took written and iconographic form contemporaneously, it will be difficult in many cases to determine the origins of specific motifs and the directions of the influence.

23. For the emphasis on women in Śākta ideology and practice, see Sanjukta Gupta, "Women in the Śaiva/Śākta Ethos," pp. 206–8. In popular Śākta practice, the tendency of female deities to possess, or manifest through, women has been observed in northwestern India by Kathleen Erndl, *Victory to the Mother*, pp. 105, 109, 112f., 134.

24. These parallels are discussed here in chap. 3.

25. In the Hindu context the worship of women is designated *kumārīpūjā, nāyikāpūjā, yonipūjā*, and a range of other terms. The Buddhist version of the practice is discussed here in chap. 6.

26. Theoretical justification for worship of women is seen, for example, in *Kaulāvalīnirṇaya* 12.178–79: "If only one young woman is worshipped or seen, all the great goddesses have been worshipped by the supreme practitioner. One who doesn't worship a beloved woman (*kauthā*) incurs obstructions and loses whatever merit he has attained, what to speak of whatever [merit] he gets in his next birth."

27. André Padoux, "A Survey of Tantric Hinduism for the Historian of Religions," p. 347. He also states that "to posit as separate entities on the one hand

Śāktism . . . and, on the other, Tantric . . . is, I believe, to establish an unjustified distinction" (p. 347).

28. Documenting the pan-Asian range of Pāla Indian artistic influence is the theme of Susan Huntington and John Huntington, *Leaves from the "Bodhi" Tree.*

29. To mention just a few, the philosophical works of Śāntarakṣita, Haribhadra, Kamalaśīla, Dharmakīrti, and Jñānagarbha; the ethical classics of Śāntideva; Tantric works too numerous to mention, for which one simply needs to consult the Tantric portion (rGyud-sde) of the Tibetan canons (bKa'-'gyur and bsTan-'gyur); and the Tantric scholastic overviews of the polymath Abhayākaragupta.

## CHAPTER THREE

1. Christopher George, *The Caṇḍamahāroṣaṇa Tantra*, critical edition, p. 103: *gzungs ma yid 'ong 'di khyod kyis / bsten byar sangs rgyas rnams kyis gsungs / rmongs pa gang zhig 'da' byed pa / de la mchog gi dngos grub med.*

2. David Snellgrove, *Indo-Tibetan Buddhism*, p. 287.

3. Alan Sponberg, "Attitudes toward Women and the Feminine in Early Buddhism," p. 28. See also Hanna Havnevik, *Tibetan Buddhist Nuns*, p. 35.

4. Sudhir Kakar, *Shamans, Mystics and Doctors*, p. 153. This claim is also made for Buddhism as a whole, generally in the form of blanket assertions of the male authorship and ideological ownership of all Buddhist texts, as recently reasserted by José Cabezón when he states that "by examining the textual traditions we are for the most part examining culture as seen through the eyes *of men*"; emphasis his, "Mother Wisdom, Father Love," p. 189.

5. *Cakrasaṃvara-tantra*, Mal translation, fol. 15b.3–4 (lines corresponding to sDe-dge 368, fol. 231a.1–2): *bdag gi pho nya ma kun 'gro / pho nya ma de kun grub ster / mthong ba dang de ni reg pa dang / tsum ba na dang rtag par 'khyud / rnal 'byor gnas ni khyad par nyid / ji srid rnal 'byor ma yi tshogs / thams cad dngos grub byed par bshad / bde can kun la sbyin bya yi.*

6. Ibid., fol. 16a.5–6 (lines corresponding to sDe-dge 368, fol. 231b.4–5): *rab dga' nyid dang dngos grub ni / zhing rnams gnas su grub pa yi / mkha' 'gro ma dag rnam par gnas / der gnas pa yi 'zlas pa bya / zas rnyed pa ni gnyis pa'o / de ni rol par yang dag gnas.*

7. Monier Monier-Williams, *A Sanskrit-English Dictionary*, p. 858a.

8. The etymology of *ḍākinī* remains a puzzle. One of the most promising suggestions is a derivation from the root √*ḍī*, meaning "to fly," a derivation that is supported by its translation into Tibetan as *mkha'-'gro-ma*, literally, "woman who travels in the sky." For a detailed history of non-Buddhist and Buddhist uses of the term, see Adelheid Hermann-Pfandt, *Ḍākinīs*, pp. 115–18.

9. The Sanskrit term *dūtī* (Tib. *pho-nya-mo*), is often abbreviated in Tibetan as *pho-nya*, without the feminine suffix, since there is no masculine equivalent with which it might be confused. For a discussion of this term, see Alex Wayman, "Messengers, What Bring Ye?"

10. The "heroine" or *vīrā* (Tib. *dpa'-mo*) has a masculine counterpart, the hero (*vīra*, Tib. *dpa'-bo*).

11. Christopher George, *The Caṇḍamahāroṣaṇa Tantra*, critical edition, p. 33:

*saṃsevayet striyaṃ / striyaḥ svargaḥ striyo dharmaḥ striya eva paraṃ tapaḥ / striyo buddhaḥ striyaḥ saṃghaḥ prajñāpāramitā striyaḥ.*

12. Critical edition by Malati Shendge, *Advayasiddhi*, verse 21, p. 19: *sarvavarṇasamudbhūtā jugupsā naiva yoṣita / saiva bhagavatī prajñā sa(ṃ)vṛtyā rūpamāśritā.* The Tibetan translation neutralizes *jugupsā*, meaning to censure, denigrate, or disrespect, by rendering it as *brtag-bya*, meaning to discriminate; sDe-dge 2220, fol. 61b.5.

13. Critical edition by Malati Shendge, *Advayasiddhi*, verses 4–5, p. 15: *jananībhaginīścaiva duhitṛbhāginehikān / prajnopāya-vidhānena pūjayedyogavit sadā / ekāṁgavikalāṁ hīnāṁ śilpinīṁ śvapacikāṁ tathā / yoṣitām pūy*[should be *j*]*ayet nityam jnāna-vajraprabhāvanaih.*

14. See chap. 6, section entitled "Union as Worship of the Female Partner."

15. Christopher George, *The Caṇḍamahāroṣaṇa Tantra*, critical edition, p. 32: *yāvad dhi dṛṣyate loke strīrūpaṃ bhuvanatraye / tan madīyaṃ mataṃ rūpam.* This *yoginī-tantra* was important in India and has remained important for the Vajrācāryas in Nepal and the Sa-skya sect in Tibet. The Sa-skya sect maintains a Caṇḍamahāroṣaṇa transmission lineage as part of the *rGyud sde kun btus.*

16. Christopher George, trans., *Caṇḍamahāroṣaṇa Tantra*, pp. 81–83.

17. Skt. *devatāgarva*; Tib. *lha'i nga-rgyal, yi-dam nga-rgyal*, or *yi-dam lha'i nga-rgyal.*

18. Christopher George, *The Caṇḍamahāroṣaṇa Tantra*, critical edition, p. 96: *bud med gang gis nga mi shes / bud med kun gyi lus la gnas / bdag ni de rnams phan don phyir.*

19. Ibid., p. 121: *bdag gi gzugs ni bsgom byas nas / nga rgyal mchog 'di byas gyur na / gal te tshangs 'joms de yang ni / sdig pa yis ni gos mi 'gyur / . . . . / rtse med g.yo dang khro ba dang / gsod pa'i don phyir sems dpa' can / rnal 'byor sdig pas gos mi 'gyur.*

20. For a suggestive personal account of the benefits that a contemporary woman has derived from meditating on a female deity, see Rita Gross, "I Will Never Forget to Visualize that Vajrayoginī Is My Body and Mind." Anne Klein has clarified that women aspiring to progress on the Buddhist path need both ontological deconstruction, or "an ontological critique of the self," and psychological affirmation, or "an appropriately functioning psychological self"; see "Finding a Self," p. 194. Klein provides a vocabulary for distinguishing between the ontological and psychological levels at which identification with deity can function, as it serves both to deconstruct the unenlightened self and, on the psychological level, to dismantle conventional patterns of unenlightened experience while recovering, or creating, positive modes of thought and behavior.

21. Christopher George, *The Caṇḍamahāroṣaṇa Tantra*, critical edition, p. 28: *strīm ekāṃ jananīṃ khalu trijagatāṃ satsaukhyadātrīṃ śivāṃ / . . . . / kin tu vācyo guṇaḥ strīṇāṃ sarvasattvaparigrahaḥ / kāpā vā yadi vā rakṣā strīṇāṃ citte pratiṣṭhitā / āstāṃ tāvat svajanaṃ parajanam api puṣṇāti bhikṣayā / sā ced evaṃrūpā nānyatā strī vajrayoginyā.*

22. Ibid., p. 27: *kalpayet svastriyan tāvat tava rūpeṇa nirbharāṃ / gāḍhenaivātiyogena yathaiva sphuṭatāṃ vrajet.*

23. George Roerich, trans., *Blue Annals*, p. 701.

24. Martin Willson, *In Praise of Tārā*, p. 197.

25. Slightly amended version of translation by Lama Chimpa that appears in Tāranātha, *History of Buddhism in India*, p. 281.

26. Ibid., pp. 281–82.

27. This genre of passage, generally spoken by a female deity, identifies women and goddesses and on this basis urges respect and worship of women and extends threats for mistreating or failing to honor women. Non-Buddhist examples can be found in *Kulacūḍāmani-tantra* 3.46–57; *Kaulāvalīnirṇaya* 10.66, 10.82, 10.87, 10.91, 15.104–5; *Lakṣmī-tantra* 43.60–65, 43.70–72; and *Kulārṇava-tantra* 11.62–65. *Kaulāvalīnirṇaya* 12.179 extends its penalties to the omission of worship, in addition to the commission of transgressions.

28. *Cakrasaṃvara-tantra*, sDe-dge 368, fol. 229b.5: *dam tshig can gang rjes chags pa / dpa' bo'i longs spyod sa gzhi yin / gzhi ni sa gzhir byas nas su / rnal 'byor pa yi sdom pa mchod.*

29. This comparison of the female partner and the earth should not be mistaken for the Western equation of woman-as-nature versus man-as-culture that has been made explicit by Sherry Ortner in "Is Female to Male as Nature is to Culture?" In the Indian context, the *śakti*, or life force, that is present in the earth and also in women vivifies culture and social institutions like the family, religious ritual, and kingship, as well as biological growth, the seasons, and cosmic rhythms; see Frédérique Marglin, "Gender and the Unitary Self."

30. gNyan Phu-chung-pa, *Mu tig phreng ba*, p. 334.2.4–5: *byin gyis rlob byed kyi rnal 'byor mar ngo shes shing sgrub pa po la mnyes kyang rnal 'byor ma dang chags bar byas nas ma mchod na / sgrub pa po la byin gyis mi rlob cing dngos grub mi 'byung bas.* Tantric Buddhists use the term *adhiṣṭhāna* where Hindus would use *śakti*, that is, to express the power or energy that women can bestow upon men, strengthening them psychically. *Adhiṣṭhāna* has a wide range of applications in the Buddhist context and is not always linked to gender, whereas *śakti* generally has a gender connotation. Tibetan translations of *śakti* include *mthu*, meaning "power" or "energy," and *nus-pa*, which generally refers to spiritual ability or power that a practitioner has attained through religious discipline.

31. gNyan Phu-chung-pa, *Mu tig phreng ba*, p. 334.3.3–4.1.

32. "Behavior of the left" translates the Tibetan translation (*g.yon-pa'i spyod*) of *vāmācāra*, a term that is generally interpreted in secondary works on Hindu Tantra as referring to the non-Vedic or heterodox nature of Tantra. Debiprasad Chattopadhyaya reads *vāmācāra* not as *vāma-ācāra*, "practice of the left," implying a perverse, impure, or reverse practice, but as *vāmā-ācāra*, "practice centering on women," in *Lokāyata*, p. 65. The Tibetan translation, using the word "left," suggests that Buddhist sources read *vāmācāra* as "practice of the left," but Buddhist uses of the term nonetheless link it solely to interactions with women and the symbolism of femaleness.

33. Activities to be done on or from the left are specified by Tsongkhapa on fol. 308.5–309.2. See *Cakrasaṃvara-tantra*, chap. 28 (and chap. 20 regarding the secret signs), and Tsongkhapa, *sBas don kun gsal*, fol. 275.5f., on the eight vows of *yogini-tantra*. Tsongkhapa cites differing explanations of why the left side is associated with women, e.g., because women give birth with the left leg

stretched out, and they give birth to all things just as emptiness gives rise to all things; see fol. 309.3–310.6.

34. Tsongkhapa, ibid., fol. 309.3–4: *g.yon pa'i kun spyod bsngags pa'i rgyu mtshan ji ltar yin.*

35. Ibid., fol. 311.2–3: *mkha' 'gro ma'i pho nya mo mang po zhig g.yon pa'i kun spyod la dgyes shing bya ba des 'jug pas / gyon pa'i kun spyod de rnams dang mthun bar spyad pas de dag yid dga' bar 'gyur ba dang yin no.*

36. Ibid., fol. 280.4–5: *bud med dag ni mthong ba na / g.yon nas lan gsum bskor bya zhing / spyi pos phyag ni byas nas kyang / lan gsum bar du gsol ba gdab / khyod ma bdag ni bu yin te / ji srid byang chub'byung bar du / byang chub yan lag nu ma las / byung ba'i rang gi o mas skyangs zhes kyang gsungs te / gsol gdab ni.* Tsongkhapa does not identify the Indian commentary or commentaries he is citing here.

37. The root vow is "unite well with a powerful woman" (*bud med dbang phyug legs bar sbyor*), *Cakrasaṃvara-tantra*, sDe-dge 368, fol. 231.5–6; Tsongkhapa comments in *sBas don kun gsal*, fol. 283.4–5.

38. Tsongkhapa, ibid., fol. 226.6–227.1: *dpa' bo ste ming po dang / sring mor shes par byed pa ni brda 'di dag gis rang dang mkha' 'gro ma rnams yid shing tu nye bar byed pa'i don / . . . 'di rnams grub pa'i rnal 'byor ma rnams kyi brdar bshad pa ltar yin pas / dnyos grub brnyes pa'i pho nya mo'i brda yin no.*

39. These are among the many messages for which signs are described in *Cakrasaṃvara-tantra*, chaps. 20, 22, 24. See also *Hevajra-tantra*, chap. 7.

40. See *Cakrasaṃvara-tantra*, chap. 23.

41. Terms used in Tantric Buddhist literature to express a man's reliance and dependence on a woman as his religious refuge are *niśraya*, *āśraya*, and *anubhava* (Tib. *brten-pa*). Honor and service is *sevā* (Tib. *bsten-pa*), reverence and devotion are *bhakti* and *śraddhā* (Tib. *gus-pa, dad-pa, dad-mos*), devotional servitude is *upāsanā* and *upacāra* (Tib. *bsnyen-bskur*), giving gifts is *dāna* (Tib. *sbyin-pa*), and ritual worship is *pūjā* (Tib. *mchod-pa*).

42. *Caṇḍamahāroṣaṇa-tantra*, sDe-dge 431, opening of chap. 10.

43. An illuminating discussion of this vow can be found in Rita Gross, *Buddhism after Patriarchy*, pp. 100–102.

44. *Caṇḍamahāroṣaṇa-tantra*, sDe-dge 431, fol. 318b.3–5: *de nyid gal te sdug bsngal gyur / 'chi dang 'ching ba'i 'jigs pa yang / de rnams thams cad bzod bya yis / 'dir ni bud med spang mi bya / . . . / g.yo dang spobs can 'tsher ngo bral / rtag tu 'dod pa'i dpung gnyen no / dngos grub ster ba 'di nyid ne / dngos po kun gyis bsten par bya.*

45. Ibid., fol. 319a.1–2: *bud med smad par yong mi bya / . . . / snyan pa 'chag gis smra bya zhing / rjes su mthun par sbyin bar bya / dngos po kun gyis phyag byas te / ji bzhin gdug can shes mi bya / gang du'ang bud med mi spong ba / 'di ni sangs rgyas gsung du thos / gang du khyod kyis gzhan byas nas / de yi sdig pas dmyal bar 'gyur.*

46. Tsongkhapa, *sBas don kun gsal*, fol. 294.6: *pho nya la zhe sdang bskyed na / byang chub tu sems bskyed nas bskal pa bye bar bsod nams kyi tshogs bsags pa yang skad cig la 'joms pas.* Tsongkhapa cites Lvavapa and Lha-sbas as his sources for this view.

47. Translation by Christopher George, *The Caṇḍamahāroṣaṇa Tantra*, p. 79.

48. See n. 27.

49. *Kaulāvalīnirṇaya* 10.69: *strīṇaṃ śatāparādhena puṣpeṇāpi na tāṅyet.*

50. Translation by Christopher George, *The Caṇḍamahāroṣaṇa Tantra*, p. 70.

51. Ibid., p. 66.

52. Slightly amended version of translation by Mark Tatz in "The Life of the Siddha-Philosopher Maitrīgupta," p. 705. In a recent case of erasure of the female founders of Tantric Buddhism, a work by a Western author attributes these acts and words to a man; see Jampa Thaye, *A Garland of Gold*, pp. 35–36.

53. Mark Tatz, "The Life of the Siddha-Philosopher Maitrīgupta," pp. 704–5, 709; Tāranātha, *Mystic Tales of Lāmā Tārānātha*, p. 9.

54. Tāranātha, *Tāranātha's Life of Kṛṣṇācārya/Kāṇha*, pp. 9–11, 13.

55. Tāranātha, *Seven Instruction Lineages*, pp. 70–72, supplemented by dPa'-bo gTsug-lag, *Dam pa'i chos kyis 'khor lo bsgyur ba rnams kyi byung ba gsal bar byed pa mkhas pa'i dga' ston*, p. 1496, a reference kindly shared with me by Pema Losang Chogyen of Columbia University. The account by dPa'-bo gTsug-lag (ca. 1504–66) differs slightly from and apparently represents a different tradition from that of Tāranātha. These incidents also occur in the account of Sum-pa mKhan-po (1704–88), although his account follows that of Tāranātha.

56. There are parallel classifications of men, although these are less detailed. For classifications of men, see Christopher George, trans., *Caṇḍamahāroṣaṇa Tantra*, pp. 63, 85, and David Snellgrove, *The Hevajra Tantra*, vol. 1, pp. 118–19.

57. The concept and some of the terms of the classification of women (*nāyikāprakāra*, Tib. *bu-med-rtags*) were adopted from secular Indian *kāmaśāstra* literature, wherein they have been featured since their appearance in the earliest surviving erotic manual, the *Kāmasūtra* of Vātsyāyana (third century C.E.). Other classical works of this genre are the *Ratirahasya* by Kokkoka and the *Anaṅgaraṅga* by Kalyāṇamalla. The secular literature classifies men and women (*nāyakanāyikābheda*) according to their physical and psychological traits, rating their suitability as sexual partners for one another. For an overview of these schemes, see Ram Kumar Rai, *Encyclopedia of Indian Erotics*, pp. 143ff. Although the Tantrics pattern some of their classification schemes on this secular branch of study, they adapted the inherited model to reflect their own religious values.

58. dGe-lugs oral commentary on *sBas don kun gsal*.

59. These are the women of different Buddha families, albeit not the standard set of five, as described in *Cakrasaṃvara-tantra*, chap. 18.

60. These types of yoginis are described in *Cakrasaṃvara-tantra*, chap. 19.

61. Ibid., Mal translation, fol. 15b.3–4 (lines corresponding to sDe-dge 368, fol. 238a.6–7): *gal te dpa' bo mi 'jigs na / lag pa g.yon pas bzung nas ni / rang gi gnas su khyer bar byed / mi rnams mkha' 'dro de dag dang / rtag tu mngon par rtse byed de / bde ba can gyi gnas 'drar 'gyur.*

62. Slightly edited version of translation by Lama Chimpa in Alaka Chattopadhyaya, *Atīśa and Tibet*, pp. 407–8.

63. George Roerich, trans., *Blue Annals*, p. 242.

64. For the story of Saraha and the arrow-making yogini according to Karma Phrin-las-pa, see Herbert Guenther, *The Royal Song of Saraha*, pp. 5–7.

65. Abhayadatta identifies the woman only as a servant girl in his account of this incident; see James Robinson, trans., *Buddha's Lions*, p. 43. A disjuncture

between the accounts by Karma Phrin-las-pa and Abhayadatta makes it difficult to determine if the same woman is intended in both accounts. What links them is that the women are Saraha's spiritual mentors in both accounts and deliver closely similar lessons on nonduality.

66. Translated by David Snellgrove in Edward Conze, ed., *Buddhist Texts through the Ages*, p. 238.

67. Keith Dowman, *Masters of Mahāmudrā*, p. 34.

68. James Robinson, trans., *Buddha's Lions*, pp. 216–17; Keith Dowman, *Masters of Mahāmudrā*, pp. 325–26; and Sonam Tobgay Kazi, *Tibet House Museum*, pp. 48–49.

69. Translation by Keith Dowman in *Masters of Enchantment*, p. 163.

70. Ibid., p. 162.

71. *Guhyasamāja-tantra* 5.6; critical edition by Yukei Matsunaga, p. 15: *mātṛbhaginīputrīś ca kāmayed yas tu sādhakaḥ / sa siddhiṃ vipulāṃ gacchen mahāyānāgradharmatām.*

72. *Cakrasaṃvara-tantra*, Mal translation, fol. 17a.6–7 (lines corresponding to sDe-dge 368, fol. 233a.1–2): *ma dang sring mo bu mo dang / chung ma pho nya mo nyid gnas / . . . / 'khor los de bzhin grub pa la / gzhan du bya ba ma yin no.*

73. Ibid., fol. 17b.4–5 (lines corresponding to sDe-dge 368, fol. 233a.7): *dam tshig la gnas mkha' 'gro mar / gang gis yang dag shes 'gyur ba'o / ming po'am yang na pha dang ni / bdag po nyid du skad cig mthong.*

74. See Tsongkhapa, *sBas don kun gsal*, fol. 279.1f. Other sets of correspondences can also be found in scholastic treatises. Casting the female relatives as levels of insight or other doctrinal categories helped this tradition adapt in a monastic context. For example, in his Guhyasamāja exegesis the philosopher Candrakīrti holds that the mother corresponds to *dharmakāya*, the sister to *sambhogakāya*, and the daughter to *nirmāṇakāya*; see Alex Wayman, *The Buddhist Tantras*, pp. 191–92. Alternate exegeses can be found in G. W. Farrow and I. Menon, trans. and ed., *The Concealed Essence of the Hevajra Tantra*, pp. 257, 269–70.

75. Christopher George, trans., *The Caṇḍamahāroṣaṇa Tantra*, p. 74.

76. Keith Dowman, *Sky Dancer*, pp. 259–60.

77. David Snellgrove, *The Hevajra Tantra*, vol. 1, p. 17.

78. Mircea Eliade, *Yoga: Immortality and Freedom*, p. 261, n. 204.

79. Keith Dowman, *Sky Dancer*, p. 259.

80. Mircea Eliade, *Yoga: Immortality and Freedom*, p. 261, n. 204. Eliade's view is widely accepted and espoused in literature on this subject.

81. The qualifications of female practitioners are discussed in chap. 6.

82. Frédérique Marglin, *Wives of the God-King*, pp. 98, 231–32, 290–91, 302–3.

83. This power represents, in Marglin's terms, a "transformative principle" rather than a dualistic hierarchical principle; Frédérique Marglin, *Wives of the God-King*, pp. 21, 298–99.

84. Kathleen Erndl makes some valuable observations on low-caste women in *Victory to the Mother*, pp. 99–101.

85. Translations of their biography can be found in James Robinson, trans., *Buddha's Lions*, pp. 34–35, and Tāranātha, *Seven Instruction Lineages*, pp. 19–23.

86. See Keith Dowman, *Masters of Mahāmudrā*, p. 57.

87. He highlights this in the first verse of his work; see the translation by Malati Shendge, "*Śrīsahajasiddhi*," p. 145.

88. Tāranātha, *Seven Instruction Lineages*, p. 22.

89. Her name appears as "Ḍombiṇī" in the colophon. The song occurs in a Newari manuscript of the *caryāgīti*. The manuscript, a four-hundred-year-old copy of a much older text, is owned by Ratna Kaji Vajracharya, a Newari priest in Kathmandu, Nepal, who was kind enough to share it with me.

90. Songs attributed to Ḍombīpa can be found in sDe-dge 2368 and scattered throughout other canonical anthologies.

91. Tāranātha reports that Ḍombīyoginī figures in two Hevajra lineages. One is traced from Ḍombīpa through Ḍombīyoginī to Ratnavajra and Kāṇha; the other is traced from Ḍombīyoginī through Caryāpa, a "yoginī of Singhala" (Sri Lanka), Durjayacandra, and Rahulavajra; see *Seven Instruction Lineages*, pp. 22–23.

92. Rita Gross, *Buddhism after Patriarchy*, parts 2 and 3.

93. Insightful analyses of the range of attitudes toward women expressed in early Buddhist writings can be found in Alan Sponberg, "Attitudes toward Women and the Feminine in Early Buddhism," and Rita Gross, *Buddhism after Patriarchy*, chap. 4.

94. *Caṇḍamahāroṣaṇa-tantra*, sDe-dge 431, fol. 318b.4: *'dir ni bud med spang mi bya*.

## CHAPTER FOUR

1. Tāranātha, *Tāranātha's Life of Kṛṣṇācārya/Kāṇha*, p. 63.

2. George Roerich, trans., *Blue Annals*, pp. 915–20.

3. Tāranātha, *Seven Instruction Lineages*, pp. 54–55. One of the two male students was Śāntigupta, who was the teacher of Tāranātha's teacher, which is why so much information about the various students was available to Tāranātha. It is fortunate for later historians that he preserved so many of the details with which he was entrusted.

4. Ibid., p. 100.

5. Ibid., p. 25. Her story is also related by Lakṣmīṅkarā, *Lhan cig skyes grub kyi gzhung 'grel*, sDe-dge 2261, fol. 6b.5–8a.3, under the name Rol-pa-mo (Skt. Līlādevī), but the biography is the same, and Tāranātha cites Lakṣmīṅkarā's work as one of his sources.

6. According to Tāranātha, there were "five hundred"—i.e., many—yoginis in his circle, along with five hundred yogis, and they all attained supernatural powers; Tāranātha, *Tāranātha's Life of Kṛṣṇācārya/Kāṇha*, p. 104.

7. Takpo Tashi Namgyal, *Mahāmudrā*, p. 118.

8. Elisabeth Schüssler Fiorenza has critiqued the reading of generic language as if it were gender-specific language referring only to men in the context of New Testament studies and concludes, as a general principle, that "a historically adequate analysis must take into account that androcentric language functions as generic language until proven otherwise. . . . Those passages . . . that

directly mention women cannot be interpreted as providing all the information on women." See "The 'Quilting' of Women's History," pp. 38–40.

9. The provision by a reader of information and organizing schema that are not present in a text is a well-known and extensively researched phenomenon, often discussed under the rubric of "schema theory." For a useful guide to the literature that highlights the role of gender in this process, see Mary Crawford and Roger Chaffin, "The Reader's Construction of Meaning."

10. A similar psychology of translation is at work in the translation of Vedic sources, where the dual form of "father," *pitarau*, and the plural, *pitaraḥ*, meaning "parents," are consistently translated as "fathers."

11. For an application of this principle, see Reginald Ray, "Accomplished Women in Tantric Buddhism of Medieval India and Tibet," p. 228, where he asserts without the benefit of any statistics that "there were always far fewer women Tantric practitioners than men."

12. Even when extensive information is available to historians, a process of selection will be at work. For example, in historical accounts written in modern America, which presumably is much more advanced in its record-keeping practices than medieval India, women have an extremely low rate of representation. A survey of American history textbooks in use in the 1980s revealed that an average of 2 percent of each text was devoted to coverage of women, despite the fact that women have had prominent, documented leadership roles in suffrage movements, civil rights, labor history, education, social services, and religious and mission history. See Dolores Schmidt and Earl Schmidt, "The Invisible Woman."

13. Songs that Padmalocanā, Jñānalocanā, and Śavari sang to "Advayavajra," i.e., Maitrīpa, are preserved as *Phyag rgya chen po rdo rje'i glu zhes bya ba*, sDe-dge 2287.

14. The erasure of women from historical records continues to the present day. In a recent work by a Western author, the words and actions of these two women are credited to Śavari, the male guru; see Jampa Thaye, *A Garland of Gold*, p. 36.

15. On Tāranātha's historiography, see David Templeman, "Tāranātha the Historian."

16. For a discussion of soteriology and magical ritual in Tantric Buddhism, see Stephan Beyer, *The Cult of Tārā*, pp. 92–94, 245–51, 277–79, 303.

17. Tāranātha, *Seven Instruction Lineages*, pp. 99–100. Her story is preserved in some detail by Tāranātha because Tāranātha's three gurus studied with her. The spelling of Dinakarā or -ī, meaning "one who makes or brings light," seems more likely than Tāranātha's Dīnakarā, meaning "one who distresses or makes miserable." Tāranātha's mishandling of Sanskrit spellings is consistent enough to justify a correction here.

18. Ibid., p. 22; and James Robinson, trans., *Buddha's Lions*, p. 35.

19. Tāranātha, *Tāranātha's Life of Kṛṣṇācārya/Kāṇha*, pp. 62–63.

20. Tāranātha, *Seven Instruction Lineages*, p. 12.

21. Tāranātha, *Tāranātha's Life of Kṛṣṇācārya/Kāṇha*, pp. 65–67.

22. Ibid., p. 74.

23. George Roerich, trans., *Blue Annals*, p. 368.

24. Martin Willson, *In Praise of Tārā*, p. 205. Willson spells the guru's name as Lokapradāpa or Lokapradhā, but since neither is a documented Sanskrit word, I have amended the name to the more likely Lokapradīpa here.

25. George Roerich, trans., *Blue Annals*, p. 368. Without more information it is not possible to ascertain if they were prostitutes (*veśyā*) or courtesans (*gaṇikā*), since Tibetan translators use the generic term *smad-tshong-ma*.

26. Martin Willson, *In Praise of Tārā*, p. 194.

27. Tāranātha, *Seven Instruction Lineages*, p. 90.

28. Tāranātha, *Tāranātha's Life of Kṛṣṇācārya/Kāṇha*, p. 73.

29. Ibid., p. 100.

30. See discussion here in chap. 5.

31. Yaśodattā, *'Phags pa 'jam dpal rin po che'i cho ga*, sDe-dge 2588; and Yaśobhadrā, *'Phags pa 'jam dpal gyi sgrub pa'i thabs*, sDe-dge 2587.

32. Women are usually included in the standard sequence of things to be mastered, but Lakṣmīṅkarā omits women from one of her lists; see *rNal 'byor ma'i sgrub pa'i thabs*, sDe-dge 1547, fol. 96a.4, where, unless there is a scribal error, she eliminates the recitation of the mantra two hundred thousand times.

33. *rTa mgrin gyi sgrub thabs*, sDe-dge 2142.

34. *'Phags pa 'jig rten dbang phyug gsang ba'i sgrub thabs*, sDe-dge 2140.

35. *Tshe dpag tu med pa'i sbyin sreg gi cho ga zhes bya ba*, sDe-dge 2144.

36. [*Togs pa brjod ba mkha' 'gro ma'i gsang mdzod na gnas pa*], sDe-dge 2450, fol. 87b4–5: *kho la ma lta nga la ltos / nga ni ye shes chen po yin / kho ni nga yi sprul pa yin / gnyis med ye shes blo las 'das*.

37. Tib. *tshogs kyi 'khor-lo* and *tshogs kyi mchod-pa*.

38. These practices are the topic of chaps. 6 and 7, here.

39. The feast is explicitly cited in this regard by Mircea Eliade in *Yoga: Immortality and Freedom*, p. 261, n. 204, in his reference to the cakra, or "Tantric wheel"; Shiníchi Tsuda, "'Vajrayoṣidbhageṣu Vijahāra,'" p. 607; and David Snellgrove, *Indo-Tibetan Buddhism*, p. 168.

40. As is often the case for collections of songs in the Tibetan canon, sDe-dge 2450 does not have a formal title. The colophon says they are "songs of realization from a secret ḍākinī treasury": *rtogs ba brjod ba mkha' 'gro ma'i gsang mdzod na gnas pa*.

41. *dPal rdo rje mkha' 'gro ma'i mgur zhes bya ba*, sDe-dge 2441. The Tibetan name of this cremation ground is Ha Ha sGrogs-pa.

42. Tāranātha, *Tāranātha's Life of Kṛṣṇācārya/Kāṇha*, p. 65.

43. In some descriptions in classical literature, equal numbers of men and women are required for a feast. In other instances, women preside over the feast and men may be invited to attend. In all cases, women are present in numbers at least equal to the men. Adelheid Hermann-Pfandt has traced the male appropriation of this women's practice; see *Ḍākinīs*, chap. 10.

44. For information on Jvālāmukhī, a pilgrimage site shared by both Hindus and Tantric Buddhists, see Kathleen Erndl, *Victory to the Mother*, pp. 44–48.

45. The yogi was rGod-tshang-pa mGon-po rdo-rje (born 1189 C.E.); see George Roerich, trans., *Blue Annals*, p. 682. A longer version of the story ap-

pears in Giuseppe Tucci, "Travels of Tibetan Pilgrims in the Swat Valley," pp. 380–81.

46. Tāranātha, *Tāranātha's Life of Kṛṣṇācārya/Kāṇha*, p. 13.

47. George Roerich, trans., *Blue Annals*, p. 242. Chattopadyaya notes that there is nothing to corroborate 'Gos Lotsaba's report that Atīśa practiced in Uḍḍiyāna for three years, but neither is the report contradicted or cast into doubt by anything else that is known about his career; Alaka Chattopadhyaya, *Atīśa and Tibet*, p. 76.

48. Tāranātha, *Seven Instruction Lineages*, p. 8.

49. *mKha' 'gro ma'i 'jam glu ring mo zhes bya*, sDe-dge 2451.

50. *Hevajra-tantra* I.vii.8–9, translated from the critical edition in David Snellgrove, *The Hevajra Tantra*, vol. 2, p. 22: *mālām abhipreṣitāṃ kṛtvā samaye tistha suvratā / bhajeti tatra melāyaṃ divya-gocaram āśritya / yad (dhi) vadanti yoginyas tat sarvan (eva) kartavyaṃ.*

51. David Snellgrove, trans., *The Hevajra Tantra*, vol. 1, pp. 115–16.

52. See, for example, Kalhaṇa, *Rājataraṅgiṇī* 2.104, 2.108; and Somadeva, *Kathāsaritsāgara* 2.104, 2.106, 3.49, 3.95, 9.58, 9.63. These terms are generally translated into English as such colorful but misleading phrases as "band of witches" or "sorceress convention."

53. Kalhaṇa, *Rājataraṅgiṇī* 2.98–109. Another description of a women's nocturnal gathering for mantra, ritual, and sacrament that bears parallels to Buddhist yogini-circles is the story of the yogini-queen Kuvalayāvalī in *Kathāsaritsāgara* 2.98–112.

54. The Tibetan term for female Buddha is *sangs-rgyas-ma*, a title frequently applied to Tārā in the Tantric context, although in the Mahāyāna context she remains a bodhisattva.

55. George Roerich, trans., *Blue Annals*, p. 851. Black Bhairava is also known as Kṛṣṇayamāri, Tib. gShin-rje-gshed nag-po.

56. Tāranātha, *Seven Instruction Lineages*, p. 100.

57. Ibid., p. 22.

58. Ibid., p. 26.

59. sDe-dge nos. 2587 and 2588.

60. *'Phags pa 'jam dpal ngag gi rgyal po'i sgrub thabs*, sDe-dge 3442. This form of Mañjuśrī is also known as Vāgrāja and Vādirāja.

61. The contributions of Vajravatī, Lakṣmīṅkarā, Mekhalā, and Kanakhalā are discussed here in chap. 5.

62. Tāranātha, *Tāranātha's Life of Kṛṣṇācārya/Kāṇha*, p. 65. Women continue to master this attainment to the present day; for recent examples, see Hanna Havnevik, *Tibetan Buddhist Nuns*, pp. 70–73.

63. These are discussed here in chap. 6.

64. Niguma's works, or works recording Niguma's oral instructions, on the inner yogas are the [*Thabs lam sgom pa'i rnal 'byor*], Peking 4648; [*Thabs lam gtum mo sgom pa*], Peking 4647; [*rTsa kha 'byed pa'i man ngag*], Peking 4645; [*rTsa rlung la sogs sgom pa*], Peking 4646; and [*Rang lus rtsa yi 'khor lo*], Peking 4649.

65. *Rim pa lnga'i don gsal bar byed pa zhes bya ba*, sDe-dge 1842.

66. *gYung drung 'khyil ba gsum gyi zhal gdams kyi nyams len zhes bya ba*, sDe-dge 2415, discussed here in chap. 5.

67. Tāranātha, *Tāranātha's Life of Kṛṣṇācārya/Kāṇha*, pp. 73–74.

68. *Urgyen gyi rim pa'i sgrol ma'i sgrub thabs zhes bya ba*, sDe-dge 1711, fol. 74b.3: *'di yi rnal 'byor ma yi rnal 'byor gyis.*

69. Tantric songs are variously called *dohā*, *caryāgīti*, and *vajragīti*. Some songs are straightforward and didactic descriptions of enlightened awareness. These songs employ a special vocabulary, shared with *mahāmudrā* and *rdzogs-chen* literature, that utilizes terms with the prefix *rang-*, meaning "self," or "innate," indicating something that inherently or spontaneously has a certain characteristic or quality. For discussions of this terminology, see Takpo Tashi Namgyal, *Mahāmudrā*; Samten Karmay, *The Great Perfection (rDzogs-chen)*; and John Reynolds, *Self-Liberation through Seeing with Naked Awareness.*

70. The term *rdzogs-chen* is additionally used in Tibetan literature. The terms have been accepted as synonymous in regard to the goal, but different in terms of the methods used to reach that goal. *Mahāmudrā* (Tib. *phyag-rgya chen-po*) is generally associated with the gSar-ma schools and *rdzogs-pa chen-po* with the rNying-ma sect. For discussion of rNying-ma views on the Indian origins of *rdzogs-chen*, see Samten Karmay, *The Great Perfection (rDzogs chen)*, pp. 137–42, 144f., 197–200. Tibetan debates regarding the history and technicalities of various *mahāmudrā* teachings are analyzed by David Ruegg, *Buddha-Nature, Mind and the Problem of Gradualism in a Comparative Perspective.*

71. *Rang grol phyag rgya chen po zhes bya ba*, Peking 4641, fol. 162b.8–163a.6: *gang yang yid la mi bya bar / ma bcos snyug ma'i nang du bzhag / rang sems ma yengs chos kyi sku / de la ma yengs sgom pa'i gnad / mtha' bral chen por rtog par bya / . . . . / ji ltar dangs pa'i rgya mtsho la / chu sbur byung zhing chu la thim / de bzhin rnam par rtog pa yang / chos nyid min pa gzhan med kyi / skyon du ma lta glod la zhog / gang shar gang skyes de nyid la / der 'dzin med par rang sar grol / snang grag chos rnams rang gi sems / sems las ma gtogs chos gzhan med / sems ni skye 'gag spros dang bral / sems kyi de nyid shes pa des / 'dod yon lnga la spyang gyur kyang / chos nyid dang las g.yos pa med / . . . . / spang blang mnyam bzhag rjes thob med.*

72. [*rTogs pa brjod ba mkha' 'gro ma'i gsang mdzod na gnas pa*], sDe-dge 2450. The Tibetan term for "song of realization" in this case is *rtogs-pa brjod-pa'i mgur.*

73. *dPal rdo rje mkha' 'gro ma'i mgur zhes bya ba*, sDe-dge 2441.

74. sDe-dge 2450, fol. 86a.4: *kye ho padma'i ge sar snying gi dbus su sad / gsal ba'i me tog 'dam gyi dri ma bral / dri dang kha dog ldan pa gang gis rkyen / 'di la dgag dang bsgrub pa yod dam ci.*

75. sDe-dge 2450, fol. 87a.5: *kye ho gang gis mthong dang thos pa dang / dran dang tshor ba'i bye brag kun / yid kyi ye shes dangs pa la / gzugs brnyan tsam du shar ba las / gzhi la ma grub ngo bos stong.*

76. *Thugs kyi gsang ba glur blangs pa zhes bya ba*, sDe-dge 2443, fol. 70a.2–3: *brag ci'i sgra 'di su yis smras / me long gzugs brnyan su yis bris / rmi lam ltad mo gang du gyis / gang na'ang med do sems kyi ngang.*

77. sDe-dge 2450, fol. 86b.1–2: *kye ho stong nyid rig pa'i rtsal dang ldan / skye med skye ba'i cho 'phrul stong / dgag sgrub med de rang sar grol / 'di la bya rgyu ngas ma rnyed.*

78. sDe-dge 2450, fol. 86a.4–5: *kye ho nam mkha' las byung cho 'phrul ni / nam mkha' nyid kyis byas pa'i phyir / nam mkha'i ngang du rang byung ste / 'di la skyon du ma 'dzin cig.*

79. sDe-dge 2450, fol. 86a.2: *kye ho chos rnams gzhi med rmi lam 'dra / snang bar rkyen skyes gzugs brnyan 'dra / rang byung rang zhi lbu ba 'dra / rtsa bral chen po nam mkha' 'dra.*

80. This is a central theme of Nāgārjuna's *Mūlamadhyamakakārikā*, especially chaps. 1, 8, 10, 13, 15, 24–25.

81. sDe-dge 2450, fol. 86b.2–3: *kye ho yod do byas na ngos gzung med / med do byas na sna tshogs 'char / yod med mkha' las 'das pa la / 'di shes nga yis mtshon mi nus.*

82. sDe-dge 2450, fol. 87a.3: *lam gyi de nyid bsgom du med.*

83. sDe-dge 2443, fol. 70a.4–5: *ma yengs bsgom du med ba la / nyams su lan na mkhas pa yin / sna tshogs rjes med chen po ru / lam du 'khyer na grol ba yin.* In the final line, the term for practice, *lam du 'khyer*, means carrying the practice, or path, into everyday life and all one's activities.

84. sDe-dge 2450, fol. 86a.7: *thams cad thams cad thar pa'i lam.*

85. sDe-dge 2450, fol. 87b.1–2: *kye ho ye shes chen po mchog gi lam / ma bkrod de bzhin nyid kyi sa / ma bsgrubs lhun gyis grub pa'i don / e ma rnal 'byor skal bar bzang.*

86. sDe-dge 2450, fol. 86a.6–7: *kye ho sna tshogs snang ba'i cho 'phrul 'di / dran pa'i gzugs brnyan yin shes shing / dran pa rang ngos stong shes na / dbying kyi bde ba btsal mi dgos.*

87. sDe-dge 2450, fol. 86b.4: *kye ho snang srid 'di ni phyag rgya che / 'dod yon 'di ni dngas pa yis / gnyug ma'i don la 'du 'bral med / bde chen thang la rgyug tu gsol.*

88. sDe-dge 2450, fol. 87a.5–6: *gang gis ma mthong de mthong na / yid ni rang grol chos kyi sku / rlung gi rta pho shul du lus / sems kyi mi pho mkha' la 'gro.*

89. *dPal rdo rje mkha' 'gro ma'i mgur zhes bya ba*, sDe-dge 2441, fol. 64b.7: *mkha' la bya 'phur rten sa med.*

90. sDe-dge 2450, fol. 86a.3: *kye ho de nyid nyams su myong ba'i skyes bu gang / bde chen nam mkha'i khams su mi shong ngo / 'di la mtshon du 'dug gam khyod kyis smros / nga yis ci yang mthong ba med par mthong.*

91. sDe-dge 2450, fol. 87b.3–4: *kye ho rang byung bde chen ye shes 'di / ma rtogs smra bar mi nus te / rtogs nam brjod du ga la yod / myong ba smra med lkugs pa'i kha.*

92. sDe-dge 2441, fol. 63a.7–b.1: *hūṃ ri rab chen po'i rtser phyin te / ri bran ma lus blta bar bya / gyi ling sgrog tu bcug pa la / phyogs mtshams kun du rgyug par bya / bung bas rtsi bcud kun sdud de / ro rnams gcig tu bsre bar byed / . . . . / skyes bus nam mkha'i dbying mthong bas / phyogs su 'dzin pa 'jig par 'gyur.*

93. Peking 4641, fol. 163a.6–7: *gang gi tshe na mngon du gyur / de tshe lhun gyis grub par 'gyur / 'gro ba'i re 'dod skongs mdzad pa'i / yid bzhin nor bu lta bur 'gyur.*

94. sDe-dge 2443, fol. 70b.2–3: *stong nyid nam mkha'i glegs bam la / rang rig ye shes yi ger bris / sna tshogs thabs kyi gdams pa bkod / rgyun chad med pa'i bstan pa sgrogs.*

95. sDe-dge 2443, fol. 70b.3–4: *mi 'gyur nam mkha'i rdo rje la / g.yo 'kul 'byung ba'i cho 'phrul shar / sna tshogs skye 'gro'i bya ba byas / rang grol nam mkha'i dbyings su yal.*

96. See Robert Thurman, trans., *Holy Teaching of Vimalakīrti*, pp. 8–9, 12–13, 51–55, 79–81, 84–85, 93–95.

97. There are several anthologies of such songs by women in the Tibetan canon, including a collection of fifty-five songs compiled by Padmalocanā, *Phyag rgya chen po rin po che brda'i man ngag*, sDe-dge 2445; a set of songs entrusted to Pha-dam-pa sangs-rgyas, *rDo rje mkha' 'gro ma'i brda'i mgur zhes bya*

*ba,* sDe-dge 2442; and a set collected by a yogini named Kurukullātārā and others, *Phyag rgya chen po brda'i brgyud pa,* sDe-dge 2439.

98. sDe-dge 2441, fol. 63b.2–3: *hūṃ lhangs kyis 'bod pa de ci sems / cer gyis lta ba gang la yengs / nam mkha' ji ltar gsal bar 'gyur / mar me 'di yi rtog pa gang / chu bur zhig pa'i rjes mi rnyed / rmi lam rtog pa sad pas stong / . . . / bu zhi'i a ma'i gces 'dzin su / chu bo'i brol la ro drug gang / lkugs mas smras pa'i tshig de ci.*

99. In addition to its characteristically startling, paradoxical language, this poetry uses a range of images from rural and village life expressed in idiomatic expressions that are often difficult to translate (especially via the Tibetan translation) because of their references to agriculture, food preparation, occupations, folk customs, ornaments, utensils, dance, music, kinship, etc., which must be deciphered before one can begin to discern the logic that is being violated. Culturally as well as religiously these works are enigmatic, as they are intended to be, and forbiddingly difficult to translate. Discussions can be found in Atindra Mojumder, *The Caryāpadas,* pp. 10–55, 93–102, and the translations in part 2.

100. The language of these poems resembles the *ulaṭ(ṭa)bāṃsī,* or "upside-down language," of the medieval poetry of Kabir and the Nath yogis, with which it may instructively be compared; see Linda Hess, *The Bījak of Kabir,* pp. 145–61. Kabir also uses the form of direct address, which is discussed by Hess in the same work, pp. 10–11. The enigmatic language of the Buddhist verses is termed *sandh(y)ābhāṣā;* see Agehananda Bharati, *The Tantric Tradition,* pp. 164–84, and David Ruegg, "Allusiveness and Obliqueness in Buddhist Texts."

101. *Sems nyid kyi rtog pa 'joms pa'i lta ba zhes bya ba,* sDe-dge 2433, fol. 47b.5–48a.3: *mar sar mgo bo bcad ba yis / sta re'i so ni 'chag par byed / sbal bas glang po mid par 'gyur / kye ma shing thun dgod par byed / kye ma ngo mtshar me go kye / sems la the tshom ma byed cig / mtshar na a ba dhū tī pa / sems la rtog pa ma byed cig / kho yis ma bshad 'di ma go / nam mkha' las ni me tog 'byung / kye ma ngo mtshar me go kye / sems la the tshom ma byed cig / mtshar na a ba dhū tī pa / sems kyi the tshom ci zhig bya / kye ma mo gsham bu skyes na / khri yang gar ni byed par 'gyur / ras bal dkon par thob 'gyur bas / nam mkha'i gos can ngu bar byed / . . . . / kye ma glang chen khri la 'dug / sbrang bu gnyid kyis 'degs par byed / dmus long lam ston ngo mtshar che / lkugs bas gtam ni smra bar byed / . . . . / byi bas byi la 'ded pa mtshar / de mthong ngo mtshar skye bar 'gyur / bong bu myos pa mthong 'gyur bas / glang po rnams kyang bros par byed / kye ma ngo mtshar me go kye / sems la the tshom ma byed cig / mtshar na a ba dhū tī pa / sems kyi the tshom ci zhig bya / kye ma spre'i ltogs pa ni / rdo ba kham gyis za bar byed / kye ma sems kyi nyams myong ni / sus kyang brjod par nus ma yin.*

102. Lakṣmīṅkarā is clearly addressing an inner yoga adept, or *avadhūta,* but it is not clear whether she is using the term as a descriptive title or addressing a disciple by that name. It is difficult to determine without having the Sanskrit original of this piece and without knowing whether Lakṣmīṅkarā had a disciple of this name. Pending more conclusive evidence, I have chosen to translate this in the generic, leaving open the possibility that the other person intended is the other woman who recorded the song, Kanakhalā, who was an adept at making the wind enter the central channel. The other possibility is that *avadhūtī-pa* is an alternate way of addressing Mekhalā, for poetic effect.

103. 'Gos Lotsawa gZhon-nu-dpal, *Deb gter sngon po bzhugs,* fol. 754.2–3: *khye'u khyod skye 'chis 'jigs nas chos la dka' las byed pa ngo ma tshar bas / rdo rje theg*

*pa thun mong ma yin pa ma nor ba cig nged kyis sbyin kyis / bus kyang nyams su long cig gsung nas zhabs sbyi bor blangs so*. This account is also translated in George Roerich, trans., *Blue Annals*, p. 851.

104. 'Gos Lotsawa gZhon-nu-dpal, *Deb gter sngon po bzhugs*, fol. 753.1–5. Cf. George Roerich, trans., *Blue Annals*, pp. 850–51.

105. One of the Tibetan terms for this "direct pointing" is *rig-pa ngo sprod*.

106. Taranatha, *Seven Instruction Lineages*, p. 3; and Herbert Guenther, *The Royal Song of Saraha*, pp. 5–7.

107. Mark Tatz, "The Life of the Siddha-Philosopher Maitrīgupta," pp. 704–5.

108. Her name in Tibetan is given as Gaṅga bzang-mo; George Roerich, trans., *Blue Annals*, p. 868.

109. Ibid., p. 869.

## CHAPTER FIVE

1. Translation of *Pratyutpanna-buddha-sammukhāvasthita-samādhi-sūtra* 8.14–17 by Paul Harrison, in *The "Samādhi" of Direct Encounter with the Buddhas of the Present*, pp. 76–77. This text, which is traceable to the earliest strand of Mahāyāna literature, heralds *buddha-sammukhāvasthita-samādhi*, the meditative state in which one can directly perceive a Buddha.

2. This passage, from the *Ārya Sarvapuṇya-samuccaya-samādhi-nāma-mahāyānasūtra* (sDe-dge 134), is translated by Tulku Thondup Rinpoche, *Hidden Teachings of Tibet*, p. 59. A similar belief is expressed by Śāntideva, *Bodhicaryāvatāra* 10.37, where he expresses the bodhisattva's aspiration that "by means of all birds and trees, and even by rays from the sky, may the sound of Dharma be heard unceasingly by all beings"; translation by Marion Matics, *Entering the Path of Enlightenment*, p. 231. Janet Gyatso, in "Sign, Memory and History," discusses Buddhist understandings of revelation on pp. 9–11 and 28–29 and the revelation of Dharma teachings through natural phenomena such as birds and plants on pp. 14 and 31, n. 34. For general Mahāyāna understandings of revelation, see Graeme McQueen, "Inspired Speech in Early Mahāyāna Buddhism."

3. Women continued to introduce new practices in Tibet. These include the *gcod* practice introduced by Ma-gcig Labs-sdron-ma; the Dharma-protector Achi Chos-kyi sGrol-ma introduced by 'Bri-gung Achi, the matriarch of the 'Bri-gung hereditary lineage; and a Seng-gdong-ma (Siṃhamukhā) lineage started by Jetsun Lochen. Women's reception of revelation in Tibet seems especially to have been acknowledged in the rNying-ma sect, the sect that institutionalized ongoing revelation in the form of the *gter-ma* tradition. There are women among the *gter*-concealers and *gter*-revealers, such as Ye-shes mtsho-rgyal (eighth century), Jo-mo sMan-mo (1248–83), sMin-gling rje-btsun mi-'gyur dpal-sgron (1699–1769), sMin-gling rje-btsun 'gyur-med phrin-las chos-sgron (early nineteenth century), and Se-ra mkha'-'gro kun-bzang bde-skyong dbang-mo (early twentieth century).

4. The following religious biography of Vajravatī is from a text by Lakṣmīṅkarā (colophon: Lha-lcam rJe-btsun-ma dpal-mo), *Lhan cig skyes grub*

*kyi gzhung 'grel*, sDe-dge 2261, fol. 11a.2–11b.5. Only at first mention does Lakṣmīṅkarā refer to her as Vajravatī Brāhmaṇī; thereafter she shortens this to Brāhmaṇī, making it easy to overlook the subject of the biography. This quotation is a translation of fol. 11a.7: *gal te khrus kyis 'dag lta na / nya pa rnams kyang don byas shing / nyin dang mtshan du gnas pa yi / nya sogs pa smos ci dgos*. Ānandavajra transmitted *sahaja* realization to Vajravatī, which means that he awakened her to the nature of her own mind, but no mention is made of the Pīṭheśvarī practice, a practice that by all evidence she introduced.

5. sDe-dge 2261, fol. 11b.3–4: *bram ze mo nam mkha' yongs su dag ba'i dbyings nas sprin dag byung nas de nyid du thim pa'am / chu klung yongs su dag pa las nya dag byung ba ji lta ba bzhin du bram ze mo khyod kyis sems la lta bar gyis dang / gdod sangs rgyas thams cad kyi yul la 'jug pa'i ye shes kyi chu zhes bya bas bdag tu lta ba'i dri ma ma lus par 'dug par 'gyur ro.*

6. sDe-dge 2261, fol. 11b.4–5.

7. Vajravatī (Tib. rDo-rje ldan-ma), *Urgyen gyi rim pa'i sgrol ma'i sgrub thabs zhes bya ba*, sDe-dge 1711, fol. 72a.2. She also claimed that her "adamantine words were written in former *sādhana*(s) of Tārā in *vajra* secret *tantra*," using the term *rdo-rje gsang-ba'i rgyud* (fol. 74b.6). Special thanks to Ngawang Jorden for counsel on difficult passages in this text.

8. The way she uses the term *rdo-rje gsang-ba'i rgyud* does not suggest that it is a title, and indeed there is no "*Vajraguhya-tantra*" in the Tibetan canon. There is a *Guhyavajra-tantrarāja* (sDe-dge 383), but it does not bear any discernable relation to Vajravatī's text.

9. See n. 7.

10. Tulku Thondup Rinpoche, *Hidden Teachings of Tibet*, pp. 57–60. Although all the Tibetan Buddhist sects share this belief, the process of transmission and revelation seems to be articulated most extensively by the rNying-ma school in association with its *gter-ma* tradition; see Eva Dargyay, *The Rise of Esoteric Buddhism in Tibet*, pp. 85–91ff. Other symbolic forms through which *ḍākinīs* might communicate include seed-syllables, gems, crystals, and drawings.

11. In *Urgyen gyi rim pa'i sgrol ma'i sgrub thabs zhes bya ba*, sDe-dge 1711, she directs the yoginis (*rnal-'byor-ma*) to begin self-generation (fol. 73b.7) and calls the perfection stage the "yoga of yoginis" (fol. 74b.3); see also fol. 73b.5.

12. sDe-dge 1711, fol. 73b.6–7.

13. sDe-dge 1711, fol. 74b.6–7: *ma dad pa'am ma sbyin bya ba ngan dang / chags can khro ba can min slob min bu la min / sdug bsgnal blo can la min slob dbon gyis / gzhan la sgrub thabs 'di sbyin byang phyogs kyi / ū rgyan nas 'ong bram ze'i gnas kyi nang zhing gi bu mo'i rnal 'byor ma tshogs rdo rje'i tshig de grub.*

The term translated here as "human" is "field-born," a Tantric term for designating human women or women born in a Buddha-land, which is ambiguous since it can refer to a human woman born in this Buddha-land or a "nonphysical" birth in another Buddha-field, which might seem nonphysical from our perspective. Here, human women are indicated by the qualification of women born in "*brāhmaṇa* places," i.e., priestly households or places in India under the cultural sway of Hindu priests.

14. It is possible that the system has survived outside the monasteries, for the

transmission of practices is not confined to the monasteries in Tibet, although survival in the monastic context assures greater historical visibility.

15. Whether the practice was restricted to women is unclear in part because one canonical version of the practice specifies women as its practitioners (sDe-dge 1711), whereas the other does not (sDe-dge 1706).

16. Thus, there is no reason to tokenize these women and conclude, as Hanna Havnevik does in *Tibetan Buddhist Nuns*, that recent instances of women having female students are "exceptions" (p. 132).

17. Tib. gNas-chen gyi dbang-phyug-ma; the Sanskrit version of her name as given in the title of the texts is Urgyan (i.e., Uḍḍiyāna)-krama Tārā, meaning "Tārā as visualized according to the Uḍḍiyāna method," or "Tārā in the form in which she revealed herself in Uḍḍiyāna."

18. The location of Uḍḍiyāna (variously spelled Oḍḍiyāna, Udyāna, Orgyan, Urgyan) has been debated, but it appears from the routes of Chinese and Tibetan pilgrims that the present-day Swat Valley is intended; see Alexander Cunningham, *The Ancient Geography of India*, pp. 68–70; Bimala Churn Law, *Historical Geography of Ancient India*, p. 132; and D. C. Sircar, *The Śākta Pīṭhas*, pp. 12–13, 16. It has also been suggested that Uḍḍiyāna was Orissa, but it appears rather that the term Uḍḍīśa or Oḍiśa (also spelled Oḍḍāvisa, Oḍraviṣaya, Oḍra) was once the pronunciation of Orissa, another important center of Tantric activity, and was in some texts mistaken for Uḍḍiyāna; see D. C. Sircar, *Śākta Pīṭhas*, pp. 13, 21. The historical presence of Tantric practices in the Swat Valley region is suggested by the folklore and symbolism of the present inhabitants of the valley, who use sexual and fertility symbolism (an ancient *yab-yum* motif) to denote prosperity and well-being and believe in *ḍenik* (= *ḍākinī*), women who are skilled at magical arts and can transform themselves at will; see Maximilian Klimburg, "Male-Female Polarity Symbolism in Kafir Art and Religion," pp. 487–88.

19. For Uḍḍiyāna forms of Mārīcī, see sDe-dge nos. 3231, 3340, 3344, 3345, and 3529; S. K. Saraswati, *Tantrayāna Art*, pp. 45, 89–91, and figs. 257–58; and Benoytosh Bhattacharyya, ed., *Sādhanamālā*, vol. 2, nos. 138–40. For Uḍḍiyāna forms of Kurukullā, see sDe-dge nos. 3370 and 3566; and Benoytosh Bhattacharyya, ed., *Sādhanamālā*, vol. 2, no. 179. An Uḍḍiyāna form of Mahāmāyā was introduced by a woman, Vajraḍākinī; see *sGyu 'phrul chen mo zhes bya ba'i sgrub pa'i thabs*, sDe-dge 1626.

20. According to Giuseppe Tucci, "there are many Tantras that were commonly acknowledged as having been first revealed in Uḍḍiyāna. One of the most esoteric methods of Tāntric realisations relating chiefly to the cycle of the *ḍākinī* was even known as the Uḍḍiyānakrama [Uḍḍiyāna method]"; Giuseppe Tucci, "Travels of Tibetan Pilgrims in the Swat Valley," pp. 369–70. There are many traditional accounts that Tantric teachings originated in Uḍḍiyāna. For example, a sixteenth-century bKa'-brgyud text says that Vajrapaṇi first entrusted the *tantras* on *mahāmudrā* to *ḍākinīs* (translated by Lhalungpa as "awakened women") in Uḍḍiyāna, from which they passed to a king and then to Saraha, who spread the teaching more widely; see Takpo Tashi Namgyal, *Mahāmudrā*, p. 116.

21. *dBang phyug ma'i sgrub pa'i thabs*, sDe-dge 1706, fol. 63b.7–64a.1: *phyogs bcur gnas ba'i sangs rgyas rnams / sgrol ma'i gzugs rnams rnam bsgom bya / . . . . / ye shes 'od zer rnam dag nya / sangs rgyas de nyid rab gnas bya / bang chub snying po mchis kyi bar / myur du sangs rgyas sgrol ma can*. The term translated as "Buddha Tārā" is *sangs-rgyas sgrol-ma*.

22. sDe-dge 1711, fol. 74a.7–b.1. The term "worldly *ḍākinī*" (*lokaḍākinī*, Tib. *'jig-rten-pa'i mkha'-'gro-ma*) can refer to a human *ḍākinī* with magical powers, as I am interpreting it here, although it has a range of meanings in other contexts, for which see Adelheid Hermann-Pfandt, *Ḍākinīs*, pp. 118–22.

23. sDe-dge 1711, fol. 72a.3–4, 6.

24. sDe-dge 1711, fol. 73b.7–74a.2: *ri dags gdan can sna tshogs pad nyi la / bdag nyid rje btsun sgrol ma'i gzugs 'dzin ma / . . . zhabs bzhib rkyang bskum du / yang dag brtan bzhugs . . . . mi rus rgyan 'dzin skra grol ba / spyan gsum dmar bas mdzes pa'i gzugs can*.

25. sDe-dge 1711, fol. 72b.2–4: *dmar dang sngon po ljang gu cung zad khro / dpa' bo zhi ba ser po steng gi zhal / thod pa'i phreng bas dbu brgyan ye shes lnga / rgyan rnams ma lus thams cad brgyan ba yi / rdo rjer la gri utpala rin po che / thod pa khaṭvāṅ dril bu ḍa ma ru / 'dzin ching bde ba'i ye shes 'bras bu 'byung / stag lpags sham thabs phed krung gar gyis gnas / sna tshogs pad zla'i dkyil brtan snying rje khros / spyan gsum dmar bas kun la gzigs g.yon du / . . . / zhing du spros pa mchog gi rnal 'byor mtshogs dbus*.

26. sDe-dge 1711, fol. 73a.5, where she is called dGa'-bde'i dbang-phyug-ma.

27. sDe-dge 1711, fol. 72b.7–73a.4. A slightly varying list of the twenty-four goddesses occurs in the Pīṭheśvarī *sādhana* in Benoytosh Bhattacharyya, ed., *Sādhanamālā*, vol. 2, no. 311.

28. sDe-dge 1711, fol. 73b.5–6: *rnal 'byor ma grogs bzang dang sgom pa po / rtag tu bza' dang bza' min de bzhin du / btung dang btung min bgrod bya bgrod min spyod / rnal 'byor ma tshogs dkyil 'khor 'di dag ni / sdig pas ma gos nyam nyid brtan pa'i chos*.

29. *dPal 'khor lo sdom pa myur du sgrub pa zhes bya ba'i thabs*, Peking 4637. According to the colophon, fol. 158a.5–6, this text contains "secret oral instructions" (*zhal-gdams*) recorded by Khyung-po rnal-'byor, who claims to have met people who knew Niguma but only to have met her himself in a visionary state. Since he knew others who knew her, it is possible that he gathered her secret oral instructions from them as well. Although it is called a five-deity *maṇḍala*, it includes six deities: the divine couple in the center and a yogini in each of the cardinal directions. These deities form the inner circle of the Cakrasaṃvara *maṇḍala*, which may be expanded into more elaborate forms, such as the sixty-two-deity version in the root-*tantra* and Luipa's system.

30. Peking 4637, fol. 157a.4.

31. Peking 4637, fol. 157a.1–3: *gsang ba kho na nyid mchod pas / yab yum snyoms 'jug sbyor 'tshams nas / byang sems dkar la dmar mdangs chags / chu rgyun rang gi spyi gtsug zug / 'khor bzhi kha ṭvaṃ snyoms 'jug pas / gsang gnas byang sems rgyun rnams babs / spyi gtsug gcig tu gyur nas ni / gnas bzhir babs pas sdig sgrib dag*. Some of Khyung-po rnal-'byor's explanatory notes appear in the translation in parenthesis.

32. The crown *cakra*, ignorance, heat ailments, and bodily defilements; the throat *cakra*, cold ailments and defilements of speech; and the heart *cakra*, anger, phlegm disorders, and mental defilements; Peking 4637, fol. 157b.2–8.

33. Peking 4637, fol. 157a.6–b.1: *dbus su bde mchog yab yum ni / padmar ga'i mdog 'dra ba / rus pa thod pa skram rlon brgyan / gar dgu'i nyams dang ldan pa'o / phyogs bzhir lha mo gri thod can / mdog dmar kha ṭvaṃ bcas pa'o / rtsobs kyi raṃ las gong bzhin du / ye shes me 'bar mchod bas mnyes / gtsho 'khong yab yum sbyor 'tshams nas / byang sems dmar ba'i chu rgyun byung / mgrin pa man chad khengs ba yis / nad gnod sdig sgrib dag par bsam / chu rgyun 'khor lo me dpung rlung.*

34. Peking 4637, fol. 157b.2–6: *snying khar bruṃ sngon bo dur mdog / rno ngar ldan pa'i 'khor lo bsam / nyi zla 'jigs byed dus mtshan steng / hūṃ dang rdo rje'i spro bsdu las / bde mchog sngon po yum dmar zhing / drag po'i rang bzhin 'khor bcas bsgom / rtsibs la me dpung sngo nag 'bar / yab yum snyoms 'jug . . . / zag med bde ba cher rgyas shing / hūṃ phaṭ gad mo 'brug stong sgrogs / sbyor 'tshams byang sems 'thing shun mdog / snying kha man chad khengs pa yis / sems kyi nad gdon sdig sgrib dag / khyad par gdon dang zhe sdang rnams / 'khor los stubs shing me dpung bsregs / ye shes rlung gis gdengs par bya / byang sems chu rgyun drag po yis / sdig sgrib thal ba'i ri bo bkru.*

35. *dPal 'khor lo sdom pa'i dkyil 'khor gyi cho ga*, Peking 4638. Tāranātha's commentaries on the practice and initiation, *Ni gu lugs kyi bde mchog lha nga'i mngon rtogs* and *Ni gu lugs kyi bde mchog lha lnga'i dbang cho ga*, are available in a reprint edition. Tāranātha's works currently serve as the major written resource for Shangs-pa practitioners.

36. Tib. *rGyud sde kun btus*; see bSod nams rgya mtsho and Musashi Tachikawa, *The Ngor Mandalas of Tibet: Plates*, p. xix and plate 121.

37. Since the nineteenth century, the dPal-spungs branch of the Karma bKa'-brgyud sect, stemming from Kong-sprul bLo-gros mTha'-yas (1813–99), has been the major preserver of Shangs-pa practices; see Matthew Kapstein, "The Shangs-pa bKa'-brgyud," p. 142.

38. *dPal dgyes pa rdo rje'i dkyil 'khor gyi cho ga zhes bya ba*, sDe-dge 1296.

39. Niguma's teachings on the "stages of the path of magical illusion" (*māyādhanakrama*) can be found in *sGyu ma lam gyi rim pa (dri med snying po) zhes bya ba*, Peking 4643; and *sGyu ma lam gyi rim pa'i 'grel pa zhes bya ba*, Peking 4644. They are analyzed by Matthew Kapstein in "The Illusion of Spiritual Progress."

40. My narrative combines incidents related by Abhayadatta and others; see James Robinson, trans., *Buddha's Lions*, pp. 250–53; and Sonam Tobgay Kazi, *Tibet House Museum*, pp. 60–61. My description of Lakṣmīṅkarā's daily activities as a princess is based upon Sanskrit literary descriptions of life in the women's quarters of a royal court as summarized by Jeannine Auboyer, *Daily Life in Ancient India from Approximately 200* BC *to 700* AD, pp. 268–73.

41. Lakṣmīṅkarā wrote meditation manuals that have been preserved in the Tibetan canon, i.e., *rNal 'byor ma'i sgrub pa'i thabs*, sDe-dge 1547, and *rDo rje phag mo dbu bcad ma'i sgrub thabs*, sDe-dge 1554 (colophon: Śrīmatīdevī, an epithet of Lakṣmīṅkarā). The severed-headed form of Vajrayoginī/Vajravārāhī (Tib. dbU-bcad-ma) is similar to the Hindu goddess Chinnamastā, which raises the question of shared origins and borrowing; see David Kinsley, *Hindu God-*

*desses*, pp. 172–77. Elisabeth Benard analyzes the history and symbolism of these goddesses in *Chinnamastā*.

42. For a translation of this song, see chap. 4.

43. For example, see Lokesh Chandra, *Buddhist Iconography*, no. 1183.

44. *dbU bcad ma'i sgrub thabs zhes bya ba*, sDe-dge 1555, fol. 208a.

45. George Roerich, trans., *Blue Annals*, p. 360.

46. Ibid., p. 390: "The majority of the Tantric yogins in this Land of Snows (Tibet) were especially initiated and followed . . . the system." The author of the *Blue Annals* refers to the system as Phag-mo gzhung-drug, something like the "sixfold system" or "six treatises" of Vajravārāhī, and identifies their textual locus as sDe-dge nos. 1551–56. Lakṣmīṅkarā's texts are sDe-dge nos. 1547 and 1554. The next four in the lineage were Avadhūtipa, Paiṇḍapātika, lDong-ngar-ba, and Jinadatta; George Roerich, trans., *Blue Annals*, pp. 390–91f. Tāranātha comments on this practice in *sKu gsum rdo rje phag mo zhes bya ba dbu bcad mar grags pa'i sgrub mchod ngag 'don*.

47. In this variation of the practice, Vajrayoginī does not have a severed head, but the root mantra and other symbolism are those introduced by Lakṣmīṅkarā, who is identified as the founder of the practice. The *sādhana* in current use is by Rig-'dzin Chos-bdag.

48. The Sa-skya *sādhana*, in which Severed-Headed Vajrayoginī is envisioned as red rather than yellow, is preserved in the *sGrubs thabs kun btus*. For painted depictions, see Adelheid Hermann-Pfandt, *Ḍākinīs*, p. 265, and the outer ring of the Sa-skya Hevajraḍāka *maṇḍala*.

49. For example, Lakṣmīṅkarā is not mentioned among Virūpa's teachers in the detailed religious genealogy given in Chogay Trichen, *The History of the Sakya Tradition*, pp. 8–12.

50. Tāranātha, *Tāranātha's Life of Kṛṣṇācārya/Kāṇha*, pp. 62–63; James Robinson, trans., *Buddha's Lions*, pp. 211–13; and Keith Dowman, *Masters of Mahāmudrā*, pp. 317–18. Dowman offers a creative retelling of the story in *Masters of Enchantment*, pp. 187–88, in which he describes the sisters as "impish," "mischievous," "impulsive," and the cause of their own misery.

51. Tibetan folio reproduced in James Robinson, *Buddha's Lions*, p. 376, fol. 259.3–4: *e ma rnal 'byor chen mo gnyis / yin tan mchog thob dge ba ste / rang nyid zhi bde dman bas na / 'gro ba'i don phyir gnas par mdzod*.

52. Keith Dowman, *Masters of Mahāmudrā*, pp. 319–20. Dowman also notes the similarity of their iconography to that of the Severed-Headed Goddess, but he explains this as a further reference to their destruction of ego rather than as a reference to the specific content of their meditation practices.

53. Ibid., p. 319.

54. Tāranātha, *Seven Instruction Lineages*, p. 36.

55. The colophon states that the song was sung by Lakṣmīṅkarā and "transmitted" (*brgyud*) by Mekhalā and Kanakhalā; see Miranda Shaw, "An Ecstatic Song by Lakṣmīṅkarā," p. 55. For discussion of the song, see chap. 4 of the present work.

56. Tāranātha even suggests that Vajravārāhī herself got the idea of a headless form from them; see Tāranātha, *Tāranātha's Life of Kṛṣṇācārya/Kāṇha*, p. 63.

57. *gYung drung 'khyil ba gsum gyi zhal gdams kyi nyams len zhes bya ba*, sDe-dge 2415.

58. sDe-dge 2415, fol. 34b.6–35a.2: *ye shes me spar rang lus ni / mkhrin pa'i gnas nas rkang mthil bar / gnyis ni g.yas skor gyon skor ro / slar yang rlung gis phu byas nas / g.yung drung gnyis la byim byas nas / dbus kyi 'khyil pa thim par bsam / ye shes me spar rang lus ni / mkhrin pa'i gnas nas rkang mthil bar / rim kyis zhu lte chos dbyings su / mnyam nyid thig ler sems gtad do / brtags pas ma grub dngos med yin / dmigs pa'i mtshan nyid thams cad bral / de ltar ma bsgoms ci byas kyang / lhan skyes ma rtogs 'khor bar 'khyams / thig le de las blangs byas nas / bdag nyid dbu bcad yum du bskyed / de nas lte bar hrīṃ yig bsam / sum mdor rlung ldang khyen la rgyu / hri ni thig le gsum du zhu / i ni rlung gi thig le ste / ha ste byang chub thig le'o / rakta'i thig le raṃ yig ste / mdor na rim par sdo dkar dmar / ma shar rlung gis gyen la 'ded / dbu bcad rtsa sbubs rgyu na ni / steng du sor bzhi 'thon par bsam / g.yon pa g.yon skor g.yas pa g.yas / dbus kyi thig le 'par zhing thim.*

59. sDe-dge 2415, fol. 35a.2–3: *lha mo gnyis kyis phus btab bas / g.yas g.yon thig le dbus la thim / de nyid mar la rngub byas pas / snying ga'i hūṃ la thim par bsam /de ni gsal la dri ma med / gnyis med thig le rang rig ste / bde dang sdug bsngal thams cad bral / 'khor ba snang ba rang rig stong / kye ho rnal 'byor bsgoms nas ni / gnyis med ye shes thob par 'gyur.*

60. This date is based on the dates of two of her prominent students, Ras-chung-pa (1084–1161) and Khyung-po rnal-'byor (born 1086).

61. Mainly through interviews of abbots and scholars of various schools, conducted in March through May of 1990 in the Kathmandu Valley, I confirmed that Siddharājñī's system is used by all the gSar-ma schools, i.e., the three Sa-skya sects, the three bKa'-brgyud sects, and the dGe-lugs. There is evidence of the presence of a Siddharājñī transmission within the rNying-ma school, but I have not been able to ascertain the specifics.

62. A lama might prescribe a long-life ritual when someone's life is deemed to be endangered by illness or a threat from unseen forces. Recently a Tibetan lama determined through divination that a woman's life was in serious danger and prescribed one hundred "long-life consecrations." Soon thereafter, a heart attack cemented her resolve to obtain the consecrations.

63. Robert Paul, *The Tibetan Symbolic World*, pp. 109–10. In some cases the Mani Rimdu is a *gtor-ma* blessing focusing on Padmanarteśvara, another deity taught by Siddharājñī; see pp. 122–24 here.

64. L. Austine Waddell, *Tibetan Buddhism*, p. 445.

65. Christoph von Fürer-Haimendorf, *The Sherpas of Nepal*, pp. 184–85.

66. See, for example, L. Austine Waddell, *Tibetan Buddhism*, pp. 444–48 (under the name "Eucharist of Lāmaism"); Christoph von Fürer-Haimendorf, *The Sherpas of Nepal*, pp. 214–16; and David Snellgrove, *Himalayan Pilgrimage*, pp. 141–46. For some photographs of the ritual, see Mario Fantin, *Mani Rimdu.Nepal*, plates 51–56.

67. *rJe btsun ras chung rdo rje grags pa'i rnam thar rnam mkhyen thar lam gsal ba'i me long ye shes snang ba bzhugs so* (hereinafter, Ras-chung-pa's *rNam-thar*), fol. 42ff. Her association with Ras-chung-pa makes it possible to date Siddharājñī to the late eleventh and twelfth centuries. According to his biography, he was

forty-four when he met her, which, if accurate, places their meeting in about 1127. It is possible that Siddharājñī was in her twenties at this time, as some adepts had remarkable accomplishments at relatively early ages. The biography does not shed light on this issue, for it says that when they met she was five hundred years old but looked sixteen as a result of her mastery of the longevity practices, an almost inevitable hagiographical claim in view of her mastery of the long-life practices associated with the Buddha of Infinite Life.

68. Shamarpa Rinpoche, current regent of the Karma bKa'-brgyud sect, told me that he thinks her inner, outer, and secret biographies may be extant, but I have not yet been able to locate these.

69. Specifics regarding her education and religious training are not given, but apparently she had studied Amitāyus scriptures. One of her text colophons notes that she had used "the vase chapter of the root *tantra* and the *Od-zer dra-ba* ('Net of Light-Rays') commentarial *tantra*," texts whose identities cannot be ascertained on the basis of this scant information, but the mention of which indicates that she was versed in Amitāyus literature.

70. E.g., Helmut Hoffmann, *The Religions of Tibet*, p. 156. Giuseppe Tucci does not mention any of his teachers by name. David Snellgrove considers the ritual that Rechungpa reportedly learned from her to have an indigenous Tibetan or Nestorian origin, because of its "non-Buddhistic" emphasis upon health and longevity, although it is not clear whether he offers this theory without knowing the Tibetan account of the origin of the ritual or in refutation of it; see *Himalayan Pilgrimage*, p. 143. To my knowledge, the only Western-language publication that identifies her as the founder of this system is a publication of the Karma bKa'-brgyud sect; see Kalu Rinpoche, "Women, *Siddhi*, and Dharma," pp. 94–96.

71. Ras-chung-pa's *rNam-thar*, fol. 48a–b.

72. Literally, "five precious substances."

73. Ras-chung-pa's *rNam-thar*, fol. 45b.5–46a.3: *rdo rje phag mo sprul ba'i sku / rgyal ba'i rgyal yum gos dkar mo / sangs rgyas thams cad skyes pa'i yum / grub pa'i rgyal mo la phyag 'tshal / . . . . / mtshan mchog sum chu rtsa gnyis ldan / dkar dmar 'od ldan yid 'ong ma / 'ja' lus rdo rje'i tsham par mdzes / lang tshor ldan zhing bde ster ma / rin chen rus pa'i rgyan drug gsol / gri gug bdud rtsi thod pa bsnams / dar gyi lhab lhub cod pa'i can / mkha' 'gro rgya mtsho'i tshogs dbus su / gandho shel gyi gtsug lag du / rin chen sna lnga'i khri stengs su / ma cig grub pa'i rgyal mor grags.*

74. On the symbolism of this bower, or chamber, see John Strong, "*Gandhakuṭī*."

75. The three realms in this case are below the ground, on the earth, and in the sky.

76. Peaceful, prospering, empowering, wrathful.

77. Ras-chung-pa's *rNam-thar*, fol. 46a.3–47a.2: *tshe lha yongs kyi zhal gzigs te / tshe dbang khrid dang bcas pa gsan / rig 'dzin tshe'i dngos grub thob / . . . / 'og min stug po bkod par byon / longs sku rdo rje 'chang chen mjal / gsang sngags dbang bzhi rdzogs par zhus / bla med ku mngon du byur / rdo rje phag mo zhes su grags / rgyal brgya mtsho'i 'khor gyis bskor / . . . / bde mchog 'khor lo dang mjal te / sa rdo rje theg pa gsan / gsang sngags mchog gi dngos grub brnyes / rdo rje mkha' 'gro zhes su grags / gnas gsum dpa' bo mkha' 'gros bskor / . . . . / mkha' 'gro seng gdong ma dang mjal /*

*bde chen gsang ba'i ngo sprod gsan / phrin las rnam bzhi'i dngos grub brnyes / dur khrod ro zan zhes su grags / mkha' 'gro sprul pa'i stag gzig dang / dom dang ce spyang mang pos bskor.*

78. Ras-chung-pa's *rNam-thar*, fol. 46b.5–47a.1.

79. *bCom ldan 'das tshe dang ye shes dpag tu med pa'i dkyil 'khor gyi cho ga*, sDe-dge 2146.

80. The two Amitāyus *sādhanas* by Siddharājñī in the Tibetan canon are nearly identical, with only a few words' difference between them, so I am treating them as one text that has survived in two slightly differing versions. They are *Tshe dang ye shes dpag tu med pa zhes bya ba'i sgrub thabs*, sDe-dge 2143, and *Tshe dang ye shes dpag tu med pa'i grub thabs*, sDe-dge 2145. The form of Amitāyus that she taught is now the standard form; see "Grub-rgyal Tshe-dpag-med" in Lokesh Chandra, *Buddhist Iconography*, no. 1685.

81. For example, the 'Brug-pa bKa'-brgyud sect uses a Siddharājñī Amitāyus *sādhana* entitled *Tshe dpag med gsang ba 'dus pa*, written by Ratna gLing-pa (1403–78), a rNying-ma treasure-discoverer (*gter-ston*). Most Karma bKa'-brgyud monasteries use a *sādhana* by the first 'Jam-mgon Kong-sprul (1813–99) found in the *gDams ngags mdzod*. An exception is the Pawo monastery, which uses a text by Śrī Dharmasiddhi, or dPal Chos-gyi grub-thob. The 'Bri-gung sect uses a *sādhana* by dKon-mchog bsTan-'dzin Padma'i rGyal-mtshan, of Drikung Thel monastery (1770–1826; held seat of Drikung Thel monastery from 1788–1810).

82. This sculpted offering is termed *bali* in Sanskrit, Tib. *gtor-ma*. Her text is *rTa mgrin gyi sgrub thabs*, sDe-dge 2142. I have not located a surviving lineage of Siddharājñī's transmission of Hayagrīva.

83. *Tshe dpag tu med pa'i sbyin sreg gi cho ga zhes bya ba*, sDe-dge 2144.

84. Tib. Padma-gar gyi dbang-phyug.

85. Tib. rGyal-ba rgya-mtsho.

86. For example, a poster-sized image of Padmanarteśvara *yab-yum*, with Siddharājñī at the top of the painting as the lineage founder, was published as the illustration on a 1991–92 calender printed in Bhutan.

87. For other forms of Padmanarteśvara, see Walter Clark, ed., *Two Lamaistic Pantheons*, p. 193, fig. 6A9; p. 233, fig. 34; p. 265, fig. 164; and p. 266, fig. 165. For *Sādhanamālā* examples, see Benoytosh Bhattacharyya, *The Indian Buddhist Iconography*, pp. 133–36.

88. On the basis of my interviews, these appear to be the only sects of Tibetan Buddhism that do the Padmanarteśvara practice. Each sect has developed its own practice manual. The Karma bKa'-brgyud sect uses a text by the Sixth Karmapa (1416–53). The dGe-lugs-pas use a text by Shakya Bhikhu Lobsang Kalsang Gyatso, translated into English by Gelong Thubten Chödag Yuthok with Lama Thubten Zopa Rinpoche and Michele Perrott as "The sadhana of the Great Compassionate Gyalwa Gyatso, the so-called 'Treasury of Attainments,'" in typescript form. For a commentary on the dGe-lugs-pa practice, see Lama Yeshe, *Gyalwa Gyatso*.

89. The five families are 1) Buddha, white, wheel, 2) lotus, red, lotus, 3) *vajra*, blue, *vajra*, 4) jewel, yellow, jewel, and 5) karma, green, double *vajra* (*viśvavajra*).

90. *'Phags pa 'jig rten dbang phyug gsang ba'i sgrub thabs*, sDe-dge 2140.

91. sDe-dge 2140, fol. 208b.5–7: *gsang gnas lha tshogs me 'bar te / 'khor lo bzhi yi gtso bo rnams / ltos chags med ba'i me 'bar te / lte ba'i a la gtugs nas ni / me 'bar hūṃ la reg pa yis / byang chub sems kyi rgyun ba babs / 'khor lo bzhi gang lha tshogs rnams / bde ba chen por 'bar ba dang / dus gsum sangs rgyas ma lus dang / skye 'gro sems can byams sdang sogs / . . . / rlung dang dbyer med bsdus la bstim / me 'bar nyon mong rab bsregs nas / stong nyid snying rje chen po'i dang / gnyug ma yid la mi byed pa / tha mal shes pa ma bcos ngang / rang rig dri med bskyang byas la / rlung bzung rig pa phogs med sbyang.*

92. sDe-dge 2140, fol. 209b.2–210a.2: *dben gnas pyi ru mi btsal te / lus 'di gzhal yas khang nyid yin / lha sku logs su mi btsal te / sems nyid skye 'gag med pa de / rigs kyi bdag po bla ma yin / ma rtogs nyon mong gti mug 'di / rtogs grol thugs rje chen po yin / yid byed rtog chogs 'phro ba de / rtogs pas sangs rgyas stong rtsa yin / zhe sdang gdug rtsub ldan pa de / gzhi med rtogs pas rta mgrin yin / 'dod sems gdung ba tur tur de / rtsa bral rtogs pas gsang ye yin / nyon mongs nga rgyal rtog tshogs rnams / ngar 'dzin bral bas dpa' bo yin / phrag dog rlung ltar 'tshub pa de / re dogs zad pas dpa' mo yin / . . . . / de ltar sems kyi ngo bo de / ma rtogs 'khrul pas 'khor ba ste / de shes rtogs pas mya ngan 'das / lha sku sems kyi rang rtsal de / dngos bor bzung bas 'khrul pa ste / lha yang sems nyid chos skur gsal / . . . . / smras tshad grag stong brjod med yin / gdod nas dag pa'i rig pa 'di / ye nas chos skur gnas pa la / ngo sprod de ngo shes pa yin / chos dbyings ye shes [dharmadhātu-jñāna] rtogs pa la / sangs rgyas zhes su grags pa'o.*

93. Ross Kraemer, in "Women's Authorship of Jewish and Christian Literature in the Greco-Roman Period," argues that an attribution of female authorship is evidence of female authors and teachers in the milieu in which the attribution is made. The argument that she makes for a letter that is either written by a woman or attributed to a woman could also apply to these texts by or attributed to Siddharājñī: "Regardless of the author's actual identity, the fact remains that someone composed a letter in the name of a woman. . . . The author of this work did not think a letter in the name of a woman to be at all implausible. . . . We may conclude, then, that women who wrote letters addressing important theological and political issues were not unknown to the author's community, and thus not inherently unacceptable" (p. 226).

94. George Roerich, trans., *Blue Annals*, pp. 1007–8, 1044; see also 1008–18 for information about her lineal descendants. Her student Jñānabhadra taught Rin-chen bzang-po (958–1055), who transmitted the teaching to Atīśa (982–1054; met Rin-chen bzang-po in 1042). These well-known successors are the basis for establishing her date.

95. This biographical account is drawn from a detailed oral biography of Bhikṣuṇī Lakṣmī that Sherry Ortner gathered in Nepal. The oral biography is clearly based on a written version or versions unspecified by her informant. Prof. Ortner has most kindly allowed me to cite her typescript version of this biography, which is briefly introduced in *High Religion*, p. 181, and will appear in her forthcoming work.

96. This version occurs in the brief biography related in Kalu Rinpoche, "Women, *Siddhi*, and Dharma," pp. 96–97.

97. Episode 17 in Sherry Ortner's typescript version of the biography.

98. Episodes 18–21 in ibid.

99. Sherry Ortner, *Sherpas through Their Rituals*, chap. 3.

100. Ibid., p. 130. She reports on p. 36 that the ritual is also unique in being the only communal ritual devoted to a peaceful deity.

101. Ibid., pp. 164–65. Although the ritual is usually devoted to personal liberation, Stan Mumford reports an innovative application of the ritual in Tshap village in Nepal. A fasting ritual is staged during the Dasain festival, a major occasion of animal sacrifice, and the participants dedicate the merit to the liberation of the slaughtered animals; see Stan Mumford, *Himalayan Dialogue*, p. 113.

102. Sherry Ortner, *Sherpas through Their Rituals*, p. 59.

103. For descriptions of the ritual, see Emil Schlagintweit, *Buddhism in Tibet*, pp. 240–42; Christoph von Fürer-Haimendorf, *The Sherpas of Nepal*, pp. 180–84, although Haimendorf misidentifies a story told on the occasion of the ritual as the origin story of the ritual; and an insightful discussion based on participant observation by Stan Mumford in *Himalayan Dialogue*, pp. 25, 57, 111–13.

104. Sherry Ortner, *Sherpas through Their Rituals*, pp. 51, 55, and 173, n. 3; Christoph von Fürer-Haimendorf, *The Sherpas of Nepal*, p. 182.

105. A three-month *smyung-gnas* is undertaken annually by the nuns at Hemis convent in Ladakh. For this long session, food is eaten every other day. In another case, a two-week fasting ritual is led annually in California by Lama Lodo, a Karma bKa'-brgyud lama. People may take a vow to perform a fast monthly or to complete a certain number of fasts during their lifetime, sometimes numbering in the hundreds; see George Roerich, trans., *Blue Annals*, pp. 1014–15, 1017.

106. Samuel Beal, trans., *Si-yu-ki*, vol. 1, p. 160. It is not clear whether the monastic institution in question is a monastery or a convent.

107. Within Tantric Buddhism the fasting practice is a relatively exoteric one. There is no perfection stage (*sampannakrama*) of advanced yogic practices, so as a *tantra* of the *kriyā-tantra* class it can be taught and practiced more widely than an *anuttara-yoga tantra* practice.

108. He was a disciple of 'Jam-mgon Kong-sprul bLo-gros mtha'-yas (1813–99), which makes this a nineteenth-century or possibly early twentieth-century text. It is used by the Karma bKa'-brgyud sect. My thanks to Melbourne Taliaferro for locating and obtaining a copy for me.

109. Full title: *dGe slong ma dPal mo'i lugs kyi thugs rje chen po zhal bcu gcig pa'i sgrub thabs smyung gnas dang bcas pa'i cho ga sdig sgrib rnam sbyong*. It is used by the Sa-skya sect and included in the *sGrubs thabs kun btus*.

110. This manual and a short commentary upon it by the Fifth Dalai Lama (1617–82) are translated in Glenn Mullin, trans., *Meditations on the Lower Tantras*, pp. 73–84.

111. *'Phags pa spyan ras gzigs dbang phyug la bstod pa*, sDe-dge 2738, fol. 125b.4–126a.1: *zhal ras rgyas pa zla ba lta bur mdzes pa po / spyan gyi padma mchog tu bzang zhing yangs pa po / kha ba dung ltar rnam dkar dri ngad ldan pa po / dri med 'od chags mu tig tshom bu 'dzin pa po / mdzes pa'i 'od zer skya rengs dmar pos brgya pa po / padma'i mtshe ltar phyag ni mngar bar byas pa po / ston ka'i sprin gyi mdog dang ldan zhing gzhon pa po / rin chen mang pos dpung pa gnyis ni brgyan pa po / lo ma'i mchog ltar phyag mthil gzhon zhing 'jams pa po / . . . . / lte ba'i ngos ni padma'i 'dabs ltar 'jam pa po / . . . . / rtag tu bde ba 'byung gnas rga nad sel ba po.*

112. sDe-dge 2738, fol. 126a.2–3.

113. The passage is in chap. 25: "To those who can be conveyed to deliverance by the body of . . . bhikṣuṇī [nun] . . . or upāsikā [laywoman] he preaches Dharma by displaying the body of bhikṣuṇī . . . or upāsikā. To those who can be conveyed to deliverance by the body of the wife of elder, householder, official, or Brahman he preaches Dharma by displaying the body of a woman." Translation by Leon Hurvitz, *Scripture of the Lotus Blossom of the Fine Dharma (The Lotus Sūtra)*, pp. 314–15.

114. *rJe btsun thugs rje chen po la bstod pa*, sDe-dge 2740, fol. 127b.1–2: *zla ba'i 'od ltar rgyal ba'i yum / gzugs kyi lha mo yid 'od sku / . . . . / rang bzhin mi dmigs stong pa'i ngang / bud med gzugs kyis 'gro ba 'dul.*

115. The visualizaton manual is *rJe btsun 'phags pa spyan ras gzigs dbang phyug zhal bcu gcig pa'i sgrub thabs*, sDe-dge 2737; the heads and hands are described on fol. 124b.6–125a.3. She interprets the hand implements and gestures in *'Phags pa spyan ras gzigs dbang phyug gi bstod pa*, sDe-dge 2739, fol. 126b.1–2.

116. The image is known as "Eleven-Headed Avalokiteśvara according to (Bhikṣuṇī) Lakṣmī's system" (Lakṣmī-krama Ekādaśamukha Avalokiteśvara, Tib. sPyan-ras-gzigs bcu-gcig-zhal dpal-mo-lugs). This form, with four subsidiary figures, can be found in the Sa-skya Ngor pantheon of the *rGyud sde kun btus*, compiled in the nineteenth century; see bSod nams rgya mtsho and Musashi Tachikawa, *The Ngor Mandalas of Tibet: Plates*, p. xx and plate 135. It also occurs in the nineteenth-century sNar-thang pantheon, or "sNar-thang Five Hundred"; see Lokesh Chandra, *Buddhist Iconography*, no. 614.

117. The major works are *mahāsiddha* biographies in the Tibetan canon, the *Grub thob brgyad cu rtsa bzhi'i lo rgyus*; Tāranātha's collection of *siddha* lineages, the *bKa' babs bdun ldan*, translated into English most recently and most accurately by David Templeman under the title *Seven Instruction Lineages*; various biographies and lineages in works of the *chos-byung*, or Buddhist history, genre, especially in the *Debs ther dngon po* by gZhon-nu-dpal, translated into English by George Roerich under the title *Blue Annals*; and various sectarian annals and lineage histories, such as the Sa-skya version by 'Phags-pa in the *Sa skya gsung 'bum*, vol. PA. Lineages of particular teachings are additionally given in works discussing those teachings.

118. The problems stem from such features as multiple names for a single person, discrepancies among chronologies, some persons being listed as both the predecessor and successor of a given person, and similar stories becoming associated with several figures. General issues and specific problems in identifying and dating the adepts are discussed in Giuseppe Tucci, "Animadversiones Indicae," pp. 138–58; Râhula Sâṅkṛtyâyana, "Recherches Bouddhiques, part 2, L'Origine du Vajrayâna et les 84 Siddhas," pp. 218ff.; Giuseppe Tucci, *Tibetan Painted Scrolls*, pp. 227–32; David Snellgrove, *The Hevajra Tantra*, vol. 1, pp. 12–15; Turrell Wylie, "Dating the Death of Nāropa"; and Keith Dowman, *Masters of Mahāmudrā*, pp. 389–94 and the commentaries following each *mahāsiddha* biography, in which he summarizes information from the aforementioned sources.

119. According to the historian Jo-nang Tāranātha, Saraha was a contemporary of Pāla dynasty king Dharmapāla (reigned ca. 775–812). However, ac-

counts in other Tibetan sources variously make him a contemporary of kings Mahāpāla, Candanapāla, and Ratnapāla, so it is almost impossible to determine a date for even so pivotal a figure as Saraha; on his date (and place of birth), see Herbert Guenther, *The Royal Song of Saraha*, pp. 3–4, 7–8.

120. The bKa'-brgyud lineages regard Saraha as the authoritative source of their *mahāmudrā* tradition and sGam-po-pa (1079–1153) as their authoritative formulator of the *mahāmudrā* system. Saraha is seen as the authoritative "founder" but is not necessarily placed at the head of the *mahāmudrā* lineages, although in some cases he is—for example, in a classical *mahāmudrā* treatise written in the sixteenth century, the *Nges don phyag rgya chen po'i sgoms rim gsal bar byed pa'i legs bshad zla ba 'od zer* by bKra-shis rNam-rgyal (1512–87), translated by Lobsang Lhalungpa under the title *Mahāmudrā*.

121. According to gZhon-nu-dpal, after Saraha the system passed through Śavari, Luipa, Dārika, Deṇgi, Vajraghaṇṭa, Kurmapāda, Jālandhara, Kāṇha, Vijayapāda, Tilopa, and Nāropa; see George Roerich, trans., *Blue Annals*, p. 380. gZhon-nu-dpal also places Saraha early in the Guhyasamāja lineage (p. 359), whereas 'Phags-pa reports some versions of the Guhyasamāja lineage that place Saraha at the head; Giuseppe Tucci, *Tibetan Painted Scrolls*, p. 231.

122. That is, as its first public teacher after centuries of secrecy; Tāranātha, *History of Buddhism in India*, pp. 151–52.

123. Line as translated by Herbert Guenther in *Royal Song of Saraha*, p. 5. This version of his biography is summarized from Herbert Guenther's translation of the account by Karma Phrin-las-pa (fifteenth century). The *rnam-thar* in Abhayadatta's *mahāsiddha* collection does not recount Saraha's training, mention a guru, or explain why he is portrayed with arrows in his iconography. It does tell that he lived in the mountains for over twelve years with a low-caste woman who supported him during his retreats and offered key spiritual insights and keen psychological observations at critical points; see James Robinson, trans., *Buddha's Lions*, pp. 41–42.

124. Tāranātha, *Seven Instruction Lineages*, p. 3.

125. Slightly amended version of translation by David Snellgrove in Edward Conze, ed., *Buddhist Texts through the Ages*, pp. 235–36. The main changes are additional line breaks and retranslation of *sahaja* as "enlightened spontaneity" rather than "the innate."

126. Tāranātha, *Seven Instruction Lineages*, pp. 2–3.

127. Tibetans authors often refer to this group of three as "Lu-Nag-Dril," meaning Luipa, Kāṇha (Tib. Nag-po spyod-pa), and Ghaṇṭapa (Tib. Dril-bu-pa), showing how closely they are associated with the Cakrasaṃvara tradition and with each other.

128. Keith Dowman, *Masters of Mahāmudrā*, p. 273, drawing on Bu-ston's version. Dārika had received his initiation from Luipa (James Robinson, trans., *Buddha's Lions*, p. 237), whose female teachers are discussed presently.

129. Tāranātha, *Seven Instruction Lineages*, p. 31. Tāranātha identifies the Vilasyavajrā of this narration as "Yoginī Cinto" (p. 31), i.e., Sahajayoginīcintā. For her teachings on liberation through passion, see chap. 7 of the present work.

130. James Robinson, trans., *Buddha's Lions*, pp. 176–79. According to Tāranātha, it was a beer-seller's daughter; see *Seven Instruction Lineages*, p. 32.

131. Tāranātha, ibid., p. 8. Elsewhere Tāranātha credits Luipa with introducing the "yogini cult," i.e., practice focusing on Vajrayoginī or Vajravārāhī, although Luipa was initiated into this practice at a yogini feast in Uḍḍiyāna.

132. James Robinson, trans., *Buddha's Lions*, pp. 23–24. Luipa seemed to have a conviction in the spiritual importance of male Tantrics living in proximity to women; at least, he sent two of his main disciples, Dārika and Deṅgipa, to serve as servants to a dancer-courtesan and a wine-seller, respectively.

133. Tāranātha, *Seven Instruction Lineages*, p. 8.

134. Ibid., p. 36. Jālandhari's initiator into Hevajra was a wisdom-*ḍākinī* who appeared to him in bodily form; see James Robinson, trans., *Buddha's Lions*, p. 162.

135. Tāranātha, *Tāranātha's Life of Kṛṣṇācārya/Kāṇha*, pp. 9–11.

136. Atīśa considers Kambala (Tib. Lva-va-pa) and Padmavajra to be the founders of *anuttara-yoga tantra*, in contrast to Tāranātha, who credits Saraha with this role; Tāranātha, *History of Buddhism in India*, p. 152, citing Atīśa's *Spyod bsdus sgron ma*, sDe-dge 3960. gZhon-nu-dpal also notes this tradition; see George Roerich, trans., *Blue Annals*, p. 362. Kambala is also important, along with Padmavajra, for the introduction of the *Hevajra-tantra*; see Tāranātha, *History of Buddhism in India*, p. 152, n. 20.

137. James Robinson, trans., *Buddha's Lions*, pp. 118–19. A very short work by Kambala's mother (colophon: Kambala'i Yum) has been preserved in the Tibetan canon, as sDe-dge 2643.

138. Kambala's works on the Cakrasaṃvara are sDe-dge nos. 1443 and 1444.

139. Keith Dowman, *Masters of Mahāmudrā*, p. 234.

140. David Snellgrove, *The Hevajra Tantra*, vol. 1, pp. 12–13, citing Tāranātha and other sources. gZhon-nu-dpal also places Padmavajra first in a mKha'-spyod bsnyen-sgrub lineage maintained by the Kar-ma bKa'-brgyud sect; George Roerich, trans., *Blue Annals*, p. 1041. Padmavajra (Tib. Tsho-skyes rdo-rje) was also known as Saroruha.

141. Her teachings on this subject are the topic of chap. 7 herein.

142. Tāranātha, *Seven Instruction Lineages*, pp. 26–28.

143. Chogay Trichen, *The History of the Sakya Tradition*, pp. 8–10.

144. George Roerich, trans., *Blue Annals*, pp. 390–91.

145. XIIth Khentin Tai Situpa, *Tilopa (Some Glimpses of His Life)*, pp. 3–7. This book is based on an oral telling of Tilopa's life by a modern bKa'-brgyud master; it is a traditional account based on dispersed information about Tilopa in ancient sources (p. vii), but the written sources are not named. This is also mentioned in the short biography given in Nik Douglas and Meryl White, compilers, *Karmapa*, p. 5.

146. Although her name is preserved as a Barima in this Tibetan telling, its proximity to the Sanskrit *dārima*, "courtesan," suggests that originally it was probably Dārima.

147. A bodhisattva living as a courtesan is also seen in classical Mahāyāna sources, as in the *Avataṃsaka-sūtra*, *Gaṇḍavyuha* episode 25, wherein the pilgrim Sudhana receives teachings from the courtesan-bodhisattva Vasumitrā. For a translation of this episode, see Thomas Cleary, *The Flower Ornament Scripture*, vol. 3, pp. 146–49.

148. Tai Situpa, *Tilopa (Some Glimpses of His Life)*, pp. 11–12, 14–16.

149. Ibid., pp. 29ff.

150. According to Tai Situpa's account in ibid., Tilopa's first expulsion from his monastery came about when he climbed onto the roof and threw a copy of a Prajñāpāramitā text into the river below (pp. 11–12); however, he continued to stay in monasteries from time to time, but other monks disapproved of him because he was not maintaining celibacy, so he was again, and decisively, expelled from their midst (pp. 14–15).

151. Tāranātha, *Seven Instruction Lineages*, p. 45.

152. Maitrīpa (or Maitrīgupta) was also known as Advayavajra and Avadhūtipa, as ascertained on the basis of Sanskrit texts discussed by Giuseppe Tucci in "Animadversiones Indicae." His other gurus were Nāropa, Jñānaśrīmitra, Ratnākaraśānti, and Sāgara; Giuseppe Tucci, *Tibetan Painted Scrolls*, vol. 1, p. 232.

153. Mark Tatz, "The Life of the Siddha-Philosopher Maitrīgupta," pp. 704–5, 709; Tāranātha, *Mystic Tales of Lāmā Tārānātha*, p. 9. This episode is discussed in more detail here in chap. 3.

154. Mark Tatz, "The Life of the Siddha-Philosopher Maitrīgupta," p. 709.

155. Tāranātha, *Seven Instruction Lineages*, p. 12.

156. Possible gender markers include a *-ma* or *-mo* ending or title of *lcam*, *rnal-'byor-ma*, or *rje-btsun-ma*. An example of a female name with no gender marker is Lhan-gcig rdo-rje (Skt. Sahajavajra), a name that appears among the *sahaja* masters listed in Indrabhūti's *Sahajasiddhi*, sDe-dge 2260, fol. 1b.2. Without the additional information given in the commentary on this text by Lakṣmīṅkarā, which reveals that Sahajavajrā was a woman, it would be impossible to discern on the basis of the name alone that the adept in question was a woman.

157. See Ross Kraemer, "Women's Authorship of Jewish and Christian Literature in the Greco-Roman Period." Following lines of inquiry already opened in Jewish and Christian biblical scholarship, it will be fascinating to begin to consider to what degree and in what ways Buddhist scriptures convey women's insights, perspectives, and authorial intention. An example of a strong candidate for this line of speculation would be the *Kun byed rgyal po'i mdo*, translated by Eva Neumaier-Dargyay under the title *The Sovereign All-Creating Mind—The Motherly Buddha*.

## CHAPTER SIX

1. *Cittaviśuddhiprakaraṇa* verses 42 and 112: *durvijñai sevita kāmaḥ kāmo bhavati bandhanam / sa eva sevito vijñai kāmo mokṣaprasādhakaḥ / . . . / sarvakāmopabhogaistu ramatha muktito 'bhayāt*. *Kāma* could be translated as "love," "desire," or "erotic attraction."

2. A major exception to the general trend of misapprehension can be found in the work of Herbert Guenther, who has consistently defended these practices against trivialization and interpretation within a parochially Western framework. His insightful analyses can be found in *The Life and Teaching of Nāropa*, pp. 202–21; *The Tantric View of Life*; and *Buddhist Philosophy in Theory and Practice*,

pp. 194–95. Sir John Woodroffe (Arthur Avalon) also championed the religious genuineness of ritual union in Śākta Tantra, going against a strong current of disapproval and misapprehension; see Sir John Woodroffe, *Shakti and Shākta*, pp. 553–55, 559–61, 581–83, 588–91.

3. A most effective example of this type of defense is that of Paul Muller-Ortega, *The Triadic Heart of Śiva*, pp. 52–54. One of the wittiest examples is that of Agehananda Bharati in *The Tantric Tradition*, pp. 284–85. Such defenses are also common in works that advocate or provide instruction in the practice, such as André Van Lysebeth, *Tantra, le culte de la Féminité*, pp. 269–70, and Swami Saraswati, *Kundalini Tantra*, pp. 112–13.

4. Agehananda Bharati, "Making Sense out of Tantrism and Tantrics," p. 53.

5. Psychological and affective requirements for the effective performance of ritual is a widespread feature of ritual cross-culturally, not a special feature of Tantric union. See Stanley Tambiah, *Culture, Thought and Social Action*, chap. 1, "Form and Meaning of Magical Acts," and chap. 4, "A Performative Approach to Ritual."

6. In India, the terms *yoginī-tantra* and *mahāyoga-tantra* originally held sway, whereas in Tibet these texts were grouped into a class officially termed *anuttara-yoga tantra* (*bla-na med pa'i rgyud*) in gSar-ma school terminology; see David Snellgrove, *Indo-Tibetan Buddhism*, pp. 209, 462–63, 475. The rNying-ma school uses a different classification system altogether and classifies Tantric union as one of two perfection stage methodologies, designating the method with sexual union as *thabs-lam* and that without sexual union as *'gro-lam*.

7. The *Guhyasamāja-tantra*, a foremost text of the *mahāyoga* class, also richly repays study on this theme.

8. The Tibetan term for this, at least in the Cakrasaṃvara system, is *spyod-pa byed-pa*. It implies the normal activities of daily life as the context for the spontaneous expression of nondual awareness, or the expression of Tantric insight while moving and going about one's daily activities.

9. *Cakrasaṃvara-tantra*, Mal translation, fol. 17b.6–7 (lines corresponding to sDe-dge 368, fol. 233b.2–3): *gsang sngags 'di las 'byung ba yin / sngags dang phyag rgya yang dag ldan / sgrub byed sgrub la rab brtson dang / phyag rgya dang bral gsang sngags ni / lus can rnams la 'byin mi rlob / ji ltar rol pa'i bya ba dag / mngon par 'bad pas rtogs par bya*.

10. *Cakrasaṃvara-tantra*, sDe-dge 368, fol. 233b.4: *dper na la la mar 'dod pas / 'bad pas chu ni bsrubs gyur kyang / mar sar 'byung bar mi 'gyur gyi*.

11. *Caṇḍamahāroṣaṇa-tantra*, sDe-dge 431, fol. 319a.7–b.1: *lha mo sgyu 'phrul sras mkhas pas / pho brang 'khor gyi btsun mo ni / stong phrag brgyad khri sbangs nas slar / nai rañ ja nā'i 'gram gshegs na / sangs rgyas dngos grub rab gsangs dang / gang du bdud ni 'dul mdzad pa / de nyid gzhan don kho na yin*.

12. Ibid., fol. 319a.1–2: *go pā dang bcas bde ldan grub / rdo rje padma mnyam sbyor bas / gang phyir bde ba las thob po / bde ba las thob sangs rgyas ni / bde ba bud med dang bral min*. In the *Lalitavistara* and other traditions, Gopā (Tib. Sa-mtsho) is given as the name of the wife of Śākyamuni. In Pali literature the name Gopā is used for Sujatā, the milkmaid who revived Siddhārtha after his ascetical trials, which may raise a question about who is intended here. The chronology of this narra-

tive makes it clear that the event described took place before he left the palace. Other internal elements in the text also confirm that Gopā is the wife in this account.

13. *Caṇḍamahāroṣaṇa-tantra,* sDe-dge 431, fol. 319a.3–4: *khro bo gtum po'i sgrub thabs ni / dka' thub kyis ni 'grub mi 'gyur / yid ni dri med ma byas par / 'bras med gti mug dra bas bcings / 'dod ldan 'dod pa spong byed pa / brdzun gyis 'tsho ba skye 'gyur te / brdzun gyis gang 'tsho skig pa ste / sdig pas dnyal bar 'gro bar 'gyur.*

14. Ibid., fol. 319a.4–6: *de phyir bsgrub bya bsgrub par bya / rgyal ba'i bdag nyid 'dod pas so / 'dod yon lnga po de spangs nas / bdag nyid dka' grub gdung mi bya / gzungs rnyed pa ni blta bya zhing / sgra yang de bzhin mnyan par bya / dri ni mnam par bya ba ste / ro yi mchog ni bza' bar bya / reg bya reg par bya ba ste / 'dod pa lnga po bsten par bya / . . . / myur du sangs rgyas mchog 'gyur ro / . . . / btsun mo'i skye gnas yang dag bsten / khro bo gtum po'i go 'phang mthong.*

15. Ibid., fol. 319b.2–3: *gang du sbyor bral bya ba ni / 'jig rten nyams pa spang phyir ro / 'jig rten gang gis 'dul ba na / de dang de yi sangs rgyas 'gyur / rgyal ba'i sgyu ma'i gar nyid kyis / de dang de nyid tshul gyis so / mdo sde chos mngon thams cad nas / bud med rnams ni smod mdzad pa / sna tshogs slob ma'i snod phyir bshad / de kho na nyid sbas nas gsung.*

16. Ibid., fol. 319b.6–7: *phyir nyan thos la sogs pa rnams bud med sun 'byin par byed / bcom ldan 'das kyis bka' stsal pa / gang zhig 'dod pa'i khams gnas pa'i / nyan thos la sogs grags kun gyis / bud med la ltos kun ster ba'i / thar pa'i lam ni me shes so.*

17. Ibid., fol. 319b.7–320a.1: *dad pa dman pa'i skye po 'di / de nyid la ni sems mi 'jug.*

18. Ibid., 320a.1.

19. Ibid., fol. 319b.7.

20. Tsongkhapa, *sBas don kun gsal,* fol. 317.3.

21. The term for spiritual friend is *kalyāṇamitra,* Tib. *dge-ba'i bshes-gnyen.*

22. Tsongkhapa, *sBas don kun gsal,* fol. 316.3–4: *phyag rgya de rnams ni grol ba'i dngos grub kyi don du / dge ba'i bshes gnyen te rnal 'byor pa thams cad kyi thun mong du rjes su 'gro ba ma'o.*

23. Tsongkhapa, ibid., fol. 38.6, summarizing the main themes of the *Cakrasaṃvara-tantra.*

24. There is a widespread impression that the dGe-lugs sect deemphasizes the sexual yogas, but I have found that dGe-lugs-pas generally maintain a less casual, more classical approach than other sects, therefore accomplishing greater secrecy and also adhering to some of the original teachings regarding qualifications and attitudes toward women. In addition, the discouragement of lay clergy in the dGe-lugs sect prevents the blurring of lines and resultant confusion that can arise when a guru indulges in ordinary, exploitative, or abusive sexual relations. Such activities are not Tantric, but their performance by holders of religious office confuses Westerners who are trying to understand the parameters of Tantric union. Persons knowledgeable about the tradition know that such behavior bears no similarity to Tantric union and finds no justification in Tantric texts.

25. Lama Yeshe, *Introduction to Tantra,* p. 147. This view is also expressed by Geshe Dhargyey, *A Commentary on the Kālacakra Tantra,* p. 137.

26. He writes: "In fact, a person . . . *must* accept an action seal [human partner], if he or she is to achieve the isolated mind of ultimate example clear light before death"; Geshe Kelsang Gyatso, *Clear Light of Bliss*, p. 126.

27. He writes: "If you are not yet qualified to embrace an action seal [human consort] and have not yet met the necessary conditions, you can still practise by visualizing a wisdom seal (jnana mudra)"; ibid., p. 128.

28. dGe-lugs oral tradition.

29. Geshe Kelsang Gyatso, *Clear Light of Bliss*, p. 126. Geshe Dhargyey, in his Kālacakra commentary, specifies that the fifth of the five major inner winds (*prāṇa, apāna, vyāna, udāna, sāmana*) is the most difficult to bring into the heart center, and it is in order to bring the *sāmana* into the heart that "it is indispensable for the yogin to meditate in union with an actual consort or a ḍākinī (Skt. *karma-mudrā*)"; Geshe Dhargyey, *A Commentary on the Kālacakra Tantra*, p. 137. For a more detailed discussion of the process of opening and clearing the central channel and heart *cakra*, see Robert Thurman, "Tantric Practice According to Tsongkhapa."

30. A rNying-ma biography relates how the master Guru Chos-kyi dbang-phyug (also known as Guru Chos-dbang; 1212–70) could not understand a certain text until Jo-mo sMan-mo, his female companion, unraveled the knot in his heart, enabling him to gain complete understanding; see Eva Dargyay, *The Rise of Esoteric Buddhism in Tibet*, p. 121.

31. This passage, from a Kālacakra commentary by the First Dalai Lama (1391–1474), is from a translation by Glenn Mullin in *Bridging the Sutras and Tantras*, p. 152. The ascension of the imagined partner, or *jñānamudrā*, over the human partner in Kālacakra commentaries, seen here as early as the First Dalai Lama, continued as a feature of this strand of commentarial literature and is reiterated in a recent commentary by Geshe Dhargyey, *A Commentary on the Kālacakra Tantra*, p. 151.

32. The presence of a partner in the initiation ritual reflects the descent of the ritual from royal enthronement, or coronation, ceremonies. Only a householder, or married person, can be coronated; see Frédérique Marglin, *Wives of the God-King*, p. 158. On the genesis of Tantric Buddhist initiation rituals in relation to the symbolism and insignia of sovereignty, see David Snellgrove, "The Notion of Divine Kingship in Tantric Buddhism," esp. pp. 205, 207, 211, 213–14.

33. On the practice of *maithuna*, or ritual union, in the wisdom consecration (*prajñābhiṣeka*) and secret initiation (*guhyābhiṣeka*) and the fact that this disqualified fully ordained monks adhering to a vow of celibacy, see David Ruegg, "Deux problèmes d'exégèse et de pratique tantriques," pp. 213–16. As Atīśa instructed in *Bodhipathapradīpa* 64: "The Secret and Insight Initiations should not be taken by religious celibates, because it is emphatically forbidden in the *Great Tantra of Primal Buddha*" (i.e., chap. 5 of the *Kālacakra* root *tantra*); translation by Richard Sherburne in *A Lamp for the Path and Commentary*, pp. 12 and 172; see also p. 185, n. 19.

34. mKhas-grub-rje (1385–1438 C.E.) attributed the substitution of union with a visualized partner in the wisdom-initiation to a scarcity of persons of sufficient qualification to unite with a human partner: "Nowadays, we do not find

such hierophants, neophytes, along with a *vidyā* [female Tantric], that possess the complete characteristics as have been set forth. Hence . . . [the disciple] imagines he has been made to enter into union." Translation by F. D. Lessing and A. Wayman in *Introduction to Buddhist Tantric Systems*, p. 323.

35. For example, see Geshe Dhargyey, *A Commentary on the Kālacakra Tantra*, p. 12.

36. On this preliminary, see Geshe Kelsang Gyatso, *Clear Light of Bliss*, pp. 126–27. He describes the yogic practices that develop this ability in chaps. 1–3.

37. Any phrase in a *tantra* can be taken to refer to almost any aspect of Tantric practice, and the homologous structuring of the doctrinal categories of meditation, ritual, yoga, cosmology, and philosophy reinforces the interreferentiality of the language, creating a thick weave of potential associations. For an overview of this system of correlations, see David Snellgrove, *The Hevajra Tantra*, vol. 1, pp. 22–31, 35–39.

38. The first of the "four methods" (*tshul bzhi*) of Tantric exposition is literal expression (*tshig gi don*), which is intended for the most elementary level of understanding.

39. Robert Thurman, "Vajra Hermeneutics," pp. 124–26, 137–38, 144. Thurman attributes the literary form of Tantric texts largely to their role in the "experiential, personal, sacramental transmission" of Tantra from master to disciple (p. 129).

40. The term for "secret level" is *garbhī*, Tib. *sbas-pa'i don*, meaning concealed, as if in a womb, sometimes translated as "pregnant meaning" or "mystic meaning." The four methods or levels (*tshul*) of explanation and those to whom the four are aimed are described in Candrakīrti's *Pradīpoddyotana* and further systematized by commentators like Bhavyakīrti. A charting of the levels and stages based on these works can be found in Ernst Steinkellner, "Remarks on Tantristic Hermeneutics," pp. 453–56. Steinkellner concludes that the system was fully developed and in use by the ninth century. Since it was developed in the context of Guhyasamāja exegesis, the stages of practice reflect the fivefold perfection stage (*pañcakrama*) of this system and do not correlate precisely with other formulations of the inner yogas; however, the progressive nature of the explanations and their simultaneity as valid interpretations are applicable to other *tantras*.

41. Giuseppe Tucci, *Rati-Līlā*, p. 44.

42. For example, see the key in Agehananda Bharati, *The Tantric Tradition*, pp. 174–76.

43. *Cakrasaṃvara-tantra*, sDe-dge 368, fol. 214a.2–3: *ri bo tshang tshing sman ljongs sam / chu bo che rnams ngogs dgu dang / gdod nas grub pa'i dur khrod du / der ni dkyil 'khor bri bar bya.*

44. Tsongkhapa, *sBas don kun gsal*, fol. 99.1–3: *bud med kyi phyag rgya ni bde ba chen po'i bdag nyid kyis mu stegs byed kye bdag tu lta bas mi gyo bas na ri bo'o / sems can dman pas gting dpag par mi nus pas na tshang tshing ngo / bdud rtsis bkang ba'i khung bu yin pas na phug go / thams shes sbyor bas zab pa dang rgya che ba'i chu'i 'gram mo / gdongs nas grub pa ni skye 'gag spangs pa'i de kho na nyid la / bde chen gyis dmigs pas de'i rang bzhin du byas pa'o / 'dod chags chen po'i mes nyan rang gi byang chub bsreg pas na dur khrod do.*

45. These are respectively termed *bhaga-maṇḍala* and *bodhicitta-maṇḍala*. See mKhas-grub-rje's comments in F. D. Lessing and A. Wayman, trans., *Introduction to Buddhist Tantric Systems*, pp. 318, n. 7; 319, and 323.

46. *Cakrasaṃvara-tantra*, sDe-dge 368, fol. 213b.3–4: *bsrub bya srub byed yang dag sbyar / ji lta ba ni de bzhin du / sngags bzlas bsam gtan la sogs ldan / sbyor nyid cho ga'i ye shes ni / rnal 'byor bla na med pa yi / rgyud las gsungs pa mnyan par gyis.*

47. Tsongkhapa's Indian sources include commentarial *tantras* such as the *Vajraḍāka*, *Abhidhanottara*, and *Saṁvarodaya*; meditation systems of early masters such as Kambala, Kāṇha, Ghaṇṭapa, Nāropa, and Luipa; and commentaries that he finds particularly helpful, such as those of Bhavabhadra and Bhavyakīrti. Thus, his detailed commentary represents a repository of Indian interpretations and provides a useful compendium of and indispensable guide to those interpretations. Significant portions of Tsongkhapa's commentary have been summarized by Geshe Kelsang Gyatso in *Guide to Dakini Land*, although he does not discuss the portions pertaining to Tantric union.

48. Tsongkhapa develops this argument in *sBas don kun gsal*, fol. 85.6–86.6, principally citing Kāṇha.

49. This analogy was suggested by Agehananda Bharati in *The Tantric Tradition*, pp. 259–60, where he describes how the *kulāmṛta*, or *kula*-nectar, is understood as both the residuum of ritual intercourse (mirroring the divine intercourse) and the nectar produced by churning the ocean of milk, during which process Śakti herself was the main product.

50. These latter analogies are suggested to me by the applications of the term "churning" in Kashmir Śaivism, whose Tantric methodologies were part of the same cultural matrix as Buddhist Tantra; see Lilian Silburn, *Kuṇḍalinī*, pp. 41–43.

51. The Sanskrit terms used in Buddhist texts are *strīpūjā* and *yoṣitpūjā*, Tib. *bud-med mchod-pa* and *phyag-rgya mchod-pa*.

52. "Secret worship" is a translation of the Sanskit *guhyapūjā* and Tibetan *gsang-ba'i mchod-pa*. "Great worship" is from the Tibetan *mchod-pa chen-po*, the term used in chap. 36 of the *Cakrasaṃvara-tantra*. Tsongkhapa comments on this, characterizing chap. 36 as dealing with the "great offering" that relies on a human partner: "Relying on the partner is called 'great worship.' . . . Indeed, placing the syllables on their two pure organs is also mantra. Having placed those (i.e., imagined them on the organs), they do activities together. This is what is known as the great worship"; *sBas don kun gsal*, fol. 373.5–6.

53. Louis de la Vallée Poussin, s.v. "Tantrism (Buddhist)," p. 196b: "The most conspicuous topic of this literature is what is called the *strīpūjā*, worship of women . . . looked upon as the true 'heroic behavior' (*duḥkaracharya*) of a *bodhisattva*."

54. In Vaiṣṇava Sahajiyā, this conflation of ritualized worship and sexual union is termed *nāyikāpūjā*. Edward Dimock has published a translation of the *Nāyikāsādhanaṭīkā*, a text that describes the ritual, in *Place of the Hidden Moon*, pp. 239–42; see also pp. 218–19. In the *Yoni-tantra*, another text of Vaiṣṇava orientation, the practice is termed *yonipūjā*, or "worship of the female organ"; for a description of this ritual, see J. A. Schoterman's introduction to his critical edition, *The Yonitantra*, pp. 26–27. Agehananda Bharati summarizes and translates

from such a ritual as it is presented in the *Vāmamārga*; see *The Tantric Tradition*, pp. 264–65. A Pāñcarātra version of the practice occurs in *Lakṣmī Tantra* 43.73–85; see Sanjukta Gupta, trans., ibid., pp. 292–93. A Śākta version is commended and summarily described in *Kaulāvalīnirṇaya* 9.106, 9.111–12, 9.114–20, 16.45–51, 17.130–40.

55. *Caṇḍamahāroṣaṇa-tantra*, sDe-dge 431, fol. 318b.6: *skyes pa bud med lha mo dang / bud med kyi ni skyes pa lha / rdo rje padma rab sbyor bas / phan tshun du ni mchod par bya / mchod par bya ba gzhan du min.*

56. Tsongkhapa, *sBas don kun gsal*, fol. 89.4–5.

57. Christopher George, trans., *The Caṇḍamahāroṣaṇa Tantra*, p. 80, n. 75, cites an unspecified commentary interpreting the five *maṇḍalas* as the five limbs, which are touched to the ground in a prostration. The five *maṇḍalas* can also refer to the five *cakras* (in the partners' bodies), which are brought together in Tantric union; the meditators can visualize the female deities in the woman's body uniting with the male deities in the man's body.

58. "Tantric yogini" here is a translation of *caṇḍālī* (Tib. *gtum-mo*), which can refer to a rough or fierce woman, an ardent and passionate woman, or a female Tantric practitioner who has aroused her own inner fire (*gtum-mo*) and helps a male practitioner to arouse his own. The multivalence of the term makes it difficult to translate adequately.

59. *Caṇḍamahāroṣaṇa-tantra*, sDe-dge 431, fol. 318b.6–319a.1: *de phyir rnal 'byor brtse ldan pas / dkyil 'khor mdun du byas nas ni / de la nyer zhugs bud med ni / shes rab phar phyin rnam pa la / rtag tu me tog gis mchod cing / de bzhin spos dang mar me sogs / dkyil 'khor lnga ni rab sbyor bas / phyi nas phyag ri btsal par bya / de nas g.yas su bsgo rab bya / gtum mo la ni mchod par bya / gus pa dang bcas sems kyis ni / de bzhin skyes bus bud med mchod.*

60. Ibid., fol. 319a.1–2: *snyan pa 'chag gis smra bya zhing / rjes su mthun par sbyin bar bya.*

61. Christopher George, trans., *The Caṇḍamahāroṣaṇa Tantra*, p. 78.

62. Ibid., pp. 56, 73–79.

63. Translation by Christopher George in ibid., p. 56.

64. Christopher George, ibid., pp. 81–83.

65. *Caṇḍamahāroṣaṇa-tantra*, critical edition by Christopher George, p. 123: *chang dang bza' ba me tog sogs / rnams mchod lus la gos kyis mdzes / yang dag smra bas 'dud byas nas / thal mo yang dag sbyar byas te / blta dang reg pa nyid dang ni / dran pa yis ni smras par bya / rtag tu 'o dang lag bas 'khyud / rdo rje rnal 'byor ma mchod bya / lus kyis nus pa rnams byas nas / mi nus pa rnams ngag yid kyis / mchod pas brnyes des bdag la ni / dngos grub thams cad rtsol bar byed / bud med kun gyi lus spang nas / bdag ni gzhan du gyur pa med / sna tshogs spangs nas bud med mchod / . . . / rang gi bud med 'dod bsten bya / rdo rje pa dmo mnyam sbyor bas / bdag la byang chub ster ba mo.*

66. *Cakrasaṃvara-tantra*, Mal translation, fol. 20b.7 (lines omitted from sDe-dge edition): *pad ma'i 'od ni dri med pa'i / rnal 'byor ma la mkhas pas mchod.*

67. *Caṇḍamahāroṣaṇa-tantra*, critical edition by Christopher George, p. 104: *a ho bdag gi pa dma 'di / bde ba thams cad yang dag ldan / gang zhig cho gas sten byed na / bdag ni dngos grub stsol mdzad ma / blo ldan brtan par rab sbyor bas / pa dma bya ba ji bzhin gyis.*

68. Christopher George, trans., *The Caṇḍamahāroṣaṇa Tantra*, pp. 67–68.

69. *Caṇḍamahāroṣaṇa-tantra*, critical edition by Christopher George, pp. 112–13: *bu khyod . . . / bdag gis zhabs la skyabs su song / gang phyir bdag ni 'phel byed ma / khyod la rin chen nye bar 'ongs / bu khyod byas gzor gyis shig kye / rdo rjes bde skyed bdag la byin / dbus su ze 'brus brgyan pa yi / chu skyes 'dab ma gsum par gzigs / a ho bde ba can gyi zhing / sangs rgyas sku mdog dmar pos mdzes / chags can zhi bde ster mdzad ma / rtog pa thams cad rnam par spang / bdag ni gan rgyal yang dag sbyar / chags pas yid ni rnam par mos / phrag par rkang pa zung byin nas / bdag gi steng dang 'og tu stos / de nas rdo rje rab bsad pas / pad dbus ran dha ra* [*sic*] *rab tu gzhug / brgya stong 'bum dang bye ba phrag / de nas bskyod pa nyid du gyis / bdag pad 'dab me gsum ldan pa / sha yis rab tu gang ldan la / rang gi rdo rjer de gzhugs pas / sems nyid bde bas rab tu mchod / rlung dang rlung gis bdag pad la / snying po las ni snying po mchog / rdo rje rtse mor rab tu rig / ba ndhu dmar po dang mtshungs pa.*

70. Christopher George, trans., *The Caṇḍamahāroṣaṇa Tantra*, p. 78.

71. Secular Indian texts such as the *Kāmasūtra* of Vātsyāyana were available to the Tantrics for study and reference, and texts on the topic were included in the Tibetan Buddhist canon (e.g., Surūpa, *'Dod pa'i bstan bcos*, sDe-dge 2500), but the Buddhist Tantric sources seem to draw upon or represent a different tradition, because they use a different vocabulary with only occasional overlap with the secular systems. The difference in intent between the secular and sacred arts of love is that in the secular context the goal is to enhance pleasure, while in the religious context it is to enhance meditation.

72. *Caṇḍamahāroṣaṇa-tantra*, chap. 6; see Christopher George, trans., pp. 71–72; for other positions, see pp. 73–77. Their context herein is the discussion of the advanced inner yogas, or *rtsa-rlung* practice, of the perfection stage, performed on the final stages of approach to liberation. These positions might occur in another text or body of teachings, written or oral, to which the Tantrics had access; however, Christopher George has observed that these positions do not occur by these names in the *Kāmasūtra* of Vātsyāyana (p. 71, n. 65), and I have not found them in other works of the same genre.

73. E.g., *Cakrasaṃvara-tantra*, sDe-dge 368, fol. 237a.2–3. The Sanskrit term for reverse union is *viparītarati*. Agehananda Bharati, *The Tantric Tradition*, p. 224, n. 2, suggests that the favor shown for this position reflects its popularity in certain regions of India. Frédérique Marglin discusses the gender dynamics and religious implications of this position in "Types of Sexual Union and their Implicit Meanings," pp. 302, 310.

74. This is not to suggest that the temple carvings themselves are Tantric in origin or intent. The theory of Tantric origins was considered in the 1950s, but more recently an apotropaic function of the carvings has been identified by Thomas Donaldson, "Propitious-Apotropaic Eroticism in the Art of Orissa," and Devangana Desai, *Erotic Sculpture in India*, while Purāṇic inspiration for some of the erotic scenes at Khajuraho has been identified by Shobita Punja, *Divine Ecstasy*, chaps. 9–10.

75. The term is *guhyapūjā*, Tib. *gsang-ba'i mchod-pa*. The practice is also called "great worship" (Tib. *mchod-pa chen-po*), as in chap. 36 of the *Cakrasaṃvara-tantra*.

76. This entire passage, which is elided from David Snellgrove's translation, is *Hevajra-tantra* 11.11–14 in Snellgrove's critical edition, vol. 2, p. 99: *tshal dang skye bo med gnas dang / bdag gi khyim gyi nang du yang / gcer bur phyag rgya che byas nas / rnal 'byor rigs* [*sic*, should be *rig*] *pas rtag tu mchod / o dang 'khyud pa byas nas ni / de bzhin bha gar reg par nyid / skyes pa'i sna ni gzhib pa nyid / ma mchu'i sbrang rtsi btung de nyid / rtag tu myos pa'i mtshan ma las / bo la ldan pas lag pas bya / khyogs dang brla zhes bya ba dang / de bzhin shin tu bskal pa yis / yang yang rdo rjes 'dod pa bya / stengs dang 'og tu blta ba nyid / dngos grub rgyas pa thob pa ste / sangs rgyas kun dang mnyam par 'gyur.*

77. The term is *śukra*, Tib. *khu-ba*. For instance, Agehananda Bharati makes this mistake in "Making Sense out of Tantrism and Tantrics," wherein he queries: "It is the man who controls the seminal upward and downward flow. What about the woman?" On this basis, he proceeds to define a Tantric as an "Indian male" (p. 53).

In the West, "semen" is assumed to be a male term in part because of a late recognition in the West of the female effluviant and its corresponding anatomy. For a history of its discovery in Western science, see Josephine Sevely, *Eve's Secrets*, chap. 3. The female fluid, or ejaculate, has been acknowledged and its precise biological mechanism debated in Indian medical thought for more than a millenium; see Ram Kumar Rai, *Encyclopedia of Indian Erotics*, pp. 233–35, 291–92. Although the production of this liquid by both women and men is implicit throughout Tantric literature, it is explicitly stated in the *Hevajra-tantra*: "In man there is this twofold nature, *śukra* (relative) and the bliss arising from it (absolute); in woman too it is the same, *śukra* and the bliss arising from it"; David Snellgrove, trans., *The Hevajra Tantra*, vol. 1, p. 76.

78. E.g., *Hevajra-tantra* 9.12, as well as the passage translated above. The Tibetan translation is *sbrang-rtsi*.

79. The Tibetan term is *me-tog-chu*. *Cakrasaṃvara-tantra*, sDe-dge 368, chap. 42: "Then the hero, having drunk flower-water, should remember the mantra." Tsongkhapa glosses this: "Drink the self-arisen flower-water (*rang-byung gi me-tog gi chu*) with the *vajra*"; *sBas don kun gsal*, fol. 405.1–2.

80. "Musk of desire," as a translation of *madanāṅga*, is an attempt to retain both the meaning of *madana* as passion, love, a kind of embrace, or an intoxicating drink or liquor, and the meaning of the compound, confirmed by the Tibetan translation, as "musk."

81. Some Hindu *tantras* advocate ritual union during the menses and attribute numinosity to menstrual blood, e.g., *Kaulāvalīnirṇaya* 15.117, 16.41–46. I have not found this to be the case in Buddhist Tantra, although future research may reveal some Buddhist attention to this theme.

82. The term "red" in this case refers to an Ayurvedic medical theory that the mother's contribution to the fetus is the red elements of the body (blood, flesh, marrow, etc.), whereas the father contributes the white elements (bone, brain, fat, etc.). Therefore, the term "red" refers to the endocrinal content of the female sexual fluid rather than its color. The nature of the fluid is revealed by its synonyms, such as *śukra* (sexual fluid), *strīśukra* (female sexual fluid), *strīkāmadravam* ("liquid of a woman's desire"), and *madhu* (honey). The misun-

derstanding stems both from the use of menstrual blood in other Tantric contexts and from the ambiguity created by the use of the term *rajas* for both menstrual blood and sexual fluid. An ethnographic confirmation of this can be found in Frédérique Marglin, "Types of Sexual Union," p. 309, wherein she reports her discovery that in Orissa the *rajas* that is collected as the fifth of the *pañcamakāra* is sexual fluid, not menstrual blood.

83. From the Tibetan edition reproduced in James Robinson, *Buddha's Lions*, p. 353, fol. 167.4–168.1: *gzhan lus thabs ldan khyad par can / bha ga'i rnam pa'i dkyil 'khor du / rakta'i rgya mtsho chen po la / byang sems 'o ma bsres shing len / gnas su 'khyol nas khong du gram / bde brgyun chags de lta min / bde bas bde ba 'joms ba na / de yang stong dang dbyer med sgom.*

84. Tsongkhapa, *sBas don kun gsal*, fol. 313.4.

85. Christopher George, trans., *The Caṇḍamahāroṣaṇa Tantra*, critical edition, p. 109: *lce yis kun nas 'zib par bya / . . . / 'dir ni rang gi bza' ba mchog / sangs rgyas kun gis rab tu bzas.*

86. Women as well as men control this fluid in Tantric *sādhanā* and even in *haṭha-yoga* disciplines. The *Haṭha-yoga-pradīpikā* specifies that men and women both perform *vajrolī-mudrā*, or reabsorbing discharged sexual fluid, as in verse 3.84: "By the practice of absorbing the *bindu* [discharged] during cohabitation, a man or a woman will succeed in the practice of *vajrolī*." Verse 3.91 says: "The man and woman anoint their limbs (probably meaning internally spread through their bodies) with what was drawn in by the *vajrolī-maithuna*. The two, joined in union, at that very moment are pervaded and liberated by bliss" (*vajrolīmaithunād strīpuṃsoḥ svāṅgalepanam / āsīnayo sukhenaiva muktavyāpayoḥ kṣaṇāt*). I here take *mukta-vyāpayoḥ* as a *dvandva* compound. Cf. Swami Saraswati, *Kundalini Tantra*, pp. 107–11.

The exchange of semen (*śukra*) that takes place during *vajrolī-mudrā* is described in more experiential terms by a modern Hindu Tantric, Aghori Vimalananda, as recorded by Robert Svoboda in *Aghora*. He describes the exchange, or mingling, of the male and female *śukra* and stresses that "both partners must be thoroughly prepared"; p. 289. "When both partners have full knowledge of Vajroli there is mutual benefit. She releases a little of her secretion to him, just enough to lubricate his prostate; he releases just enough of his prostate fluid to rejuvenate her"; p. 288. Vimalananda also describes the psychic fusion that can occur during this practice; see pp. 288–89.

87. David Snellgrove, trans., *The Hevajra Tantra*, vol. 1, p. 100. There are also passages in the *The Caṇḍamahāroṣaṇa Tantra*, chap. 6, telling how a man should drink the red and white from her lotus, in one case with a "pipe" and another with the mouth.

88. Tsongkhapa, *sBas don kun gsal*, fol. 285.5–6, quoting Lvavapa.

89. *Hevajra-tantra* 8.7: Nairātmyā has asked what kind of vow should be made. The last part is: "May I be born from birth to birth, proclaiming this doctrine profound and ringing the *vajra*-bell, concentrating in myself the essence of woman"; translation by David Snellgrove in *The Hevajra Tantra*, vol. 1, p. 116. "Concentrating the essence" (*yoṣicchukrasamāhārī*, Tib. *btsun mo'i khu ba mnyam zas can*) could also be translated as "gathering (or absorbing) the vaginal fluids (or female fluids)."

90. In ordinary union, it is believed that both partners reabsorb a tiny amount of their mixed fluids, but that the woman absorbs far more as a matter of course. For an ethnographic account of this belief in Tamilnadu, see E. Valentine Daniel, *Fluid Signs*, pp. 164–70.

91. O'Flaherty states that "the female fluid is consumed in clear contrast to its role in non-Tantric Hindu thought, where the male fluid is consumed and the female fluid is 'consuming,'" in Wendy O'Flaherty, *Women, Androgynes, and Other Mythical Beasts*, p. 39. She argues on p. 78 that this signals the direction of the transfer of power from the woman to the man. As I am doing here, O'Flaherty bases her analysis in part on that of Frédérique Marglin, "Types of Sexual Union and their Implicit Meanings." Marglin bases her discussion on a distinction among three types of union: 1) hierarchical or conjugal, as between Viṣṇu and Lakṣmī; 2) between equals, as in the case of Śiva and Pārvatī; and 3) inverse or ritual union (*viparītarati*), in which the female is above the male and is the active partner; see p. 302. Basing her analysis on Śākta Tantra practices in Orissa, Marglin observes that "what characterizes this type of sexual intercourse is that instead of the woman's receiving within her the male sexual fluid, the opposite process occurs: here it is the man who ingests the female sexual fluid. This rite is thus graphically and specifically the inverse of conjugal intercourse and well merits the appellation 'inverse sexual intercourse,'" (p. 310).

92. Wendy O'Flaherty, *Women, Androgynes, and Other Mythical Beasts*, p. 78.

93. Tsongkhapa, *sBas don kun gsal*, fol. 89.5–6, discussed on fol. 89.6–90.4.

94. The term for "measureless mansion" is *vimāna*, Tib. *gzhal yas khang*.

95. For the Indian anatomical terms, see Ram Kumar Rai, *Encyclopedia of Indian Erotics*, s.v. *bhaga*, pp. 206–7.

96. The equation between the vulva and the *maṇḍala* is discussed by Anne Klein in "Nondualism and the Great Bliss Queen."

97. Tsongkhapa, citing the *Vajraḍāka-tantra* (a commentarial *tantra* of the Cakrasaṃvara group) as his source, in *sBas don kun gsal*, fol. 96.3–4: *sor mos rdo rje'i sa gzhi ste rten padma'i rtsa bskul ba dang / rtsa sad pa'i phyi nas rdo rje bcing ba ste rtsa gnyis mi phyed par 'ching ba'i sbyor ba yis snyoms 'jug byed par gsungs pa.*

98. This description of a yogic process accords with what is known of female anatomy, namely, that during sexual arousal the uterus descends, bringing the tip of the vaginal channel close to the tip of the spinal column. For a diagram comparing the uterus and vagina in the normal and lowered positions, see Josephine Sevely, *Eve's Secrets*, p. 125, fig. 47. Although Western physiology is aware of this lowering, its significance is lost, for, as seen in this diagram, the channel terminates in what is regarded as an anatomical vacuum, rather than in the nexus of veins and nerves posited by the Indian system. Taoist sexual yogas describe the vaginal physiology in a similar manner and with more detail than is found in Western anatomical descriptions.

99. Tsongkhapa, *sBas don kun gsal*, fol. 96.1–2: *de gnyis kyi rtse gnyis sbyar ba'i nges don ni / yab kyi gsang gnas kyi rtse'i dhū tī'i mar sna dang / yum gyi gsang gnas kyi rtse'i bya rog gdong zhes grags pa'i rtsa gnyis kha sbyor ba yin te.*

100. Ibid., fol. 405.6–406.2: *chang gis myos pa'i sngags pa zhes pa ni / rigs ldan chen mo zhes pa ni sngags dang ldan ma bcud kyis myos ma can no / . . . / rang gi phyag rgya rigs ldan ma chen mor byas ba byang chub kyi sems 'bab pa'i bcud kyis myos ba*

*can ma zhes pa'i don no / gang gi phyir de bzhin gshegs pa thams cad ni sgrub pa po'i lus kyi dkyil 'khor du 'dus shing / de bzhin du lha mo thams cad kyang rang gi phyag rgya rigs ldan ma chen mo reg bya rdo rje mar bsgoms pa'i lus kyi kyil 'khor du 'dus ba de'i phyir / phyag rgya mo de nyid mchod par bya'o.*

101. Kambala (Lvavapa), who had female teachers, explicitly addresses the women's performance of this yogic process: "'Exhale' means, according to Lvavapa, the descent of the winds of wisdom. On the occasion of the wind in the central vein of a female messenger, by virtue of (the wind) having entered the door of the central channel, the drops will descend"; Tsongkhapa, ibid., fol. 409.3.

102. *Urgyen gyi rim pa'i sgrol ma'i sgrub thabs zhes bya ba*, sDe-dge 1711, fol. 74b.2–3: *spyi bo'i steng du zla ba'i dkyil 'khor gyi / steng na bdud rtsi lnga 'bab yang dag 'phro / gang zhig brtan pas oṃ yig bsgom par bya / mi phyed byas pa ji ltar rnal 'byor gyis / steng nas 'bab pa 'byung bar byed pa yi / 'di yi rnal 'byor ma yi rnal 'byor gyis.*

103. The term is *khecarī*, Tib. *mkha'-spyod.*

104. Tsongkhapa, *sBas don kun gsal*, fol. 414.5–415.3, citing Saraha's mirage analogy.

105. *Cakrasaṃvara-tantra*, sDe-dge 368, fol. 236a.7–b.2.

106. The elaboration given here is drawn from gNyan Phu-chung-pa, *dPal 'khor lo bde mchog gi rtsa ba'i rgyud kyi ṭīkā mu tig phreng ba*, p. 299.2.6–4.4. This Cakrasaṃvara commentary dates to about the eleventh century according to Ven. Khenpo Abbe, a leading Sa-skya scholar and former abbot of Sakya College. This explanation occurs as an exegesis of the root-*tantra* lines: "At a special time the yogi should continuously worship a woman of his Buddha family, a female messenger who has attained enlightened spontaneity (*sahaja*)—superior, middling, lesser. . . . One should worship the Buddhas and bodhisattvas with life-drops (*bindu*), one's own substance"; *Cakrasaṃvara-tantra*, sDe-dge 368, fol. 213b.4–5.

107. Tsongkhapa, *sBas don kun gsal*, fol. 96.4–5: *'di ni rigs ldan ma mchod pa'i gnad dam par snang ngo*. Tsongkhapa specifies a "woman of one's Buddha lineage."

108. Ibid., fol. 95.6.

109. Ibid., fol. 257.5–6.

110. Ibid., fol. 376.1–2.

111. In Tibetan the ten are sometimes called *dam-tshig gi rdzas*, or "substances of Tantric commitment."

112. See, for example, *Chāndogya Upaniṣad* 3.16.1–7 and 5.9, *Kauṣītaki Brāhmaṇa Upaniṣad* 2.5, and *Maitrī Upaniṣad* 6.9, 6.36, and 6.38, the latter presenting mystical contemplation as the ultimate fire sacrifice.

113. *Bṛhadāraṇyaka Upaniṣad* 6.4.1–4; edited version of translation by S. Radhakrishnan, *The Principal Upaniṣads*, pp. 321–22. A similar passage occurs as *Chāndogya Upaniṣad* 5.8, in which the woman is the sacrificial fire, the male organ the fuel, the vulva the flame, the lovemaking the coals, the sexual pleasure the sparks, the semen the libation, and the end result a child. In the same vein, *Chāndogya Upaniṣad* 2.13 equates sexual intercourse with a hymn to

Vāmadeva, a form of Śiva. Each stage of lovemaking is equated with a phase of the hymnal chant. See Sir John Woodroffe, *Shakti and Shākta*, p. 559, for the *maithuna-mantra*.

114. For descriptions of this pattern, see Agehananda Bharati, *The Tantric Tradition*, pp. 261–62.

115. The Tibetan canon includes a number of manuals for performing fire offerings, and many ritual texts were written subsequently in Tibet. English translations of texts in active use today can be found in Sharpa Tulku and Michael Perrott, trans., *A Manual of Ritual Fire Offerings*, and Geshe Kelsang Gyatso, *Guide to Dakini Land*, pp. 439–501.

116. According to Tsongkhapa in his commentary on chap. 28, after the heroes and yoginis have feasted together, they make the secret offering, or "offering of self," by uniting (*sbyar*), thereby worshipping all the Buddhas, bodhisattvas, heroes, yoginis, and everything animate and inanimate. Tsongkhapa's sources (e.g., Kambala, Bhavabhadra, Bhavyakīrti) take this as the secret offering, which is followed by an inner fire offering that occurs in chap. 34 of the *Cakrasaṃvara-tantra*; Tsongkhapa, *sBas don kun gsal*, fol. 304.1–3, 304.5–6.

117. Described by Tsongkhapa, *sBas don kun gsal*, fol. 357.5–359.3, summarizing Indian commentaries on chap. 34 of the *Cakrasaṃvara-tantra*.

118. Tsongkhapa, *sBas don kun gsal*, fol. 358.1–4: *gnas gsum gyi sems can dkyil 'khor par byas ba rnams kyi bar du snang bar byas pas / de dag thams cad kyis bde ba chen po nyong bar bsam mo / bde ba nyong bas phyi'i gnas gsum gyi dpa' bo dpa' mo zhu bar gyur ba dur khrod la dang / dur khrod zhu ba gzhal yas khang la bsdu ba nas / mkha' 'gro ma la sogs pa bzhi'i bar du bsdu ba ni / dpa' bo kun dang zhes pa'i rkang pa gyis kyi don no / de rnams zhu ba shal bzhi'i sna bug gyon pa nas zhugs te / smin mtshams nas dhūtīr zhugs nas byang sems babs pas 'khor lo bzhi la yang khyab pa ni smin ma'i bar du zhes pa'i rkang ba gnyis don no / de nas rang dang phag mo bde ba chen bor zhu ba.*

119. Ibid., fol. 362.3, quoting Ghaṇṭapa: "From the A at the navel, the fire rises, burning. . . . Burn the five offerings there."

120. As cited by Tsongkhapa, ibid., fol. 361.4–5.

121. The root text only specifies nine offerings to be burnt, allowing for different sets that can include the five sense-faculties, five *skandhas*, etc. The process was not totally systematized; for alternative sets of offerings, see ibid., fol. 362.3–5.

A similar conception of the inner fire offering in Kashmir Śaivism is seen in a Abhinavagupta's *Tantrāloka* 3.259.b–264: "The disappearance obtained by this violent digestion . . . consumes by fire the kindling wood of differentiation. . . . All existing things hurled forcibly into the fire that rages in the stomach of one's own consciousness abandon all differentiation and feed the fire with the fuel of its own powers. When the finite form of all things is dissolved by this violent digestion, then the All, which feeds and sustains the divinities of consciousness, becomes the ambrosia of immortality." Translation by Paul Muller-Ortega in *Triadic Heart of Śiva*, p. 195.

122. Tsongkhapa recommends a series of repeated sessions for twenty-five days; *sBas don kun gsal*, fol. 359.1. The signs of success will be a series of five

visions, and then the *maṇḍala* will appear clearly and vividly before the meditator's eyes.

123. Tsongkhapa, ibid., fol. 364.3: *rnam rtog sreg pa'i nges don gyi sbyin sreg 'od gsal du zhugs pa dang.* There is some disagreement about what to call the "real fire offering," as outlined by Tsongkhapa, fol. 365.2–3:

> Although it may be said, along with Bhavabhadra, that "the fire offering comes from union with the female messengers," one can also follow Lvavapa in identifying the internal yogic process of melting drops of nectar dripping into the fire at the navel as the "real meaning" (*nges-don*) of the fire offering, which he explains in detail. For dKa'-rgyal, "the true meaning of fire offering is visualizing the short 'A' (A-*thung*) at the navel, which is the meeting place of all the yoginis, or female messengers, while the common meaning of fire offering is union with the female messengers."

Tsongkhapa gathers these opinions and concludes that the entry into clear light is the real meaning of the fire offering: "According to Lvavapa, *kha-sbyor* (kissing union, joining of mouths) is the real meaning (*nges-don*) of fire offering, which he explains in detail" (fol. 364.4). He gives more details of what Lvavapa means by the "joining of mouths": "Taking the first letter (A), if you visualize it, it will quickly begin to blaze. The meaning of the two (to be joined), method and wisdom, is: method is the moonlike drop (where the *dhūtī* terminates between the eyebrows), wisdom is the A at the navel. They unite by burning and dripping, which is expressed by 'joining mouths'" (fol. 362.2).

124. Tsongkhapa, ibid., fol. 360.4: *'od gsal gyi rlung sems tsam las dkyil 'khor gyi 'khor lor langs pa ni.*

125. Ibid., fol. 363.4–6: *ye shes sems dpa'i thugs kar padma dkar po la . . . . dkyil 'khor bde chen gyi rang bzhin rdul phra mo tsam du bsdus pa las 'phros pa'i ye shes kyi 'od zer gyi phreng ba las / sna tshogs pa'i sangs rgyas kyi sku 'phros pas.*

126. Technically this subtle form of experience and divinized embodiment is known as an "illusory body" (*māyādeha*, Tib. *sgyu-ma'i lus*).

127. The mutual resonance that propels the partners through various mental-bodily states is implicit in Buddhist descriptions of the process but rarely explicitly described. The resonance is described in more experiential terms in Kashmiri Śaivite sources; see Lilian Silburn, *Kuṇḍalinī*, p. 169. It is also described more phenomenologically by Aghori Vimalananda as recorded by Robert Svoboda in *Aghora*, wherein he describes the psychic fusion that can occur after the practice of *vajrolī-mudrā*: "Then there are higher practices of *sahajoli* and *amaroli*, in which the man and woman enter each other's subtle bodies and feel what each other are experiencing and enjoying. This requires two very advanced partners" (p. 288). He also claims that "Vajroli is . . . a union of two personalities into one. . . . The union . . . can be used for great spiritual advancements. It is the achievement of a lifetime" (p. 289).

128. According to June McDaniel, "in these traditions, there is also a disintegration of intimacy, an element of sexual alienation and distancing. The *tāntrika* and Bāul have sex without sensuality. . . . There is no relationship of intimacy with an individual—the woman (or in rare cases the man) involved is an object, a representation of power itself or of other persons or deities. For the *tāntrika*,

sensuality is reserved for the dark goddess of mystery and danger . . . while physical women are merely spiritual batteries" (*Madness of the Saints*, p. 274).

129. *Cakrasaṃvara-tantra*, sDe-dge 368, fol. 239b.7–240a.1: *phyag rgya gcer bur mchod pa yi / las nyid kyis ni yongs su grol / gos nyid kyis ni bkab pa'am gzhan / 'dod pa rnams kyis gos mi 'gyur / las rnams thams cad brtsam par bya / rtsa ba'i sngags dang de bzhin gzhan / phyogs bcing par ni 'jug pa yis / lha dang lha yi tshogs kyis kyang / ma mthong bar ni mchod par gyis.*

130. Tsongkhapa, *sBas don kun gsal*, fol. 415.5–416.1.

131. Tib. *chags-pa chen-po* or *'dod-chags chen-po*; see Tsongkhapa, ibid., fol. 234.3.

132. Mircea Eliade, *Yoga: Immortality and Freedom*, p. 261, n. 204.

133. Christopher George, *The Caṇḍamahāroṣaṇa Tantra*, critical edition, p. 31: *na virāgāt paraṁ pāpaṁ na puṇyaṁ sukhata paraṁ.*

134. *Cakrasaṃvara-tantra*, sDe-dge 368, fol. 233a.1–2: *'dod la rmongs pas 'gro mi byed / pho nya la rtag zhen thar pa / . . . / skye gnas dman dang cig shos la'ang / bsnyen bkur nyid ni bya ba min.*

135. Tsongkhapa, *sBas don kun gsal*, fol. 306.2: *pho nya mo dam tshig dang ldan pa ma gtogs pa 'dod ma'i khyad par gzhan dag la / 'dod pa la rmongs pas bgrod par ma bya'o.*

136. Ibid., fol. 307.1–4: *pho nya'i mtshan nyid phun sum tshogs par ma gyur na / skye gnas dman pa yin la / de la mi gnas pa ni mtshan nyid tshangs ba yin pas de la bsnyen bkur gyis gus par bya ba nyid de de tsam ni bya ba min no / Lva va pas / pho nya mo mtshan nyid dang ldan pa la bza' btung la sogs pas bsnyen bkur bnyid de kho na'am de tsham zhig bya ba min gyi / snyoms par 'jug par bya ste / ji skad du / . . . / chags pas 'dus par dga' ba ste / de phyir 'khyud par rab tu bya / rjes su chags dang ldan pas 'thob / gzhan du bde bar mi 'gyur ro.*

137. Ibid., fol. 312.5.

138. Ibid., fol. 313.2–3: *sgrub pa po de yi pho nya mo mchog . . . btshon par ldan pa ste le lo med par dngos grub sgrub pa la rjes su chags pa'o / de 'dra ba de rnyed nas de dang legs par sbyor ba las kun nas te shin tu chags pa'i dga' ba yi longs spyod bya'o.*

139. Ibid., fol. 351.6–352.1.

140. Ibid., fol. 89.1–2. "Disciplined" here is a translation of *sbyangs-pa*, which means accomplished at meditation and thus disciplined, skillful, and experienced.

141. Ibid., fol. 290.5–6: *kun mtshan nyid ma tshang bar de ltar byed pa la nyes dmigs shin tu che bar gsungs pa rnams.*

142. Ibid., fol. 91.4–5.

143. We find similar belief in the necessity of the adeptness of both partners in Kashmir Śaivite Tantra, Sahajiya Vaiṣṇava Tantra, and Aghora Tantra. For the Kashmiri Śaivite convictions on this matter, see Lilian Silburn, *Kuṇḍalinī*, pp. 180–81. Edward Dimock, in *Place of the Hidden Moon*, summarizing Bengali sources he studied in great depth, reports on pp. 220–21 that "the implications throughout are that both male and female can attain the ultimate goal" and that the man and woman must both have religious motivations and be "alike" (*sāmāna*); he translates from *Caṇḍīdāser padavālī*, a Bengali text that warns: "The man and woman should be of one type in order to worship in that *rati* . . . . If a woman of good type takes an evil man for *sādhana*, her heart will be torn like a

flower by thorns. And if a man of good type takes a lesser woman as an object of *rati*, he will wander as if dead, as a man possessed by an evil spirit" (p. 220). For the requirements for both partners in Aghora Tantra, see Robert Svoboda, *Aghora*, pp. 288–90.

144. Keith Dowman, *Masters of Mahāmudrā*, p. 217.

145. The vocabulary of the *kāmaśāstra* classifications is sometimes used in Tantric literature as a classificatory scheme, but not as a hierarchical grading, as it is in the secular literature.

146. E.g., Tsongkhapa, *sBas don kun gsal*, fol. 295.1 and 314.4–6. The Tibetan term *dam-tshig-ldan* is generally used to translate *samayin*.

147. *Cakrasaṃvara-tantra*, Mal translation, fol. 17b.1 (corresponding to sDe-dge 368, fol. 233a.3): *bsgrub po de ni dam tshig brtson / dam tshig rigs la spyod pa yis*. Another passage at the beginning of chap. 29 refers to "*ḍākinīs* established in [i.e., keeping] Tantric vows" as the ones with whom a yogi should practice.

148. Tsongkhapa, *sBas don kun gsal*, fol. 278.6–279.1: *dam tshig dang ldan pa'i rnal 'byor ma mthong na / bza' ba dang ston mo dang tsā ru dang . . . la sogs pa thams cad sbyin par bya ste dam tshig dang mi ldan pa la nam yang sbyin par bya ba ma yin no*.

149. Discussions of the Tantric vows can be found in Geshe Dhargyey, *A Commentary on the Kālacakra Tantra*, pp. 17–28. Tsongkhapa's work on the subject, *rTsa ltung gi rnam bshad*, provides an encyclopedic overview of opinions in Indian sources.

150. Tsongkhapa, *Zab lam Nā ro'i chos drug gi sgo nas 'khrid pa yid ches gsum ldan zhes bya ba bzhugs so*, fol. 64.6–65.4: *rang dang phyag rgya gnyis ka gang zag dbang po rab tu gyur ba / rnam par dag pa'i dbang bskur ba thob nas / rtsa ba dang yan lag gi dam tshig la mkhas shing / ji lta ba bzhin du srung ba / dkyil 'khor lo'i sgrub thabs la mkhas shing / thun bzhir bsgoms pas legs par byang ba / dga' ba'i bstan bcos bas 'byung ba'i sgyu rtsal la drug cu rtsa bzhi la mkhas pa / stong nyid kyi lta ba phu thag chod cing / dga' bzhi'i rim pa dang / khyad par du lhan cig skyes pa'i ye shes skye ba'i sa mtshams la mkhas pa dang / byang sems phyir mi 'pho bar 'dzin nus pa sogs rgyud sde dang / grub chen gyi gzhung khungs ma nas bshad pa'i mtshan nyid tshang ba cig gis byed ba yin pa la / de ltar bshad pa'i brda chang rags pa tsam yang ma chags par / zab mo yin zer ba'i man ngag ltar snang re la ngas ba drangs nas / lag tu len pa ni / shin tu mi bzad pa'i ngan 'gro'i sgo 'byed par shes par gyis shig / he ru ka mngon 'byung las kyang*.

151. Offering a new interpretation is not simply a matter of presenting evidence that will stand or fall on its own merits. Like Wittgenstein's proverbial fly in a jar, whose flight pattern is circumscribed, any philosophical or interpretive discourse remains bounded by implicit and explicit interpretive categories and by the terms set by the operative rules of inquiry. The only possibility of escape is by the removal or destruction of the jar—the operative culture-bound assumptions. For instance, Western readers will tend to equate sexual discourse and power discourse. This can be seen in the interpretation of Tantric sexual relations as power relations, or relations of domination. As long as Tantric texts are read as repositories of Western values, the fly remains in the bottle. To attempt to *prove* that they are otherwise simply reifies and legitimizes the preoccupation with sexual domination.

152. Even in the West, where sexuality and power have become closely allied, one can never pinpoint a specific location or transfer of power through sexuality, because both occur in ever-shifting matrices. Michel Foucault, in *The History of Sexuality*, vol. 1, identifies specific strategies whereby sexuality became an object of knowledge and a "mode of domination," or instrument for the transfer of power in the industrializing West, beginning in the seventeenth century, as part of the rise of specific movements and disciplines (such as psychoanalysis); see pp. 103–14. Foucault contrasts the Western objectification, pathologization, and manipulation of sexuality (what he calls *scientia sexualis*) with what he calls the *ars erotica* of the East (of which Tantra would be one), which he characterizes as sexuality developed and explored for its own sake, for a bliss that leads to transcendence; see pp. 57–58.

153. Third World feminists have criticized Western scholarship and feminism for their emphasis upon dominance and exploitation, contending that Western values preclude appreciation of some of the highly nuanced balances of interdependence and autonomy that can characterize gender relations in other societies. For example, see Trinh Minh-ha, *Woman, Native, Other*.

154. *Cakrasaṃvara-tantra*, Mal translation, fol. 20a.3–4 (corresponding to sDedge 368, fol. 236a.4–5): *dngos bo kun gyis sgrub pa pos / de nas phyag rgya mchod par bya / mchod pas mchod par 'dod pa ste / brnyas pa yis ni nges par sreg / rnal 'byor rgyud du mi rnams kyi / phyag rgya chen po dang po 'grub / kun nas dag bas mchod par bya.*

155. Tsongkhapa, *sBas don kun gsal*, fol. 307.4–5: *de rnams kyang shin tu brtse zhing gdung ba'i dbang gis ma dang sring mo dang bu mo dang chung ma bzhin du / . . . lhag par sdugs pa'i sems kyis rtag tu mchod par bya'o / de 'dra ba de la bshung zhing dman pa'i sems kyis dka' thub byed na / phun sum tshogs ba thams cad nges par zad par 'gyur la.*

## CHAPTER SEVEN

1. Janice Willis, "Nuns and Benefactresses," p. 77.

2. A man cannot on his own can have sufficient knowledge of female anatomy and responsiveness, which he must know if he is to master this yoga. For example, when the Tibetan Gedün Chöpal sought to perfect this practice, even with a number of textual sources available to him he could not complete his knowledge without instruction by a female practitioner of the art, toward which end he interviewed women until he found one who would instruct him; see *Tibetan Arts of Love*, pp. 43, 45.

3. Tāranātha, *Seven Instruction Lineages*, p. 31. This Padmavajra is sometimes designated as Mahāpadmavajra to distinguish him from one who comes later in the lineages and who may have been named after him. Tāranātha identifies Vilasyavajrā (Tib. sGeg-mo rdo-rje) as "Yoginī Cinto," i.e., Sahajayoginīcintā.

4. Tāranātha, ibid., p. 25.

5. Ibid., p. 36.

6. Tāranātha, *Tāranātha's Life of Kṛṣṇācārya/Kāṅha*, pp. 10–11.

7. Alaka Chattopadhyaya, *Atīśa and Tibet*, p. 408.

8. George Roerich, trans., *Blue Annals*, p. 701.

9. Ibid., pp. 729, 731.

10. Ibid., pp. 847, 851–52. "Lakṣmī the Great of Kashmir" is an epithet of Bhikṣuṇī Lakṣmī.

11. Ibid., p. 367.

12. This is the case in Tsongkhapa's detailed commentary on the *Cakrasaṃvara-tantra*. Tsongkhapa frequently cites these adepts on the yoga of union; see *sBas don kun gsal*, chaps. 27–29.

13. George Roerich, trans., *Blue Annals*, p. 368; Tāranātha, *Seven Instruction Lineages*, p. 56.

14. According to the Tibetan translation of Abhayadatta, the mother was a courtesan; see James Robinson, *Buddha's Lions*, p. 364, fol. 212.1. Cf. Tāranātha, *Seven Instruction Lineages*, p. 32, according to which his companion was a beer-seller's daughter.

15. Mark Tatz, "The Life of the Siddha-Philosopher Maitrīgupta," p. 709.

16. This widespread assumption is discussed in chaps. 3 and 8.

17. Alex Wayman, *The Buddhist Tantras*, p. 183.

18. This group is discussed in Benoytosh Bhattacharyya, *An Introduction to Buddhist Esoterism*, pp. 77–79. The Buddhist historian gZhon-nu-dpal, author of the *Blue Annals*, identifies seven texts written by these figures as fundamental texts of Tantric Buddhist history; the seven texts (*sgrub-pa sde-bdun*) are sDe-dge nos. 2217–23. According to gZhon-nu-dpal, these were among the teachings that Vajrapāṇi (a human figure, eleventh century) transmitted to Nepal and Tibet; George Roerich, trans., *Blue Annals*, pp. 856–57. The Sanskrit manuscripts survive in Newari script versions; see the following note for editions and translations.

19. The *Advayasiddhi* of Lakṣmīṅkarā (sDe-dge 2220) has been edited and translated by Malati Shendge, *Advayasiddhi (A Study)*. The *Prajñopāyaviniścayasiddhi* of Anaṅgavajra (sDe-dge 2218) and the *Jñānasiddhi* of Indrabhūti (sDe-dge 2219) have been edited by Benoytosh Bhattacharyya in *Two Vajrayāna Works*. The *Śrīsahajasiddhi* of Ḍombīheruka (sDe-dge 2223) is edited and translated by Malati Shendge, "*Śrīsahajasiddhi*."

20. *dNgos po gsal ba'i rjes su 'gro ba'i de kho na nyid grub pa*, sDe-dge 2222. A Newari script version of the Sanskrit text is preserved in the collection of the Oriental Institute of Baroda.

21. Tāranātha, *Seven Instruction Lineages*, p. 31.

22. sDe-dge 2222, fol. 68a.3–5: *dpal u rgyan gyi rdo rje chen po mchog gi gnas su rang byung gi ye shes phun sum tshogs pa'i dpal rnal 'byor ma rnams 'dus nas yang dag pa'i don la gzigs mo las byung ba'i ma nor ba'i chos kyi de kho na nyid kyi mod la byin gyis rlob bar byed ba / sa gsum rdo rje lta bu'i ting nge 'dzin* (*trilokavajrasamādhi*) *la snyoms par zhugs pa'i dus su / nem nur mi mnga' pa'i zhal gyi padma rab tu rgyas pa las bde ba phun sum tshogs pa'i sbrang rtsi'i rgyun 'bab par gyur pa dngos po gsal ba'i rjes su 'gro ba de kho na nyid grub pa rdzogs so.*

23. The term *adhiṣṭhāna*, translated here as "power-enriched energy," refers among other things to a power that flows from Buddhas and bodhisattvas, or the realm of truth, and inspires its recipient to attain certain meditative concentrations, visions of reality, etc., and to speak from that deep inspiration. So

*adhiṣṭhāna* is a term used to indicate when something is genuine revelation. According to the *Laṅkāvatāra-sūtra,*

> Whatever the Bodhisattva accomplishes in the way of Samādhi, psychic attainments, or preaching, is done by being sustained in two ways by the power (*adhiṣṭhāna*) of the Buddhas. If the Bodhisattva could at all preach intelligently without being sustained by the power of the Buddhas, the ignorant would also preach intelligently. Why? It all depends upon whether or not one is sustained by the Buddhas' power. (Translation by Daisetz Suzuki, *Studies in the Laṅkāvatāra Sūtra*, pp. 204–5)

With this Mahāyāna belief in the background, the reference to Sahajayoginī's inspiration from this source expresses her authority to speak religious truths.

24. sDe-dge 2222, fol. 63a.7–b.2: *'dir gnyis su med cing rang bzhin gyis rnam bar dag pa'i lhan cig skyes pa'i gnas skabs su / bdag nyid gyis don te rtogs par bya ba'i phyir / bdag nyid skyes pa dang bud med kyi gzugs su mngon par sprul te / rang gi ngo bo nyid 'byin pa po'i rang bzhin du dnyos po gsal ba'i rjes su ston par mdzad de.* One of her key terms is *sahaja*, a term that is important in works of this period and is not easy to define precisely. It designates what is innate, pure, and spontaneous; see Shashibhusan Dasgupta, *Obscure Religious Cults*, pp. 77–86, and Per Kværne, "On the Concept of Sahaja in Indian Buddhist Tantric Literature."

25. sDe-dge 2222, fol. 64a.7–b.2, followed by a technical description of the development of the embryo.

26. For the soteriological aspects of Tantric physiology, see William Stablein, "The Medical Soteriology of Karma in the Buddhist Tantric Tradition."

27. Tib. *chags-'joms-pa.*

28. sDe-dge 2222, fol. 63b.2: *lhan cig skyes pa'i rnam par sprul pa'i nyams dga' ba'i bu mo la kun tu bltas nas dga' ba dang bde ba'i 'dod pa'i yid du gyur nas / bcom ldan 'das shin tu chags pa dang bcas pa'i rol pa dang bcas nas kun du gzigs par mdzad do.*

29. Sahajayoginīcintā's terms are general enough to apply to both approaches and to be used with any of the Buddha couples that the women in her immediate audience might be practicing. She has been associated with the Buddha couple of Cakrasaṃvara and Vajrayoginī, into whose practice she is reported to have given initiation; Keith Dowman, *Masters of Mahāmudrā*, p. 273.

30. sDe-dge 2222, fol. 63b.5–6: *de nas kyang mgrin pa nas gya gyu'i zab mo sgrogs pa . . . rol pa'i rang bzhin gyi rnam pa lnga rmi lam lta bu la bdag nyid gar mkhan lta bus kun du rtse bar mdzad do.* "Play," or "sport," translates Tib. *rol-pa*, corresponding to Skt. *lalita, līlā*, and *krīḍā.*

31. This interpretation of the "five" was suggested to me by an oral commentator and is reinforced by a parallel passage from the *Laṅkāvatāra-sūtra*; see Daisetz Teitaro Suzuki, *Studies in the Laṅkāvatāra Sūtra*, p. 195. The five, according to Suzuki's commentary, are the *vijñāna* of the five sense faculties. A more remote possibility is that the "five" may refer to the five basic forms (*bandha*) of intercourse as categorized by Vātsyāyana, that is, supine (*uttānaka*), lateral (*tiryak*), seated (*āsita* or *upaviṣṭa*), standing (*sthita*), and prone (*vyānata*, i.e., woman face down). Since the "reverse," or female superior, position, a Tantric

favorite, is not counted as one of the "standard" forms, it seems unlikely that this list of five is intended here.

32. sDe-dge 2222, fol. 63b.2–4: *de nas shin tu 'jam zhing nges pa'i gsung gis thugs 'dzin bar mdzad cing / de'i 'og tu de la dri zhim pos mthug por byug pa'i dri bsung chags pa bsnams pas thugs tshim par mdzad do / de nas thugs nyams su lon pa'i bdud rtsi'i bum pa brgyas bkus pa bzhin du dga' ba dang bde ba chen po thob nas / tsham tshom med par bde ba'i bye brag dag gis 'khyud do.*

33. sDe-dge 2222, fol. 63b.6–7: *mdza' bos chags pas kun tu blta zhing de yi rjes su sbrang rtsi 'dzag 'dra'i tshig 'jam dang / de nas dga' ba'i char 'babs lags pa'i mtsho skyes bskyod pas de la kun 'khyud pa'i.*

34. Technical descriptions of these processes can be found in Garma Chang, *Teachings of Tibetan Yoga*, and Geshe Kelsang Gyatso, *Clear Light of Bliss*.

35. sDe-dge 2222, fol. 63b.4–5: *de nas bdag nyid don byas pa bzhin du yid la sems shing dpe med pa'i ro nyang ba'i phyir 'o bya ba'i rnam pa dag mdzad do / de las kyang sos 'debs pas gcod pa dang / 'bigs ba la sogs pa'i bye brag dag khyad par du mdzad do / de'i rjes la yang shin tu bde pa skyes pas rmongs pa bsal ba'i phyir / skabs skabs su shin tu 'jam pa'i sen mos 'debs bas sad par byed do.*

36. sDe-dge 2222, fol. 63b.7–64a.1: *rim gyis chags pa'i ro yis de ni su yin bdag kyang cir 'gyur ma shes te / grogs rnams sngar mi bde ba tshig gis brjod du ma btub pa zhig skyes par 'gyur.*

37. sDe-dge 2222, fol. 64a.1–2: *yid las byung ba las skyes pa'i spros pa'i rgyun gyis 'ching ba 'dis gnyis ka bcing ste gang gi gnyi ga'i sems kyi 'jug pa ji srid du gzhan mi dran zhing dga' ba'i dran pa la phyogs pa ste.*

38. sDe-dge 2222, fol. 64a.3–4: *gnyi ga yang sir ces zer zhing thams cad la cher ltos pa med cing tsham tshom med pa dang bcas pas shin tu rgya che ba'i dga' sgrub pa spel bar gyur to / de las kyang bde ba'i bya ba shin tu goms pa'i longs spyod kyis thibs po kun sad par byas te / dga' ba dang bde bas yang dag par spel ba 'jug pas bskyed pa ni.*

39. sDe-dge 2222, fol. 64a.4–5: *'gro ba rnams kyi bde ba mtshan mar bcas pa ni / gang yin de nyid mtshan ma spangs par gyur pa na / rang byung ye shes nyid kyi ngo bor gyur pa ste / rtog pa rnams kyi stong pa'i bde ba chen po yin.*

40. sDe-dge 2222, fol. 66a.4–5: *rlung gi blo ni rjes su btsal bas ni / bde ba dam pa'i ngo bo rang sems ni / tshim byed de dag las bzhan mi g.yo ba / shes rab thams kyi rang bzhin 'ga' zhig yin / thabs dang shes rab kyi rang bzhin gsal ba de kho na nyid du sems gnas so.*

41. sDe-dge 2222, fol. 66a.7: *bla na med pa'i longs spyod du nye bar 'gro zhing byed pa'i grong khyer rnams rjes su zhugs pa dang ldan pas 'dro ba 'di dag nyid bde ba chen po'i rnam par ro gcig par 'gro bar 'gyur te.*

42. sDe-dge 2222, fol. 68a.1: *rab dga' gzhan don la dga' mchog gis bde ba dam pa legs par gnas.*

43. sDe-dge 2222, fol. 66b.6.

44. sDe-dge 2222, fol. 66b.6–7: *yang thog ma med pa'i bag chags kyi tshogs kyi zil gyis mnan pa'i byis pa rnams 'byed par byed pas ci zhig bya ste.*

45. sDe-dge 2222, fol. 67a.2–3.

46. sDe-dge 2222, fol. 67a.2–4: *rang bzhin dag pa'i byang chub kyis gang yang lhan cig skyes shing rnam par sprul pa'i yan lag bskyod pa ji snyid pa de dag phyag rgya rab tu dbye bar 'gyur la / gang yang ngag gis brjod pa'i ji snyid sngags kyi rnam*

*pa'o / . . . / bya ba rnams 'di ltar sgeg pa dang / dpa' ba dang / 'jigs su rung pa byed pa dang / snying rje dang / rngam pa dang / zhi ba la sogs pa'i 'dod chags dang / zhe sdang dang / dregs pa dang / ser sna dang / phrag dog la sogs pa cung zad skyes pa de dag ma lus par rang bzhin dag pa'i ye shes kyi rnam pa yongs su rdzogs pa yin no.*

47. sDe-dge 2222, fol. 67b.7.

48. sDe-dge 2222, fol. 67a.5.

49. sDe-dge 2222, fol. 67a.5–b.7.

50. sDe-dge 2222, fol. 67b.7–68a.1: *sna tshogs 'di dag rang bzhin dag pas spyod pa'i dgongs ldan mkhas pa ni / de yi lag na bde gshegs go 'phang bdag chen rtsom pa cher ldan pa.* I chose the feminine pronoun here in view of the all-female audience.

51. U. N. Ghoshal in *The Age of Imperial Kanauj*, ed. R. C. Majumdar, pp. 368–69, citing two twelfth-century sources, the *Kāvyamīmāṃsā* of Rājaśekhara and the *Sūktimuktāvalī* by Jalhaṇa. Since the family background of some of the famous female poets, philosophers, and doctors is not known, it is impossible to say conclusively that an education was not available, perhaps on a tutoring basis, to other sectors of society; A. S. Altekar, *The Position of Women in Hindu Civilization*, p. 19.

52. According to the *Kāmasūtra*, attributed to Vātsyāyana, the women most likely to be trained in the sixty-four arts were courtesans and daughters of princes and ministers. The sixty-four arts include singing, music, dance, drama, perfumery, magic, mantras, logic, cryptography, poetic composition, versification (how to scan poems), languages and dialects, dictionaries and vocabularies, and mathematics; see *Kāmasūtra*, chap. 3.

53. For example, a famous martial ode in Tamil was written by a woman who is identified simply as "a potter's wife"; A. L. Basham, *The Wonder That Was India*, p. 178. Any woman attached to the palace, even a servant, could be trained in the sixty-four arts; see *Kāmasūtra*, chap. 3.

54. Frequent references in Tantric biographies would indicate that many *ḍākinīs* made their living by selling alcohol or running taverns. For information about this occupation, see A. L. Basham, *The Wonder That Was India*, pp. 214–15, and Jeannine Auboyer, *Daily Life in Ancient India from Approximately 200* BC *to 700* AD, pp. 88–89.

55. Jeannine Auboyer, ibid., pp. 86–87, 197.

56. Many court retainers lived in the palace. Wine-servers, who wore the national dress of the country of origin of the wine they served, lived in the palace; see ibid., p. 260. The person in charge of the royal wine storehouse would have lived in the palace. Although Sahajayoginīcintā's activities indicate access to the palace, there is nothing to indicate whether or not she lived there.

57. Tāranātha, *Seven Instruction Lineages*, pp. 30–31.

58. For dancers as living in the palace, see Jeannine Auboyer, *Daily Life in Ancient India from Approximately 200* BC *to 700* AD, pp. 260, 273. Dance was an accepted part of the education of cultured women and was not associated only with courtesans, as it later came to be—after medieval times, according to A. L. Basham, *The Wonder That Was India*, p. 179. *Kṣatriya* women might be trained in dance, painting, and music, although a *brāhmaṇī* could not; Jeannine Auboyer, *Daily Life in Ancient India from Approximately 200* BC *to 700* AD, p. 172. This is seen

in the *Kāmasūtra*, where dance appears near the top of the list of arts to be mastered by women (1.3), and also known from descriptions of heroines in medieval Sanskrit literature, reports of private dance performances staged by palace ladies, and reports that a dance teacher typically was retained as a royal official; see A. S. Altekar, *The Position of Women in Hindu Civilization*, pp. 20–21. *Mahābhārata* 3.232 describes how Princess Uttarā and her companions studied dance in the palace.

59. Parts of her work that have not been discussed in this exegesis evoke the subtleties of these intellectual systems in a precise, technical way. We may find a parallel example in the case of Maṇimēkalai, a famous Buddhist nun of Tamilnadu who was the daughter of a leading courtesan and dancer. As an artist, Maṇimēkalai would have received a basic artistic and literary education; as a Buddhist nun, she received a comprehensive philosophical and doctrinal education, including syllogistic logic, from her guru. A description of Maṇimēkalai's education at the hands of her guru can be found in *Maṇimēkalai* chaps. 26–30; see Paula Richman, *Women, Branch Stories, and Religious Rhetoric in a Tamil Buddhist Text*, pp. 22–23.

60. Tāranātha, *Seven Instruction Lineages*, pp. 26–28.

61. sDe-dge 2222, fol. 68a.3–4.

62. Ghaṇṭapa's biography as it occurs in the *mahāsiddha* collection of Abhayadatta does not name or include any discussion of his Tantric guru; see James Robinson, trans., *Buddha's Lions*, pp. 174–79. However, other sources identify his female teachers; see Keith Dowman, *Masters of Mahāmudrā*, p. 273, citing Bu-ston, and Tāranātha, *Seven Instruction Lineages*, p. 31.

63. Tāranātha, ibid., p. 8.

64. Ibid., p. 45; XIIth Khentin Tai Situpa, *Tilopa (Some Glimpses of His Life)*, pp. 29–30. This account and pp. 30–33 discuss the different types of *ḍākinīs* to be found there: human or worldly *ḍākinīs*, more advanced *ḍākinīs*, and disembodied wisdom-*ḍākinīs*.

65. Keith Dowman, *Masters of Mahāmudrā*, pp. 272–73, drawing on Bu-ston's version; Tāranātha, *Seven Instruction Lineages*, p. 30.

66. Also known as Jñānapāda; George Roerich, trans., *Blue Annals*, p. 367.

67. Tāranātha, *History of Buddhism in India*, p. 287.

68. Tāranātha, *Seven Instruction Lineages*, p. 26.

69. In the course of my field research I did discover cases of Tibetan Buddhist practitioners and gurus who allow the general reputation of Tantra to lend an aura of legitimacy to their seductions, but closer inquiry (generally an interview of one of the parties involved) in each case revealed that the man in question was not knowledgeable about Tantric teachings regarding sexual yoga and that the partners did not consider themselves to be practicing Tantra.

## CHAPTER EIGHT

1. The conflation of the monastic Mahāyāna and noncelibate Tantric paradigms required explicit synthesis. One locus of this type of discussion is the *sdom-gsum* literature, wherein the relationship among the monastic, bodhisattva, and Tantric vows are explored. Some place the vows and related

behaviors in ascending order, each one supplanting the next, while others regard them to be simultaneous, corresponding to a practitioner's outer, inner, and secret conduct. The Sa-skya school Lam-'bras and the dGe-lugs Lam-rim literatures are also encyclopedic syntheses of the general Mahāyāna and more specialized Tantric teachings and practices.

2. Veena Das, "The Imaging of Indian Women," p. 218.

3. The "reproduction of patriarchy" is a complex process. It refers not only to a perpetuation of patriarchy into the future but to a projection of patriarchy onto the past. Patriarchy is served by historical "proof" of universal male dominance, which confirms the inevitability of present social arrangements and gender relationships. Conversely, it challenges present arrangements to reveal in history and in other cultures peoples whose social ideals are more inclusive, equitable, just, harmonious, or cooperative. I would argue that an unconscious motivation to reproduce patriarchy, and not purely historiographical considerations, have fueled denials that women were full participants in Tantric circles and co-creators of the Tantric Buddhist tradition.

4. Historians who were unaware of female authorship in this tradition prematurely announced that all the works in the Buddhist canons are of male authorship; for example, see Janice Willis, "Nuns and Benefactresses," pp. 60 and 78, n. 3.

5. For example, James Robinson provides partial lists of the texts by the female *mahāsiddhas* in his appendix in *Buddha's Lions*, pp. 304, 306. These lists are not complete or authenticated, but they provide a helpful point of departure for someone searching for texts by women.

6. Herbert Guenther, *The Life and Teaching of Nāropa*, p. x; see also pp. ix and x, n.1.

7. Alan Sponberg, "Attitudes toward Women and the Feminine in Early Buddhism," p. 28. Sponberg argues that the *ḍākinīs* are of benefit to men because they are of the opposite sex and thus complementary to them, but he does not extend his argument and claim that the male figures of Tantric iconography are irrelevant to men and solely benefit women.

8. Nathan Katz, "Anima and mKha'-'gro-ma." Although Katz acknowledges that a *ḍākinī* may be a human woman, he focuses on the role of this figure in male spiritual development.

9. Fokke Sierksma, *Tibet's Terrifying Deities*, p. 197; see also pp. 158, 198, 273, 275. A similar interpretation reappears in Keith Dowman's analysis of Severed-Headed Vajrayoginī as "the yogin's female energy fulfilling the function of ego-destruction"; *Masters of Mahāmudrā*, p. 320.

10. Shashibhushan Dasgupta, *Obscure Religious Cults*, p. 99; see also pp. 116, 173. For an overview of interpretations of the *ḍākinī* figure, see Janice Willis, "Ḍākinī."

11. Willis, ibid., p. 72. Her explanation for this claim follows on pp. 72–73.

12. One does find occasional acknowledgments in the works mainly of Indian and several Tibetan scholars. N. N. Bhattacharyya, *History of Tantric Religion*, p. 110: "The Lāmās therefore constituted a mystic group of adepts who had their own special practices. The Ḍākinīs . . . were also women of flesh and blood, later raised to the standard of divinity." Also, *ḍākinī* is translated as

"awakened women" (p. 116) and "female mystics" (p. 118) by Lhalungpa in *Mahāmudrā*; see also p. 460, n. 197. Pioneering Western studies that treat the yoginis and *ḍākinīs* in Buddhist and Śaiva Tantric movements as human women are those of Martin Kalff, "Selected Chapters from the *Abhidhānottara-tantra*," pp. 46–48, 93–97, and Alexis Sanderson, "Purity and power among the Brahmans of Kashmir," pp. 201–2, and "Śaivism and the Tantric Traditions," pp. 671–72.

# *Bibliography*

## TIBETAN SOURCES

Tibetan sources are listed here in Tibetan alphabetical order. Sanskrit names of Indian authors, when known or when reconstruction is generally agreed upon, are used.


Indrabhūti. *Lhan cig skyes grub* (Skt. *Sahajasiddhi*). sDe-dge 2260, bsTan-'gyur, rGyud, ZHI, 1b–4a.

Kanakhalā. See Mekhalā.

Kambala'i Yum. *De kho na nyid gsal bar byed pa'i sgron ma zhes bya ba*. sDe-dge 2643, bsTan-'gyur, rGyud, JU, 246b–247a.

Kambala. *bCom ldan 'das dpal 'khor lo bde mchog gi sgrub thabs rin po che gtsug gi nor bu zhes bya ba*. sDe-dge 1443, bsTan-'gyur, rGyud, WA, 243b-251a.

———. *dPal 'khor lo bde mchog gi dkyil 'khor gyi cho ga rin po che rab tu gsal ba'i sgron ma zhes bya ba*. sDe-dge 1444, bsTan-'gyur, rGyud, WA, 251a–272b.

Kurukullātārā et al. *Phyag rgya chen po brda'i brgyud pa*. sDe-dge 2439, bsTan-'gyur, rGyud, JI, 50a–55b.

*mKha' 'gro ma'i 'jam glu ring mo zhes bya*. sDe-dge 2451, bsTan-'gyur, rGyud, ZI, 88a–90a.

'Gos Lotsawa gZhon-nu-dpal. *Deb gter sngon po bzhugs*. Published as *The Blue Annals, Completed in* A.D. *1478*, reproduced by Lokesh Chandra from the collection of Prof. Raghu Vira. Śata-Piṭaka Series, Indo-Asian Literatures, vol. 212. New Delhi: International Academy of Indian Culture, 1974.

*rGyud gyi rgyal po dpal bde mchog nyung ngu* (Skt. **Laghusaṃvara-tantrarāja*, abbreviated herein as *Cakrasaṃvara-tantra*). sDe-dge 368, bKa'-'gyur, rGyud, KA, fol. 213a–246b.

*rGyud gyi rgyal po dpal bde mchog nyung ngu* (Skt. **Laghusaṃvara-tantrarāja*, abbreviated herein as *Cakrasaṃvara-tantra*). Mal translation. Printed in Tibet, n.p., n.d.

*Cakrasaṃvara-tantra*. See *rGyud gyi rgyal po dpal bde mchog nyung ngu*.

*Caṇḍamahāroṣaṇa-tantra*. See *dPal gtum po khro bo chen po'i rgyud kyi rgyal bo dpa' bo gcig pa zhes bya ba*.

*rJe btsun ras chung rdo rje grags pa'i rnam thar rnam mkhyen thar lam gsal ba'i me long ye shes snang ba bzhugs so*. (Abbreviated herein as Ras-chung-pa's *rNam-thar*.) Kulu-Manali: Apo Rinpoche [1989].

gNyan phu-chung-pa. *dPal 'khor lo bde mchog gi rtsa ba'i rgyud kyi ṭīkā mu tig phreng ba. Sa skya bka' 'bum*, vol. KA, fol. 153–337a. In *Complete Works of the Great Masters of the Sa Skya Sect of the Tibetan Buddhism*, edited by Bsod nams rgya mtsho, vol. 1, pp. 288.3.1–380.4.1. Tokyo: Toyo Bunko, 1968.

Tāranātha. *sKu gsum rdo rje phag mo zhes bya ba dbu bcad mar grags pa'i sgrub mchod ngag 'don*. Reprint edition, *The Collected Works of Jo-naṅ Rje-btsun*

*Tāranātha*. Reproduced from a set of prints from the Rtag-brtan Phun-tshogs-gliṅ blocks preserved in the library of the Stog Palace in Ladak. Vol. 4, pp. 653–62. Leh: C. Namgyal and Tsewang Taru, 1985.

Tāranātha. *Ni gu lugs kyi bde mchog lha nga'i mngon rtogs* and *Ni gu lugs kyi bde mchog lha lnga'i dbang cho ga*. Reprint edition, *The Collected Works of Jo-naṅ Rje-btsun Tāranātha*. Reproduced from a set of prints from the Rtag-brtan Phun-tshogs-gliṅ blocks preserved in the library of the Stog Palace in Ladak. Vol. 11, pp. 345–87. Leh: C. Namgyal and Tsewang Taru, 1985.

[*rTogs pa brjod ba mkha' 'gro ma'i gsang mdzod na gnas pa*]. sDe-dge 2450, bsTan-'gyur, rGyud, ZI, 85b–88a.

*Thugs kyi gsang ba glur blangs pa zhes bya ba*. sDe-dge 2443, bsTan-'gyur, rGyud, ZI, 67a–71b.

Niguma. *sGyu ma lam gyi rim pa (dri med snying po) zhes bya ba*. Peking 4643, bsTan-'gyur, rGyud, PU, 165a–176a.

———. *sGyu ma lam gyi rim pa'i 'grel pa zhes bya ba*. Peking 4644, bsTan-'gyur, rGyud, PU, 176a–199a.

———. [*Thabs lam sgom pa'i rnal 'byor*]. Peking 4648, bsTan-'gyur, rGyud, PU, 200a–b.

———. [*Thabs lam gtum mo sgom pa*]. Peking 4647, bsTan-'gyur, rGyud, PU, 199b–200a.

———. *dPal 'khor lo sdom pa myur du sgrub pa zhes bya ba'i thabs*. Peking 4637, bsTan-'gyur, rGyud, PU, 156b–158a. (Also Narthang 4554, bsTan 'gyur, rGyud, PU, 150a–151b.)

———. *dPal 'khor lo sdom pa'i dkyil 'khor gyi cho ga*. Peking 4638, bsTan-'gyur, rGyud, PU, 158a–160a. (Also Narthang 4555, bsTan- 'gyur, rGyud, PU, 151b–153b.)

———. *dPal dgyes pa rdo rje'i dkyil 'khor gyi cho ga zhes bya ba*. sDe-dge 1296, bsTan-'gyur, rGyud, TA, 187a–188b.

———. *dPal 'chi med ye shes chen po*. Peking 4639, bsTan-'gyur, rGyud, PU, 160b–161b.

———. *Phyag rgya chen po*. Peking 4640, bsTan-'gyur, rGyud, PU, 161b–162b.

———. *'Phags pa smon lam gyi rgyal po (zhes bya ba)*. Peking 4650, bsTan-'gyur, rGyud, PU, 201a–203a.

———. [*rTsa kha 'byed pa'i man ngag*]. Peking 4645, bsTan-'gyur, rGyud, PU, 199a.

———. [*rTsa rlung la sogs sgom pa*]. Peking 4646, bsTan-'gyur, rGyud, PU, 199a–b.

———. *Rang grol phyag rgya chen po zhes bya ba*. Peking 4641, bsTan-'gyur, rGyud, PU, 162b–164b.

———. [*Rang lus rtsa yi 'khor lo*]. Peking 4649, bsTan-'gyur, rGyud, PU, 201a.

———. *Lam khyer gyi chos gsum zhes bya ba*. Peking 4642, bsTan-'gyur, rGyud, PU, 163a–164b.

Padmalocanā, compiler. *Phyag rgya chen po rin po che brda'i man ngag*. sDe-dge 2445, bsTan-'gyur, rGyud, ZI, 74a–79a.

Padmalocanā, Jñānalocanā, and Śavari. *Phyag rgya chen po rdo rje'i glu zhes bya ba*. sDe-dge 2287, bsTan-'gyur, rGyud, ZHI, 150a–152b.

dPa'-bo gTsug-lag. *Dam pa'i chos kyis 'khor lo bsgyur ba rnams kyi byung ba gsal bar byed pa mkhas pa'i dga' ston*. Beijing: Mi rigs dpe skrun khang, 1986.

*dPal gtum po khro bo chen po'i rgyud kyi rgyal bo dpa' bo gcig pa zhes bya ba* (Skt. *Śrī Ekavīracaṇḍamahāroṣaṇa-tantrarāja*, abbreviated herein as *Caṇḍamahāroṣaṇa-tantra*). sDe-dge 431, bKa'-'gyur, rGyud, NGA, fol. 304b–343a.

*dPal rdo rje mkha' 'gro ma'i mgur zhes bya ba*. sDe-dge 2441, bsTan-'gyur, rGyud, ZI, 62a–64b.

Pha-dam-pa sangs-rgyas, compiler. *rDo rje mkha' 'gro ma'i brda'i mgur zhes bya ba*. sDe-dge 2442, bsTan-'gyur, rGyud, ZI, 64b–67a.

Bu-ston. *bDe mchog rtsa rgyud kyi rnam bshad gsang ba'i de kho na nyid gsal bar byed pa*. In *Collected Works of Bu-ston*, edited by Lokesh Chandra, part 6 (CHA), 141–717. New Delhi: International Academy of Indian Culture, 1966.

———. *bDe mchog rtsa ba'i rgyud kyi bsdus don gsang ba 'byed pa*. In *Collected Works of Bu-ston*, edited by Lokesh Chandra, part 6 (CHA), 119–40. New Delhi: International Academy of Indian Culture, 1966.

Bhikṣuṇī Lakṣmī (Tib. dGe-slong-ma dPal-mo; Kha-che Lakṣmī). *'Jig rten dbang phyug la bstod pa*. sDe-dge 2729, bsTan-'gyur, rGyud, NU, 107a–b.

———. *rJe btsun thugs rje chen po la bstod pa*. sDe-dge 2740, bsTan-'gyur, rGyud, NU, 127a–b.

———. *rJe btsun 'phags pa spyan ras gzigs dbang phyug zhal bcu gcig pa'i sgrub thabs*. sDe-dge 2737, bsTan-'gyur, rGyud, NU, 123b–125b.

———. *'Phags pa spyan ras gzigs dbang phyug gi bstod pa*. sDe-dge 2739, bsTan-'gyur, rGyud, NU, 126a–127a.

———. *'Phags pa spyan ras gzigs dbang phyug la bstod pa*. sDe-dge 2738, bsTan-'gyur, rGyud, NU, 125b–126a.

———. *Rim pa lnga'i don gsal bar byed pa zhes bya ba*. sDe-dge 1842, bsTan-'gyur, rGyud, CHI, 187b–277a.

Bhavabhadra. *dPal 'khor lo sdom pa'i dka' 'grel zhes bya ba*. sDe-dge 1403. Co-ne 1344, bsTan-'gyur, rGyud, BA, 144a–246b.

Bhavyakīrti (Tib. sKal-ldan grags-pa). *dPal 'khor lo sdom pa'i dka' 'grel dpa' bo'i yid du 'ong ba zhes bya ba*. sDe-dge 1405. Co-ne 1346, bsTan-'gyur, rGyud, MA, 1b–45b.

Mi-pham 'Jam-dbyangs rnam-rgyal. *'Dod pa'i bstan bcos bzhugs so*. Dharamsala: Tibetan Cultural Printing Press, n.d.

Mekhalā and Kanakhalā. *gYung drung 'khyil ba gsum gyi zhal gdams kyi nyams len zhes bya ba*. sDe-dge 2415, bsTan-'gyur, rGyud, ZI, 34a-35a.

Tsongkhapa. *dPal 'khor lo sdom par brjod pa bde mchog bsdus pa'i rgyud kyi rgya cher bshad pa sbas pa'i don kun gsal* (abbreviated herein as *sBas don kun gsal*). From the *rJe yab sras gsung 'bum*, bKra shis Lhun po edition, published as *The Collected Works of Tsong Khapa, rGyal Tshab, and mKhas Grub*, vol. NYA. Delhi: Ngawang Gelek Demo, 1980.

———. *Zab lam Nā ro'i chos drug gi sgo nas 'khrid pa'i rim pa yid ches gsum ldan zhes bya ba bzhugs so*. From the *rJe yab sras gsung 'bum*, vol. TA, 5–123. Lhasa edition, n.p., n.d.

Zhu-chen Tshul-khrims Rin-chen. *dGe slong ma dPal mo'i lugs kyi thugs rje chen po zhal bcu gcig pa'i sgrub thabs smyung gnas dang bcas pa'i cho ga sdig sgrib rnam sbyong*, expanded by 'Jam-dbyang mKhyen-brtse dBang-po. In *sGrub thabs kun btus*, vol. GA, fol. 92–144.

Yaśodattā. *'Phags pa 'jam dpal rin po che'i cho ga*. sDe-dge 2588, bsTan-'gyur, rGyud, NGU, 154a–156a.

Yaśobhadrā. *'Phags pa 'jam dpal gyi sgrub pa'i thabs*. sDe-dge 2587, bsTan-'gyur, rGyud, NGU, 151b–154a.

Ras-chung-pa's *rNam-thar*. See *rJe btsun ras chung rdo rje grags pa'i rnam thar rnam mkhyen thar lam gsal ba'i me long ye shes snang ba bzhugs so*.

Lakṣmīṅkarā. *gNyis su med par grub pa'i sgrub thabs* (Skt. *Advayasiddhi-sādhana*). sDe-dge 2220, bsTan-'gyur, rGyud, WI, 60b–62a.

———. *rDo rje theg pa'i rtsa ba'i ltung ba bcu bzhi pa'i 'grel pa*. sDe-dge 2485, bsTan-'gyur, rGyud, ZI, 181a–185a.

———. (Colophon: Lha-mo dpal gyi blo-gros-ma). *rDo rje phag mo dbu bcad ma'i sgrub thabs*. sDe-dge 1554, bsTan-'gyur, rGyud, ZA, 205a–206a.

———. *rNal 'byor ma'i sgrub pa'i thabs*. sDe-dge 1547, bsTan-'gyur, rGyud, ZA, 195b–196a.

———. *Lhan cig skyes grub kyi gzhung 'grel*. sDe-dge 2261, bsTan-'gyur, rGyud, ZHI, 4a–25a.

———. *Sems nyid kyi rtog pa 'joms pa'i lta ba zhes bya ba*. sDe-dge 2433, bsTan-'gyur, rGyud, ZI, 47b–48a.

Vajraḍākinī. *sGyu 'phrul chen mo zhes bya ba'i sgrub pa'i thabs*. sDe-dge 1626, bsTan-'gyur, rGyud, YA, 226b–228a.

———. *'Phags pa 'jam dpal ngag gi rgyal po'i sgrub thabs*. sDe-dge 3442, bsTan-'gyur, rGyud, MU, 101a–102b.

Vajravatī. *Urgyen gyi rim pa'i sgrol ma'i sgrub thabs zhes bya ba*. sDe-dge 1711, bsTan-'gyur, rGyud, SHA, 72a–75a.

———. *dBang phyug ma'i sgrub pa'i thabs*. sDe-dge 1706, bsTan-'gyur, rGyud, SHA, 63b–67b.

Virūpa. *dbU bcad ma'i sgrub thabs zhes bya ba*. sDe-dge 1555, bsTan-'gyur, rGyud, JA, 206a–207a.

Śrīmatīdevī (Tib. Lha-mo dpal gyi blo-gros-ma). See Lakṣmīṅkarā.

Sahajayoginīcintā. *dNgos po gsal ba'i rjes su 'gro ba'i de kho na nyid grub pa* (Skt. *Vyaktabhāvānugatatattvasiddhi*). sDe-dge 2222, bsTan-'gyur, rGyud, WI, 63a–68b.

Siddharājñī (Tib. Grub-pa'i rgyal-mo). *bCom ldan 'das tshe dang ye shes dpag tu med pa'i dkyil 'khor gyi cho ga*. sDe-dge 2146, bsTan-'gyur, rGyud, TSHI, 223a–231a.

———. *rTa mgrin gyi sgrub thabs*. sDe-dge 2142, bsTan-'gyur, rGyud, TSHI, 215b–216a.

———. *'Phags pa 'jig rten dbang phyug gsang ba'i sgrub thabs*. sDe-dge 2140, bsTan-'gyur, rGyud, TSHI, 205a–210a.

———. *Tshe dang ye shes dpag tu med pa zhes bya ba'i sgrub thabs*. sDe-dge 2143, bsTan-'gyur, rGyud, TSHI, 216a–219a.

———. *Tshe dang ye shes dpag tu med pa'i grub thabs*. sDe-dge 2145, bsTan-'gyur, rGyud, TSHI, 220a–223a.

———. *Tshe dpag tu med pa'i sbyin sreg gi cho ga zhes bya ba*. sDe-dge 2144, bsTan-'gyur, rGyud, TSHI, 219a–220a.

Surūpa. *'Dod pa'i bstan bcos zhes bya ba*. sDe-dge 2500, bsTan-'gyur, rGyud, ZI, 274b–277a.

## SANSKRIT AND WESTERN LANGUAGE SOURCES

Allione, Tsultrim. *Women of Wisdom*. London: Routledge and Kegan Paul, 1984.

Altekar, A. S. *The Position of Women in Hindu Civilization: From Prehistoric Times to the Present Day*. Delhi: Motilal Banarsidass, 1959.

Atkinson, Jane Monnig, and Shelly Errington, eds. *Power and Difference: Gender in Island Southeast Asia*. Stanford: Stanford University Press, 1990.

Auboyer, Jeannine. *Daily Life in Ancient India from Approximately 200 BC to 700 AD*. Trans. Simon Watson Taylor. 1961. English trans., New York: Macmillan, 1965.

Bagchi, P. C. See *Kaulajñānanirṇaya*.

Banerji, S. C. *Tantra in Bengal: A Study in Its Origin, Development, and Influence*. Calcutta: Naya Prokash, 1978.

Basham, A. L. *The Wonder That Was India: A Survey of the Culture of the Indian Sub-Continent before the Coming of the Muslims*. 1954. Evergreen ed., New York: Grove Books, 1959.

Beal, Samuel, trans. *Si-yu-ki: Buddhist Records of the Western World. Translated from the Chinese of Hiuen Tsiang (A.D. 629)*. 1884. Reprint, New York: Paragon Book Reprint Corp., 1968.

Benard, Elisabeth. *Chinnamastā: The Aweful Buddhist and Hindu Tantric Goddess*. Motilal Banarsidass, forthcoming.

Beyer, Stephan. *The Cult of Tārā: Magic and Ritual in Tibet*. Berkeley and Los Angeles: University of California Press, 1973.

Bharati, Agehananda. "Making Sense out of Tantrism and Tantrics." *Loka 2: A Journal from Naropa* (1976): 52–55.

———. *The Tantric Tradition*. 1965. Revised ed., New York: Samuel Weiser, 1975.

Bhattacherjee, Bholanath. See Bholanath Bhattacharya.

Bhattacharya, Bholanath. "Some Aspects of the Esoteric Cults of Consort Worship in Bengal: A Field Survey Report." *Folklore: International Monthly* 18, no. 10 (October 1977): 310–24; no. 11 (November 1977): 359–65; no. 12 (December 1977): 385–97.

Bhattacharya, Brajamadhava. *The World of Tantra*. Delhi: Munshiram Manoharlal, 1988.

Bhattacharyya, Benoytosh. *The Indian Buddhist Iconography: Mainly Based on the Sādhanamālā and Cognate Tāntric Texts of Rituals*. Calcutta: Firma K. L. Mukhopadhyay, 1968.

———. *An Introduction to Buddhist Esoterism*. Delhi: Motilal Banarsidass, 1980.

———. *Sādhanamālā*. Vol. 1: Gaekwad's Oriental Series, no. 26. Baroda: Oriental Institute, 1925. Vol. 2: Gaekwad's Oriental Series, no. 41. Baroda: Oriental Institute, 1928.

———. *Two Vajrayāna Works*. Gaekwad's Oriental Series, no. 44. Baroda: Oriental Institute, 1929.

Bhattacharyya, Narendra Nath. *History of the Tantric Religion (A Historical, Ritualistic, and Philosophical Study)*. New Delhi: Manohar, 1982.

———. *The Indian Mother Goddess*. 1970. 2d ed., New Delhi: Manohar, 1977.

Bode, Mabel. "Women Leaders of the Buddhist Reformation." *Journal of the Royal Asiatic Society of Great Britain and Ireland* 25 (1893): 517–66 and 763–98.

Brock, Peggy, ed. *Women, Rites and Sites: Aboriginal Women's Cultural Knowledge*. Sydney: Allen and Unwin, 1989.

Brock, Rita Nakashima, et al., eds. "The Questions That Won't Go Away: A Dialogue about Women in Buddhism and Christianity." *Journal of Feminist Studies in Religion* 6, no. 2 (Fall 1990): 87–120.

Brooks, Douglas Renfrew. *The Secret of the Three Cities: An Introduction to Hindu Śākta Tantrism*. Chicago: University of Chicago Press, 1990.

———. "The Śrīvidyā School of Śākta Tantrism: A Study of the Texts and Contexts of the Living Traditions in South India." Ph.D. dissertation, Harvard University, 1987.

Brooten, Bernadette J. "Early Christian Women and Their Cultural Context: Issues of Method in Historical Reconstruction." In *Feminist Perspectives on Biblical Scholarship*, ed. Adela Yarbro Collins, pp. 65–91. Chico, Calif.: Scholars Press, 1985.

Bynum, Caroline Walker. *Holy Feast and Holy Fast: The Religious Significance of Food to Medieval Women*. Berkeley and Los Angeles: University of California Press, 1987.

Cabezón, José Ignacio. "Mother Wisdom, Father Love: Gender-Based Imagery in Mahāyāna Buddhist Thought." In *Buddhism, Sexuality, and Gender*, ed. José Ignacio Cabezón, pp. 181–99. Albany: State University of New York Press, 1992.

Chandra, Lokesh. *Buddhist Iconography*. Compact ed., New Delhi: International Academy of Indian Culture and Aditya Prakashan, 1987.

———. *Tibetan-Sanskrit Dictionary*. New Delhi: International Academy of Indian Culture, 1959. Compact ed., Tokyo: Rinsen Book Co., 1982.

Chang, Garma C. C. *Teachings of Tibetan Yoga*. New Hyde Park: University Books, 1963.

Chattopadhyaya, Alaka. *Atīśa and Tibet: Life and Works of Dīpaṅkara Śrījñāna in Relation to the History and Religion of Tibet*. With Tibetan sources translated under Lama Chimpa. 1967. Reprint, Delhi: Motilal Banarsidass, 1981.

Chattopadhyaya, Debiprasad. *Lokāyata: A Study in Ancient Indian Materialism*. 1959. 6th ed., Delhi: People's Publishing House, 1985.

Chögyam, Ngakpa. *Rainbow of Liberated Energy: Working with Emotions through the Colour and Element Symbolism of Tibetan Tantra*. Longmead: Element Books, 1986.

Chöpel, Gedün. *Tibetan Arts of Love*. Trans. Jeffrey Hopkins. Ithaca: Snow Lion, 1992.

*Cittaviśuddhiprakaraṇa*. Sanskrit and Tibetan editions by Prabhubhai Bhikhabhai Patel. N.p., Visva-Bharati, 1949.

Clark, Walter Eugene, ed., *Two Lamaistic Pantheons*. 1937. Reprint, New York: Paragon Book Reprint Corp., 1965.

Cleary, Thomas. *The Flower Ornament Scripture: A Translation of the Avatamsaka Sutra*. Vol. 3: *Entry into the Realm of Reality*. Boston: Shambhala, 1987.

Conze, Edward, ed. *Buddhist Texts through the Ages*. 1954. Harper Torchbook ed., New York: Harper and Row, 1964.

Crawford, Mary, and Roger Chaffin. "The Reader's Construction of Meaning: Cognitive Research on Gender and Comprehension." In *Gender and Reading: Essays on Readers, Texts, and Contexts*, ed. Elizabeth A. Flynn and Patrocino P. Schweickart, pp. 3–30. Baltimore: Johns Hopkins University Press, 1986.

Cunningham, Alexander. *The Ancient Geography of India*. 1871. New enlarged ed., Varanasi: Bhartiya Publishing House, 1975.

Daniel, E. Valentine. *Fluid Signs: Being a Person the Tamil Way*. Berkeley and Los Angeles: University of California Press, 1984.

Dargyay, Eva. (See also E. K. Neumaier-Dargyay.) *The Rise of Esoteric Buddhism in Tibet*. 1977. Revised ed., Delhi: Motilal Banarsidass, 1979.

Das, Veena. "The Imaging of Indian Women: Missionaries and Journalists." In *Conflicting Images: India and the United States*, ed. Sulochana Raghavan Glazer and Nathan Glazer, pp. 203–20. Glenn Dale, Md.: Riverdale, 1990.

Dasgupta, Shashibhusan. *Introduction to Tantric Buddhism*. 1958. Reprint, Berkeley: Shambhala, 1974.

———. *Obscure Religious Cults*. Calcutta: Firma KLM Private, 1976.

David-Neel, Alexandra. "Women of Tibet." *Asia* 34, no. 3 (March 1934): 176–81.

Denton, Lynn Teskey. "Varieties of Hindu Female Asceticism." In *Roles and Rituals for Hindu Women*, ed. Julia Leslie, pp. 211–31. Rutherford, N.J.: Fairleigh Dickinson University Press, 1991.

Desai, Devangana. *Erotic Sculpture in India: A Socio-Cultural Study*. New Delhi: Tata McGraw-Hill, 1975.

Dhargyey, Geshe Ngawang. *A Commentary on the Kālacakra Tantra*. Trans. Gelong Jhampa Kelsang (Allan Wallace). Dharamsala: Library of Tibetan Works and Archives, 1985.

Dimock, Edward. *Place of the Hidden Moon: Erotic Mysticism in the Vaiṣṇava-Sahajiyā Cult of Bengal*. Chicago: University of Chicago Press, 1966.

Donaldson, Thomas. "Propitious-Apotropaic Eroticism in the Art of Orissa." *Artibus Asiae* 37 (1975): 75–100.

Douglas, Nik, and Meryl White. *Karmapa: The Black Hat Lama of Tibet*. London: Luzac, 1976.

Dowman, Keith. *Masters of Mahāmudrā: Songs and Histories of the Eighty-Four Buddhist Siddhas*. Albany: State University of New York Press, 1985.

———. *Sky Dancer: The Secret Life and Songs of Lady Yeshe Tsogyel*. London: Routledge and Kegan Paul, 1984.

———, trans. *Masters of Enchantment*. N.p.: Inner Traditions International, 1988.

Dyczkowski, Mark S. G. *The Canon of the Śaivāgama and the Kubjikā Tantras of the Western Kaula Tradition*. New York: State University of New York Press, 1988.

Eliade, Mircea. *Yoga: Immortality and Freedom*. 1958. 2d ed., Princeton: Princeton University Press, 1969.

Erndl, Kathleen M. *Victory to the Mother: The Hindu Goddess of Northwest India in Myth, Ritual, and Symbol*. New York: Oxford University Press, 1993.

Falk, Nancy Auer. "The Case of the Vanishing Nuns: The Fruits of Ambivalence in Ancient Indian Buddhism." In *Unspoken Worlds: Women's Religious Lives in Non-Western Cultures*, ed. Nancy Falk and Rita Gross, pp. 207–24. San Francisco: Harper and Row, 1979.

Fantin, Mario. *Mani Rimdu.Nepal, The Buddhist Dance Drama of Tengboche*. New Delhi: English Book Store and Toppan Co., 1976.

Farrow, G. W., and I. Menon, trans. and eds. *The Concealed Essence of the Hevajra Tantra, with the Commentary of Yogaratnamālā*. Delhi: Motilal Banarsidass, 1992.

Fiorenza, Elisabeth Schüssler. *Bread Not Stone: The Challenge of Feminist Biblical Interpretation*. Boston: Beacon Press, 1984.

———. *In Memory of Her: A Feminist Theological Reconstruction of Christian Origins*. New York: Crossroads, 1989.

———. "The 'Quilting' of Women's History: Phoebe of Cenchreae." In *Embodied Love*, ed. Paula M. Cooey et al., pp. 35–49. San Francisco: Harper and Row, 1983.

Foucault, Michel. *The History of Sexuality*. Vol. 1: *An Introduction*. Trans. Robert Hurley. 1978. Vintage Books ed., New York: Random House, 1980.

George, Christopher S., trans. *The Caṇḍamahāroṣaṇa Tantra, Chapters 1–8: A Critical Edition and English Translation*. American Oriental Series, no. 56. New Haven: American Oriental Society, 1974.

Gross, Rita M. *Buddhism after Patriarchy: A Feminist History, Analysis, and Reconstruction of Buddhism*. Albany: State University of New York Press, 1993.

———. "Buddhism and Feminism: Toward Their Mutual Transformation." *The Eastern Buddhist* 19, no. 2 (Autumn 1986): 62–74.

———. "I Will Never Forget to Visualize That Vajrayoginī Is My Body and Mind." *Journal of Feminist Studies in Religion* 3, no. 1 (Spring 1987): 77–89.

———. "Yeshe Tsogyel: Enlightened Consort, Great Teacher, Female Role Model." In *Feminine Ground: Essays on Women and Tibet*, ed. Janice Willis, pp. 11–32. Ithaca: Snow Lion, 1990.

Guenther, Herbert. *Buddhist Philosophy in Theory and Practice*. Boulder: Shambhala, 1976.

———. *The Life and Teaching of Nāropa*. 1963. Reprint, Oxford: Oxford University Press, 1975.

———. *The Royal Song of Saraha: A Study in the History of Buddhist Thought*. 1968. 1st paperback ed., Berkeley: Shambhala, 1973.

———. *The Tantric View of Life*. 1969 (published under the title *Yuganaddha*). Paperback ed., Boulder: Shambhala, 1976.

Gupta, Sanjukta. "Women in the Śaiva/Śākta Ethos." In *Roles and Rituals for Hindu Women*, ed. Julia Leslie, pp. 193–209. Rutherford, N.J.: Fairleigh Dickinson University Press, 1991.

———, trans. *Lakṣmī Tantra: A Pāñcarātra Text*. Leiden: E. J. Brill, 1972.

———, Dirk Jan Hoens, and Teun Goudriaan. *Hindu Tantrism*. Leiden: E. J. Brill, 1979.

Gyatso, Geshe Kelsang. *Clear Light of Bliss: Mahamudra in Vajrayana Buddhism*. Trans. Tenzin Norbu. London: Wisdom, 1982.

———. *Guide to Dakini Land: A Commentary to the Highest Yoga Tantra Practice of Vajrayogini*. London: Tharpa, 1991.

Gyatso, Janet. "Sign, Memory and History: A Tantric Buddhist Theory of Scriptural Transmission." *Journal of the Association of Buddhist Studies* 9, no. 2 (1986): 7–35.

Harlan, Lindsey. *Religion and Rajput Women: The Ethic of Protection in Contemporary Narrative*. Berkeley and Los Angeles: University of California Press, 1992.

Harrison, Paul. *The "Samādhi" of Direct Encounter with the Buddhas of the Present*. Studia Philologica Buddhica Monograph Series, no. 5. Tokyo: International Institute for Buddhist Studies, 1990.

———. "Who Gets to Ride in the Great Vehicle? Self-Image and Identity among the Followers of the Early Mahāyāna." *Journal of the International Association of Buddhist Studies* 10, no. 1 (1987): 67–89.

Havnevik, Hanna. *Tibetan Buddhist Nuns*. Oslo: Norwegian University Press, 1990.

Hazra, Kanai Lal. *Buddhism in India as Described by the Chinese Pilgrims, AD 399–689*. New Delhi: Munshiram Manoharlal, 1983.

Hecker, Hellmuth. *Buddhist Women at the Time of the Buddha*. Kandy: Buddhist Publication Society, 1982.

Hermann-Pfandt, Adelheid. *Ḍākinīs: Zur Stellung und Symbolik des Weiblichen im Tantrischen Buddhismus*. Indica et Tibetica, vol. 20. Bonn: Indica et Tibetica Verlag, 1992.

Hermanns, Matthias. "The Status of Woman in Tibet." *Anthropological Quarterly* 26, no. 3 (July 1953): 67–78.

Hess, Linda. *The Bījak of Kabir*. San Francisco: North Point Press, 1983.

Hoffmann, Helmut. *The Religions of Tibet*. 1956. Reprint, Westport, Conn.: Greenwood Press, 1979.

Horner, Isaline B. *Women under Primitive Buddhism: Laywomen and Almswomen*. Delhi: Motilal Banarsidass, 1930.

Hummel, Siegbert. "Die Frauenreiche in Tibet." *Zeitschrift für Ethnologie* 85, no. 1 (1960): 44–46.

Huntington, C. W., Jr., with Geshé Namgyal Wangchen. *The Emptiness of Emptiness: An Introduction to Early Indian Mādhyamaka*. Honolulu: University of Hawaii Press, 1989.

Huntington, Susan L. *The "Pāla-Sena" Schools of Sculpture*. Studies in South Asian Culture, vol. 10. Leiden: E. J. Brill, 1984.

Huntington, Susan L., and John C. Huntington. *Leaves from the "Bodhi" Tree: The Art of Pāla India (8th–12th Centuries) and Its International Legacy*. Seattle: Dayton Art Institute and University of Washington Press, 1990.

Hurvitz, Leon, trans. *Scripture of the Lotus Blossom of the Fine Dharma (The Lotus Sūtra): Translated from the Chinese of Kumārajīva*. New York: Columbia University Press, 1976.

Jacobson, Doranne, and Susan S. Wadley. *Women in India: Two Perspectives*. Delhi: Manohar, 1986.

Jayakar, Pupul. *The Earth Mother: Legends, Ritual Arts, and Goddesses of India*. San Francisco: Harper and Row, 1990.

Kabilsingh, Chatsumarn. *A Comparative Study of Bhikkhunī Pāṭimokkha*. Chaukhambha Oriental Research Studies, vol. 28. Varanasi: Chaukhambha Orientalia, 1984.

Kakar, Sudhir. *Shamans, Mystics and Doctors: A Psychological Inquiry in India and Its Healing Traditions*. New York: Alfred A. Knopf, 1982.

Kajiyama, Yuichi. "Women in Buddhism." *Eastern Buddhist* 15, no. 2 (Autumn 1982): 53–70.

Kalff, Martin M. "Selected Chapters from the *Abhidhānottara-tantra*: The Union of Female and Male Deities." Ph.D. dissertation, Columbia University, 1979.

———. "Ḍākinīs in the Cakrasaṃvara Tradition." In *Tibetan Studies Presented at the Seminar of Young Tibetologists, Zürich, June 26–July 1, 1977*, ed. Martin Brauen and Per Kværne, pp. 149–62. Zurich: Völkerkundemuseum der Universität Zürich, 1978.

Kapstein, Matthew. "The Illusion of Spiritual Progress: Remarks on Indo-Tibetan Buddhist Soteriology." In *Paths to Liberation: The Mārga and Its Transformations in Buddhist Thought*, ed. Robert E. Buswell, Jr., and Robert M. Gimello, pp. 193–224. Honolulu: University of Hawaii Press, 1992.

———. "The Shangs-pa bKa'-brgyud: An Unknown Tradition of Tibetan Buddhism." In *Tibetan Studies in Honour of Hugh Richardson*, ed. Michael Aris and Aung San Suu Kyi, pp. 138–44. New Delhi: Vikas Publishing House, 1980.

Karmay, Samten. *The Great Perfection (rDzogs-chen): A Philosophical and Meditative Teaching of Tibetan Buddhism*. Leiden: E. J. Brill, 1988.

Katz, Nathan. "Anima and mKha'-'gro-ma: A Critical Comparative Study of Jung and Tibetan Buddhism." *Tibet Journal* 2, no. 3 (Autumn 1977): 13–43.

*Kaulajñānanirṇaya*. In *Kaulajñāna-nirṇaya and Some Minor Texts of the School of Matsyendranātha*, ed. P. C. Bagchi. Calcutta Sanskrit Series, no. 3. Calcutta: Metropolitan Printing and Publishing House, 1934.

*Kaulāvalīnirnayah*. Tantrik Texts, vol. 14. Ed. Arthur Avalon. Calcutta: Āgamānusandhāna Samiti, n.d.

Kazi, Sonam Tobgay. *Tibet House Museum: Catalogue Inaugural Exhibition*. New Delhi: Tibet House Museum, 1965.

Kinsley, David. *Hindu Goddesses: Visions of the Divine Feminine in the Hindu Religious Tradition*. Berkeley and Los Angeles: University of California Press, 1986.

Klein, Anne C. "Finding a Self: Buddhist and Feminist Perspectives." In *Shaping New Vision: Gender and Values in American Culture*, ed. Clarissa W. Atkinson et al., pp. 191–218. Ann Arbor: UMI Research Press, 1987.

———. "Nondualism and the Great Bliss Queen: A Study in Tibetan Buddhist Ontology and Symbolism." *Journal of Feminist Studies in Religion* 1, no. 1 (1985): 73–98.

———. "Primordial Purity and Everyday Life: Exalted Female Symbols and the Women of Tibet." In *Immaculate and Powerful: The Female in Sacred Image and Social Reality*, ed. Clarissa W. Atkinson et al., pp. 111–38. Boston: Beacon Press, 1985.

Klimburg, Maximilian. "Male-Female Polarity Symbolism in Kafir Art and Religion: New Aspects in the Study of the Kafirs of the Hindu-Kush." *East-West*, n.s., 26, nos. 3–4 (September–December 1976): 479–88.

Kraemer, Ross S. "Women's Authorship of Jewish and Christian Literature in the Greco-Roman Period." In *"Women Like This": New Perspectives on Jewish Women in the Greco-Roman World*, ed. Amy-Jill Levine, pp. 221–42. Atlanta: Scholars Press, 1991.

Kramrisch, Stella. "Unknown India: Ritual Art in Tribe and Village." In *Exploring India's Sacred Art: Selected Writings of Stella Kramrisch*, ed. Barbara Stoler Miller, pp. 85–120. Philadelphia: University of Pennsylvania Press, 1983.

*Kulacūḍāmani-tantra*. Ed. and trans. Arthur Avalon. 1915. 2d ed., Madras: Ganesh, 1956.

*Kulārṇava-tantra*. Sanskrit ed. and English trans. Ram Kumar Rai. Tantra Granthamala, no. 5. Varanasi: Prachya Prakashan, 1983.

Küng, Hans. *Christianity and the World Religions: Paths of Dialogue with Islam, Hinduism, and Buddhism*. Trans. Peter Heinegg. 1985. English ed., New York: Doubleday, 1986.

Kværne, Per. "On the Concept of Sahaja in Indian Buddhist Tantric Literature." *Temenos* 11 (1975): 88–135.

*Lakṣmī-tantra*. See Sanjukta Gupta, trans.

Law, Bimala Churn. *Historical Geography of Ancient India*. 1954. Reprint, New Delhi: Oriental Books Reprint Corp., 1984.

———. *Women in Buddhist Literature*. Varanasi: Indological Book House, 1981.

Lerner, Gerda. "Placing Women in History: A 1975 Perspective." In *Liberating Women's History: Theoretical and Critical Essays*, ed. Berenice A. Carroll, pp. 357–67. Urbana: University of Illinois Press, 1976.

Leslie, Julia, ed. *Roles and Rituals for Hindu Women*. Rutherford, N.J.: Fairleigh Dickinson University Press, 1991.

Lessing, F. D., and A. Wayman, trans. *Introduction to Buddhist Tantric Systems*. 1968. 2d ed., Delhi: Motilal Banarsidass, 1978.

Lewis, Jane. "Women Lost and Found: The Impact of Feminism on History." In *Men's Studies Modified: Impact of Feminism on the Academic Disciplines*, ed. Dale Spender, pp. 55–72. Oxford: Pergamon Press, 1981.

Lhalungpa, Lobsang P., trans. See Takpo Tashi Namgyal.

McQueen, Graeme. "Inspired Speech in Early Mahāyāna Buddhism." *Religion* 11, no. 4 (1981): 303–19; and 12, no. 1 (1982): 49–65.

Majumdar, R. C., ed. *The Age of Imperial Kanauj. The History and Culture of the Indian People*, vol. 4. 1955. 3d ed., Bombay: Bharatiya Vidya Bhavan, 1984.

Majupuria, Indra. *Tibetan Women (Then and Now)*. Lashkar, India: M. Devi, 1990.

Marglin, Frédérique Apffel. "Gender and the Unitary Self: Locating the Dominant When Listening to the Subaltern Voice." *International Journal of Indian Studies*, forthcoming.

———. "Rationality, The Body, and the World: From Production to Regeneration." In *Decolonizing Knowledge: From Development to Dialogue*, ed. Frédérique Apffel Marglin and Steven A. Marglin. Oxford: Clarendon Press, forthcoming.

———. "Refining the Body: Transformative Emotion in Ritual Dance." In *Divine Passions: The Social Construction of Emotion in India*, ed. Owen M. Lynch, pp. 212–36. Berkeley and Los Angeles: University of California Press, 1990.

Marglin, Frédérique Apffel. "Types of Sexual Union and Their Implicit Meanings." In *The Divine Consort: Rādhā and the Goddesses of India*," ed. John Stratton Hawley and Donna Marie Wulff, pp. 298–315. Berkeley: Berkeley Religious Studies Series, 1982.

———. *Wives of the God-King: The Rituals of the Devadasis of Puri*. Delhi: Oxford University Press, 1985.

———. "Woman's Blood: Challenging the Discourse of Development." *Ecologist* 22, no. 1 (January–February 1992): 22–32.

Marriott, McKim. "Hindu Transactions: Diversity without dualism." In *Transaction and Meaning*, ed. Bruce Kapferer, pp. 109–42. Philadelphia: Institute for the Study of Human Issues, 1976.

Matics, Marion, trans. *Entering the Path of Enlightenment: The "Bodhicaryāvatāra" of the Buddhist Poet Śāntideva*. London: Macmillan, 1970.

Matsunaga, Yukei, ed. *The Guhyasamāja-tantra: A New Critical Edition*. Osaka: Toho Shuppan, 1978.

McDaniel, June. *The Madness of the Saints: Ecstatic Religion in Bengal*. Chicago: University of Chicago Press, 1989.

Miller, Beatrice D. "Views of Women's Roles in Buddhist Tibet." In *Studies in History of Buddhism*, ed. A. K. Narain, pp. 155–66. Delhi: B. R. Publishing, 1980.

Mojumder, Atindra. *The Caryāpadas*. 2d ed., Calcutta: Naya Prokash, 1973.

Monier-Williams, Monier. *A Sanskrit-English Dictionary*. 1899. Reprint, Oxford: Oxford University Press, 1982.

Muller-Ortega, Paul Eduardo. *The Triadic Heart of Śiva: Kaula Tantricism of Abhinavagupta in the Non-Dual Shaivism of Kashmir*. New York: State University of New York Press, 1989.

Mullin, Glenn, trans. *Bridging the Sutras and Tantras: A Collection of Ten Minor Works by Gyalwa Gendun Drub, the First Dalai Lama*. Ithaca: Gabriel/Snow Lion, 1982.

———. *Meditations on the Lower Tantras*. Dharamsala: Library of Tibetan Works and Archives, 1983.

Mumford, Stan Royal. *Himalayan Dialogue: Tibetan Lamas and Gurung Shamans in Nepal*. Madison: University of Wisconsin Press, 1989.

Murcott, Susan. *The First Buddhist Women: Translations and Commentaries on the Therigatha*. Berkeley: Parallax Press, 1991.

Nālandā Translation Committee, trans. *The Life of Marpa the Translator: Seeing Accomplishes All* (Tsang Nyon Heruka). Boulder: Prajñā Press, 1982.

Namgyal, Takpo Tashi. *Mahāmudrā: The Quintessence of Mind and Meditation*. Trans. and ed. Lobsang P. Lhalungpa. Boston: Shambhala, 1986.

Nandy, Ashis. *At the Edge of Psychology: Essays in Politics and Culture*. Delhi: Oxford University Press, 1980.

———. *The Intimate Enemy: Loss and Recovery of Self under Colonialism*. Delhi: Oxford University Press, 1983.

Neumaier-Dargyay, E. K. (See also Eva Dargyay.) *The Sovereign All-Creating Mind—The Motherly Buddha: A Translation of the Kun byed rgyal po'i mdo*. Albany: State University of New York Press, 1992.

Nikhilananda, Swami, trans. *The Gospel of Sri Ramakrishna*. New York: Ramakrishna-Vivekananda Center, 1973.

O'Flaherty, Wendy Doniger. *Women, Androgynes, and Other Mythical Beasts.* Chicago: University of Chicago Press, 1980.

Ortner, Sherry B. "The Founding of the First Sherpa Nunnery, and the Problem of 'Women' as an Analytic Category." In *Feminist Re-visions: What Has Been and Might Be,* ed. Vivian Patraka and Louise A. Tilly, pp. 98–134. Ann Arbor: University of Michigan, 1983.

———. *High Religion: A Cultural and Political History of Sherpa Buddhism.* Princeton: Princeton University Press, 1989.

———. "Is Female to Male as Nature Is to Culture?" In *Woman, Culture, and Society,* ed. Michelle Rosaldo and Louise Lamphere, pp. 56–87. Stanford: Stanford University Press, 1974.

———. *Sherpas through Their Rituals.* Cambridge: Cambridge University Press, 1978.

———. Typescript biography of Bhikṣuṇī Lakṣmī. N.d.

Padoux, André. "A Survey of Tantric Hinduism for the Historian of Religions." *History of Religions* 20, no. 4 (May 1981): 345–60.

Parikh, Indira J., and Pulin K. Garg. *Indian Women: An Inner Dialogue.* New Delhi: Sage Publications, 1989.

Paul, Diana Y. *Women in Buddhism: Images of the Feminine in Mahāyāna Tradition.* Berkeley: Asian Humanities Press, 1979.

Paul, Robert A. *The Tibetan Symbolic World: Psychoanalytic Explorations.* Chicago: University of Chicago Press, 1982.

Pitzer-Reyl, Renate. *Die Frau im frühen Buddhismus.* Marburger Studien Zur Afrika- und Asienkunde, series B, Asien, vol. 7. Berlin: Verlag Von Dietrich Reimer, 1984.

Punja, Shobita. *Divine Ecstasy: The Story of Khajuraho.* New Delhi: Viking, 1992.

Radhakrishnan, S., trans. *The Principal Upaniṣads.* New York: Harper and Brothers, 1953.

Raheja, Gloria Goodwin. *Poison in the Gift: Ritual, Prestation, and the Dominant Caste in a North Indian Village.* Chicago: University of Chicago Press, 1988.

Rai, Ram Kumar. *Encyclopedia of Indian Erotics.* Varanasi: Prachya Prakashan, 1983.

Ray, Reginald A. "Accomplished Women in Tantric Buddhism of Medieval India and Tibet." In *Unspoken Worlds: Women's Religious Lives in Non-Western Cultures,* ed. Nancy Falk and Rita Gross, pp. 227–42. San Francisco: Harper and Row, 1979.

Reynolds, John Myrdhin. *Self-Liberation through Seeing with Naked Awareness.* Barrytown, N.Y.: Station Hill Press, 1989.

Rhie, Marylin M., and Robert A. F. Thurman. *Wisdom and Compassion: The Sacred Art of Tibet.* New York: Harry N. Abrams, 1991.

Richman, Paula. *Women, Branch Stories, and Religious Rhetoric in a Tamil Buddhist Text.* Foreign and Comparative Studies, South Asian Series, no. 12. Syracuse: Maxwell School of Citizenship and Public Affairs, Syracuse University, 1988.

Ricouer, Paul. *Hermeneutics and the Human Sciences: Essays on Language, Action and Interpretation.* Trans. John B. Thompson. Cambridge: Cambridge University Press, 1981.

Rigzin, Tsepak. *Tibetan-English Dictionary of Buddhist Terminology.* Dharamsala: Library of Tibetan Works and Archives, 1986.

Rinpoche, Kalu. "Women, *Siddhi*, and Dharma." In *The Dharma That Illuminates All Beings Like the Light of the Sun and the Moon*, trans. Janet Gyatso, 91–108. Albany: State University of New York Press, 1986.

Rinpoche, Tulku Thondup. *Hidden Teachings of Tibet: An Explanation of the Terma Tradition of the Nyingma School of Buddhism*. London: Wisdom, 1986.

Robinson, James B., trans. *Buddha's Lions: The Lives of the Eighty-Four Siddhas* (a translation of the *Caturaśīti-siddha-pravṛtti* by Abhayadatta). Berkeley: Dharma, 1979.

Roerich, George N., trans. *The Blue Annals*, by 'Gos Lo-tsa-ba gZhon-nu-dpal. 1949. 2d ed. Delhi: Motilal Banarsidass, 1976.

Roy, Satindra Narayan. "The Witches of Orissa." *Journal of the Anthropological Society of Bombay* 14, no. 2 (1927–28): 185–200.

Ruegg, David Seyfort. "Allusiveness and Obliqueness in Buddhist Texts: *Saṃdhā, Saṃdhi, Saṃdhyā* and *Abhisaṃdhi*." In *Dialectes dans les litteratures indo-aryennes*, ed. C. Caillat, 295–328. Paris: College de France, 1989.

———. *Buddha-nature, Mind and the Problem of Gradualism in a Comparative Perspective: On the Transmission and Reception of Buddhism in India and Tibet*. London: School of Oriental and African Studies, 1989.

———. "Deux problèmes d'exégèse et de pratique tantriques." In *Tantric and Taoist Studies in Honour of R. A. Stein*, ed. Michel Strickmann, pp. 212–26. Mélanges Chinois et Bouddhiques, vol. 20. Brussels: Institut Belge des Hautes Etudes Chinoises, 1981.

Sangari, Kumkum, and Sudesh Vaid, eds. *Recasting Women: Essays in Indian Colonial History*. New Brunswick, N.J.: Rutgers University Press, 1990.

Sanderson, Alexis. "Purity and Power among the Brahmans of Kashmir." In *The Category of the Person: Anthropology, Philosophy, and History*, ed. Michael Carrithers et al., pp. 190–216. Cambridge: Cambridge University Press, 1985.

———. "Śaivism and the Tantric Traditions." In *The World's Religions*, ed. Stewart Sutherland et al., pp. 660–704. London: Routledge, 1988.

———. "Vajrayana: Origin and Function." Paper presented at Dhammakaya Foundation, Bangkok, Thailand, February 1990.

Sâṅkṛtyâyana, Râhula. "Recherches Bouddhiques, part 2, L'Origine du Vajrayâna et les 84 Siddhas." *Journal Asiatique* 225 (October–December 1934): 209–30.

Saraswati, S. K. *Tantrayāna Art: An Album*. Calcutta: Asiatic Society, 1977.

Saraswati, Swami Satyananda. *Kundalini Tantra*. Munger, Bihar: Bihar School of Yoga, 1984.

Schlagintweit, Emil. *Buddhism in Tibet, Illustrated by Literary Documents and Objects of Religious Worship*. London: Trübner, 1863.

Schmidt, Dolores Barracano, and Earl Robert Schmidt. "The Invisible Woman: The Historian as Professional Magician." In *Liberating Women's History: Theoretical and Critical Essays*, ed. Berenice A. Carroll, pp. 42–54. Urbana: University of Illinois Press, 1976.

Schoterman, J. A., ed. *The Yonitantra*. Delhi: Manohar, 1980.

Schott, Robin May. *Cognition and Eros: A Critique of the Kantian Paradigm*. Boston: Beacon Press, 1988.

Schuster, Nancy. "Changing the Female Body: Wise Women and the Bodhisattva Career in Some *Mahāratna-kūṭasūtras*." *Journal of the International Association of Buddhist Studies* 4, no. 1 (1981): 33–46.

Scott, Joan Wallach. *Gender and the Politics of History*. New York: Columbia University Press, 1988.

Sevely, Josephine Lowndes. *Eve's Secrets: An Evolutionary Perspective on Human Sexuality*. 1987. London: Paladin/Grafton Books, 1989.

Shaw, Miranda. "An Ecstatic Song by Lakṣmīṅkarā." In *Feminine Ground: Essays on Women and Tibet*, ed. Janice Willis, pp. 52–56. Ithaca: Snow Lion, 1989.

Shendge, Malati J. *Advayasiddhi (A Study)*. M. S. University Oriental Series, no. 8. Reprinted from *Journal of the Oriental Institute*. Baroda: Oriental Institute, 1964.

———. "*Śrīsahajasiddhi*." *Indo-Iranian Journal* 10, nos. 2 and 3 (1967): 126–49.

Sherburne, Richard, trans. *A Lamp for the Path and Commentary*. Wisdom of Tibet Series, vol. 5. London: George Allen and Unwin, 1983.

Siegel, Lee. "Bengal Blackie and the Sacred Slut: A Sahajayāna Buddhist Song." *Buddhist-Christian Studies* 1 (1981): 51–58.

Sierksma, Fokke. *Tibet's Terrifying Deities: Sex and Aggression in Religious Acculturation*. Rutland, Vermont, and Tokyo: Charles E. Tuttle, 1966.

Silburn, Lilian. *Kuṇḍalinī: The Energy of the Depths*. Trans. Jacques Gontier. Albany: State University of New York Press, 1988.

Singh, Renuka. *The Womb of Mind: A Sociological Exploration of the Status-Experience of Women in Delhi*. New Delhi: Vikas Publishing House, 1990.

Sircar, D. C. *The Śākta Pīṭhas*. 2d ed. Delhi: Motilal Banarsidass, 1973.

Situpa, XIIth Khentin Tai. *Tilopa (Some Glimpses of His Life)*. Ed. and trans. Kenneth Holmes. Eskdalemuir, Scotland: Dzalendara, 1988.

Smith, Kendra. "Sex, Dependency, and Religion—Reflections from a Buddhist Perspective." In *Women in the World's Religions, Past and Present*, ed. Ursula King, pp. 219–31. New York: Paragon House, 1987.

Snellgrove, David L. *Buddhist Himālaya*. Oxford: Bruno Cassirer, 1957.

———. *The Hevajra Tantra: A Critical Study*. 2 vols. London: Oxford University Press, 1959.

———. *Himalayan Pilgrimage: A Study of Tibetan Religion by a Traveller through Western Nepal*. 1981. Reprint, Boston: Shambhala, 1989.

———. *Indo-Tibetan Buddhism: Indian Buddhists and Their Tibetan Successors*. London: Serindia, 1987.

———. "The Notion of Divine Kingship in Tantric Buddhism." In *The Sacral Kingship*. Contributions to the Central Theme of the VIIIth International Congress for the History of Religions (Rome, April 1955), pp. 204–18. Leiden: E. J. Brill, 1959.

bSod nams rgya mtsho and Musashi Tachikawa. *The Ngor Mandalas of Tibet: Plates*. Bibliotheca Codicum Asiaticorum, vol. 2. Tokyo: Centre for East Asian Cultural Studies, 1989.

Sponberg, Alan. "Attitudes toward Women and the Feminine in Early Buddhism." In *Buddhism, Sexuality, and Gender*, ed. José Ignacio Cabezón, pp. 3–36. Albany: State University of New York Press, 1992.

Spradley, James. *Participant Observation*. New York: Holt, Rinehart and Winston, 1980.

Srinivasan, Amrit. "Reform or Conformity? Temple 'Prostitution' and the Community in the Madras Presidency." In *Structures of Patriarchy: The State, Community, and Household*, ed. Bina Agarwal, pp. 175–98. London: Zed Books, 1990.

Stablein, William. "The Medical Soteriology of Karma in the Buddhist Tantric Tradition." In *Karma and Rebirth in Classical Indian Traditions*, ed. Wendy Doniger O'Flaherty, pp. 193–216. Berkeley and Los Angeles: University of California Press, 1980.

Steinkellner, Ernst. "Remarks on Tantristic Hermeneutics." In *Proceedings of the Csoma de Körös Memorial Symposium*, ed. Louis Ligeti, pp. 445–58. Bibliotheca Orientalis Hungarica, vol. 23. Budapest: Akadémiai Kaidó, 1978.

Stone, Merlin. *When God Was a Woman*. San Francisco: Harcourt Brace Jovanovitch, 1976.

Strong, John S. "*Gandhakuṭī*: The Perfumed Chamber of the Buddha." *History of Religions* 16 (1977): 390–406.

Suzuki, Daisetz Teitaro. *Studies in the Laṅkāvatāra Sūtra*. 1930. Reprint, Boulder: Prajñā Press, 1981.

Svoboda, Robert E. *Aghora: At the Left Hand of God*. Albuquerque: Brotherhood of Life, 1986.

Takakusu, J., trans. *A Record of the Buddhist Religion as Practised in India and the Malay Archipelago (A.D. 671–695), by I-Tsing*. 1896. Reprint, Taipei: Ch'eng Wen, 1970.

Tambiah, Stanley. *Culture, Thought and Social Action*. Cambridge: Harvard University Press, 1985.

Tāranātha. *History of Buddhism in India*. Trans. Lama Chimpa and Alaka Chattopadhyaya, ed. Debiprasad Chattopadhyaya. Atlantic Highlands, N.J.: Humanities Press, 1981.

———. *Tāranātha's Life of Kṛṣṇācārya/Kāṇha*. Trans. David Templeman. Dharamsala: Library of Tibetan Works and Archives, 1989.

———. *Mystic Tales of Lāmā Tāranātha: A Religio-Sociological History of Mahāyāna Buddhism*. Trans. Bhupendranath Datta. Calcutta: Ramakrishna Vedanta Math, 1944.

———. *The Seven Instruction Lineages: Tāranātha's* bKa'.babs.bdun.ldan. Trans. and ed. David Templeman. Dharamsala: Library of Tibetan Works and Archives, 1983.

Tatz, Mark. "The Life of the Siddha-Philosopher Maitrīgupta." *Journal of the American Oriental Society* 107, no. 4 (1987): 695–711.

Templeman, David. (See also Tāranātha.) "Tāranātha the Historian." *Tibet Journal* 6, no. 2 (Summer 1981): 41–46.

Thaye, Jampa. *A Garland of Gold: The Early Kagyu Masters of India and Tibet*. Bristol: Ganesha Press, 1990.

Thurman, Robert A. F. "Tantric Practice According to Tsongkhapa." Typescript.

———. "Vajra Hermeneutics." In *Buddhist Hermeneutics*, Kuroda Institute Studies in East Asian Buddhism, no. 6, ed. Donald S. Lopez, pp. 119–48. Honolulu: University of Hawaii Press, 1988.

Thurman, Robert A. F., trans. *The Holy Teaching of Vimalakīrti*. University Park and London: Pennsylvania State University Press, 1976.

Tiwari, Laxmi. *The Splendor of Worship: Women's Fasts, Rituals, Stories, and Art*. Delhi: Manohar, 1991.

Trichen, Chogay. *The History of the Sakya Tradition: A Feast for the Minds of the Fortunate*. Trans. Jennifer Scott. Bristol: Ganesha Press, 1983.

Trinh, Minh-ha. *Woman, Native, Other: Writing Postcoloniality and Feminism*. Bloomington and Indianapolis: Indiana University Press, 1989.

Tsomo, Karma Lekshe, ed. *Sakyadhītā: Daughters of the Buddha*. Ithaca: Snow Lion, 1988.

———. "Tibetan Nuns and Nunneries." In *Feminine Ground: Essays on Women and Tibet*, ed. Janice Willis, pp. 118–34. Ithaca: Snow Lion, 1989.

Tsuda, Shiníchi. *The Saṃvarodaya-tantra: Selected Chapters*. Tokyo: Hokuseido Press, 1974.

———. "'*Vajrayoṣidbhageṣu Vijahāra*': Historical Survey from the Beginnings to the Culmination of Tantric Buddhism." In *Indological and Buddhist Studies: Volume in Honour of Professor J. W. de Jong on his Sixtieth Birthday*, ed. L. A. Hercus et al., pp. 595–616. Canberra: Faculty of Asian Studies, 1982.

Tucci, Giuseppe. "Animadversiones Indicae." *Journal of the Asiatic Society of Bengal*, n.s., 26, no. 1 (1930): 125–60.

———. *Rati-Līlā: An Interpretation of the Tantric Imagery of the Temples of Nepal*. Geneva: Nagel, 1969.

———. *Tibetan Painted Scrolls*. 1949. Reprint, Kyoto: Rinsen Book Co., 1980.

———. "Travels of Tibetan Pilgrims in the Swat Valley." In *Opera Minora*, vol. 2, pp. 369–418. Università di Roma Studi Orientali Pubblicati a Cura della Scuola Orientale, vol. 6. Roma: Dott. Giovanni Bardi Editore, 1971.

Tulku, Sharpa, and Michael Perrott, trans. *A Manual of Ritual Fire Offerings*. Dharamsala: Library of Tibetan Works and Archives, 1987.

Tulku, Tarthang, trans. *Mother of Knowledge: The Enlightenment of Ye-shes mTsho-rgyal*, by Nam-mkha'i snying-po, ed. Jane Wilhelms. Berkeley: Dharma, 1983.

Vallée Poussin, Louis de la. S.v. "Tantrism (Buddhist)" in *Encyclopedia of Religion and Ethics*, ed. James Hastings, vol. 12, pp. 193–97. New York: Charles Scribner's Sons, 1922.

Van Lysebeth, André. *Tantra, le culte de la Féminité*. Paris: Flammarion, 1988.

Vaudeville, Charlotte. *Bārahmāsā in Indian Literatures*. 1965. English ed., Delhi: Motilal Banarsidass, 1986.

Von Fürer-Haimendorf, Christoph. *The Sherpas of Nepal: Buddhist Highlanders*. Berkeley and Los Angeles: University of California Press, 1964.

Waddell, L. Austine. *Tibetan Buddhism: With Its Mystic Cults, Symbolism and Mythology*. London: W. H. Allen, 1895 (published under the title *The Buddhism of Tibet, or Lamaism*). Reprint, New York: Dover Publications, 1972.

Wayman, Alex. *The Buddhist Tantras: Light on Indo-Tibetan Esotericism*. New York: Samuel Weiser, 1973.

———. "Messengers, What Bring Ye?" In *Indo-Tibetan Studies: Papers in Honour and Appreciation of Professor David L. Snellgrove's Contributions to Indo-Tibetan*

*Studies*, ed. Tadeusz Skorupski, pp. 305–22. Tring, United Kingdom: Institute of Buddhist Studies, 1990.

Wiethaus, Ulrike. "Sexuality, Gender and the Body in Late Medieval Spirituality: Cases from Germany and the Netherlands." *Journal of Feminist Studies in Religion* 7, no. 1 (Spring 1991): 35–52.

Willemen, Ch. *The Chinese Hevajratantra: The Scriptural Text of the Ritual of the Great King of the Teaching, The Adamantine One with Great Compassion and Knowledge of the Void*. Orientalia Gandensia, vol. 8. Leuven: Uitgeverij Peters, 1983.

Willis, Janice D. "Ḍākinī: Some Comments on Its Nature and Meaning." In *Feminine Ground: Essays on Women and Tibet*, ed. Janice Willis, pp. 57–75. Ithaca: Snow Lion, 1989.

———. "Nuns and Benefactresses: The Role of Women in the Development of Buddhism." In *Women, Religion and Social Change*, ed. Yvonne Haddad and Ellison Findlay, pp. 59–85. Albany: State University of New York Press, 1985.

———. "Tibetan *Ani*-s: The Nun's Life in Tibet." In *Feminine Ground: Essays on Women and Tibet*, ed. Janice Willis, pp. 96–117. Ithaca: Snow Lion, 1989.

Willson, Martin. *In Praise of Tārā: Songs to the Saviouress*. London: Wisdom, 1986.

Woodroffe, Sir John. *Shakti and Shākta: Essays and Addresses on the Shākta Tantrashāstra*. 1918. 3d ed., Madras: Ganesh, 1929.

Wylie, Turrell. "A Standard System of Tibetan Transcription." *Harvard Journal of Asiatic Studies* 22 (1959): 261–67.

———. "Dating the Death of Nāropa." In *Indological and Buddhist Studies: Volume in Honour of Professor J. W. de Jong on His Sixtieth Birthday*, ed. L. A. Hercus et al., pp. 687–92. Canberra: Faculty of Asian Studies, 1982.

Yeshe, Lama. *Gyalwa Gyatso*. London: Wisdom, 1984.

———. *Introduction to Tantra: A Vision of Totality*. Compiled and ed. Jonathan Landaw. London: Wisdom, 1987.

Yün-hua, Jan. "Buddhist Relations between India and Sung China." *History of Religions* 6 (1966): 24–42, 135–68.

# Index

*mahāsiddha*, 74, 76–77, 135, 238nn. 117 and 118
Mahāsukhāsiddhī, 283
Mahāyāna Buddhism, 20, 79, 95, 128, 211n.1, 240n.147; women in, 4, 27, 68
Mahāyāna philosophy, 20, 23–24, 62, 89, 94, 101, 136, 195
*mahāyoga-tantra*, 14, 141, 242nn. 6 and 7
*maithuna* (sacred union), 31, 109, 143, 184, 200, figures 15–17. *See also* Buddha couple
Maitrīpa, 50–52, 77, 79, 99, 131, 134, 137–38, 180
male dominance: as universal postulate of Western scholarship, 4, 9, 196, 210n.36, 263n.3
*maṇḍala*, 46, 84–85, 106–8, 121, 125, 153, 161, 164, 166, 168; definition of, 26, 106, 151; vulva as, 151, 159–60, 162
Mani Rimdu, 117–18
Maṇibhadrā, 22, figure 2
Maṇimēkalai, 262n.59
Mañjuśrī, 26, 80, 84
mantra, 22, 25, 38, 40, 62, 80, 108–9, 127, 151, 161, 170, 174
*mantrayāna*, 211n.1
*maṇtrinaḥ*, 76
Marglin, Frédérique, 61, 158, 251n.91
Mārīcī, 229n.19
Matāṅgi, 136
*māyādeha*, 254n.126
measureless mansion, 159, 164. See also *maṇḍala*
Mekhalā, 79, 85, 87, 96, 102, 113–17, 138, 226n.102, figure 11
men in Tantric Buddhism: admission to yogini feasts of, 82–84, 104, 134; cooperation with women of, 4, 36–38, 54, 72, 139–40, 174, 179, 195, 200–201, 203–4; as "founders" of Tantric Buddhism, 102, 130–39, 192–94, 201, 204; proper attitudes and behavior toward women of, 4, 6, 11, 37–38, 40–43, 45–50, 53, 70–73, 153, 174, 176, 179, 199, 217n.41; purported ruthlessness of, 8, 204; as spiritual companions of women, 14, 65, 68–73, 134–35, 137–38, 146–47, 158, 168, 170–71, 180, 192, 204–5, 255n.143, figure 17; textual characterizations of, 37, 76–77, 138, 174. *See also* Tantric partner; worship of women
Menakā, 80
menstrual blood, 111, 154, 158, 249n.81, 250n.82
monastic universities, 20–21, 177
monastic vows, 52, 131, 146, 195. *See also* celibacy
monasticism and Tantric practice, 20, 22, 53, 60, 105, 148, 177, 179, 194–95, 204, 207–8n.10, 212n.6, 241n.150, 244n.33, 262n.1
mother-*tantra*. See *yoginī-tantra*
*mudrā* (hand gesture), 38, 170, 172

*nāḍī*, 147. *See also* yogic anatomy
*nāḍīgranthi-nirṃocana* (untying the knots), 147
Nāgārjuna, 92
Nairātmyā, 28, 63, 84, 136
Nālandā, 21
Nāropa, 15, 74, 107, 136, 172, 246n.47
nectar, 26, 38, 57, 67, 122; sexual fluid as, 152, 157–58, 160, 162
Nepal, 15, 67, 98, 101, 113, 136, 215n.15, 237n.101
Niguma, 87–88, 94, 102, 107–10, 180, 198, 230n.29, 231n.29
nondual awareness, 95, 97, 116–17, 134, 163, 165, 186–87
nuns, 4, 20, 207n.8. *See also* Bhikṣuṇī Lakṣmī

Odantapurī, 21
O'Flaherty, Wendy, 158
*Oral Instructions on the Three Whirling Crosses*, 114–17
Orissa, 8, 134–35, 229n.18, 250n.82, 251n.91
Ortner, Sherry, 127, 216n.29, 236n.95

*padma*. *See* lotus
Padmalocanā, 22, 50, 77, 98, 134, 225n.97, figure 6
Padmanarteśvara, 122–25, 235n.88
Padmapādā, 99
Padmasaṃbhava, 33, 131, 193
Padmavajra, 25, 84, 131, 135, 138, 179, 182, 192–93, 240nn. 136 and 140, 257n.3
Padoux, André, 32–33
Pāla period, 20, 33–34, 101, 177
*pañcakrama*, 87, 245n.40
Pañcarātra, 247n.54
Paṇḍaravāsinī, 119
Pārvatī, 32
passion, 3, 21, 25, 28, 31, 73, 149, 151, 184, 190, 193, 195, 199–200; as basis for Tantric practice, 24, 135, 140, 152, 162, 167, 169, 172, 182, 186–88, 192, 205, 207–8n.10

## TIBETAN NAMES AND TERMS

# PASSIONATE ENLIGHTENMENT